the gap-year guidebook 2016

Editor: Samantha Wilkins

John Catt Educational Ltd

JOHN CATT
EDUCATIONAL
LIMITED

Published in 2015 by John Catt Educational Ltd,
12 Deben Mill Business Centre, Old Maltings Approach,
Melton, Woodbridge, Suffolk IP12 1BL

Tel: +44 (0) 1394 389850   Fax: +44 (0) 1394 386893
Email: info@gap-year.com   Website: www.gap-year.com

First published by Peridot Press in 1992; Twenty-fourth edition 2016
© 2015 John Catt Educational Ltd

British Library Cataloguing in Publication Data.

ISBN: 978 1909 717 48 0

Designed and typeset by Theoria Design
Printed and bound in Great Britain by Hobbs the Printer Ltd, Totton, Hampshire.

Contacts

Editor
Samantha Wilkins
Email: editor@gap-year.com

Production - James Rudge

Distribution/Booksales
Tel: +44 (0) 1394 389863
Email: booksales@johncatt.com

Advertising
Tel: +44 (0) 1394 389853
Email: info@gap-year.com

contents

contents ... continued

Your gap-year abroad

contents ... continued

Your gap-year in the UK

contents ... continued

Appendix

Many thanks to all those who have given their time, advice and expertise to help us keep this book as up-to-date as possible, with particular thanks to Stefan Wathan at Year Out Group, Jon Arnold at Oyster Worldwide, Richard Nimmo at Blue Ventures and Linsey MacLeod at Gapwork.com. Thank you also to those who have shared their gap-year adventures with us.

Cover image, courtesy of John Taylor, SACI Sculpture and Drawing Instructor 'SACI Drawing students on site at San Miniato al Monte above Florence, Italy'

Preface

How gap-years have changed...

Preface: How gap-years have changed

Stefan Wathan, chief executive of the Year Out Group, offers an outline of what a 'gap-year' means in 2016

In 2014-15 the member organizations of Year Out Group arranged structured gap-year placements for 25,000 people in over 90 countries across the globe. 72% of the participants were aged between 17 and 25 predominantly taking time between school and university or leaving university and taking up full-time work; 18% were between 26 and 40 mostly taking a sabbatical or career break or even looking for a change of career, while the remaining 10% were catching up on travel opportunities they may have missed out on and offering valuable skills in the process – or even deciding that they too have a new potential career ahead of them.

How have gap-years changed?

Taking a gap later in life

The trend of taking a 'gap' later in life seems to be continuing but it is more popular across the globe with 60% of participants coming from outside the UK in 2014 compared to 34% in 2006.

The driver for this may be that more people are looking for opportunities to gain experience outside of their own country. In the USA demand is growing and their universities are becoming more proactive in their support of well-structured and purposeful 'gap' experiences. A growing number of middle class students in China and India may also be a factor.

Competition for gap-year places

The average length of structured activity during a gap is 10 weeks. It can be as little as 2 weeks or as many as 52 weeks. Participants are leaving it later to book, which makes it harder for providers to plan effectively and to guarantee a place. It's not clear if this trend will continue but probably has something to do with ease of searching and booking via mobile devices.

Year Out Group places an emphasis on telling participants to do some planning and to remember that there are selection processes for many programmes even if it is a telephone interview. With oversees participants now dominating the market there is danger UK young people will miss out if they are not thinking ahead.

Shorter Placements

Over the past four years there has been a demand for shorter placements of a few weeks rather than a few months. There is no doubt that the state of the economy has been a major driver but it might also be because there is an element of CV building for its own sake or as perhaps in most cases, leaving things to the last minute, knowing you can find something online is a now a habit of most consumers.

Employers have always required evidence of commitment and an ability to plan ahead as well as deal with things in the moment or under pressure, people looking to impress need to bear all these attributes in mind.

Multiple experiences

Independent travel combined with an expedition or some work, paid or unpaid is not new but there it seems there may be more people combining different packages during their year out. People are also booking more high value experiences.

Responsible travel and safety

More overseas operators are now offering activities and schools themselves may begin to partner with operators in the country they visit. Year Out members need to be aware of this and ensure they continue to operate at the highest standards but potential participants also need to be vigilant when considering who to travel with, as some packages may appear too good to be true.

Amongst other questions, ask how long they have been operating in the country, who is responsible for your safety and how your money is spent? The Year Out Group has always encouraged people to ask these types of questions and the increase in driven in part by media stories questioning the validity of some programmes including orphanages and lion sanctuaries.

Why take a gap-year?

Those taking a gap-year between leaving school/college and going to university arrive refreshed and focused. After all you may not have an opportunity like this for many years. Evidence shows students are more likely to complete their chosen course if they have taken a gap-year – so long as, that is, they have planned for it.

For those less certain about their degree subject, a gap-year may mean they decide university isn't for them or they may change their choice of degree. Some may take time to get back into academic mode but this is more than compensated for in their social maturity. Their completion of a demanding challenge that they have initiated, planned and implemented successfully boosts their self-confidence significantly. They are also more globally aware which enables them to provide a more broadly based contribution in tutorials. In short they are better placed to make the most of their time at university and to succeed. They will also have acquired skills and experiences that will enhance their employability.

As with any new experience the real learning often takes place back at home, when you time to reflect on what you've done and what you'll do next. You keep a diary or blog or photo album on your phone to remind you have the thoughts, experiences and incidents you've had. You can then draw on these to illustrate your attributes as you draft a CV or prepare for an interview.

For more information on Year Out Group, visit: www.yearoutgroup.org

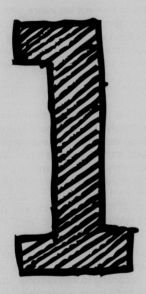

Tips for travellers

DownUnder Insurance – The Best Cheap Backpacking Insurance Providers

The most important tip we can offer travellers is to take out insurance with us to ensure they are covered in the event of any emergency whether medical, flight related or a loss of personal belongings. Insurance is a vital part of planning a trip, however it is thought around 1 in 3 young backpackers aged 18-24 travel without it – this is a terrifying thought considering backpackers often participate in high risk adventure activities whilst abroad.

So why choose DownUnder?

Well, besides being having 20 years' experience in the travel insurance market, we believe our product is one of the best value for money policies around giving you high quality but low cost insurance. Our backpacking, gap-year and traveling policies are specifically designed with young people in mind and for example more than 60 adventure activities or extreme sports are covered at no extra cost – meaning you're protected in the event of injury without having to worry about sky high medical bills. Our list of adventure activities would take even the most enthusiastic traveller some time to complete so as long as what you want to do is on our list and you inform us beforehand you can bungee jump, canoe, horse ride, scuba dive and "zorb" etc. to your heart's content.

When you are young you want to experience as much as possible while you have the time and energy and this often includes hazardous activities which is where travel insurance becomes an absolute essential. According to International Student Insurance, medical cover is the most important part of a travel insurance policy and this is where our 24 emergency service comes in – you can call anytime, 365 days a year for immediate help in the event of illness or injury abroad and our staff will help you out in whatever you need, for example, providing a multilingual service, liaising with doctors or arranging repatriation.

Our policies are also extremely flexible, allowing for that last minute change of plan that can often occur during backpacking holidays as you or a member of your group decides they absolutely must-see a specific landmark or city. All you need is internet access or a phone to inform us of your change of plan and you will still be covered for the new leg of your journey. On top of this, if you choose to extend your trip you can extend your policy with us for up to 18 months as opposed to having to take out a new policy. Our policies also allow you to spend up to 25% of your time travelling in other worldwide destinations outside of those originally covered on your policy. This means for a 12 month policy to Australia, for example, you could spend 3 months travelling outside of Australia and still be covered!

We also provide some of the most affordable policies to cover you whilst working abroad if you so wish to. We cover a variety of work including office and clerical work, retail and light manual work such as fruit picking as standard on our backpacking and gap-year policies. Many backpackers find that at some point during their trip money can start to become tight therefore some part time work while you explore a city can be an excellent way of both topping up your funds, gaining work experience and meeting new people.

Many young people like to travel with smartphones, expensive cameras, tablet computers or laptops, even whilst backpacking, we provide baggage cover of up to £1,500 depending on which policy you choose (3) as well as providing an additional extension for high value items to ensure your peace of mind whilst traveling with your valued equipment. We do, however, suggest backing up information and photos whenever possible to avoid losing those memorable holiday snaps in the event of theft, loss or breakages etc.

Another advantage of our insurance packages is that you can remove standard policy excess fees by choosing to take out our Excess Waiver – this is extremely popular as it allows you to simply pay a one-off fee on top of your standard policy price and therefore avoid paying a standard excess for every claim and meaning that you pay nothing, however many times you choose to claim. We also pride ourselves on customer satisfaction and therefore allow all customers a 14 day cooling off period to cancel your policy and receive your money back as long you have not claimed or travelled.

So come on, book that trip of a lifetime you've always wanted or that gap-year holiday you've been dying to take and travel around the world safe in the knowledge you're covered by one of the best insurance products on the market.

Tips for travellers

For starters, what do we mean by gap-year?

Well, according to the Oxford Dictionary, a gap-year is defined as:

'a period, typically an academic year, taken by a student as a break between school and university or college education.'

Typically, yes, but we'd contend that a gap-year can be and is much more than that nowadays. It's certainly not limited to school leavers. Nowadays people travel to volunteer, work and study. You might be taking a year out from work, spending a redundancy pay-out or enjoying your retirement.

Don't think your break would have to be for a year either – it could be as long and short as you like, or can afford!

But the one thing all such trips have in common is the fact that they're all about taking time out of the normal routine to do **something different, challenging, fulfilling, memorable** – so that is our definition of a gap.

Who goes on a gap?

As we've just explained, anyone *can*. But who does?

It's difficult to give exact numbers because of the wildly different ways you can spend your gap, but we're likely to be talking hundreds of thousands – that includes young people (teenagers and those in their early 20s), career breakers and retired people.

The Year Out Group, which represents 34 of the leading gap-year providers in the UK, arranged structured gap-year placements for 25,000 people in over 90 countries across the globe in 2014-15.

They say 72% of the participants were aged between 17 and 25, predominantly taking time between school and university or leaving university and taking up full-time work; 18% were between 26 and 40 mostly taking a sabbatical or career break or even looking for a change of career, while the remaining 10% were catching up on travel opportunities they may have missed out on and offering valuable skills in the process or even deciding that they too have a new potential career ahead of them.

"We work with all age groups" says Ellen Sziede of African Conservation Experience. "We have seen the average age go up a bit over the years, with many students now opting to travel and volunteer in their summer break while they are at university rather than between school and university. There are also many non-students volunteering, so it is not uncommon to have some teenagers, university students in their 20s, a career breaker in their 40s or 50s and a retiree working together at a project."

So the answer is people of all ages and walks of life go on a gap.

Why should you take a gap?

There are as many reasons to take a gap as there are different opportunities on offer. Time out before further study? A break from the daily work routine? A memorable experience? To give something back? To learn something new? A way to gain work experience that will boost your career prospects? All are valid reasons.

The benefits of taking a gap-year are considerable. Younger gappers who have taken a structured trip are likely to arrive at university refreshed and focused and research shows they are more likely to finish their chosen course.

And if you feel like you're fed up with the daily grind of a 9-to-5 job, a career break can help you get out of your rut. Working full-time for even just ten years means roughly around 20,000 hours of sitting in an office staring at your computer screen. A career break will help you gain a new perspective on life and work and will be an experience you remember for the rest of your life.

Increasingly, young people planning a gap-year do so with improving their CV in mind and making sure they are more attractive to employers when they return. A well-planned gap-year that includes a work placement and learning new skills is likely to be of a huge benefit when you're back and looking for a job, particularly in tough economic times when work may be hard to come by.

Stefan Wathan from the Year Out Group highlights the key skills that employers are looking for and can be acquired through a structured gap-year; "More people with gap experiences means you may have to try that bit harder to impress so the important thing is to do something you really think you will enjoy and learn from. It is not just about ticking a box on the CV list." Employers are looking for:

· Communication skills The ability to express oneself clearly verbally and in writing so that one can argue a position, persuade and inspire. The ability to relate to customers is also important.

15

SACI Florence

· Courage to challenge and take risks The ability to manage a project, to identify and manage risk and to experience and learn from failure.

· Planning and organization The ability to have an idea, to develop a plan and to implement that plan successfully.

· Initiative and adaptability The ability to think on ones feet, to act on one's own accord and to adjust a plan as and when circumstances change.

· Teamwork The ability to play a full part in a team. This links to adaptability as teams will often change as a project progresses.

· Internationalism Knowledge of languages and being at ease in diverse cultures is becoming increasingly important.

· Business acumen Understanding figures, an ability to negotiate and having some knowledge of maths and science in order to appreciate and make best use of emerging technology.

· The self-confidence that comes from a successful gap-year that enables you to start a job and draw on all your skills so that you become an effective member of staff as soon as possible.

16

Guy Whitehead, managing director of leading gap-year company The Leap, told us: "It has never been harder to gain meaningful employment, the job market is increasingly competitive especially for graduates. There are numerous stories in the media of employers complaining that young people do not have the necessary soft skills to take their place in the 'world of work'.

"Universities are increasingly on record highlighting the benefits of structured time out – students arrive having really thought through their choice of course, they may have spent some time overseas focused on an aspect of their future course, demonstrating a genuine passion and desire to learn that subject and as a result they are less likely to drop out of their course.

"Students are learning that if they take a gap-year they need to fill their time wisely. Consequently, gap-year participants are choosing projects that will enable them to acquire new skills or hone existing ones and gain experience that will positively enhance their CV. Either by setting their sights on paid work and internships or volunteering projects where the skills and experience required to succeed in a paid job, such as teamwork, good communication, problem solving, thinking on one's feet, learning a language and risk management, can be acquired just as readily by participating as a volunteer.

"Doing this overseas can take you out of your comfort zone and requires you to learn how to adjust to different customs and cultures and to open your mind to new ideas and opportunities".

Have tuition fees and the economy had an impact?

It's true that the uncertain economic times and the introduction of tuition fees of up to £9000 a year have made people think much harder about what they do and how they spend their money.

Jon Arnold from Oyster Worldwide finds that, "Some people say they want to get straight on with university and not take a gap-year because of the high tuition fees. I say to them, think again, if you rush in to university and decide that you have chosen the wrong course or location and leave, it will be an expensive mistake. A gap-year might cost you a few thousand pounds, but the benefits far outweigh the drawbacks, particularly if you go on to study a course that you will be far more committed to."

As we've already mentioned, with the traditional route of going straight to university after finishing A levels not proving as dependable as in previous years and a sluggish jobs market, more youngsters are considering vocational training or work experience on a gap-year abroad, allowing them to gain the hands-on experience that employers are looking for.

What's more, experts say the number of young professionals booking extended trips and work sabbaticals is still rising – up 30% in the past five years.

So, if anything, industry leaders are expecting to see more people taking a gap, despite the economy.

Planning your gap – the first steps

What do you want to do?

The beauty of the modern gap-year is the amount of choice and variety on offer: each is as unique as the individual participant, and each is an opportunity to create a tailored programme to meet their own personal ambitions.

17

You know your own personality, your interests, your strengths and weaknesses. Are you someone who likes to get stuck into something for a while – or do you want to be on the move a lot?

If you're not confident about coping alone with unfamiliar situations you might want a more structured, group setting. On the other hand if you know you need time away from the crowds, you're bound to want to build in some independent travel.

Voluntary work attracts the most placements and the greatest variety of projects, with placements available in nearly every country where gap-year providers operate.

Teaching is the most popular activity and is the ideal way to experience a country's culture and customs. When volunteering as an individual it generally follows that the longer the placement, the greater the benefit to both the volunteer and the host organisation.

Or perhaps you want to explore things you've always wanted to pursue but never had time? It could be anything from a spiritual retreat to meditation and yoga, art, photography, a new language or particular places and cultures.

Maybe you're particularly concerned about the state of the world and would like to do your bit environmentally or contribute to helping disadvantaged people? The possibilities are endless and many gappers end up constructing a programme that combines several elements.

Those with a full year at their disposal will perhaps have time for more than one activity, and might want to combine a structured element to their gap with some travel. The increase in cheap flights and wider access to previously unreachable destinations has made this even more possible.

Choosing the activity, destination and organisation most suited to the individual can be a difficult and time-consuming task. However, proper planning and research is

visit: www.duinsure.com

crucial and will help ensure you get the most out of your time; a gap or career break can easily be wasted without planning ahead.

It is also important that you are aware of your responsibilities. Dropping out of a placement or programme before it has finished can be disruptive not only to you but also to others directly and indirectly involved.

A gap-year can also be used for spiritual reasons or for personal development and there are companies that specialise in emotionally and spiritually-enriching trips.

But don't worry if all this sounds a bit heavy: the planning and preparation stage can be almost as much fun as the trip itself. And of course, this is where *the gap-year guidebook* comes into its own...

Where do you want to go?

Here, the Year Out Group talk us through the most popular destinations for gappers:

"South Africa is consistently popular stemming from the diverse nature of the country and the availability of a wide range of suitable and worthwhile projects. These projects range from conservation work in the numerous private and national game parks, a wide variety of teaching placements, many opportunities to coach sports and volunteer placements in the care field including orphanages, health centres and HIV/Aids awareness programmes. Projects can last from a few weeks to a whole year. South Africa is also seen as a comparatively safe destination with plentiful flights and the cost of living is good value. Because of the scale of opportunities its important to chose wisely by asking questions of the provider about the benefits any projects are bringing to conservation and communities alike.

"Tanzania is home to some of the most famous of East Africa's attractions – from Africa's highest mountain, the snow-capped Mount Kilimanjaro to the incredible

the gap-year guidebook 2016

my
gap-year
Kenny

Having just graduated from university, I was not prepared to immediately start working. I wanted to travel to an exotic country but do something that benefited the people of that nation. Little did I know that my time in Nepal would benefit me more than I could have ever given back.

Oyster Worldwide's programme to Nepal allowed me to live with a family in a majestic village on the outskirts of Kathmandu. My host family welcomed me with open arms and allowed me to take part in every local function, party and wedding. Time spent with my family gave me an opportunity that most tourists did not have in Nepal - the chance to fully immerse myself into the beautiful Nepalese culture.

My four months in Nepal were packed with incredible food, breathtaking views and amazing company. Eating traditional meals by candle light became the norm along with the morning blue sky pierced by the peaks of the Himalayan Mountains. The family, new friends and most importantly, my students accompanied me throughout this life-changing journey.

The trip was an endless adventure with every day beginning with a traditional meal with my family. Following breakfast, I would walk to school through the rice paddies and yellow mustard fields while receiving smiles and waves from every local person I passed. I would teach 9-13 year olds and in the early afternoon was able to head back home and enjoy the flexibility of this programme.

At first, the idea of teaching was daunting and I was unsure how well I would do. However, the eagerness of the students and positive energy at the school made everyday a pleasure. Art lessons, story telling and outdoor relay races made the time fly and kept the students entertained, happy and looking forward to their next class with the volunteers! After school, students would accompany me on hikes through the local jungle and invitations for dinner were always in abundance. On weekends, we were free to travel through the chaotic and historical city of Kathmandu where foreigners from around the world would congregate before their treks.

This trip now feels like a dream that was too good to be true. Dancing in traditional Nepali clothes, learning local dialect and making friendships that will last as long as my memories. Oyster Worldwide gave me the opportunity to teach English, explore the mountains of Nepal and challenge myself in profound and life-changing ways that I never knew were possible.

For more information about Oyster Worldwide, see Chapter 6 - Volunteering Abroad

Serengeti National Park and the Ngorogoro Crater, which hold some of the largest concentrations of wildlife on the continent. Low living costs and safety make it an attractive option and there is real need away from the tourist areas for support in education. However a high visa cost does detract which may act against it if other countries like Kenya become safer in future.

"Both countries saw a drop in bookings during the Ebola crisis, despite the fact they are located far away from the outbreak. It shows that some travellers can be ignorant of geography and also of the importance of the programmes they volunteer on and their commitment to it. It highlights the importance of researching gap-year options and knowing why you want to commit to any particular programme.

"Madagascar is the world's fourth biggest island and home to 5% of the known animal and plant species. Singing lemurs, giant baobab trees and some of the world's best street food make it an inviting place in which to trek and volunteer.

"Thailand continues to be popular. It is a very popular tourist destination so there are plenty of flights and there are hundreds of volunteering opportunities especially in teaching, community and conservation projects.

"Cambodia - a wide variety of activities are available including teaching, care work and conservation projects. It is comparatively safe, the people are very warm and welcoming and once again the cost of living is low.

"Canada - there are now several more organizations offering winter sports activities ranging from ski and snowboard instructor courses that invariably lead to offers of paid work as an instructor on completion of the course, something which may lead to full-time career or a way of earning money during university holidays. For those that wish to venture further into the mountains there is now the possibility to train as a mountain leader. The companies are also making good use of the facilities in the summer months: as mountain biking increases in popularity so does the demand

for instructors and the Canadian countryside provides the ideal terrain to gain the necessary skills and experience.

"Australia and New Zealand remain popular despite higher cost of living. Both countries are ideal staging post to stop off for a few weeks or months, get a job and then move north to Indochina. The higher living costs are somewhat offset by higher earnings but many people will work in return for accommodation and food, on farms for instance and they can also get assistance through operators to find work whilst they are there. Needless to say the natural environment of these countries is a draw and if you are looking to train in something technical like sailing then they are hard to beat.

"Costa Rica and Ecuador - Costa Rica's popularity again stems from the wide variety of activities available, comparative ease of access and its geographic position that enables gap-year travellers to go on to South America or the States. Costa Rica has a vibrant culture and good infrastructure (helped by the fact that it has no army and so spends more on public services) and fantastic wildlife accessible through National Parks. Ecuador is a nature lovers dream and also a place of epic adventures that can take in the Andes, jungle, the Galapagos and Pacific Coast.

"Nepal and India both are gaining in popularity as discerning British and international students and graduates seek to learn more about the culture and customs of an important and rapidly developing country like India, which offers a wide range of voluntary work placements and an increasing number of internship opportunities. Nepal remains both mystic and friendly and is much loved despite the earthquakes of this year, which means it'll need the support of tourists and volunteers to recover. Check with operators about their plans and how they make a difference to the country.

"European Countries - don't dismiss the UK's near neighbours. Whilst they may sound less exotic they have centuries of old art, culture, political history and industrial heritage, not forgetting amazing natural habitats, landscapes and cities. Travel cost will be less though you'll need more day-to-day budget but you are unlikely to need vaccinations or visas. You will be able to practice several languages and meet a more diverse range of gappers from around the globe than you might in far flung countries. You can also get home that much quicker if needed and you are entitled to work in other EU nations.

That gives you an idea of where others have gone. So where do you fancy?

If you want to visit several places you can let a cheap round-the-world ticket decide the framework for you. Otherwise you need to get your route clear in your mind.

Do you feel attracted to a particular area or to a particular climate? Unexplored territory or the popular backpacker places you've heard about? If you're unsure, try connecting with people who've been, through the many gap-year internet messageboards.

Heading for unknown territory off the backpacker routes in search of something more unusual will usually mean higher costs, perhaps a longer wait for visas and less efficient transport systems – therefore more preparation and travelling time. A bit of netsurfing, a check with any contacts who know a country and a chat with a travel agent will help you get a better idea of what this might mean.

Then there's the risk factor. Obviously family and friends will want you to avoid danger zones. The political situation in some places around the world is serious, unstable and can't be ignored.

You want your gap travels to be stimulating, fun, to let you experience different cultures and meet new people, but do you really want to end up in the middle of a war zone with your life in danger? Foreign news correspondents and war reporters with large back-up organisations prepare properly, with proper insurance and safety and survival courses – and it makes sense for gappers too!

A good starting point is the Foreign & Commonwealth Office website (**www.fco. gov.uk**) where you can find country profiles and assess the dangers and possible drawbacks to places you're thinking of. The FCO updates its danger list regularly as new areas of unrest emerge, but it's not, and never can be, a failsafe.

How long have you got?

Now you have at least a rough idea of where you want to go and what you want to do. The next step is to consider how long you might need to get it all in. How much time you can spare depends on *when* you're taking your gap.

That's going to be dictated by when you have to be back for starting university or college or, for career breakers, how much time your employer's prepared to let you have, or even whether you're willing to risk quitting your job for more gap time.

We are hearing plenty of evidence that shorter placements of a few weeks rather than a few months are in increasing demand. Here, you need to consider what you want to get out of your gap, and whether you are getting value for money. University entrance tutors and employers will want to see how your gap made a real difference – they will be looking for commitment, determination to see a project through, planning ability, the ability to think on one's feet, to assess and manage risks, and to raise money and manage finances. If you've taken on a short placement just to 'tick the gap-year box', you may find you haven't really gained these skills at all.

And, while it may be tempting to look for last-minute bargains, there are plenty of

my gap-year
Caroline

Before I went on my expedition to Borneo I was working at Rolls Royce as a customer services manager, where I worked for nine years. I felt like I needed a change and thought that a career break would be ideal. My friend recommended Raleigh International to me and I looked into the charity. I agree with their ethos about focusing on giving people a new outlook on life and the use of fundraising to spread Raleigh International's name.

I was the project manager responsible for overseeing the construction of a kindergarten in Sonsogon Magandai and my role was to ensure that it was built on time. I also had to ensure all the venturers were safe and I supported them throughout the project. Building a kindergarten in Borneo was important because Malaysia does not provide pre-school education and children are only accepted into primary education if they already have basic knowledge, which is very difficult for remote villages. It was the first time that Westerners and Raleigh International went to Sonsogon Magandai so it was important we made a good impression. I encouraged the venturers to interact with the local community so I organised for venturers to teach at the local school. I also got the venturers involved in community days, where we played games and we became involved with the local church. I think everyone, all venturers and the local community enjoyed this interaction.

My most challenging moment was when we were dropped off with 500kg of kit and had to trek two hours to get to the project site. The team decided the best way to carry the heavy kit was by carrying for 200m then hand over to another venture, just like a relay. I did not think we would get all the kit to the project site, but we did, the team's spirit made the difference.

My best moment was the opening ceremony for the kindergarten because at the beginning there was a green space and at the opening ceremony there was this beautiful yellow building with blue window sills just sitting there in the luscious green rainforest. I was so proud about what we had achieved. We had actually made a school, and to see the little children's eyes as they sat in the stools for the first time was really special. On the same day we handed the keys over. It was quite a moment for me as I handed the keys over to the head of the village.

Overall, Raleigh International is an absolutely awesome organisation. You are stretched, you're challenged, and you have these huge highs when you've achieved something you never thought you could achieve before. You get these real rollercoaster journeys at times when you hit a low, but then that becomes a high because the team really pulls together. Raleigh makes you understand how lucky you are, makes you aware of what you have, and to enjoy life.

For more information about Raleigh International, see Chapter 6 - Volunteering Abroad

reasons to get organised in good time.

Here, Jon Arnold, of Oyster Worldwide, gives his top five reasons for booking your gap-year early.

1. Secure your place – many projects book up months ahead of time, some can book up as far in advance as a year ahead of departure. If you leave your plans until the last minute, your chosen project may not be available.

2. Spread the cost – the earlier you book the longer you have to raise the money and save for your gap-year. When booking early you will generally pay a small deposit to hold your place, with the balance due much closer to departure.

3. Secure any work permits you need – if you want to get a paid job overseas on your gap-year you may need to get a work permit. For certain countries there may only be a small number of permits available which will run out quickly each year. As an example, for departures to Canada in November 2014, the work permits ran out in January 2014 for British passport holders!

4. Have something to look forward to – if you are still at school with one year left, the next 12 months are going to be the toughest of your education to date. Give yourself some light at the end of the tunnel, book your gap-year early, then you'll have something to look forward to at the end of all of those exams and essays.

5. Impress university admissions tutors when applying for deferred entry – by planning your gap-year before you apply for university you are really going to impress the admissions tutors when they look at your application. They will see someone who is organised, motivated and will have had a worthwhile experience overseas.

Ellen Sziede from African Conservation Experience says that, "A balance between being well prepared and keeping an open mind is good. Being prepared logistically prevents last minute stress. Reading up a bit on your destination and the topics you'll be exposed to during your placement are also a great idea, but try to avoid the pitfall of anticipating every last detail. You'll have a far more enjoyable time if you keep a bit of an open mind as to what things will be like."

How much do you want to spend?

Estimates vary widely, but the average cost for a full year's gap is £5000 for young people, around £6000 for mature travellers and up to £9000 for career breakers.

Much depends on where you're going and what you plan to do, and these days, if you care about the planet, climate change and ethical travel, you need also to include the costs of carbon offsetting. It's important to do as much research as possible,and a good place to start is **Chapter 2 – Finance**.

Do you want to go alone, or with friends and family?

It's totally understandable that you may want to share your experiences with friends or close family, and you may feel safer and more confident with company – and no doubt it will help the peace of mind of the family you leave behind. But, while safety should always be your first priority, don't be afraid of heading out on your own.

"My greatest advice would be not to wait around until you can persuade your friends and family to come with you," says Heilwig Jones, of Kaya Responsible Travel. "That is the most common reason that people end up not doing it and missing out. The

travelling community is so friendly, and participation in organised programs, such as ours, mean that it is easy to make friends along the way."

If you do travel with a friend or family, you have to be 100% certain you can spend 24 hours a day with them. We often hear of people going their separate ways during their trip.

Before you go, get to know where you're going

The more you know about your destination, the easier your trip will be: India, for example, is unbearably hot and humid in pre-monsoon April to June, Australia has seasons when bush fires are rampant and then there are the cyclone seasons in South Asia and rainy seasons in South America – and the consequent risk of flooding.

It's also worth finding out when special events are on. It could be very inconvenient to arrive in India during Diwali, when everyone's on holiday and all the trains are full! Similarly Japan – gorgeous in cherry blossom season but avoid travelling in Golden Week.

Before visiting any country that has recently been politically volatile or could turn into a war zone, check with the FCO (**www.gov.uk/knowbeforeyougo**) for information.

Note: If you're from a country that qualifies for a Visa Waiver for the USA (and that includes UK citizens) you must now register online your intent to visit the USA and you *must* receive travel authorisation. Authorisation still doesn't guarantee you'll be granted entry and you may still be asked to go to the US embassy for an interview, but you have to go through the process before you can do anything else. You'll find the details here: **travel.state.gov/content/visas/en.html**

If you're intending to visit for longer, or are planning to work, you will need the correct visa (see **Chapter 5 – Working abroad**).

Sort the paperwork

If you need to get yourself a passport for the first time, application forms are available from Post Offices or you can apply online. But remember: passport interviews are a new part of the process and are required by all applicants, aged 16 or over, who are applying for a passport for the first time.

You can apply for and renew passports online (**www.gov.uk/browse/abroad/passports**), but remember also that first time applicants can't use the fast track service.

There are interview offices around the country and you have to go to the correct one for where you live – see the map on the IPS (Identity and Passport Office) website: **maps.direct.gov.uk/LDGRedirect/MapAction.do?ref=passportinterviewoffices**

The standard adult ten-year passport currently costs £72.50 and you'll need your birth certificate and passport photos. It should take no more than a month from the time you apply to the time you receive your passport, but the queue lengthens coming up to peak summer holiday season.

You can use the Passport Office 'Check and Send' service at selected Post Offices throughout the UK or send it direct. The 'Check and Send' service gets your application checked for completeness (including documentation and fee) and is given priority by the IPS – they are usually able to process these applications in two weeks and it currently costs £82.25.

If your passport application is urgent and you're not applying for the first time, you can use the guaranteed same-day (Premium) service or the guaranteed one-week (Fast Track) service. Both services are only available by appointment at one of the seven IPS offices around the UK (phone the IPS Advice Line on 0300 222 0000), and both are more expensive (£128 for Premium, £103 for Fast Track).

The services are only available for renewals and amendments. And although you'll get a fixed appointment you'll almost certainly have to wait in a queue after this for your passport.

To apply online visit: **www.gov.uk/government/organisations/hm-passport-office**

The FCO provided us with a checklist to help sort your travel documents:

- Check your passport is valid for the country you are travelling to – some countries require six months left to run after your return date to the UK so check this as soon as you can to allow plenty of time.

- Keep your passport in a safe place while you're away, ideally in the hotel safe. Pack a photocopy of the main personal details and photograph page for ID purposes, so it's easier to replace if it goes missing.

- If your passport does get lost, stolen or damaged while you are away, you'll need an Emergency Travel Document (ETD) issued by the Foreign and Commonwealth Office. It's important to remember that an ETD does not guarantee you entry to every country and will cost you time and money.

- Make sure you've got the correct visa for the country you are visiting and allow plenty of time to research and prepare. Visit the Foreign and Commonwealth Office's travel advice page at **www.gov.uk/knowbeforeyougo** to read up on country specific travel advice, information and entry requirements.

27

my
gap-year
Milly Whitehead

Milly Whitehead travelled with The Leap to experience their new Madagascar program.

3 flights, 2 days and one boat later... I finally arrived in Madagascar... It's not every day you say to friends "Sorry can't do – I'm off to Madagascar." They look at you with a blinking eye as their brain scrambles to conjure up an image other than King Julian shaking his booty on a baobab. And so it was, I embarked on a journey to reach the remote island of Nosy Komba. An island, covered in rainforest and edged with the whitest beaches on Africa's remotest corner.

Nosy Be As I chugged out on my island taxi, a buzz of excitement started bubbling... over the years, I've visited a few places but I've never seen anything like this! The water is the prettiest shade of bluey-green, looking down I could see sparkling coral, looking across I saw the bobbing heads of turtles, and ahead, Nosy Komba - Heaven.

Nosy Komba As I got closer, I could see a large thatched building emerging in the forest; Turtle Cove, our volunteer base, an enormous thatched super stylish structure, which is the main communal base for the volunteers. This is where everyone congregates for meetings or chills with a beer. Dotted behind are six thatched dorms and showers nestled amongst the palm trees. All in all, there are about 35 volunteers here at any one time, from all over the world creating a fun, dynamic environment.

Projects

Marine research This is run by Kyle, who trains volunteers up to advanced PADI so that they're ready to help collate reef data to send onto worldwide studies. You won't believe how beautiful the underwater world can be. You spend four weeks amongst stingrays, turtles and Nemo's friends.

Outreach program on a 50 ft. catamaran AKA "The Admiral". Leapers spend twp weeks on board, sailing around tiny islands and visiting remote communities, teaching and contributing on each. A big highlight.

Teaching When Turtle Cove started, the islanders couldn't speak any English; they were subsistent with limited horizons, whereas now they feel liberated. The children race to get to school and the chiefs from other islands are now turning up asking for help in their own communities. David's parting words were "Milly, we need more teachers...." I'm on the case!

Forestry conservation Run by Julia, who hauls volunteers into the rainforest to study the wildlife (mainly lemurs) and bio-diversity of the area. Totally

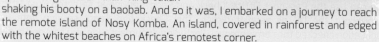

dedicated, she motivates, teaches and challenges the volunteers to battle their way through the jungle and to ignore the bugs.

On reflection To me, this is one of the best programs The Leap offers, as it is totally unique. The journey to get there is an adventure in itself, the final destination extraordinary and so off the beaten track you'll feel like an early explorer. At times, I had to pinch myself as I relished the next visual feast. All in all, it will blow your mind, and that's a promise.

For more information about The Leap, see Chapter 6 - Volunteering Abroad

Leave someone in charge at home

Make sure you have someone reliable and trustworthy in charge of sorting things out for you – especially the official stuff that won't wait. Get someone you really trust to open your post and arrange to talk to them at regular intervals in case something turns up that you need to deal with.

However, there are some things you just have to do yourself, so make sure you've done everything important before you go. This particularly applies to any regular payments you make – check all your standing orders/direct debits and make sure to cancel any you don't need; and that there's money in your account for any you do need.

It's also worth contacting your bank about giving permissions to someone else that you trust whilst you're away. Should you encounter any issues with credit card bills, or withdrawing cash *etc*, it's always handy to have someone back home to help you out – even if to save on the long distance phone calls to the bank!

If you have a flat or house you're planning to sub-let, either use an accommodation agency or make sure someone you trust will keep an eye on things – it may be necessary to give them some written form of authority to deal with emergencies. There's more on all this in **Chapter 3 – Career breaks and older travellers**.

What to take

Start thinking early about what to take with you and write a list – adding to it every time you think of something. Here's a general checklist to get you started:

- Passport and tickets
- Padlock and chain
- Belt bag
- Daypack (can be used for valuables in transit/hand luggage on plane)
- First aid kit: including any personal meds: split between day pack and rucksack
- Notebook and pen
- Camera (with spare battery, memory cards and a lead)
- USB stick (to periodically back up any photos you take)

29

- Mobile phone and charger
- Headphones with built-in microphone (mic for when you are making a video call)
- MP3 player
- Money: cards/travellers' cheques/cash
- Torch/candle
- Sheet sleeping bag
- Universal adapter
- Pack of playing cards
- Spare specs/contact lenses
- Guidebook/phrasebooks – if doing several countries trade in/swap with other travellers en route
- Spare photos for ID cards if needed
- Photocopies of documents/emergency numbers/serial numbers of travellers' cheques (Also, use online storage such as Dropbox to keep a digital copy as back-up)
- Clothes and toiletries *etc*

Some of these checklist items will be more relevant to backpackers and people on treks, than to people on a work placement or staying in a family home. The list can be modified for your own particular plans.

Handy items

We love this advice from gap-year veteran Becci Coombes, from GirlsTravelClub. co.uk, where you'll find gear, gifts and advice, for her top tips on packing for your trip:

"The key to a well-packed rucksack is not to fill it up," Becci told us, "but leave plenty of room for your necessary holiday purchases. When you are packing, lay everything out you think you are going to need, then halve it, before halving it again!"

Here is a list of some handy items Becci has found useful that you might never have considered...

· Dental floss Have you ever thought about how handy 50 metres of strong string (albeit minty-flavoured) all neatly packaged in a cute little box with a handy integral cutter could be? Many times I have used it for hanging mozzy nets, as an emergency bootlace, as a strong sewing thread, and it also makes a great washing line for drying your swimming gear.

· Forget those universal sink plug things; when you fill the sink up with water then try and actually wash something in it, the plug will either be knocked out by your vigorous sock-washing or just float about annoyingly as all your precious hot water drains away. A squash ball is much more useful; you can wedge firmly it into the hole and then use it to play squash afterwards.

· Micropore medical tape is marvellous stuff for the thrifty packer. Not only can you use it as an emergency plaster on blisters and little cuts, you can hold dressings on with it or put it on tiny splinters to yank them out of your thorn-ravaged flesh.

· Clear ziplock bags in different sizes. You can use them for storing wet swimming costumes; keeping those less-than-pleasant socks from tainting the rest of your gear, and also keep any maps nice and dry as you tramp through unexpected downpours looking for shelter.

· Bin bags also come in handy in many more ways than you'd think. Aside from using them for litter, you can always use one as a rucksack cover or an emergency poncho in a downpour; just cut a head hole and sit under it, keeping your arms nice and warm next to your body. Fill one with dry leaves as a mattress to insulate you from the ground damp as well; on one of our travel skills courses we stuffed them really full and used them as beanbags, and they were surprisingly comfy!

· I always make sure I've got a few elastic bands about my person as they are always being used for different purposes. Roll up your biggest items of clothing and secure with a couple of bands so they take up less space, and also put a couple round your flip-flops to keep them nice and tidy. Hang towels from trees by securing round one corner.

· I tend to keep my most useful bits and pieces in a plastic lunchbox, just because damp plasters/matches/Twixes aren't half as much fun as dry ones, and I have found the box very handy for all sorts of bits and pieces. Again, it can be used for collecting water from streams, as an ingenious receptacle for emergency cornflake consumption or, well, as a lunchbox.

· Lastly, and most importantly for us girls, my mum's top piece of travel advice is only pack very good quality chocolate with a high cocoa content, as it doesn't melt when it gets hot, it just bends!

There are other useful items you might want to consider: a miniature-sized room spray, for example (Yankee Candle do a great selection): useful to give your rucksack or even your dorm room a quick spray.

Water purifying tablets are great in an emergency, although they won't deal with all the possible waterborne parasites. Sometimes boiling water and adding iodine are also necessary. It's best to stick to bottled mineral water if available – even for

the gap-year guidebook 2016

my
gap-year
Pete Morrow

I always had an interest in volunteering abroad. I found that university wasn't an immediate interest of mine, but travelling definitely was. Projects Abroad came to my school and offered a safe opportunity (very popular to my parents) to go somewhere and do something cool (very popular to me).

The people of Peru are some of the funniest, kindest, and most inspirational people I have met. I was in Peru for a total of two months, living and working in a town named Calca. It became my home in every sense of the word. I had family, food, neighbours, friends, cousins, fiestas, and, in my case, even an adoptive dog named Poncho. By the end of two months I had a complete routine. Go to work, then meet a friend and Poncho to go to our regulars; the internet café, visit the juice bar lady, and later hit the pastry shop.

I was working as a care programme volunteer and five days of the week I got to work with 25 of the cutest kindergarten kids I've ever seen. I'll admit, I had no idea what I was doing on the first day of class. I thought, how am I supposed to deal with a class full of five year olds, and do it all in Spanish? The answer? Be a kid again, let down all guards, and remember how to play. Trust me, one of the most important pieces in volunteering abroad is to really get involved with what you're doing. My first week I helped the kids cut things out, paint, peeled fruits for them at break, and became a human jungle gym during recess. Later, I got more comfortable and involved by teaching a weekly animal in English, and making picture books for the class.

For more information about Projects Abroad, see Chapter 6 - Volunteering Abroad

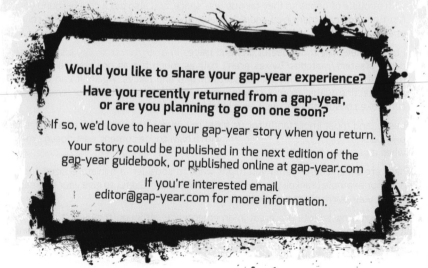

Would you like to share your gap-year experience?

Have you recently returned from a gap-year, or are you planning to go on one soon?

If so, we'd love to hear your gap-year story when you return.

Your story could be published in the next edition of the gap-year guidebook, or published online at gap-year.com

If you're interested email editor@gap-year.com for more information.

brushing your teeth – but always check that the seal is intact before you buy. That way you will be sure it's not a mineral water bottle refilled with the local dodgy supply.

Lifesaver Systems produces a bottle that converts even the nastiest stuff into drinkable water without the use of chemicals. It's not cheap but being ill through drinking bad water while travelling can be expensive or even life threatening.

Remember it's easy to get dehydrated in hot countries so you should always carry a bottle of water with you and drink frequently – up to eight litres a day. You should also take a few sachets of rehydration salts with you. Many people suffer with diarrhoea when they're away, and rehydration therapy such as Dioralyte is a great treatment.

Less is best

As airlines struggle with rising fuel costs, and diminishing passenger numbers, they are becoming increasingly inventive in dreaming up extra charges. Excess and overweight check-in baggage is one particularly fruitful area – and it's confusing as the rules vary from airline to airline. This makes it even more crucial to think very carefully about what you need to take – and what you could do without.

Basically, some charge per piece and others by weight, but that's not all. Some carriers limit you to one check-in piece, others, like BA, allow two. It can also depend on your route and your destination. Weight limits vary from as little as 20kg per bag to 30kg. Charges can even be different on outward and return journeys, with some carriers charging as much as £30 per kilogram over the permitted weight, or £90 per extra bag. It won't take much to wipe out all the money you've saved by searching for the cheapest available flights!

Inevitably if you fly business or first class the allowances are more generous but the above assumes that most people on a gap will be flying economy.

my
gap-year
Rory Fraser

For me the 'gap yah' was never the plan. It was not until Cambridge Pre-U lost one of my exam papers that I decided to take some time off in order to rethink my options. At first the prospect of a totally unstructured year was terrifying, but the more I planned, the more excited I became, for the more I came to realise that an adventure was precisely what I needed. Plans developed quickly, from ideas to conversations, conversations to contacts, contacts to three concrete zones of the year: work, travel and charity. It was during the planning phase, when sorting through the enormous pile of gap-year leaflets on the kitchen table, that my mother fished out the John Hall Course brochure, had a quick browse, and murmured "this looks good". Indeed it did, for before I could say Botticelli, I found myself whizzing across the Adriatic gawping at the looming spires of Venice.

John Hall, for those who don't know, is a two month long course which takes you from Venice through to Florence and Rome and gives you, in many ways, the modern grand tour experience through lectures in art, opera, architecture, history, photography, painting and film from some of the top experts in their field. Although these lectures were extremely good, undoubtedly hugely expanding my frame of reference for university, they were not the reason that I so loved the course. For me John Hall was about plugging into a different world, a world outside the lecture room.

The thrill that I experienced time and again wandering through these wonderful cities was extremely special, and at times even spiritual. Whether it was Venice, with her electric sense of history and echo of water against the crumbling pallazi, or Florence, enjoying a cappuccino under duomo which glitters in the early morning haze, John Hall offered the opportunity, not only to fall in love with Italy in a pretty glammy way, but fundamentally to begin to understand where the idea of Europe comes from, and so, in a sense, where I come from.

Now, six months later, after having travelled all over the world, it amuses me that the greatest adventure of my year was not in fact in Cambodia or Kenya, but in the art gallery's of Italy.

For more information about John Hall Venice see Chapter 7 - Learning Abroad

Packing tips

· Pack in reverse order – first in, last out.

· Heavy items go at the bottom.

· Pack in categories in plastic bags – easier to find stuff.

· Use vacuum pack bags for bulky items.

· Store toilet rolls and dirty undies in side pockets – easy for thieves to open and they won't want them!

· Take a small, separate backpack for day hikes *etc*. You can buy small, thin folding ones.

· Keep spares (undies, toothbrush, important numbers and documents) in hand luggage.

· Take a sleeping bag liner – useful in hostels.

· Take a sarong (versatile: can be a bed sheet, towel, purse, bag...)

· Travel towels are lightweight and dry fast.

· Remove packaging from everything but keep printed instructions for medications.

· Shaving oil takes less space than cream.

· Put liquids in squashy bottles (and don't carry liquids in hand luggage).

· Fill shoes, cups *etc* with socks and undies to save space.

· Tie up loose backpack straps before it goes into transit.

Now sit down and rationalise – cross off everything you don't really need. Pack enough clothes to see you through – about five changes of clothing should last you for months if you choose carefully. Don't take anything that doesn't go with everything else and stick to materials that are comfortable, hard-wearing, easy to wash and dry and don't crease too much. Make sure you have clothes that are

35

suitable for the climates you are visiting and don't forget that the temperatures in some dry climates can drop considerably at night! You can find very lightweight waterproofs and thermals that can be rolled up easily.

Relax, you can't prepare for every eventuality if you're living out of a rucksack. The best way to know what you need is to ask someone who's already been on a gap what they took, what were the most useful things, what they didn't need and what they wished they had taken.

Maps, directions and vital information

You won't need anything too elaborate: the maps in guidebooks are usually pretty good. A good pocket diary can be very useful – one that gives international dialling codes, time differences, local currency details, bank opening hours, public holidays and other information.

Take a list with you of essential information like directions to voluntary work postings, key addresses, medical information, credit card numbers (try to disguise these in case everything gets stolen), passport details (and a photocopy of the main and visa pages), emergency contact numbers in case of loss of travellers' cheques and insurance and flight details – and leave a copy with someone at home.

Another way of keeping safe copies of your vital documents (even if everything you have is lost or stolen) is to scan them before you leave and email them as attachments to your email address. However, it is well known that you shouldn't send sensitive information via email and it's not clear whether that advice also applies to attachments, given that they're all stored on a remote server, so you might prefer one of the many online secure data storage options. Or you could even put it all on a memory stick, which has the advantage of being small and easy to conceal and carry.

Those of you with a smartphone or an MP3 player on to which you can download apps will be able to input a mass of information and effectively 'carry' maps, timetables, hostel finders, information lists, and photographs of your valuable documents with you in one small, slim device. An app well worth looking in to is 'CityMaps2Go' as it offers an 'offline' map service. It downloads the map to your phone, so you don't have to worry about having a data connection to keep the map up to date, according to your latest position.

The FCO offers travel advice through social media updates and email alerts. You can subscribe to the alerts at **www.gov.uk/knowbeforeyougo**, selecting the country you are travelling to. Updates will also be issued via the FCO Twitter account @fcotravel and on their Facebook page: www.facebook.com/fcotravel.

Where to buy your kit

Some overseas voluntary organisations arrange for their students to have discounts at specific shops, like the YHA. The best advice on equipment usually comes from specialist shops, although they may not be the cheapest: these include YHA shops, Blacks, Millets and Camping and Outdoors Centres.

Rucksacks

Prices for a well-stitched, 65-litre rucksack can vary greatly. Remember, the most expensive is not necessarily the best, get what is most suitable for your trip.

A side-opening backpack is easier than a top-opening one. You can get all sorts of attachments but if you don't need it why pay for it? A good outdoor store should be able to advise you on exactly what you need for your particular trip. Most of these stores have websites with helpful hints and lists of 'essential' items.

You should be able to leave your rucksack in most hostels or guest houses, if you are staying for more than a day, or in a locker at the train station. Always take camera, passport, important papers and money with you everywhere, zipped up, preferably out of view.

Footwear

It's worth investing in something comfortable if you're heading off on a long trip. In hot countries, a good pair of sandals is the preferred footwear for many and it's worth paying for a decent pair, as they will last longer and be comfortable. If you're going somewhere cheap you could just pick up a pair out there but you're likely to be doing a lot more walking than usual, so comfort and durability are important.

Some people like chunky walking boots, others just their trainers, but it's best to get something that won't fall apart when you're halfway up a mountain. Take more than one pair of comfortable shoes in case they don't last, but don't take too many – they'll be an unnecessary burden and take up precious space in your rucksack.

Sleeping bags

Go to a specialist shop where you can get good advice. Prices vary widely and you can sometimes find a four-season bag cheaper than a one-season bag – it's mostly down to quality. You need to consider:

· Can you carry it comfortably and still have the energy to do all you want to do?

· Hot countries – do you need one? You may just want to take a sheet sleeping bag (basically just a sewn-up sheet).

Gap Year Travel Store, Unit C4 Evans Business Park,
Burley Rd, Leeds LS4 2PU UK
T: 0843 886 2242
E: gy-support@gapyeartravelstore.com   W: www.gapyeartravelstore.com

Established in 2006, The Gap Year Travel Store is an online store dedicated to providing gap year travellers with all the equipment they need for their trip. Our team of travel enthusiasts are always on hand to give you the best advice on travel gear, whether you're unsure which backpack to take or which sleeping bag you need for your adventure. We stock everything from travel first aid kits and travel adapters to backpacks, mosquito nets and insect repellents. Our dedicated online travel store also allows you to shop by destination, giving you a starting point when it comes to choosing the right equipment for your gap year. Check out our travel blog for destination guides, packing lists, travel kit reviews and more.

- Colder countries: what will you be doing? Take into account weight and size and the conditions you'll be travelling in – you might want to go for one of those compression sacs that you can use to squash sleeping bags into. For cold countries, you need heat-retaining materials. You can usually – but not always – rent down-filled bags for treks in, say, Nepal.

First aid kit

Useful basics:

- Re-hydration sachets (to use after diarrhoea)
- Waterproof plasters
- TCP/Tea tree oil
- Corn and blister plasters for sore feet
- Cotton buds
- A small pair of straight nail scissors (not to be carried in your hand luggage on the plane)
- Safety pins (not to be carried in your hand luggage on the plane)
- Insect repellent
- Antiseptic cream
- Anti-diarrhoea pills (only short-term; they stop the diarrhoea temporarily but don't cure you)
- Water sterilisation tablets
- Antihistamine cream
- Your own preferred form of painkiller

You can get a medical pack from most chemists, travel shops or online from MASTA (**www.masta.org**).

www.gapyeartravelstore.com also specialise in medical kits for travellers: the contents vary from sting relief, tick removers, blister kits, sun block and rehydration sachets to complete sterile medical packs with needles and syringe kits (in case you think the needle someone might have to inject you with may not be sterile).

You can also buy various types of mosquito net, water purification tablets and filters, money pouches, world receiver radios, travel irons and kettles. Not to mention a personal attack alarm.

Cameras

Picture quality on many mobile phones is now so good that you may not feel the need to take a camera as well, especially if you're going to be uploading your pictures on to one of the many photo sharing websites now available. However, very few people rely on *just* their phone when they are travelling. Firstly, taking photos will drain the phone battery quicker, and if you need your phone for staying in touch, or making a call in an emergency, a dead phone is obviously of no use. You also don't want to put all your eggs in to one basket with your devices. If you use your phone for absolutely everything, and it gets lost or stolen, you lose everything.

If you do want the back-up of a camera, check with your local photographic dealer about what will best suit your requirements. Make sure you get a camera case to protect from knocks, dust and moisture and don't buy the cheapest you can find. Cheap equipment can let you down and you need something that doesn't have software compatibility/connection problems.

Here are a few other tips:

· Digital cameras use lots of power (especially if using flash). Take plenty of batteries with you or take rechargeable batteries and a charger (you'll save money in the long run but check they're usable in your particular camera).

· Don't risk losing all your photos. Back them up as you travel. Maybe visit an internet cafe occasionally and upload your best photos to a site such as Instagram or Photobucket. Upload them on to your Facebook site. Or even send them to your home email account.

· Don't walk around with your camera round your neck. Keep it out of sight whenever possible to reduce the risk of crime.

· Remember certain countries charge extra for using a camcorder at heritage sites, safari parks and monuments, but often they don't charge for still cameras.

Looking after yourself...

Health

Note: although we make every effort to be as up-to-date and accurate as possible, the following advice is intended to serve as a guideline only. It is designed to be helpful rather than definitive, and you should always check with your GP, preferably at most eight weeks before going away.

It's not only which countries you'll be going to, but for how long and what degree of roughing it: six months in a basic backpacker hostel puts people at higher risk than two weeks in a five-star hotel.

Before you go you should tell your doctor:

· Your proposed travel route.

· The type of activities you will be doing.

Ask for advice, not only about injections and pills needed, but symptoms to look out for and what to do if you suspect you've caught something.

Some immunisations are free under the NHS but you may have to pay for the more exotic/rare ones. Some, like the Hepatitis A vaccine, can be very expensive, but this is not an area to be mean with your money – it really is worth being cautious with your health.

Also, many people recommend that you know your blood type before you leave the country, to save time and ensure safety. Your GP might have it on record – if not, a small charge may be made for a blood test.

If you're going abroad to do voluntary work, don't assume the organisation will give you medical advice first or even when you get there, though they often do. Find out for yourself, and check if there is a medically-qualified person in or near the institution you are going to be posted with.

People who've been to the relevant country/area are a great source of information. Some travellers prefer to go to a dedicated travel clinic to get pre-travel health advice. This may be especially worthwhile if your GP/practice nurse does not see many travellers.

Here are some options:

www.welltravelledclinics.co.uk is a UK travel clinic company, and part of the Liverpool School of Tropical Medicine **www.e-med.co.uk** has a useful free travel service, which you can email for advice on immunisations, anti-malaria medication and what to watch out for.

www.fitfortravel.scot.nhs.uk

www.travelhealth.co.uk

Department of Health website:

www.nhs.uk/LiveWell/TravelHealth/Pages/Travelhealthhome.aspx

For safety advice try the Foreign and Commonwealth Office:

www.fco.gov.uk/travel

Another good idea is to register with an organisation such as Medic Alert, a non-profit-making charity providing a life-saving identification system for individuals with hidden medical conditions and allergies.

The MedicAlert service is particularly helpful for those who wish to travel. The MedicAlert emblem contains the international sign of medicine, and is recognised around the world. MedicAlert also has a 24-hour emergency number that can be accessed by medical personnel anywhere in the world and has a translation service in more than 100 languages. As a MedicAlert member, you wear a bracelet or necklet (known as an emblem) engraved with a personal identification number, main medical conditions and an emergency telephone number.

my
gap-year
Jonathan Toppin

When you volunteer in Madagascar with Blue Ventures, you choose whether you want to learn fish or coral first. Both are fascinating and diverse, however fish appears to be the more popular choice and it was for me as well.

You study and practice identifying 150 species of fish so that when you do a survey during a dive, you can write down how many you see of each kind. I have made a very fun activity sound very boring, and I apologize, but in reality once you know your fish, it's like seeing old friends under the ocean. You come to learn the behaviour and swimming patterns of different fish. After this, it becomes a fun hunt to find your favourites, see rare fish, or discover new behaviour and things that you hadn't seen before.

Highlights include seeing a sailfish check out a group of divers near the surface while I was watching from the boat, seeing titan triggers and napoleon wrasses, as well as hearing the regular calls of humpback whales from underwater as they migrated through the Mozambique Channel. We spotted quite a few whales, including a few lucky divers who saw one above them from underwater, which is unbelievably rare. I was lucky enough to see lots of breaching and had some close encounters on the surface while sailing.

There is no doubt that this is a very unique ecosystem that needs to be watched and protected, as it can easily be lost, and there are plenty of large fishing boats that patrol the channel collecting everything in their paths, dismaying us and the locals who are struggling with feeding their families while protecting their ecosystem.

For more information about Blue Ventures, see Chapter 6 - Volunteering Abroad

In an emergency, medical personnel have immediate access to vital information on the back of the MedicAlert disc. By phoning the emergency number, they can also gain further medical and personal information such as your name and address, doctor's details, current drug therapy and next of kin details.

Membership to the service, including a tailor-made emblem, is £30 a year.

Accidents/injuries

Accidents and injuries are the greatest cause of death in young travellers abroad. Alcohol/drug use will increase the risk of these occurring. Travellers to areas with poor medical facilities should take a sterile medical equipment pack with them. Make sure that you have good travel insurance that will bring you home if necessary.

AIDS

The HIV virus that causes AIDS can be contracted from: injections with infected needles; transfusions of infected blood; sexual intercourse with an infected person; or possibly cuts (if you have a shave at the barbers, insist on a fresh blade, but it's probably best to avoid the experience altogether). It is not caught through everyday contact, insect bites, dirty food or crockery, kissing, coughing or sneezing. Protect yourself: always use condoms during sex, make sure needles are new and if you need a blood transfusion make sure blood has been screened, and don't get a tattoo or piercing until you're back home and can check out the tattoo shop properly.

Asthma and allergies

Whether you are an asthmatic or have an allergy to chemicals in the air, food, stings, or antibiotics, ask your GP for advice before you go. You will be able to take some treatments with you.

Allergy sufferers: if you suffer from severe shock reactions to insect bites/nuts or any other allergy, make sure you have enough of your anaphylactic shock packs with you – you may not be able to get them in some parts of the world.

Chronic conditions

Asthmatics, diabetics, epileptics or those with other conditions should always wear an obvious necklace or bracelet or carry an identity card stating the details of their condition. Tragedies do occur due to ignorance, and if you are found unconscious a label can be a lifesaver. See **www.medicalert.org.uk** for information on obtaining these items.

You should also keep with you a written record of your medical condition and the proper names (not just trade names) of any medication you are taking. If you are going on an organised trip or volunteering abroad, find out who the responsible person for medical matters is and make sure you fully brief them about your condition.

43

Contraceptives

If you are on the pill it is advisable to take as many with you as possible. Remember that contraceptives go against religious beliefs in some countries, so they may not be readily available. Antibiotics, some malaria treatments, vomiting and diarrhoea can inhibit the absorption of the pill, so use alternative means of contraception until seven days after the illness.

Condoms: unprotected sex can be fatal, so everyone should take them, even if they are not likely to be used. Keep them away from sand, water and sun. If buying abroad, make sure they are a known brand and have not been kept in damp, hot or icy conditions.

Dentist

Pretty obvious but often forgotten: get anything you need done to your teeth before you go. Especially worth checking up on are wisdom teeth and fillings – you don't want to spend three months in Africa with toothache.

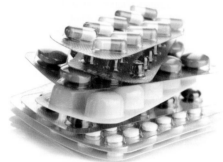

Diabetics

Wear an obvious medical alert necklace or bracelet, or carry an ID card stating your condition (preferably with a translation into the local language). Take enough insulin for your stay, although it is unlikely that a GP will give you the amount of medication needed for a full year of travelling – three to six months is usually their limit, in which case, be prepared to buy insulin abroad and at full price. Ring the BDA Careline to make sure the brand of insulin you use is available in the particular country you are planning to visit. Your medication must be kept in the passenger area of a plane, not the aircraft hold where it will freeze.

Diabetes UK, **www.diabetes.org.uk**
Careline: +44 (0) 845 120 2960, weekdays 9am-5pm.
Email: careline@diabetes.org.uk

Diabetes UK produces a general travel information booklet as well as specific travel packs for about 70 countries.

Diarrhoea

By far the most common health problem to affect travellers abroad is travellers' diarrhoea. This is difficult to avoid but it is sensible to do the best you can to prevent problems. High-risk food/drinks include untreated tap water, shellfish, unpasteurised dairy products, salads, peeled/prepared uncooked fruit, raw/undercooked meat and fish. Take a kit to deal with the symptoms (your doctor or nurse should be able to advise on this). Remember to take plenty of 'safe' drinks if you are ill and re-hydration salts to replace lost vitamins and minerals.

If vomiting and/or diarrhoea continue for more than four to five days or you run a fever, have convulsions or breathing difficulties (or any unusual symptoms), get someone to call a doctor straight away. Seek advice on the best doctor to call; the British embassy or a five-star hotel in the area may be able to offer some advice here.

To help lower the risk of diarrhoea when you're away, prepare your body before you go. For a couple months before you leave, include yogurt in your diet. It's filled with 'good' bacteria and probiotics, both of which can help regulate your digestive system whilst you're away.

Eyes

Contact lens wearers should stock up on cleaning fluid before going, especially if venturing off the beaten track; but if you're going away for a long period it might be worth switching to disposable types so there's less to carry – ask your optician for advice.

Dust and wind can be a real problem, so refreshing eye drops to soothe itchy eyes and wash out grit can be really useful. If you wear contact lenses, your optician should be able to offer you a range of comfort drops which will be compatible with your lenses.

Also most supermarket pharmacies, plus travel and camping shops, sell plastic bottles of mildly medicated hand cleanser that dries instantly. They're small and light to carry and you only use a small amount each time so it's worth packing a couple. They're really useful for cleaning hands before putting in contact lenses if the local water supply is suspect. It's also worth making sure you have glasses as a back-up, as it's not always possible to replace lost or torn contacts.

If you wear glasses consider taking a spare pair – they don't have to be expensive and you can choose frames that are flexible and durable. Keep them in a hard glasses case in a waterproof (and sandproof) pouch.

Malaria

This disease is caught from the bite of an anopheles mosquito and mosquitoes are vicious and vindictive. Highest risk areas are tropical regions like sub-Saharan Africa, the Solomon Islands and Vanuatu (Pacific), the Amazon basin in South America and parts of Asia. There's no jab, but your GP will give you a course of pills to take.

The most dangerous form of malaria is falciparum, which is particularly common in sub-Saharan Africa (places like Ghana, Gambia, DR Congo). It can cause liver, kidney, stomach and neurological problems and if left untreated, can be fatal.

One bite from a mosquito is enough. The parasite gets to your liver within 30 minutes and will reproduce there rapidly, infecting the blood stream. Once the parasites are in your blood stream you start to notice symptoms. Some versions can remain dormant in the liver, leading to repeat episodes of the illness.

The best protection is to try (as much as possible) to avoid being bitten. Here are tips for how:

· Use insect repellent, preferably containing either at least 30% DEET (diethyltoluamide), or extract of lemon eucalyptus oil.

· Keep your arms and legs covered between dusk and dawn and use a 'knockdown' spray to kill any mosquitoes immediately.

my
gap-year
Ben Robinson

Ben joined Onaris Africa for six weeks in Malindi, Kenya. His placement in a Health Clinic was carefully sourced after Ben had discussed the sort of placement he wanted and it proved to be instrumental in Ben progressing on his path towards a successful career in nursing.

Onaris Africa stood out from the crowd of volunteer organisations. The actual freedom and input I could have on my experience is something that I had not seen elsewhere. All the questions I had (and I had a lot of questions!) were talked through at length. I never once felt in the build up to my trip that I was stepping into a scenario that I wasn't 100% sure about, this was really important to me.

When I eventually landed in Kenya I was just blown away. I have never been anywhere as beautiful as the Kenyan coast. The people are incredibly friendly, the food is out of this world and I never once felt uneasy or unsafe. It took me a while to get used to the change, but you soon find yourself becoming a little more Kenyan everyday!

My placement was at Gede Health Clinic. Having discussed with Onaris Africa prior to my trip the type of experience I wanted, they suggested that this particular scenario would be ideal, and they were so right. Having an amazing number of contacts in the area meant that had I wanted a different type of medical placement, it could have been catered to by Onaris.

My placement was very hands on from day one, and it was the best time of my life. I was challenged and supported to do so many things I never thought I'd do. Everything from patching up cuts and bruises, to getting up close and personal in the maternity ward. I was very much a working piece in a busy hospital-like environment. It was a truly unforgettable experience!

For more information about Onaris Africa, see Chapter 6 - Volunteering Abroad

- Mosquito nets are useful, but they can be hard to put up correctly. It is often worth carrying a little extra string and small bits of wire so that the net can be hung up in rooms that don't have hanging hooks. Ideally the net should be impregnated with an insecticide, you can buy nets that are already treated from specialist shops and travel clinics.

- For some places, dual-voltage mosquito killer plugs are a good idea. *Holiday Which?* tested hand-held electric buzzers that claim to frighten off mosquitoes and found that they did not work on the anopheles mosquito.

- Another good idea is to spray clothes with permethrin – which usually lasts up to two weeks, although Healthguard has a product, called AM-1, which works for three months or 30 washes. Visit **www.healthguardtm.com** to find out more or call them on +44 (0)20 8275 1100.

The pills can be expensive, and some people, particularly on long trips, stop taking their pills, especially if they're not getting bitten much. Don't. Malaria can be fatal.

No one drug acts on all stages of the disease, and different species of parasites show different responses. Your GP, practice nurse or local travel clinic should know which one of the varied anti-malarials is best for you, depending on your medical history (*eg* for epileptics or asthmatics, for whom some types of anti-malarials cannot be prescribed) and the countries you are visiting. Visit your GP or travel clinic at least eight weeks before you go to discuss the options.

It's also worth doing a little research of your own before going to your GP or practice nurse. A useful website is **www.malariahotspots.co.uk** All the anti-malarial tablets have various pros and cons, and some of them have significant side effects. If you're going to an area where you have to use the weekly mefloquine tablets, MASTA recommends that you start taking the course two-and-a-half to three weeks before departure. Most people who experience unpleasant side effects with this drug, will notice them by the third dose. If you do have problems, this trial will allow you time to swap to an alternative regime before you go.

If you are in a malaria-risk area, or have recently been in one, and start suffering from 'flu-like' symptoms, *eg* fever, muscle pain, nausea, headache, fatigue, chills, and/or sweats, you should consider the diagnosis of malaria and seek medical attention immediately.

A traveller with these symptoms within several months after returning from an endemic area should also seek medical care and tell their doctor their travel history. The correct treatment involves the proper identification of the type of malaria parasite, where the traveller has been and their medical history.

Sunburn

Wherever your gap-year takes you, the advice from Cancer Research UK's SunSmart campaign is to enjoy your time in the sun safely. This means not getting caught out by sunburn which, as well as being unsightly, is a clear sign that skin cells have been damaged. Over time, this damage can build up and may ultimately lead to skin cancer.

So while everyone needs some sun in their lives, too much can be harmful. The facts are worrying – skin cancer is one of the most common cancers in the UK and the number of people who develop it is increasing faster than any other type of common cancer. Every year over 11,000 people are diagnosed with malignant melanoma – the most lethal type of skin cancer – and almost 2000 die from the disease. It is diagnosed in a disproportionately high number of younger people, being the second most common cancer in young adults (aged 15-34) in the UK.

And as well as causing skin cancer, too much UV can cause premature ageing, making skin look old and leathery before its time.

But the good news is that most cases of skin cancer can be prevented. When you're out in the sun, the most important thing is to make sure you don't burn. Get to know your skin type and how it reacts in the sun. As a general rule, the lighter your skin, the more careful you should be.

When your risk of burning is high, often during the hottest part of the day, spend time in the shade, cover up with a T-shirt or a towel and regularly apply plenty of sunscreen (at least factor 15 – but the higher the better) to protect your skin.

Whatever your skin type the message is simple – don't let sunburn catch you out. Anyone can develop skin cancer but some people have a higher risk and need to take more care, including those with fair skin, lots of moles or freckles, a history of sunburn or a family or personal history of skin cancer.

SunSmart is the UK's skin cancer awareness campaign, funded by the UK health departments. To identify your skin type, find out more about skin cancer, how to enjoy the sun safely, and the dangers of using sunbeds visit **www.sunsmart.org.uk**.

Tick borne encephalitis (TBE)

Ticks are second only to mosquitoes for carrying diseases to humans and immunisation is recommended for people who intend to walk, camp or work in heavily forested regions of affected countries between April and October when the ticks are most active. Your doctor or practice nurse can advise if you should have this immunisation for your travel destination.

Tick Alert say that TBE is "a viral disease contracted via the bite of an infected tick that is endemic in 27 countries in Europe. It leads to an annual average of 10,000 cases needing hospital treatment. Two in every 100 TBE sufferers will die from the disease."

TBE incubation is six to 14 days and at first can cause increased temperature, headaches, fever, cough and sniffles, symptoms similar to a cold or flu. The second, more dangerous phase of TBE can lead to neck stiffness, severe headaches, delirium and paralysis. There is no specific treatment for TBE. However, this is how you can protect yourself:

· Use an insect repellent that is effective against ticks.

· Avoid wearing shorts in rural and wooded areas, tuck trousers into socks, or cover all exposed skin with protective clothing (though not always practical in summer).

· Inspect your skin for ticks and remove any found as soon as possible with fine-tipped tweezers or a tick-removal tool. If using a special tool, follow instructions for use. If you are using fine-tipped tweezers, grasp the tick firmly and as close to the skin as possible. In a steady motion, pull the tick's body away directly outwards without jerking or twisting. Make sure you get the tick's head out as sometimes the head can remain embedded.

· Also, avoid unpasteurised milk which may also be infected with the TBE virus in endemic regions.

48

Vaccinations

Ones to consider:

· Hepatitis (A&B).

· Japanese Encephalitis.

· Meningitis.

· Polio.

· Rabies.

· Tetanus.

· Tuberculosis.

· Typhoid.

· Yellow Fever.

The NHS provide information on the vaccinations and diseases that you need to be aware of in the country you are visiting: **www.fitfortravel.nhs.uk** Ask your GP for advice on vaccinations/precautions six to eight weeks before you go (some may be available on the NHS). Keep a record card on you of what you've had done. Certain countries won't admit you unless you have a valid yellow fever certificate.

Seeking medical advice abroad

You can expect to be a bit ill when you travel just due to the different food and unsettled lifestyle (painkillers and loo paper will probably be the best things you've packed).

While you're away:

· Keep a record of any treatment, such as courses of antibiotics, that you have when overseas and tell your doctor when you get back;

49

my gap-year
Brooke

During my time in Mexico, I worked with children with a wide range of disabilities by doing physical therapy, feeding the children and doing intellectual exercises with them. I also felt like I contributed occupational therapy to the project because they didn't have an occupational therapist.

My fondest memory was working with a boy named Christian. When I started the project, he was being spoon-fed during all of his meals. I worked with him every day during meal time and by the time I left, he was almost eating on his own. I felt like I made an incredible difference and felt overjoyed.

If you're a picky eater you won't survive here. You need to be open to trying new things and foods. My host family was extremely nice and patient with me. They didn't speak any English, but talking to them improved my Spanish.

I felt really prepared for my project because of the pre-departure briefing with Outreach. They answered all the questions I had truthfully and they gave me the best advice possible on what to expect and take with me. Top tips are to wear a lot of bug spray because the mosquitos here are vicious and bring good walking shoes because the streets are made of uneven cobblestone.

Greta, my in-country Outreach rep, was extremely supportive and put me before herself and what she had to do. I got sick halfway into the trip and she drove 30 minutes to come and take me to a local hospital. I wouldn't have made it without her.

It definitely represented good value for money. I never went hungry and I had a place to stay for the month. This project may not be for everyone, but it certainly was for me. If you are open to new experiences and love living in and experiencing a different cultural lifestyle, this project is right for you.

For more information about Outreach International, see Chapter 6 - Volunteering Abroad

- Be wary of needles and insist on unused ones; it's best if you can see the packet opened in front of you, or you could take a 'sterile kit' (containing needles) with you; and
- If you don't speak the language, have the basic words for medical emergencies written down so you can explain what is wrong.

Is a gap-year safe?

Accidents can happen anywhere and so can earthquakes, floods, cyclones and other random events.

But there are some risks you can avoid by being alert, informed and prepared. You should take personal safety seriously and not put yourself in danger by agreeing to anything about which you have misgivings, just because you don't want to risk someone thinking that you're stupid or scared.

The Foreign & Commonwealth Office estimates that of the approximately 250,000 young people who take a gap each year, around 75,000 are prone to a reckless spirit that it calls the 'Invincibles'.

In 2014/15, the FCO handled 17,058 'assistance cases' globally. While support includes visiting those who have been admitted to hospital or arrested, to rescuing British citizens from forced marriages abroad, the FCO launched Know Before You Go because it had found that the most common problems it was being called in on were the most preventable ones, such as inadequate or no insurance.

The FCO has a Twitter service, offering easy way to stay up to date with the latest advice about travel, and to get help before and during a trip abroad. Questions to @FCOtravel are answered 9am to 6pm BST, Monday to Friday.

This service is provided by the FCO's dedicated travel advice and consular teams, who aim to respond within 30 minutes. Outside of 9am to 6pm questions are only answered in the event of a crisis situation. Others are picked up at the start of the next working day. Many questions about travel can be replied to on Twitter, but any inquiries that involve personal information are taken offline.

This service adds to the ways that British people travelling or living overseas can already get in touch with the FCO: by emailing the travel advice team – traveladvicepublicenquiries@fco.gov.uk – or contacting local consular staff: **www. gov.uk/government/world/organisations**.

The FCO has an online travel guide that you can find at:

www.gov.uk/government/news/plan-pack-explore-a-new-guide-for-travellers

While the FCO deals with all travellers, not only those on a gap, we agree with the message about being as prepared as possible before you go and that's what this guidebook is for.

We also recommend that you consider taking a gappers' safety course before you go, to teach you how to recognise danger (from people as well as natural disasters), and how to look after yourself in a bad situation – it could be the thing that saves your life.

What the experts say

Planning a gap-year can be a very exciting time. In order to get the most out of and enjoy it to the fullest you need to plan and prepare for every eventuality. Staying safe is the key to having a good time.

These days research comes in many different forms, books, websites, fairs and courses. Safety courses have increased in popularity in the last few years particularly with celebrities such as Ewan McGregor and Charley Boorman taking part and training before their high-profile motorcycle trips.

There are a number of different courses run by various companies across the country ranging from two hours to two days, the one thing they all have in common is that they are run by instructors with first-hand experience, a priceless tool.

Why attend a course? Why not? Attending a specialist gap-safety course can be a vital tool in the planning and preparation of your trip, increasing self-awareness and enabling you to recognise danger and get yourself out of tricky situations.

Most of the courses follow a similar format, covering:

Before you go – research, cultural differences, preparation, insurance, documents and money.

What to take – the clothing you will need, first aid kits, gadgets, electrical items, security of your belongings and tips on economical packing.

Over there – accommodation, food and water, transport, local authorities and awareness of a new environment and laws.

Medical Issues – emergency first aid, staying healthy, self-defence, climate, bites, bugs and vaccinations.

Many of the courses will also run a 'for girls, by girls' session.

Make sure you know enough about what you want to do and where you want to go,

visit: www.duinsure.com

talk to other travellers (there are many messageboards online). If you're travelling with an organisation, check them out; ask to speak to others that have done the same trip.

Ensure you have adequate travel insurance to cover everything you want to do including working both paid and voluntary plus any activities you have in mind to do.

Make sure you have copies of all of your documents, try an online document safe. Ensure you have telephone numbers of people to contact in an emergency; emergency medical assistance company, someone at home and if possible someone in the same country.

Travelling to unknown countries can be a great culture shock so a little preparation beforehand will ensure that you make the most of all of your opportunities without missing out. The point is that as long as you have done all you could to be well prepared with travelling essentials and knowledge, then you should go for it!

Personal safety and security checklist

We've canvassed lots of opinion about this, and we've had lots of suggestions. We think the following are among the most important:

- Don't drink too much or stay out too late, it is not like being at home and you will make yourself unnecessarily vulnerable.
- Hanging the 'Do Not Disturb' sign on your hotel door when you go out should help deter thieves.
- Always carry a business card from your accommodation. if you get lost, or want to get a taxi back, you won't have to remember the address.
- If you're worried about your belongings (whether in a hostel dorm or overnight travel), keep them in your sleeping bag with you for extra security.
- Having waterproofed documents (either laminating or in a secure plastic wallet), there is always a chance you will get caught in the rain or need to cross a river if trekking, this way your valuables and documents will stay dry.
- Walk with confidence and never use your guidebook, get out your map or start counting money in the street, find a café, sit and relax and read in peace, don't make yourself a target. Keep a small amount of change for food and drinks in a separate wallet so you don't have to keep going through your notes.
- If you have a 'weak' stomach avoid street stalls, eat in busy restaurants (where the locals are) and try and eat vegetarian if possible, although saying this salads can be some of the worst.
- If travelling alone, you are most vulnerable when you are sick (sometimes you feel like you have to travel that day) but our best advice would be don't. If you feel ill (like being drunk) don't travel and if you do make sure you are with another person you know well.
- Don't be afraid of approaching other backpackers – this is easier in non-western countries when you can generally tell who is a traveller and who isn't. Not only might you make new friends but also it's great to share experiences and good times as sometimes travelling can be very lonely.
- Talk to locals: the best way to get insight before you travel is to talk to trusted people who live there. Networks are springing up all over the place offering unique local insights based from food lovers, or culture vultures, try Tripbod: **www.tripbod.com**.

my
gap-year
Charlotte Buck

I'd heard about Typhoon Haiyan and the disaster it had wrought on the Philippines. Immediately I knew that I wanted to travel there and help in any way I could, so I headed off to Cebu!

I spent approximately five weeks in the Philippines helping with the Disaster Relief programme in Bogo City and I had the most wonderful time.

The appreciation of the people in Bogo was evident from the first day. I became friends with a girl who had grown up in Bogo, and she told me the story of what had happened to her family and their home during the typhoon. After taking shelter in one of the bigger buildings in town, they returned to their home to find it completely razed. She was so happy to have people from around the world coming to help her town recover.

Before I left home, I wasn't sure if I would be up to the challenge of all the physical labour involved with construction, but I ended up really loving it! We would arrive at the work site by van or trike. The tasks I was involved with included carrying 90 pound bags of cement, mixing cement, building walls, cutting rebar, bending rebar to make frames, and finishing the cement walls.

We worked from 8am until 4pm with a two-hour break for lunch in the middle of the day. We had a Projects Abroad staff member on site, and they were great at making sure we weren't taking on tasks we could not physically handle. I loved getting to work with the other volunteers. Everyone worked hard but had fun, and were covered in sweat and cement at the end of each day.

For more information about Projects Abroad, see Chapter 6 - Volunteering Abroad

- Whatever happens, however bad – remember people are generally good and you will find people (other backpackers, locals, hostel owners *etc*) who will go out of their way to help you and make sure that you are safe and okay.

- If you are in trouble, whatever the local police tell you, contact the local British embassy or consulate – most of them are incredibly helpful and they will have dealt with situations like yours before and will know what you should do, make sure that you have several copies of their contact details to hand.

Remember, anyone can get lost. When you are on the road don't panic. Always agree meeting places before you go somewhere and play safe by having a back-up plan. Then if you don't turn up reasonably on time someone will be alerted to raise the alarm.

Before you do anything or go anywhere think about the consequences – this isn't about not having a good time, or being boring – it's about getting through your gap without taking foolish risks.

In many places, though, you'll find people are very hospitable and curious about you and you might find their unabashed and quite frank questions intrusive. While you have to be sensible about how much information you give, equally try not to be too suspicious about their motives. What feels like an invasion of your personal space, or probing questioning, doesn't automatically mean anything sinister – remember the British in particular can be quite reserved so you'll notice the contrast. It's all a question of balance and courtesy.

Caroline's Rainbow Foundation is a charity set up to promote safety awareness for young travellers. They gave us some additional pointers, all worth emphasising:

- Leave copies of all your travel documents, visas, insurance policies and bank card details with someone back home. If you lose them or they are stolen it is easier to report if you have all the details to hand. If you can store them on the computer and email the images to yourself, you will always have the documents where ever there is internet. Lock your passport and travel tickets in a safe if possible.

- If you plan to work abroad find out if you need a work visa and get it before you leave. Some countries will not let you work while on holiday. Try not to be tempted by the offer of cash in hand; if caught you could easily be deported or even imprisoned.

- If you take regular medication ensure you have enough for your trip. Also keep a note of what it is in case you lose it. You may be able get hold of it in another country but this is not guaranteed. It may also be called a different name so try to have a note of the generic name of the drug rather than a brand name. Pharmacists can usually help with this. If taking a large amount of the prescription medication with you take a doctor's letter explaining what it is and why you need it. Easier than being mistaken for smuggling drugs.

- Try to learn a few simple phrases in the local language If you find that hard or you do not understand the dialects at least you should learn to recognise them when written down. Knowing what the sign is for a bus stop, cafe, phone, police or hostel could be very helpful, particularly when arriving somewhere at night.

- Try to book your first night's accommodation in a new location, especially if you plan to arrive after dark. Make sure you know where the place is, how far it is from your arrival point and the best way to get there. Standing around with a map and large rucksack is a give away that you are new in town and could attract unwanted attention.

- Try not to carry lots of money around with you. Lock it away in a safe if you can,

Maekok River Village Resort

Most hostels have a safe at reception. Remember you can be watched using a cash point or inside a bank.

- Remember items such as condoms are often inferior in quality, especially in places such as Africa and South America; if you think you might need them it's probably best to take your own that you know are safe.

- Be aware of the food and dietary habits in the country/countries you plan to visit. While sundried grasshoppers may not be your normal diet, you might want to be prepared to try new foods. Hygiene abroad, particularly in developing countries, may not be the same as at home so be careful not to offend when offered food even if you think it looks raw or disgusting. If you do get a 'gippy tummy' make sure you drink plenty of clean, ideally bottled, water to ensure you don't get dehydrated.

- Local transport is usually very different abroad, especially in developing countries. You may have no choice but to travel on a bus with worn tyres, too many passengers, or no seat belts to avoid being left in a deserted location, but it is worth finding out if there are any other options. Try to sit near to the main door or by an emergency exit if possible. It may seem fun to hang off the bus or sit on the roof like the locals but realistically this could be very dangerous.

- While travelling from place to place try to lock your luggage if you can not see it and do not leave any valuables in it. Take all valuables with you regardless of mode of transport.

- Be careful where and how you take photographs. It's often not a good idea to take photos of anything official, or anything which could be connected to the military, such as airports or border checkpoints. This could attract unwanted attention or hostile behavior from the local people or officials.

- In hotel or hostel rooms, check that your windows and doors lock properly and keep them locked at night. Request a room that is not on the ground floor. Check the fire evacuation procedure from your bedroom in case of emergencies.

- Make sure that someone always knows where you are and when you can be expected to return. This is especially important in rural places where mobile phones may not work.

- Never leave your drink unattended – it could be spiked.

- If you are travelling in a hire car, keep the doors locked at all times, especially when you are stuck in traffic. Make a note of contact numbers for the rental company in case of breakdown or theft. Be careful when parking you car as you may not be able to read or understand the parking rules. You do not want to return and find your car has been towed away.

- Nothing is worth more than your life. Money, cameras etc can be replaced, especially if you have insurance. If challenged do not put up a fight, letting go could save your life.

Caroline's Rainbow Foundation have a Safer Travel app which is definitely worth a look: **www.carolinesrainbowfoundation.org/safer-travel-app**

In-country advice...

Here's a quick checklist from the Foreign and Commonwealth Office:

- Familiarise yourself with your destination and its local laws and customs

- Learn some key phrases and words of the local language, this can make a huge difference to your trip and the reception you get and might help in an emergency

- Get a good guidebook and make sure you know about local laws and customs, especially those relating to alcohol and drugs.

- Book your first night's accommodation in advance. You're at your most vulnerable when you first arrive in a foreign country and are likely to be tired and uncertain of your surroundings

- Try to blend in to the local community – be conscious of any religious dress codes and dress accordingly. It's important to be respectful when you are visiting someone else's country

- Photographs – certain sites within a country can be sensitive, *eg* military bases, government buildings *etc*. Be mindful of what you are photographing. It's worth asking before you snap so as not to run into trouble or cause offence

Responsible travel

Richard Nimmo of Blue Ventures Expeditions offers some advice on travelling responsibly; "Responsible Travel covers a wide range of issues; cultural awareness and sensitivity, environmental issues, economic impact and ethical concerns like orphanage and animal tourism. I think that travellers should always try to pay a fair price for goods and services and aim to minimise the negative whilst maximising the positive impacts of their travels rather than just focussing on their own experiences and enjoyment.

"Minimise your impact: In much of the world natural resources are under pressure and waste management systems are poor or virtually non-existent. Remember to limit your water use, no long luxurious showers, especially in arid countries and regions, and try to reduce your waste footprint by avoiding packaged goods if possible and being less wasteful than you would be at home. You could also try to take home items like used batteries that can cause harm in unmanaged landfill and won't add much to your luggage weight.

my
gap-year
Naomi Clark

The two months at Sepilok with Travellers Worldwide were the best of my life. Many people want to go here because it's the only place you can get hands on with orang-utans, but it's so much more than this. At this centre you get to experience the incredible wilderness of Malaysia - which holds some extremely healthy natural habitats. We saw a wild elephant, proboscis monkeys and many other species of monkey, slow loris, tarsier, flying squirrels and lemurs, gibbons, and some absolutely crazy (and big!) insects.

I fell in love with the jungle, and actually what I miss most is not having the jungle at my doorstep, and being able to see, and hear the jungle every day and night. It was the treks (where we surveyed wild orang-utan nests) which allowed me to understand just how incredible the jungle is. You also get two weeks of trekking during the whole placement, including some night treks.

The orang-utans are amazing. Whilst doing the jobs at hand (cleaning cages, feeding them and making sure they stay on their climbing ropes) you come to understand all the individual personalities of not just the babies you're working with, but the semi-wild and wild ones that visit the centre, roaming freely. They're all so unique, funny, and curious. It's great to see these orang-utans because they're the ones who have graduated from climbing school - which is why we are there - to help orang-utans become independent adults. Bathing the tiny baby orang-utans, and trying (so hard) to make them climb (when all they want is a cuddle and their baby blanket!) was great too!

Life really won't ever be the same! Life doesn't get better than it was during these two months. Me and my partner, Mike, didn't have a single day 'off' as we chose to work on all our free days - either at the orang-utan centre or the neighbouring sun bear centre.

For more information about Travellers Worldwide, see Chapter 6 - Volunteering Abroad

"Maximise the benefits: Tourism is a tremendous source for good when it is managed well and as a tourist you can have a positive impact as you travel. Think about how you can help the country you are visiting and try to be an aware consumer; your expenditure is important to many countries. I would recommend taking a 'buy local approach' - buy locally produced clothes rather than imports when you shop, frequent smaller, locally owned food and drink establishments as more of your money will stay in the country, and avoid multi-national shops, cafes and restaurants."

Safety

Your first impression of some countries will be a swarm of people descending on you, pestering you to take a taxi or buy something – at night when you're tired from a long plane trip it can be quite scary. If you're not being met by anyone, check whether there's a pre-pay kiosk in the airport and pay for a ticket to your ultimate destination. That way the taxi driver can't take you on a detour since they won't get their money until you're safely delivered and your 'chit' has been signed.

Some people advise that, if you arrive alone in the middle of the night (which is often the case on long-haul budget flights), it might be safer to wait until daylight before heading onwards. That's not a pleasant prospect in most airports, but it may occasionally be the sensible option.

In many countries of the developing world, where there are no social security or welfare systems, life can be extremely tough and leave people close to despair. That's likely to be even more the case, in the face of growing food shortages and escalating fuel and food costs as a result of the ongoing global recession. What may seem like a cheap trinket to you may be enough to buy them a square meal for which they are desperate enough to steal from you violently, so it is sensible not to wear too much jewellery.

Stefan Wathan from the Year Out Group highlights an important safety measure you should take; "You should know that your provider has plans to get you out of a country experiencing a crisis or see you safely through it, whether it be a natural disaster, health epidemics, political unrest or conflict. They will not travel to a country against the advice of the Foreign Office and so you should keep yourself informed by visiting the Know Before You go website (**www.gov.uk/knowbeforeyougo**) which publishes regular advice bulletins about what is going on in a country."

Respect and behaviour

Equally, wandering around discarding uneaten food is a particularly tactless thing to do, when large numbers of people may not know where their next meal is coming from.

If you are carrying out a voluntary placement, Ralph from IST Plus says; "Be aware that the work you will undertake requires a strong sense of responsibility and commitment. In most cases you will become a role model and ambassador for your country, culture and language!"

Bear in mind that, in most places, even the so-called First World, rural communities are usually far more traditional and straight-laced than city ones and casual western dress codes and habits can offend.

If you don't want to find yourself in real trouble, do some research. Each culture or religion has its own codes of behaviour and taboos and, while no one would expect you to live by all their rules, as an ethical and responsible traveller, showing respect

59

for the basic principles is a must as a guest in their country, not to mention being a sensible precaution if you want to stay safe.

Also remember that a country's native people are not just part of the landscape, they are individuals who deserve respect and courtesy, so if you want to take a photo of them – ask first, or at least be discreet!

Dress codes

These are the sorts of things you should bear in mind: in most Asian and African countries don't wear a bikini top and shorts in city streets if you don't want to attract the wrong kind of intrusive attention. In any case an all-over light cotton covering will better protect you from sunburn and insect bites.

Men and women should dress modestly, particularly, but not only, in Muslim countries. Women especially should wear long sleeves and cover their legs. Uncovered flesh, especially female, is seen as a 'temptation' and you'll be more comfortable, not to mention finding people more friendly and welcoming if they can see you're sensitive to local customs.

You should also remember that, in Buddhist countries, the head is sacred and so it is unconventional to touch it.

Before entering temples and mosques throughout India and South Asia, you must remove your shoes. There are usually places at the entrances, where you can leave them with attendants to look after them.

Women are also expected to cover their hair – and in Jain temples wearing or carrying anything made of leather is forbidden. Even in parts of Europe you'd be expected to cover your head and be dressed respectfully if you go into a church.

International Volunteer HQ

visit: www.duinsure.com

Culture and beliefs

Open gestures of affection, kissing or even holding hands between married couples can be shocking to some cultures. This is particularly true of India, though it seems to be relaxing a little in the cities.

However, you will often see men or boys strolling around hand in hand or with arms around each other's shoulders in India – don't misinterpret: they are friends, *not* gay couples!

Remember also, that if you are speaking English with a local inhabitant, they may not understand or use a word with the same meaning as you do. Particularly in the area of emotional relationships and dating, remembering this and understanding the local religion, customs and morality can save a lot of misunderstanding, misery and heartache.

Sitting cross-legged, with the soles of your feet pointing towards your companions, is another example of a gesture regarded as bad manners or even insulting in some places and actually if you think about it, it's pretty logical if you're in a place where people walk around less than clean streets either barefoot or in sandals.

Since daily life and faiths are often closely interlinked, it helps to know a little about the major philosophies of life in the countries you visit.

These are the main belief systems you will encounter on your travels (we use the term belief systems because, arguably, some of these are closer to being philosophies of life than to religions or faiths in the sense most people would understand them):

- Bahá'i
- Shinto
- Taoism
- Confucianism
- Shamanism
- Humanism
- Zoroastrianism
- Islam
- Judaism
- Hinduism
- Buddhism
- Jainism
- Sikhism

For more information, or if you are interested in finding out about other religions, try: **www.bbc.co.uk/religion/religions**

the gap-year guidebook 2016

my
gap-year
Ali H

I started out on my gap-year with very basic Spanish. I could count to ten, say hello and goodbye and of course... what every gap-year student needs to know... how to order 'dos cervezas, por favour'. I knew that I wanted to spend time in two different cities and that I wanted excitement, culture and to meet as many people from all over the world as possible as well as improving my Spanish. After talking to Gemma at Live Languages Abroad she advised me that Barcelona and Madrid would give me exactly what I was looking for. She was so right. Barcelona is a dream! It's a very cosmopolitan city, full of people from all walks of life, vibrant, busy and full of excitement.

The school was amazing, I spent three months in Barcelona and my Spanish went from very basic to me holding conversations in Spanish throughout the days without even thinking about it. For the first six weeks in Barcelona I stayed with a Spanish host family. They were so welcoming and treated me as another member of the family. If you want to progress your language skills as quickly as possible, live with a Spanish family. Listening to the language being spoken and conversing with the family on a daily basis is invaluable. The last six weeks I spent in a student residence with the best group of girls that I will be lifelong friends with. I have some fantastic memories of Barcelona, from visiting la Sagrada familia to dancing with the street dancers on las ramblas. It is a truly amazing city and I can't wait to go back.

Next on to Madrid. I spent eight weeks in Madrid and to be honest as I sat on the train from Barcelona to Madrid I began to wonder how Madrid could ever top my time in Barcelona. Well it's right up there with Barcelona! Madrid is full of hidden treasures and you really need to spend some real time in Madrid to fully appreciate everything it has to offer. The school was yet again brilliant and only a few minutes' walk from the beautiful Retiro Park. I spent hours walking in the park or just sitting with a book and a coffee, watching the world go by. The teachers were so enthusiastic and they make you feel so welcome. My Spanish progressed even more and I now have a very advanced level of Spanish. One of my proudest moments of my gap-year was having a conversation about the economy of all things and putting the world to rights with an elderly Madrileño gentleman in a tapas bar just off Gran Via. Of course a little sangria for Dutch courage helped the conversation flow, but this was my moment of realisation, that I had done it... I'd learnt to speak Spanish - well! I stayed in the student residence in Madrid and again, met a fantastic group of friends.

I had the most amazing gap-year, not only did I learn to speak Spanish, I saw so much culture, made so many friends and grew as a person too. Thank you so much Live Languages Abroad, your advice was spot on and I'm so grateful for all your help in organising a fantastic gap-year. When can I go again?

Communication: Keeping in touch

Spare a thought for those you're leaving behind – friends as well as family. Not only will they be worried about your safety, but they may actually be interested in your travels – most are probably jealous and wish they could go too.

It's not just about keeping them happy: make sure you tell them where you are and where you are going – that way if something does happen to you, at least they know where to start looking. Backpackers do go missing, climbers have accidents, trekkers get lost; at least if someone is concerned that you have not got in touch when expected, they can then alert the police. If you've promised to check in regularly with close family *make sure you do*, especially when you move on to another country. Of course, if you don't stick to what you agreed, don't be surprised if the international police come looking for you.

While you probably can't wait to get away, you may be surprised how homesickness can creep up on you when you're thousands of miles away. Getting letters or emails can be a great pick-me-up if you're feeling homesick, weary or lonely, so, in order to ensure a steady supply of mail, distribute your address(es) widely to friends and family before you go. If you're not able to leave behind an exact address then you can have letters sent to the local Poste Restante, often at a main post office, and collect them from there. Also, parcels do usually get through, but don't send anything valuable.

Keeping a diary/sketchbook to record places, projects, people, how you're feeling and the effect things are having on you, can help when you get an attack of the homesick blues or just feel a bit down.

Mobile phone basics

Make sure you've set up your account to allow you to make and receive calls and text messages in all the countries you'll be travelling to (and emails if you've got a smartphone). Try to limit use of your mobile to emergencies – they usually cost a fortune to run abroad as you pay for all the incoming calls at international rates too.

It's worth insuring the handset, as mobile theft is common and if it's the latest model, try not to flash it around.

If you are staying in one country for several weeks, consider getting either a cheap local mobile phone or a local SIM card for your UK mobile. Don't forget to alert friends back home to the new number. Local texts and calls tend to be very cheap and incoming calls from abroad are free, which avoids the massive charges when using your UK mobile.

Snail mail

Aerogrammes are a cheap way of writing from most countries. Registering letters usually costs only a few pence (or equivalent) from Third World countries, and is definitely worthwhile. Postcards are quick, cheap and easy – though not very private.

www.pc2paper.co.uk: This website allows you to send letters worldwide from the internet and store addresses in your account. You type your message and they then convert it into an actual letter and post it for you. The costs vary depending on weight and size.

Email

If you can get to a cybercafé or access a wifi network on your smartphone or tablet in an airport, hotel, university, office or home when you're abroad, you can simply log in to your mailbox (remember you'll need your user ID and password if these are part of the package).

Newsletter

A great way to keep in touch with people at home is by sending out a newsletter email via a free service such as MailChimp (**www.mailchimp.com**). The service makes designing an email that is rich in images, captions, links and text easy, plus you can send the email to your whole mailing list at the touch of a button! It's a great way to keep your network back at home updated.

Internet cafés

Remember that internet cafés are much more than just a place to upload your latest batch of photos, check in with the folks at home and pick up the footie results along with your email.

visit: www.duinsure.com

In many places they're a lifeline for local people – to small farmers or traders, to families separated by war, poverty or natural disaster or a way of bringing education to children in isolated villages across the developing world – and, like any other kind of café, a place of crucial social interaction.

Equally if you are travelling independently and following your whims where better than to check with other backpackers for decent places to stay or get an idea of local customs and prices for food, transport, entertainment, whatever?

So even if you're travelling with the latest in e-technology it's worth taking your tablet or laptop to an internet café for a wi-fi hook-up. You'll get as much info from the people as you can from the machine!

Perhaps we should also include one note of caution – look for cafés with open spaces not curtained booths. Very often, particularly in very traditional societies where there is only minimal contact permitted between unmarried boys and girls, internet cafes with computers in closed booths are often male-only territory – and a place to check out the latest in 'adult' entertainment... not a good place to go if you're a female gapper just wanting to check her email and say hi to mum!

Online journals

Another easy way to keep everyone up-to-date is to set up a travel blog – as many people now do. On Facebook, your photos and comments will be available only to your 'friends' (unless you relax the privacy settings for a particular album) but there is the added advantage of being able to send messages and pictures to specific people without having to remember their email address, providing, of course, they too have a Facebook page.

Other sites you might like to check out are:

www.travelblog.org
www.offexploring.com
www.fuzzytravel.com
www.travoholic.com
www.wordpress.com

And finally... back to earth

We've talked to enough people who've already taken a gap to know that returning home can be a shock to the system.

Returning to ordinary life takes time. It doesn't matter when you took your gap, you're likely to still go through the same sequence of feelings over the three months it generally takes to readjust.

How you respond, though, will depend on what you are returning to – if you went between school and university you might find yourself switching courses or storing up something else to explore later. Or you might be quite content to take up your course with renewed enthusiasm after a travelling break from study.

It's different again for people mid-career or over-50 mature travellers, but the pattern of adjustment is pretty much the same.

InterHealth, who provide a full range of health services and pre-travel health preparation, describe the feeling as 'reverse culture shock':

"Reverse Culture Shock is a common response experienced by people returning home from another culture. It can often be worse than culture shock as it's often unexpected. Returning home should be the easiest part of the trip, and sometimes it is, however, your trip may have changed you, your values and expectations. Sometimes it may be difficult to acknowledge that you have changed and home is still the same. Your family and friends may have unrealistic expectations of you. This may be hard on you but it will also be hard on them.

"You may feel a major loss upon returning home, almost as if you have been bereaved. There may also be a communication barrier between yourself and your family and friends back home. You may not be able to express the magnitude of what you have been through abroad.

"Your view of your home country may have changed in the light of your overseas experience, and you might find yourself rejecting some of your old values and ways of living. This may cause conflict between you and your friends and family who may be affected by your lifestyle change.

"You may try to re-adapt to your old lifestyle and re-connect with your old friends but find it hard to do so. Situations and relationships back home are bound to have changed in your absence; especially if you have been away for a long time. You may feel that you no longer belong and that joining in is hard.

"If you have returned home without an immediate plan for the future you may feel as though there is a lack of purpose to your life, which sorely contrasts to when you were abroad and perhaps carrying out an important role."

All of the above can leave you feeling isolated, anxious, or depressed. It is important to remember that you are not alone in these thoughts, and that things can be done to help.

Here are some tips from InterHealth to help you adjust:

· Prepare: prepare yourself before you go by learning more about reverse culture shock.

· Keep in touch: keep in touch with your friends and family while you are away.

· Give yourself closure: say a proper goodbye to your friends and colleagues.

· Take a break: when you get home, take at least a few days off.

· Write: writing can be a cathartic experience and can help order your thoughts. If you have experienced some life-changing or difficult events, write about them.

· Avoid indulgences and rash behaviour: avoid self-indulgence in alcohol, drugs, and food – these comforts make you feel good in the short-term but are guaranteed not to help your recovery process. Also try to avoid making rash decisions; you may feel bored and want to accept the first offer that comes your way, but it is best to be patient and let your emotional state settle.

"Usually you will settle down quickly, depending on certain factors such as the effectiveness of your coping strategies and the extent of your overseas experiences. The experiences from your international assignment are likely to become incorporated into your values and the way you live. You may find yourself drawing on them to inform your decisions and thoughts, and when advising others.

"If, after a few months, you have not settled after your return we recommend you talk to a trustworthy friend or a psychological health professional. You can email **phs@interhealth.org.uk** for further advice or visit **www.interhealthworldwide.org**

The length of time you've been away makes no difference to the feelings you go through on your return and even after six months you may still need time to adjust."

We've talked to people who've taken a two-week leave of absence from work through their company's charitable foundation and to people who've spent a year or more away. They all report coming back and finding themselves looking at everything through fresh eyes and questioning the importance of various aspects of homelife that they have previously taken for granted.

On average, it seems to take about three months between stepping off that last plane after a gap and getting back into life's routines. To start with, a commonly-reported phenomenon is the odd sensation of the body decelerating while the brain's still on the move. So, after the first three weeks of initial euphoria and sharing, be prepared to come down to earth with a bump.

Having said all that, though, try and remember that you have done something really amazing. Yes, you'll be back home and missing your life on the road, but think how lucky you were to have had the chance to do something that most people only dream of.

What do you do now?

This one depends on what you had planned before you left and whether the option is still there – and if you still want to do it – once you're back.

Some people advise that, if you can manage it, putting aside some money for about three months of living expenses for your return, as part of pre-gap preparations, takes the pressure off if you're going to be job hunting. But, if taking time out isn't an option, don't panic.

If you already have work to go back to you may have to combine the post trip elation with a fairly quick return to the 'rat race'. And you'll need to think about how you interact with your colleagues. How much do you say about your trip? A spokeswoman for one major UK employer, which supports its staff in taking time out, and also has a foundation on whose projects they can do voluntary work, had this advice:

"When you are returning to work it is important to have a plan. Returning to work after 18 weeks or more can prove difficult on both a psychological and logistical level. Keep your line manager up-to-date with the timings of your return to work. This will ensure that they can factor you into their resource planning and also help you integrate back into the working environment.

"Do not rule out a degree of retraining when you return to work. Refreshing your skills will benefit most people in the work place, and, if you have been away from work for a long period of time, you should use the opportunity to familiarise yourself with new systems, procedures and practices.

"When you return to work take into consideration reverse culture shock. Whilst you might be keen to talk about your travels for many months to come, your colleagues may not be so keen to listen."

Karen Woodbridge, director of Suffolk-based Hornet Solutions (an Independent HR/ Employment Law Consultancy), also offers some important advice:

"Whilst you will quite rightly be very excited about your trip and all the anticipated adventures, it is worthwhile to take the time in advance to plan carefully your readjustment and return into the working world.

"If you have been fortunate enough to have been granted a leave of absence, it is vital that you take note of that old adage 'Out of sight, out of mind'. So plan before you go how you can stay in touch, which is so much easier now via the internet and the use of Skype.

"When you do return remember that your colleagues have been getting on with business whilst you've been away. There may even have been changes of personnel, for example your old team members or boss may have left the company. There certainly will be new alliances and different company politics. Don't expect people to remember that you were a 'star performer' before you left. That role may well be occupied by someone else now. People might also be jealous of your experiences for actually doing something they always dreamed of and this too can be a challenge.

"Therefore in many ways it will help if you think about returning to your old position as if it were a brand new job, ie expect things to be new, to have changed and realise that it will be up to you, once again, to find out how everything works and prove yourself even more capable of succeeding now because you bring all your old skills, competencies and experiences to the role plus all the new ones you developed whilst you were away. Realising you may face these challenges and planning how

to overcome them will help you to more successfully integrate and adapt to your return at work."

If you have to start earning as soon as you get back and your old job wasn't kept open for you, you can always consider temporary work. These positions are often available immediately and can be flexible enough to enable you to carry on with your permanent job search. And you never know, once working in a company, opportunities often come up that you'd never have expected.

"When putting together a CV, think through all the new skills you learnt on your trip that will be invaluable to employers. Unfortunately many people use the phrase 'travelling' to cover gaps; they may be using this term to hide an unsuccessful job that ended in dismissal or possibly even time spent in prison! Consequently, recruiters can be cynical whenever they see 'travelling' on a CV so tackle this head on by highlighting how your trip has increased the contribution you can make to the role for which you are applying. This also helps make the travelling period seem genuine but remember, in a job search situation it's the benefits to the employer that will count, not how much fun you had!"

You'll find more useful advice on this in **Chapter 3 – Career Breaks and Older Gappers.**

Deciding what next

While getting back to 'normal' life, you've no doubt been trying to process everything you've learned from your gap experience.

How do you feel? What's changed? What's been confirmed? Where to now? Is there something new you want to do next as a result? How to go about it? You'll almost certainly still be in touch with friends you made on your travels, maybe even had a couple of after-gap reminiscence meetings. Others may still be travelling and keeping you restless!

You may also still be in touch with the projects you worked on. It's a fairly common feeling to want to keep a link to something that's been a life changing, learning experience. Is this you?

The best piece of advice on dealing with the consequences of any life-changing experience is to be patient and give it time. Nothing but time can make things settle into some kind of perspective and help you work out whether you are in the grip of a sudden enthusiasm or something deeper and more long-lasting.

Change of direction?

In time you'll know whether your urge to travel has also become an urge to keep the links with the communities you visited now you're back.

What level of involvement do you want? Is it going to be something local like fundraising – doing local talks, letters to newspapers – or are you seriously looking to change career?

If you have come back with the germ of an idea for a career change as a result of a volunteer placement, for example, there's nothing to stop you slowly exploring the options and possibilities.

Have a look at your CV. Try to talk to people working in the field you're considering moving into. Armed with some basic information, you could also consider talking through issues such as what transferable skills you have to add to your volunteer experience, what training you might need and how affordable it is, with a careers counsellor or recruitment specialist – preferably with an organisation that specialises in aid/charity or NGO positions.

Try these links:

www.totaljobs.com/IndustrySearch/NotForProfitCharities.aspx

www.cafonline.org

www.charitypeople.co.uk

www.peopleandplanet.org

To keep you going you should also never underestimate the power of synchronicity. You may find unexpected connections and information come your way while you're getting on with other things. If it's meant to be, you'll find ways to make it happen.

Please see the directory pages starting on page 287 for information on companies and organisations offering services and products to help you on your gap-year.

What's in fashion?

Year Out Group CEO Stefan Wathan provides a rundown of the most popular activities for gappers

Voluntary Work attracts the most placements and the greatest variety of projects. Short and long term placements are both very rewarding. Short term bookings perhaps just for a week or two will get participants up to speed quickly so that the projects maximise the benefit of the volunteer's time which also makes a valuable contribution locally. Projects that run for 3-12 months allow more time for volunteers to get into the routine and culture of community life and deeper relationships tend to be formed as result which is more rewarding for both parties.

Courses Year Out Group members offer courses in art history, drama, diving, game ranger, languages, mountaineering, mountain leadership, sailing, windsurfing, skiing, and snowboarding amongst others. Expert instructors or guides lead these courses and most lead to internationally recognised qualifications. Some will use these to gain more expertise in their favourite past-time but for many it supplements study or offers another route to work either as a career or during holiday times.

Expeditions offer personal development opportunities through a variety of phases such as a community project, a conservation project and an adventure phase. Some organisations offer guided travel opportunities, which might see participants travelling and trekking through regions and spending time along the way completing projects in the communities they pass through, these may last several weeks. All are led by experienced and carefully chosen leaders. Expeditions have become increasingly popular with graduates in recent years with many reporting success in the job market on their return.

Structured work placements & internship The Year in Industry offers excellent opportunities for those planning to read engineering or engineer related subjects at university to gain valuable work experience in engineering companies in the UK. Subsequently these placements, who are taken on the payroll of the host company and paid a fair salary, are often supported through university by their host companies and on graduation offered full time employment.

More and more members are starting to provide internships of some nature and across quite a wide variety of skills areas, including journalism and medical and micro-finance and entrepreneurship. Unpaid internships may require a higher level of skill than volunteering placements but the distinction may be more about the intended outcome for the person taking part. For example a veterinary internship will prepare you for a job in that profession but you might be expected to be studying it at university. By contrast, volunteering on a wildlife reserve may offer a broader experience, requiring less knowledge of the subject and suitable for those who are not looking at the placement as a career stepping stone.

my gap-year
Alli

I've been travelling with my boyfriend since the beginning of 2015, doing an around the world trip on an open-ended flight.

I knew I wanted to travel and work with children even before university, but I had to save, save, save! TEFL (Teaching English as a Foreign Language) allowed me to gain my qualification online in my own time, as well as gaining seven weeks' practical experience on the LoveTEFL Cambodia Internship. This turned into four months' experience after I accepted a full-time job in Phnom Penh after the internship! My qualification means I can teach anywhere in the world... It's an overwhelming and exciting thought.

I chose Cambodia because it's somewhere I've never been before. I have several friends who visited Cambodia over the past few years and they said to just do it! I also wanted to see Angkor Wat and secretly pretend to be Lara Croft in Tomb Raider.

Signing up to the LoveTEFL Cambodia internship is the best decision I ever made. My boyfriend and I quit our jobs to go travelling and to get more life experience, and now I've found a job and way of life I'm not sure I'll ever want to leave. I have learnt so much about myself, met amazing people, and now I'm staying and working at a fantastic school in a country rich in culture and breath-taking places.

I've made some amazing friends - other interns and locals. Knowing we are helping both children and adults improve their English and confidence with the language, visiting some of the beautiful places Cambodia has to offer, learning valuable life lessons and knowing how much this is helping me grow as a person. I cannot thank LoveTEFL enough for this experience.

For more information about LoveTEFL, see Chapter 5 - Working Abroad

Finance

Finance

How much money will you need?

It all depends on what you're doing, where you're going and for how long. Long haul flights are much more expensive than regional ones, for example, and insurance and visas vary country-by-country. As we've already mentioned in **Chapter 1**, it's estimated that the average gap-year for young people is £5000, while that goes up to £6000 for more mature travellers and £9000 for career breakers, plus flights on top. The key word here is *average*, but it at least gives you a 'ball park' figure.

Stefan Wathan, of the Year Out Group, gave us this advice:

"Costs vary and need careful research as the package varies from provider to provider. A good way to gauge value for money is to add up all the costs such as the cost of the package, the flight, visa, insurance, vaccinations, specialist clothing and equipment and then divide by the number of weeks of the placement to give an average cost per week. Do this for a number of projects to see which one offers best value for money but do remember that cost should not be the only factor in deciding which project is right for you.

"It is worth asking the gap-year provider if they offer bursaries and you may find charitable trusts that do the same. Criteria usually apply because they will be targeting a particular audience or person who fits their mission or purpose."

What do you need to pay for?

A gap needn't break the bank, but it helps if you start by making yourself a list of all the things you might need to pay for, and then research how much it all comes to.

Look at your chosen locations and do a bit of research as to how much the essentials cost – accommodation, food and travel, costs between towns/countries here.

This will give you your absolute base budget per day, on top of which you can add costs for activities - seeing sights, adrenalin activities (if that's your thing) and, of course, going out!

Here's a checklist of some essentials to help you get started:

Before you go:

· Passport

· Visas and work permits (check the FCO website for the relevant embassy – **www.fco.gov.uk**)

· Insurance

· Flights

· Fees for placements/organised treks *etc*

· Special equipment if needed

visit: www.gap-year.com

· Vaccinations – they're not all free – and a travellers' medical pack

· Don't forget regular payments, such as a pay-monthly mobile phone.

When you've gone:

· Accommodation (if travelling independently)

· Transport (if travelling independently).

· Food

· Entertainment

· Shopping – gifts and souvenirs

· Emergency fund

Avoiding money disasters

The list covers the absolute basics, but if you're not careful there are plenty of extra costs that could eat into your budget – ones you wouldn't necessarily think of at first. Here are some tips from our friends at Gapwork.com:

1. Don't forget emergencies - It's a sad fact, but every traveller we've met has had some form of 'emergency' whilst travelling. These range from being scammed or needing to get home quickly for whatever reason. Ensure your budget has leeway should anything go wrong.

2. Bank accounts – Before you leave it's always a good idea to check out accounts that are beneficial for a traveller. For example, you could spend £10 a month for a current account which gives free withdrawals across the globe, and the usual commission fee for changing the currency is waived. Saving loads of money on withdrawals, and means that you can just withdraw what you need rather than walking around with stacks of cash. You can also apply for a card (not linked to your account) to top up with cash which has similar benefits. Check out **www.moneysavingexpert.com/ travel/cheap-travel-money** for more info.

75

3. And if you need cash whilst you're away? It does happen. Despite the best laid plans, people can run out of money. Don't panic and instantly think you need to go home!

A lot of travellers we know have worked in hostels both for money and to improve their language skills, others have worked in bars, some have taught languages (You can obtain a TEFL online, Teaching English as a Foreign Language qualification, see gapwork.com for options), and others write! There's also a site called 'Work Away' (www.workaway.info) which offers jobs, usually in exchange for accommodation, food and the opportunity to really experience another culture. If you need some more inspiration for what you could do whilst away then this is a good article by one of our favourite travel bloggers: www.global-goose.com/travel-tips/make-money-while-you-travel/

4. Which cash/credit cards to take? - We would recommend Travelex cash passport, especially if you are travelling through countries in quick succession and need access to variety of currencies. You can log in online and find out a list of recent transactions and gain access to your money at the current bank exchange rate.

It's useful to give parents or relatives/friends at home a second card so they could top the card up with money left at home. This is a great tip, it also allows you to budget from country to country and not get carried away. Travelex also has a 24/7 helpline where you can cancel your card at anytime and they will issue a replacement to your location within 24 hours – a life-safer when you are miles from home.

Alternatively apply for an ICE card: www.iceplc.com/prepaid-currency-card

Virgin money also offer a travel card - no need to have a bank account, works like a credit card but with credit pre applied and can be used for cash withdrawals: http://uk.virginmoney.com/virgin/travel-prepaid-card/

5. Protecting your cards! - Finally, if your cards are contact less, be aware of latest scams of people scanning your cards whilst in your pockets and bags. Unfortunately new technology brings new opportunities for scammers and carries risk. However you can protect your cards simply by using an RFID lined wallet, pouch, or waist belt. Alternatively use RFID blocking credit card covers on your cards to keep your personal credit card information safe and prevent anyone being able to scan your cards whilst in your pockets or bags. See range of RFID protection wallets on the gap year travel store: www.gapyeartravelstore.com

Raising the money

There's no doubt it's harder to raise money for gap travel in tougher economic times, when the competition for even low-skilled or part-time work is likely to be intense.

But, aside from the lucky few who can call upon major financial help from their families or wherever else, most people will have to go out and earn the money, so it may be a case of taking whatever is out there. It will be worth it to pay for your 'once in a lifetime' trip.

Do remember that how you raise the money could have lasting benefits. Raising the money for a gap year is seen as an important part of a gap year both by the company you travel with and by employers," Stefan Wathan, of Year Out Group, told us. "Done well, it demonstrates commitment, initiative, an ability to plan, to appreciate money and to negotiate as well as communication skills.

If you already have a job look at how much of your salary you can realistically put aside each month for your travelling fund. It may mean six months or so of not having quite so many cocktails each week, or not being able to buy the latest iPhone, but it will be worth it! You can set up a separate account for your travelling fund and arrange a standing order to move money each month, which is really simple to do through internet banking.

There are other ways to raise some money however, such as a car boot sales or a sponsored run, bike ride or swim *etc* (donating half to charity, half to travel funds). And the internet is a great source of money-raising ideas, from selling on eBay and Gumtree to new initiatives such as crowd-funding. Have a look at this website: www.fundmytravel.com. With a little imagination you could really lighten the financial load.

Sponsorship may be an option and local businesses may be interested if they think they can get some mileage out of it. You may able to get local media interested if you are doing something exceptional on your travels, and then you can give your business sponsors the free advertising they deserve.

Community groups, charities and religious organisations may well be interested in what you are doing and they may be willing to help in some way – particularly if you promise to give them a talk about your travels when you get back.

You could also apply for a grant. Have a look at the Directory of Grant Making Trusts. It is published each year and covers 2,500 grant-making trusts, collectively giving around £3billion.

If you are planning to do a training course during your gap-year, you may be eligible for funding via a Career Development Loan. A CDL is a deferred repayment bank loan to help you pay for vocational learning or education. The Department for Education pays the interest on your loan while you are learning and for up to one month afterwards.

You can get more info from the National CDL enquiry line: 0800 100 900; or by visiting the government website: **www.gov.uk/career-development-loans/overview**

Money savers

The International Student Identity Card (ISIC) gives you more than 40,000 travel, online and lifestyle discounts. It costs £9, is accepted in the UK and worldwide. There's also a 24/7 worldwide free call helpline for medical and legal assistance.

Many leading airlines also offer exclusive student/youth fares to ISIC (and IYTC) holders. Your travel agent can help you find the right one and advise if any age restrictions apply.

You can order your ISIC online at: **www.isic.org**

The card sees you right through the academic year: it's valid from each September, for up to 16 months, in other words until December the following year. You need to qualify for the year in which you'll hold the card:

· If you're a full-time student (15 hours weekly for 12+ weeks) at a secondary school, sixth form or further education college, language school, The Open University (60 points or more) or any UK university.

· If you've got a deferred/confirmed UCAS placement (then you can grab an ISIC for your year away).

If you're neither of the above, but under 26, you can get an International Youth Travel Card (IYTC) with a similar range of benefits. You can get the cards online at: **www.ISIC.org** or by phoning 0871 230 8546.

For budget flights and student discounts, you can check out the internet and we've included some hints in **Chapter 4 – Travelling and accomodation**.

If you're travelling independently, cut the cost of accommodation by: staying in the guest houses attached to temples and monasteries; camping or staying in a caravan park; as a guest in someone's home; sharing a room; or using budget hotels or hostels, but be careful to check for cleanliness and proper exits in case of an emergency. If you're a mature traveller, perhaps you could investigate a house swap for part of your time away, but see also **Chapter 3 – Career breaks and older travellers** for other ideas.

Buy second-hand: rather than spend a fortune on a backpack, do you know someone who's just returned from a trip and might be willing to lend or sell you any equipment they no longer need? Check the classified ads in your local paper, buy on eBay (or similar) or try some gap-year message boards.

Make sure that whatever you buy is in clean, sound condition, that the zips work, there are fittings for padlocks, and it's right for your body weight and height. If it's sound but a bit travel-worn, so much the better – you'll look like a seasoned traveller rather than a novice!

Money security

We've covered some of this earlier in this chapter, but it's worth explaining a bit further. It's best to take a mix of cash, travellers' cheques, credit/debit card and travel money cards, and here's how best to take care of them:

Cash: carry small change in pockets, not big notes. Distribute it between a belt bag, day pack and your travel bag so you have an emergency stash.

Travellers' cheques: record serial numbers and the emergency phone number for the issuer in case of theft. You sign each one when you get them from the bank but then there's a space for a second signature. Don't sign this second box until you're cashing it – if you do and your cheques get stolen, they can be cashed and you invalidate the insurance cover. Only cash a couple of travellers' cheques at any one time – get a mix of larger and small change denominations. Often street traders and snack stalls, or taxis and rickshaws, won't have change for a large note and it makes you vulnerable – you seem rich.

Hotel currency exchanges are more expensive, local banks can take a long time and require ID. If you can find a Thomas Cook centre they're the most efficient and speedy we've found. Street rates can be cheaper but be very careful. A lot of street money changers are trading illegally – don't hand over the cheque until you have your money and have counted it.

Credit card: essential back-up. The problem with a credit card is losing it or having it stolen – keep a note of the numbers, how to report the loss of the card and the number you have to ring to do so.

Both Visa and Mastercard are useful, in an emergency, for getting local currency cash advances from a cash dispenser at banks abroad. Remember, if you're using your credit card to get money over the counter then you're likely to need some form of ID (eg passport).

If you are paying for goods or restaurant meals by using your card, you should insist on signing bills/receipts in your presence and not allow the card to be taken out of your sight. This way you'll have no unpleasant surprises or mysterious purchases when you see your card statement.

Travel Money Cards: pre-pay travel cards are now a well-established alternative to travellers' cheques and can be used at an ATM using a PIN number. The idea is that you load them with funds before you leave, but beware – like credit and debit cards, most charge for every reload and for cash withdrawals. To find out more check out these two examples:

www.iceplc.com/cashcard
www.travelex.com

Wiring money

If you find yourself stranded with no cash, travellers' cheques or credit cards, then having money wired to you could be the only option. Two major companies offer this service:

MoneyGram – **www.moneygram.com**

Western Union – **www.westernunion.com**

Both have vast numbers of branches worldwide - MoneyGram has 180,000 in 190 countries and territories and Western Union has 379,000 agent locations in 200 countries and territories.

The service allows a friend or relative to transfer money to you almost instantaneously. Once you have persuaded your guardian angel to send you the money, all they have to do is go to the nearest MoneyGram or Western Union office, fill in a form and hand over the money (in cash).

It is then transferred to the company's branch nearest to you, where you in turn fill in a form and pick it up. Both you and the person sending the money will need ID, and you may be asked security questions so you need to know what the person sending the money has given as the security question *and* its answer. Make sure they tell you the spelling they've used and that you use the same.

There are now also smartphone applications for people to send money to each other. Barclays' Pingit allows its users to receive and send money, without charge, to anyone with a UK current account and a mobile phone number.

The service links users' current accounts to their mobile number. They can then 'Ping' money to another mobile phone number (the person receiving the money has to register with the service to access it). The service is protected by a passcode.

Older travellers with more assets will have specific financial concerns and perhaps more sources of funds than younger gappers, and we've included some detail in **Chapter 3 - Career breaks and older travellers.**

Sticking to a budget

How do you manage the budget when you're away? This totally depends on your style. You could be the person who loves an old fashioned spreadsheet, or someone who prefers to wing it and check your account weekly to see the damage and adjust your spending for the following week accordingly.

There are also apps that can help you with your budget, for example Expense IQ, where you input your budget, and spending each day (there's an alarm you can set up to remind you to do this). It's easy to use and very helpful if you tend to overspend! Other similar apps include Money Manager Expense and Budget. We also strongly recommend any currency converter app on your smart phone or tablet to help mange your budget.

As a general rule you'll find your money will stretch quite a long way in most of the less developed parts of the world, and once you're in-country you can find out fairly easily from other travellers/locals the average costs of buses, trains, meals and so on.

Having said that, the global recession and rises in oil and food prices have had an impact on most countries' economies. They've particularly hit costs in the less developed world and the signs are that it may take some time for things to settle down.

As you're planning some months ahead of your trip it may be sensible to add a little extra for potential inflation when you're working out your minimum and maximum spend per day. The trick then is to stick to it. Here are some tips:

Shopping: you're bound to find a zillion things that will make good souvenirs/gifts – best advice, though, is to wait. You'll see lots more wherever you are and the prices for the same goods in popular tourist and backpacker destinations will be much higher – and possibly of lower quality – than they will be in smaller towns and villages.

the gap-year guidebook 2016

Do your buying just before you move on to the next destination, or return home, so you won't have spent too much money at the start of your trip, won't have to carry it all around with you and also by then you'll have an idea of what's worth buying and for how much. Another advantage of buying locally is that more of what you pay is likely to benefit the local community, and craftspeople, rather than the middle links in the chain.

If you buy souvenirs/gifts mid-trip, you could consider posting them home to save carrying them around with you but don't risk sending anything too valuable, and make sure you know what's permitted to send (and what's not) since you'll almost certainly have to fill in a customs declaration slip, which will be stuck to the outside of the parcel.

Bargaining: make sure it's the custom before you do, and try to find out roughly what it should cost before you start. Also try to look at yourself through local eyes – if you're wearing expensive jewellery and clothes and carrying a camera or the latest mobile phone you'll find it much harder to get a real bargain.

Whatever you do, smile and be courteous. The trader has to make a living, usually in pretty harsh economic conditions, and you're a guest in their country. Not only that, but if you're a responsible traveller then ethically you should be offering a fair price, not going all-out to grab a bargain you can boast about later.

Don't give the impression you really, really want whatever it is. Don't pick it up – leave that to the market trader, then let them try to sell it to you. They will tell you how much they want and it's likely to be inflated, so offer a price the equivalent amount below the figure it should be and that you're willing to pay.

visit: www.gap-year.com

If they start the process by asking you how much you're willing to offer then mention that you've asked around local people so you know roughly what it should cost, before you name a price a little below what you're prepared to pay. From this point on it's a bit like a game of chess and it can be very entertaining – so don't be surprised if you collect an audience!

You might be told a heart-rending story about family circumstances or the trader's own costs, but you can counter that by saying that however much you like the item, you're sorry but it's outside your budget. Gradually you'll exchange figures until you reach an agreement. One technique is to pretend you're not that bothered and start to walk away, but be prepared for the trader to take you at your word.

Not getting ripped off by cabbies: find out beforehand roughly what the local rate is for the distance you want to go. Then it's much the same principle as bargaining in a market. It's generally cheaper not to let hotels find you a cab – they often get a rake-off from the fare for allowing cabbies to park on their grounds, so it will cost you more.

Agree a price before you get into the vehicle and if you're hiring a car and driver for a day (which can often work out cheaper especially if you're sharing with friends) usually you'll be expected to pay for a meal for the driver so make sure you agree that the price of a stop for food is included in the deal.

In India there's a system of pre-pay kiosks, particularly at airport exits, where you can buy a chit – a paper that states a fair, and usually accurate, price for the journey. The driver can't cash it until you're safely at your destination, can't charge you more than is on the chit, and it has to be signed – usually by your hotel/accommodation before it can be cashed. So you can be sure you'll not be taking any long detours to bump up the cost. It's worth asking whether there are similar systems wherever you are.

Tipping: it's a bit of a minefield and you need to find out what the fair rate is. A tip should be a thank you for good service, so, for example, if you're in a restaurant and there's already a percentage on your bill for service you shouldn't pay more, unless of course you feel your waiter deserves it! Remember if you over-tip you raise expectations higher than other travellers – and locals – who may not be able or willing to pay.

Finding and affording a guide: find out if there's a local scheme for licensing/approving guides and what the 'official permit' looks like. Nearly always there will be any number of 'guides' at the entrances to any interesting place you might want to visit. Some will be official – others will be trying their luck. You'll usually find out when you pay the entrance fee.

Insurance

It's important to take out comprehensive travel insurance, however long you are travelling for, and to check that it covers you for everything that you want to do while you are away. Should something go wrong while you are overseas, costs can quickly escalate with average prices ranging from £15,000 to over £100,000 (in Europe and America respectively) for treatment and re-scheduled flights back home.

Getting the proper insurance is important for when taking a gap-year. You can take out a good year or nine-month policy that will be specifically tailored to backpacker's needs.

As a backpacker your luggage is probably only going to consist of a rucksack with a few clothes in it, so most policies don't insure your luggage for a huge amount. However, the medical cover that you receive is the most important part as you may be travelling in developing countries where the medical services are not up to western standards.

It is worth noting that even in developed countries, health services work differently and you may have to pay more for certain things. Medical treatment is very expensive wherever you are, and if something really drastic happened to you whilst you were abroad, the costs could be astronomical. Most gap-year insurance packages cover repatriation costs, meaning that they would pay for you to be flown home if you were seriously ill. Some will cover the cost of having a family member flown out to you in an emergency.

It is therefore vitally important that when you take out a policy for your gap-year that you are covered for most eventualities so that you have peace of mind to really enjoy your year out. Scan all your documents and email them to yourself if everything gets lost, as long as you can find internet access you will have access to everything you need.

When taking out insurance we recommend that you ask the following questions about the insurance to ensure that you get the right one:

· How long am I going to be insured for?

· What parts of the world will the insurance policy cover me in?

· What happens if I lose or have my passport stolen or my wallet is stolen?

· What cover do I get if I decide to do an extreme sport and adventure activity?

· What happens if I need to go hospital?

· What happens if I miss my flight?

· What happens if I have to do exam retakes?

· Will I get flown home if I need to?

Some banks provide cover for holidays paid for using their credit cards, but their policies may not include all the essentials you'll need for a gap-year.

Banks also offer blanket travel insurance (medical, personal accident, third party liability, theft, loss, cancellation, delay and more). You may be able to get reductions if you have an account with the relevant bank or buy foreign currency through it.

Who to choose?

You don't have to buy a travel insurance policy as part of a travel package through a travel company and there is intense competition between insurance companies to attract your attention. It may be tedious but the best advice is shop around, check out the internet, talk to a broker and read the small print very carefully.

Medical insurance

If you're going to Europe you can get a European Health Insurance Card (EHIC), which allows for free or reduced cost medical treatment within Europe, should you need it. You can apply online: **www.ehic.org.uk** or there's an automated application service on **0300 3301350.**

If you need further help you can call Overseas Healthcare Team on 0191 218 1999.

Your card is valid for three to five years and should be delivered to you in seven days. The EHIC card only covers treatment under the state scheme in all EU countries, plus Denmark, Iceland, Liechtenstein, Norway and Switzerland. You can also pick up application forms at your post office.

However, the EHIC is not a replacement for a travel insurance policy. It only covers necessary care and won't cover things such as repatriation to the UK in the event of a medical emergency

Countries with no health care agreements with the UK include Canada, the USA, India, most of the Far East, the whole of Africa and Latin America. Wherever it happens, a serious illness, broken limb, or even an injury you might cause someone else, can be very expensive.

Medical insurance is usually part of an all-in travel policy. Costs vary widely by company, destination, activity and level of cover. Make sure you have generous cover for injury or disablement, know what you're covered for and when you've got the policy read the small print carefully. For example, does it cover transport home if you need an emergency operation that cannot be carried out safely abroad?

Some policies won't cover high-risk activities like skiing, snowboarding, bungee jumping *etc* so you'll need to get extra, specific, cover and an insurance broker can help with this. Companies may also make a distinction between doing a hazardous sport once and spending your whole time doing them. Some insurance policies also have age limits.

If you have a medical condition that is likely to recur, you may have to declare this when you buy the insurance, otherwise the policy won't be valid. Also, check whether the policy covers you for the medical costs if the condition does recur, as some will not cover such pre-existing conditions.

Already covered?

If you're going abroad on a voluntary work assignment you may find that the organisation arranging it wants you to take a specified insurance policy as part of the total cost. You may also find you have a clash of policies before you even start looking for the right policy.

For example, if your family has already booked you a one-year multi-travel insurance policy to cover travel with the family at other times of the year, you may find you are already covered for loss of life, limb, permanent disablement, some medical expenses, theft and so on.

These multi-trip policies can be basic as well as quite cheap, but it's essential to check the small print of what the policy covers as it's possible that there may be a clause compelling the insured to return to the UK after a short period of time.

Just like many of the 'free' insurance policies that come with bank accounts, many of these policies only cover for trips of up to 60 days at a time, at which point travellers had to return to the UK. In other words, great for a holiday or two or for a business traveller but no use at all if you plan to be out of the country for the whole year.

In this case you can start by finding out (through the broker or agent who sold you the policy) if any additional cover can be tacked on to your existing policy, though this can be expensive and most off-the-shelf policies won't do it. A specific gap-year or backpacking policy may be more appropriate and actually work out cheaper than trying to add stuff on.

Try to find a policy that doesn't already duplicate what is covered by an existing policy (they don't pay out twice), but some duplication is unavoidable and it's obviously better to be covered twice than not at all.

Making a claim

Read through the small print carefully before you travel and make sure you understand exactly what to do if you need to make a claim – most policies will insist that you report a crime to the police where this is possible (often within a certain time period), and that you send in the police report with your insurance claim. What you don't want to happen is to have a claim dismissed because you don't have the right paperwork to back it up.

Insurers won't pay you money unless you have complied with all their rules and many travel policies impose conditions that are virtually impossible to meet. For example, some policies demand that you report not only theft of items but also loss of items. Fine, but the police are likely to be pretty reluctant to write a crime report because you think you may have accidentally left your camera in the loo!

If you do have anything stolen and you have to get the local police to give you a report, it's a good idea to dress reasonably smartly when you visit them, be prepared to wait and try to be pleasant and polite no matter what!

The Foreign Office website (**www.fco.gov.uk/travel**) has a good page about insurance and is worth checking out for advice and links. In addition to a list of what your travel insurance should cover, which is similar to the one at the start of this chapter, it suggests the following extras, which are not always included:

· Legal expenses cover can be useful as it will help you to pursue compensation or damages following personal injury while you're abroad – very important in countries without a legal aid system.

· Financial protection if your airline goes bankrupt before or during your trip – given the state of the airline industry this may be worth serious consideration for at least the next couple of years.

Our friends at DU Insure added that it is worth noting the excess on your policy – something that is often overlooked.

"Almost all policies have an excess attached to different sections of cover. That amount is deducted from the claim, normally for each person covered and for each relevant section of the policy. If you make a number of claims whilst you are travelling this can add up so think about taking out an excess waiver so that you have to contribute nothing. It may cost a little more but could save you a small fortune."

You'll also need to let your insurers know about any existing medical conditions before you head off: "If you don't declare a pre-existing condition, the entire policy will probably be invalidated. **If you are in any doubt, talk to the insurer before you buy**. Note also that, if you have an existing injury that is exacerbated by a second accident while you are travelling, cover for this may also be excluded."

visit: www.gap-year.com

What to do if you get an emergency call to come home

We all hope there'll be no family crises while we're away on our gap but it does occasionally happen that someone close is taken seriously ill, or even dies, and then all you can think about is getting home as quickly as possible.

We've talked to a couple of insurers about this and they reinforce our advice to *always* read the policy carefully before you set off on your travels.

Generally speaking, your gap-year travel policy ceases once you return home, but some insurers offer extra cover for one extra trip home (or more, up to four, but the price rises with each one) without your policy lapsing. In a backpacker/adventure policy of three to 18 months, one home return is in the region of £5 and four would be around £24 extra on your policy.

Most insurers are used to dealing with sudden early returns and have a 24-hour emergency assistance company to help you through the whole process.

You need to let them know anyway so you can set the ball rolling for claiming for the cost and they can deal with getting you from your gap location to the airport, or, if you have one, you can use the help of your placement provider's in-country reps, or even a combination of the two, so you don't have to deal with transport hassles when all you can think about is getting home quickly.

However, there are often restrictions. First off, your family emergency has to affect an immediate relative – so husband, wife, mum, dad, grandparents, sisters and brothers, children, grandchildren – but *not* aunts, uncles and other extended family. It has to be serious injury, illness or death of a relative – family feuds and divorces do not count!

If you have home return extra on your policy you're covered for one extra flight home; you're *not* covered for an additional flight back to resume your gap. But, if you have a return ticket, as most gappers do, the best way to go is to use your existing return, if the airline will reschedule, claim for it, then book another return flight. It's often cheaper to book a return flight than an extra one-way only.

If your ticket cannot be changed and you need to purchase a new ticket for your return journey, this can be arranged via a flight-ticketing agent or direct with the appropriate airline (subject to availability of flights and seats).

Websites such as Expedia and ebookers offer a wide selection of flights including single leg and one way tickets, which you can buy online and be allocated e-tickets, or collect them from the airline sales desk at the airport.

During peak travel or holiday times you might find the quickest way to get home may be to go to the airport and wait to pick up a 'no show' seat on standby.

Finally, make sure you read the small print. This may seem like a laborious task but it can pay as there are a few things you should always bear in mind before you hand over your cash:

· If you have an on-going illness like asthma and diabetes, make sure your policy covers them, as many don't.

· Ongoing medication and vaccinations are usually not covered.

· Dental treatment costs are usually for emergency treatment only.

· If an insurance company says they'll fly you home in a medical emergency, bear in mind that it won't be up to you - the doctors and the insurance companies will decide how serious it is.

- If you can wait until you get home to be treated, it's unlikely your cover will cover any costs of treatment you think you might need.

- If you're going to do sports, make sure they're covered - don't just assume. Many companies make you pay extra for adventure sports and activity insurance.

- If you're 'off your head' when you hurt yourself then there's a good chance you'll foot the bill.

- If your airline goes bust you're unlikely to be covered - unless you've got Airline Failure Insurance.

- If you forget to report a theft to the police, you probably won't be covered for the loss.

And don't forget to take the contact phone number of your insurance company with you in case of emergency. Carry it around with you in your money belt, in your rucksack and in your wallet. Also copy the policy number and any other reference you will need if you have to contact them. Photocopy the insurance documents and take them with you on your travels, or like mentioned earlier scan them and email them to yourself too.

Please see the directory pages starting on page 293 for information on companies and organisations offering financial and insurance services for gappers.

3

Career breaks and older gappers

3 Career breaks and older gappers

What exactly do we mean?

You will read the terms 'career break' and 'sabbatical' a lot in this chapter. They will essentially refer to the same thing: stopping work for a period of time to do something new or different. You would generally consider a 'sabbatical' to be a period of time away from your job, with the agreement to return at the end of it. A career break, however, might mean cutting loose altogether – quitting your job and seeing what happens; maybe with the intention of starting a whole new career when you're back, or just a leap into the unknown. Either way, it's what we'd consider a gap, so this chapter looks at how to do it and what you'll need to think about.

An emerging trend

They may still be in the minority in the gap-year market, but the number of career breakers is definitely on the rise. Taking a month, six months or a year out of your workplace is an excellent way to add new skills to your CV, re-assess your career (or maybe your life!), or just to recharge your batteries and get away from the routine.

There may be something you've always wanted to do or somewhere you've wanted to go – and maybe now you're in a better position to afford it? Or maybe you want to 'give something back' after years in the 'rat race'?

You might have heard of the terms 'extravagapper', 'flashpacker' or 'grey gapper' to describe the more mature member of the gap community.

Extravagappers are thought of as newly-redundant city professionals with generous redundancy packages, who are taking the opportunity of a career break rather than plunge back into a possibly demoralising, recession-hit job market.

Flashpackers are those backpacking with 'flash or style', who typically spend freely, or even excessively, for activities at their chosen destination.

Grey gappers is a term used to describe people who are 50 and over, who have decided to take a gap-year.

These are caricatures, of course. People who take career breaks come from all sorts of backgrounds, and with varying degrees of affluence.

Taking a career break for one month to a year is the fastest-growing sector of gap-year activity and there's some anecdotal evidence that the global recession is increasing the numbers. Around 90,000 people take a short sabbatical each year in the UK – in other words a 'gap-month'. It may be worthwhile considering something like this, or perhaps a longer trip if you've been made redundant or taken early retirement.

Jon Arnold from Oyster Worldwide comments; "The average age of our clients is creeping up each year. For the past 12 months, the average age is 24. This has been pulled up by career breakers and short term volunteers who can be aged anything between 17-75."

visit: www.gap-year.com

Many organisations that arrange places for people on overseas projects, have told us that more than half of their activity is now focused on helping place mature travellers and/or people who are taking a career break. Our friends at Raleigh International said the number of career breakers was increasing year-on-year; "We regularly attract career breakers in our volunteer manager positions. This is a great opportunity for those wanting to use their passion, skills and experience to drive positive change in vulnerable environments and poor rural communities. Our volunteer managers will inspire and support a diverse group of young people to change their world for the better."

"We regularly hear stories about volunteer managers who, following their career break with Raleigh, return home to follow a completely different career path."

Richard Nimmo from Blue Ventures Expeditions shares his thoughts on the mature gapper trend; "Blue Ventures attract a wide variety of participants from school leavers and traditional gap-year participants to career breakers and retirees. I think that it is the retiree or 'grey gapper' that has been the most interesting trend in the last few years. This group has the time to participate in meaningful travel and enjoy joining groups, learning and developing new skills. They add to the mix and diversity of our groups and make life on an expedition more interesting and varied. The 'grey gapper' has been a very positive and welcome new entry to the gap-year market."

People are living longer and are also a lot healthier well into old age. Many, therefore, feel they want to continue to use their skills in places where they will do some good.

This, coupled with the issues of the retirement age being put back and worries about inadequate pension provision, has also prompted many older people to think about extending their working lives and perhaps also pursuing a different career altogether.

Taking a gap, perhaps to volunteer in another country, is one good way of identifying skills, wisdom and knowledge gained over a working lifetime, that may be useful in another sector and this could lead to a new career.

The VISITOZ programme provides **an introductory course** *about Australian farm work* and paid jobs in the outback

Chainsaw

Horse riding

Fencing

Motorbikes

Tractor driving

Mustering

It is a challenging adventure
in a dry, dusty and tough environment
A REAL JOB FOR A REAL PAY
With commitment and perseverance
you will have an amazing experience

Pre-travel checklist

Older travellers generally have different considerations from younger ones when making their plans. These include the effects of taking a gap on careers, what to do about the house and mortgage, financial issues and whether or not to take the children, if this applies.

This list covers the extra responsibilities older people might have to consider. It only covers the basics of what you might have to organise – but we hope it will be a useful start for you to cherry-pick what's appropriate and no doubt add your own extras!

Work:

· Talk to your employer about sabbatical/career break options

Career break:

· What do you want from it?

· What do you want to do?

· Where do you want to go?

Finance:

· Paying the bills

· Mortgage

· Financing and raising money for the trip

· Insurance

· Pensions and NI contributions.

The house: Are you going to let it? If yes, you need:

· To talk to an accommodation agency

· Safety certificates

· Insurance

· To investigate tax exemption

Storage of possessions:

· What do you want to store? And can it be stored at home?

Children:

· Talk to the school(s) about taking them

· Find out about education possibilities where you're going

· If they're coming, how long will the trip be?

Safety precautions:

· Wills and power of attorney

Your daily commute

Your 9-5

Your work colleagues

Want a break from the norm? If you want to achieve more
with your time out, we're looking for you.

raleighinternational.org/expeditions

Raleigh
International

Arranging a sabbatical

There is no legal obligation on employers to offer employees sabbaticals/career breaks. However, they are often regarded as an important part of an employee's career development, and may be granted for a variety of reasons including study research travel or voluntary work which can often be related to the employee role.

Here's some useful things to know:

· Sabbaticals can help companies retain senior staff by giving them the chance to do something different, without leaving altogether.

· Employers who grant sabbaticals will usually attach various conditions to eligibility and what happens during the sabbatical.

· Sabbaticals are usually only available to employees at senior levels and those who have completed a specified number of years of continuous service.

· Some organisations do not even have sabbatical policies.

· Where an employer does grant sabbaticals, it must ensure that part-time employees are afforded the same benefits as equivalent full-time staff.

· Normally the employee will not receive pay or benefits for a sabbatical as the employee's contract is seen as suspended.

· It's important that a strategy for the return to work is agreed in advance of the sabbatical.

· The employer should take particular care to ensure that any guarantee of re-employment is worded clearly and unambiguously in order to avoid any disagreement or challenge at a later date.

my
gap-year
Pauline

Raleigh was the perfect way to start retirement and I feel much younger at the end of expedition than I did at the beginning! I liked the variety of phases, programme structure and the length of time suited me just right. I wanted to work abroad and with a group of young people of a different age I was used to.

As a teacher you are used to helping students by giving clear directions for a task, however I learned to develop a hands off approach and allow the venturers greater control in their decision making. It's an excellent way to see young people develop. As you go on you allow the group to develop their own ways of doing things and you are much more confident that they can make the right decisions. You're not a mum or a teacher. You're not there to solve all their problems. The young person acting as day leader is the person responsible for what work is going on through the day, and also for resolving any conflicts. We as project managers mentor them and guide them, we have one-to-one sessions with them, we reflect on the phases and identify issues.

We worked on an environmental project which was split into two sections. The first half was spent at Carara National Park. The rainy season had made the park inaccessible, causing a great loss of revenue. This revenue is vital to maintain the sustainability of the area, which is a primary rainforest with exceptional biodiversity. We stayed in an old ranger station and we worked hard repairing the trail and making sure there is access for wheelchair users. This was hard physical work – a lot of digging trenches with mattocks, carrying bags of gravel and rocks.

I personally developed physical skills including greater fitness, and the ability to use a variety of tools to construct trails. The rangers took us for walks around Carara to show us the amazing flora and fauna and told us how much they appreciated our vital work and contribution, as the park was very understaffed. At the end of the project we walked the trail of 300m and flight of steps that we had constructed with Oscar, one of the rangers. He was quite emotional about the fact that without our help none of this would have happened - we had made a real difference.

The second half of the environmental phase was spent at a turtle refuge at Playa Hermosa. Thousands of turtles a year come to lay their eggs, however these fall prey to predators and poachers who sell them for profit. We again supported the rangers by doing night patrols, collecting eggs and placing them safely in a hatchery we built. Once the eggs hatched we released the baby turtles into the sea at a safe time to give them the best possible chance of surviving and the best possible chance to conserve this very important species. Releasing the newborn turtles at dawn was one of the best moments, as well as being on night patrols and seeing the sand light up sparkly like a disco floor! (bioluminescence).

The final, community phase was my favourite, staying in La Arenilla, Nicaragua where our group helped in the construction of six houses.

La Arenilla is an incredibly poor community however they welcomed us into their homes and it was a privilege to be part of their lives. In 2011 hurricanes devastated many communities in the stunningly beautiful Miraflor reserve. Heavy rain left many families in La Arenilla homeless so, in conjunction with El Foro – a non-governmental organisation responsible for the co-management of the reserve, Raleigh was keen to get involved in the disaster relief initiative.

We worked alongside the local community levelling terrain and collecting rocks to lay new foundations, made adobe blocks and helped build six new houses, meaning six families could move into new homes rather than makeshift accommodation. It was hard physical work making mud for the adobe bricks and carrying them as well as the actual construction of the houses.

Despite the age difference between myself, the venturers and the other project managers, (most of whom are in their late 20s or 30s - I'm 61) we quickly became a team.

I have enjoyed working with a different age group of young people as well as local communities and being a volunteer. I am definitely more laid-back and tolerant of others, and little things don't irritate me in the same way as they did before. I arrived at the realisation that I need very little to get along in life. I don't need to eat as much as I thought and I don't need meat. I milked a cow straight into a glass of hot coffee - frothy coffee! I am stronger, more resilient and more independent than before Raleigh. I have developed in fluency of Spanish through interactions with rangers and members of the community.

For me Raleigh International has been an amazing challenge. Whether you come as a venturer or you come as a volunteer manager, it gives you an opportunity to grow in confidence, even if you've got no firm plans for the future, you've got the confidence to go with it and to challenge yourself and not always do the conventional thing. It's been great working with such a wide variety of people. That's the great thing about Raleigh International – it's not just a group of people from one sector of society, it's not just wealthy, privileged kids, it's people from all walks of life – that's of the great things you take from it. You meet people you wouldn't have spent any time with, all different life stages, it's been really special.

For more information about Raleigh International, see their advert on page 96

What if you can't arrange a sabbatical?

Companies have no obligation to provide career breaks, so if you're turned down, you'll need to think about what to do. You may decide to resign. If not, you might want to consider how it will affect your future prospects there. It's a tricky one, and depends very much on both you and the company: your career goals, and their hopes and plans for you.

One option you might consider if you can't arrange a sabbatical and are wary of just quitting is arranging a job swap with someone from another country in a similar industry. You need to consider:

· Where do you want to travel?

· Do you speak a second, third or fourth language?

· Will you need housing?

· Do you need to be paid while away?

· How long do you want to be away for?

This may be easier in an international company where there may even be opportunities to transfer to the overseas office. Many such companies offer formal secondment programmes so it's always worth exploring these first.

If the above options are not possible, and you are prepared to resign, you could investigate whether your company might agree to guarantee you a job on your return.

Even if they don't guarantee a position for you, have regular contact with the key decision-makers whilst you are away by the occasional email *etc*. This will keep

visit: www.gap-year.com

you in their minds and make it easier for you to approach them when you come back home, to see if they have any suitable job opportunities. Just remember, in job hunting, as in everything else, it's not *what* you know but *who*. So it's absolutely vital that you make the effort not to lose touch with your professional colleagues, networks and contacts whilst you are away. If you do, you'll regret it once you are back.

If you're not already signed up to LinkedIn, you might like to consider it. This website is the business world equivalent of Facebook. It's free to use and you can link to colleagues and business contacts and post recommendations about them and, importantly, get them to post recommendations about you. You can upload your CV, and indicate that you are open to job opportunities. It could also be useful to add your list of contacts gained *whilst* you're on your career break, thus adding extra value to your LinkedIn profile. Visit **www.linkedin.com** to create a profile.

No sabbatical? Take your chances

If you're willing to quit and take your chances, what about finding work when the break's over?

What the jobs market will be like when you return is anyone's guess; however, you'll have a faster and more productive job search if you work at it before you leave.

Think now about the job you should be aiming for after the gap. Your gap is likely to develop new skills and ambitions so you might want something different from the current role.

In the various sections in the book, you'll discover the vast range of things you can do on your gap; the skills you can learn and the places you can visit. Whatever you choose, it's likely you'll be boosting your CV in a number of ways – and not always those you'd expect.

So, it's likely you'll return from your gap with new skills, a new sense of purpose, and a clearer idea of what you want to do in the future.

Your target job identified, talk to the people who'll help you find future vacancies. Research the specialist recruitment consultancies in that sector (*eg* Google them), then ask to talk to consultants with at least two years' experience of recruiting for the jobs that interest you. You want to know those consultants' best guesses about the likely state of that jobs market a year from now, what skills employers are most likely to look for in candidates and so on.

Stay in touch with the most useful of these recruitment consultants (*eg* by sharing snippets of your gap news with them). Keeping yourself at the forefront of their minds puts you on the inside track for news about developments in the jobs market. Similarly, stay in touch with ex-colleagues, university tutors and careers service advisors – they will often have huge networks for you to tap in to.

It's also a good idea to plan your career break around the natural hiring cycles of your industry. Recruitment activity tends to fall in December and early January, the Easter break and the weeks that coincide with the school summer holidays, for example. It may be harder to find jobs in these periods. The busiest times for recruitment tend to be the early spring and autumn.

Do update your CV before you go, ensuring it's ready for your return to employment. It's a good idea to keep it available on email so you can send it to interested parties while you're away, if an opportunity presents itself.

my
gap-year
Celia

For the past four years I have worked in London supporting disabled children through developmental home based play sessions. It's great, but, I was ready to spread my wings and have a nose at what's on offer elsewhere...so Thailand happened!

I had heard about the work being carried out at the Maekok River Village Education Centre and with an idea of volunteering my skills, I was excited to find a school in Thailand which was attempting to cater for special needs children. I booked my flight and off I went! Staying in the spacious 'gap house' within the school grounds was relatively luxurious after living in my tiny apartment in Camden! The accommodation was basic but with all the essentials like my own bedroom, bathroom, space for planning lessons and cooking meals.

The moment I entered the classroom I knew it was where I needed to be. I was able to work alongside the special educational needs teacher, share ideas and my experience. I was surrounded by kindness from every pupil and each teacher in the school. I felt totally included, a word that is often talked about in the world of disability.

I found it so refreshing to be around children who were determined to learn. Particularly the children with additional needs, who proudly put on their uniform and took pride in their achievements. I would recommend volunteering to anybody. If you're looking for a new challenge, fancy a break from your everyday job or care about enriching the life of others, do it!

For more information about Maekok River Village Resort, see Chapter 6 - Volunteering Abroad

Finance

You've talked to your employer, perhaps also worked out what you hope to do – there are plenty of organisations to help you plan your chosen activities in the various sections in this book. The next crucial question is finance.

Obviously the amount of money you'll need depends on where you want to go, what you want to do, and how long you want to be away. At this point, drawing up a rough budget for how much it will cost would be a good idea. (See **Chapter 2 - Finance**, for a checklist). Once you have this it's worth talking to your building society or bank to see whether they have any schemes that can meet your needs.

While banks often have student and graduate advisers who can advise on what to do about everything from travel insurance to suspending direct debits and deferring loan payment, they don't seem yet to have reached the stage of having advisers *specifically* for career breakers. They are, however, increasingly aware of the trend to take a career break and may well be able to use their experience of advising younger gappers to help you think the finances through.

One recent survey amongst older people in the UK revealed that a large majority are extremely pessimistic or fearful about the quality of their lives in old age. A significant number were taking the view that, if their old age was going to be so grim, why not have one last adventure? Consequently, they were using annuities and equity release or lifetime mortgages to unlock money from their homes to boost their retirement income and pay for such adventures.

This might seem like a good plan. However, there have also been many reports of schemes offering to buy people's homes and allowing them to rent them back for their lifetimes, only for them to be evicted after a few months or to find 'hidden charges' that meant they saw little money at the end of it. So beware! Read the small print *very* carefully.

Some companies offer lifetime mortgages, where you can release the value of your home and live in it without paying anything until you die, when the company will recover its money from the sale of the home.

Individual circumstances vary and if you feel you are 'asset rich but cash poor' it may be tempting to consider such options. You should only consider such a scheme with a reputable company and if the scheme includes protection against negative equity. We would strongly advise that if you are thinking of doing something like this you consult an independent financial adviser.

Maximise your funds: the chance for a good clear out

Is the garage crammed, are every drawer and cupboard stuffed? Is it all 'file and forget' or 'might come in handy' but never has? Admit it, you're one of those people who hasn't touched any of this stuff for years and you've kept saying you'd do a massive clearout. But the more you add over the years, the more daunting it is and the easier it is to put off. We all do it. And how much houseroom do some of us give to all that stuff our children insist they have no space for but have sentimental attachments to?

Preparing for your year out is the perfect opportunity to de-clutter your life. Have a look at what you need to get rid of and turn into funding for your gap. Consider raising some cash by selling items through online auction sites, such as eBay, holding a garage sale or a car boot sale.

my
gap-year
Lucy Healey

My life was happy, socially rocking and I had just received a promotion in my office job. However, the lure of the underwater world was making my feet itch. Undeniable. Three months later I was unemployed and on my way to Africa to join 17 others to experience a whole new culture and environment, go diving and create amazing, unforgettable memories!

Our location, the South West side of Madagascar, was mostly desert parked next to a sandy coastal town - it was dry and hot. The Baobab trees there were fat - and phat! Some of these trees are over 3000 years old! One such tree was hollowed out and would be perfect as a bar venue. Valerie and I will be starting our joint venture Baobab Bar in the near future. Flyers to come ... A typical day in our life as Blue Venture volunteers consisted of diving, marine studies, teaching English, eating, maintenance duties and sometimes a visit into town for exploring and the inevitable purchase of delicious bokubokus (doughnut type sweets). Dinner each night brought everyone together, staff and volunteers alike, for a review of the day, plans for the next day, story time and a plank off. Saturday night was party night, which lured the playfulness out of all and themed dress ups were the name of the game! The Malagasy men can really dance! The night usually ended on the sand dunes overlooking the moonlit ocean sharing stories from all corners of the world. Sundays were generally a lazy day off to explore, swim, sail, study and relax. This trip will remain on my most awesome experiences list forever.

For more information about Blue Ventures, see Chapter 6 - Volunteering Abroad

You'll create space to store your precious items (the things you want to keep but not leave lying about), you'll add some cash to your travel fund, and you'll come back to a well-organised home.

Imaginative fundraising

If you've already settled on the kind of project you want to do and it involves raising a specific sum, as volunteer projects often do, you can hold fundraising events to help you raise the cash – the options are as limitless as your imagination!

You have an untapped resource where you work – you could try asking for a contribution from your employer. It's good PR to have a link with someone doing something for a worthy cause.

If your employer agrees, what about baking cakes to sell at coffee time or holding competitions (guess the weight/number of objects in a container) or even asking colleagues to sponsor you? Even simple things like putting all those irritating bits of small change that weigh down pockets, and cram purses, into a large pot or jar can mount up surprisingly quickly.

Pensions and National Insurance contributions

If you have an occupational pension and are taking a sabbatical you should check with your employer to see if they offer a pension 'holiday' and what that might mean to your eventual pension, but it might be possible to stop or reduce your payments while you are away. If you have been with the company less than two years, it might be possible to arrange a refund of pension contributions.

For the state pension you might want to look at two issues: during the time you're away, you will be officially classified as living abroad and you won't be paying NI.

the gap-year guidebook 2016

However, you should check what that will do to your contributions' record and how it might affect your eventual state pension. You can find out if there are gaps in your record by calling the HMRC (HM Revenue and Customs) helpline (0845 915 5996) and for more information. People living abroad should call: 0845 915 4811.

Once you have that information it's worth talking to the DWP (Department for Work and Pensions). They have a help and advice service (Tel: 0845 606 0265) and you can find out what you can expect by way of state pension. A DWP adviser told us that, from 2010, to get the maximum state pension both men and women will have to have paid NI for at least 30 years.

However, another useful fact, if you're likely to reach retirement age during your gap and can afford it, is that there's an incentive for deferring your state pension. For every five weeks you agree to defer, you get 1% added to your eventual pension. After a year, you can either take that as a taxable lump sum or have it incorporated into your regular pension payments. You can defer for more than a year and continue to add this interest to your eventual state pension.

The Directgov website also has a useful page on pensions for people living abroad: **www.direct.gov.uk/en/BritonsLivingAbroad/Moneyabroad/DG_4000013**

Earning on your career break

It may even be possible to part-fund your career break by using your skills on volunteer and other projects.

United Nations Volunteers sometimes pay modest living or travel costs, for people with the skills they need for particular volunteer projects.

Have a look at their website: **www.unv.org/how-to-volunteer.html**

If you wanted a 'taster' before taking the big step of leaving the country, UNV also has a scheme for online volunteers, where you can become involved in worthwhile projects, using your computer in your spare time, at home: **www.onlinevolunteering.org/en/vol/index.html**

There are also organisations that can help with funding for specific projects: the Winston Churchill Memorial Trust (WCMT) is one of them. It provides grants for people wanting to travel abroad and work on special projects that they cannot find funding for elsewhere and, crucially, then use the experience to benefit others in their home communities. Applicants must be British citizens, resident in the UK and must apply by October each year.

The Trust awards travelling fellowships to individuals of all ages wanting to pursue projects that are interesting and unusual. Categories cover a range of topics over a three-year cycle. Roughly 100 are awarded each year and they usually provide funds for four to eight weeks.

The Trust emphasises that fellowships are *not* granted to gappers looking to fund academic studies, attend courses or take part in volunteer placements arranged by other organisations.

The advice is to study the WCMT website for examples of projects that have been funded, as they are very wide-ranging and will help you come up with your own ideas.

To find out more you can contact the Trust, see **www.wcmt.org.uk**, where you can apply online.

Tax issues

If you go to live or work abroad, and become non-resident in the UK, you might still have to pay UK tax – but *only* on your income earned in the UK (savings, dividends, rental income *etc*). If you do need to pay, you may need to complete a self-assessment tax return.

This website explains the tax implications for all the circumstances in which you might be abroad, whether temporarily or permanently. It's particularly useful if you're thinking of renting out your home:
www.direct.gov.uk/en/BritonsLivingAbroad/Moneyabroad/index.htm

What about the house?

Some mortgage lenders may allow a payment holiday of up to six months without affecting your scheme.

Another option might be to rent out your house. You may need to check terms and conditions for subletting with your mortgage lender, but it can be a good way of covering the mortgage costs while you are away.

As it is your home and you need to be sure it will be looked after while you are away, the above reinforces our advice that, if you decide to rent, it's worth using an accommodation agent to take care of things and make sure you comply with all the regulations. It would also be wise to check with the Inland Revenue to see whether you are eligible for a tax exemption certificate (on your rental income), which should be given to the accommodation agent.

When letting a house there are some rules to abide by and some safety certificates you must have if you're going to take this route. Another must is to tell your insurance company what you're planning.

107

Another possibility is a house swap

Obviously you'd have to be careful in arranging this and in satisfying yourself that you're happy with the people you're planning to swap with, but we've found a couple of agencies that can help you. The following arrange holiday swaps in many countries around the world and have plenty of advice on how to go about it. You have to sign up as a member to access some information:

www.homelink.org – annual membership is £115. It has regional websites in 30 countries and has been operating for 50 years.

www.homebase-hols.com – annual membership is £49.

Household contents: storage

Two things to think about if you really want to clear your house before renting:

· Do you really want to add this to your list of 'things to do' before you go?

· Can you afford it?

You would need a 20ft container for the contents of an average house. Most containers are 'self-service' so you would have to pack, move and unpack yourself and therefore need to add the costs of van rental and transport to the container rental costs.

You would also have to arrange your own insurance, but normally you can extend your household contents insurance to cover property on secured sites.

National removals and storage companies also provide container storage on managed sites and can sell you the packing materials and boxes you might need as well. Prices vary according to the distance from the storage site, size of container and length of time and some self storage companies do not charge VAT on household storage, but others do. It is worth bearing in mind that storage alone for a year would come to over £1000.

But remember, on top of that you have to add the packing, loading, removal and unloading costs at each end of your career break. On average the process can cost £300-£400 more than an ordinary house move and prices vary depending on whether your dates fall into peak season for house removals – such as children's school holidays and the peak times of year for house sales.

What about the kids?

There's some evidence that another growing trend is for families to take a gap together, particularly while the children are young.

While it's virtually impossible to get reliable figures, there's a lot of anecdotal evidence from gap providers. Our friends at Projects Abroad told us that "In the past year, we've also seen more family groups joining us."

The general view is that as long as the children are safe, have access to medical facilities and their education development is not harmed, family gap-years can have very beneficial outcomes. Some gap-year companies might have a minimum age limit of eight years and it's also important to clear the break with the children's school.

Whether to take the children out of school is really up to you as parents. Much will depend on the length of time you plan to be away and the point your children are at in their education.

Essentially you need to balance the effects of taking a child out of school against the benefits of the 'education' they will get from seeing something of the world.

You also need to think through health and medical issues, but that may mean nothing more than carrying essential medical supplies with you, as all travellers are advised to do when travelling abroad.

It's also possible that you can get your child into a local school for some of the time they are away, or you can organise some basic study for them with the help of their school while you are travelling.

The official view from the Department for Education is that, ultimately, it is down to the parents, but that they should talk it through with their child's school or local authority.

It is crucial that it's cleared with your child's school and headteacher, who has to authorise it, if you don't want to face court action by the local authority and a possible hefty fine for taking a child out of school during term time. But parents who have done it, even with very small children, say that it has been a very worthwhile experience and brought them closer to their kids. A few gap organisations are now providing family gap volunteer placements.

my
gap-year
Andy

Half the fun of an adventure is not knowing what you'll find: the daily challenges, unexpected pleasures, twists and turns along the way, great memories created and variety of people you meet. My wife (university research) and I (public relations/ event management) quit our jobs to see something of the world and make a difference along the way. Our two months at Kanaama in Uganda were a chance to help communities build a brighter future that have left a lasting impression on us.

South West Uganda is green, hilly and rural - a land of milk, honey and dusty tracks with big ruts. My way by bike to Nombe secondary school, half along a superb main road and half along red-dirt tracks, with views of banana and coffee plantations, avocado trees and rolling hills, was a joy. Every journey I waved to over 50 people, shared laughter over pronunciation of both my English and my Runyankole, or visited student homes to meet their families and their goats! I refereed a football match on my first day at school and got home late into the night, watched a school debate that filled the nearby church and spoke to scores of students about their studies, families and futures. Some students came round on Sunday afternoons for extra English lessons - we read and explained newspapers, poetry, books and a map of the world! Younger children from nearby houses dropped by all the time, to play outside with a rubber wheel that is steered ingeniously by a stick, to do drawings for us, or to read children's books (or just point at the pictures) from the house's growing library. Hazel was finding out about issues for people with disabilities, helping schools to prepare for school links, and number-crunching poverty indices with office staff.

At Rwoboguigo Primary School, 2km away, I found dedicated, friendly staff, despite challenges of poor pay and lack of books and learning tools. The children love to laugh and have endless enthusiasm. Differences in pronunciation were also difficult. We covered English language, poetry, drama and conversation skills, and most days PE running, balance and coordination games. The district education officer came to motivate and suggest improvements, and the next day the Management Group (largely teachers) wanted more progress in science.

Kashare sub-county has orphans with no one to care for them, single parents with barely a roof over their head and hungry mouths to feed, young adults with no education or hope of work. The difference KICS is making is impressive. Gathering case studies strongly conveyed the excellent work.

Two Crested Cranes, Uganda's national bird, landed nearby as we left - a crowning glory to an incredible adventure. We'd met wonderful people, new customs and cultures, and challenged ourselves. The chance to get stuck in and interact with so many I will always remember. Do go and join in!

Safety precautions

You will find a great deal of advice on all aspects of planning your gap in **Chapter 1 – Tips for travellers**, as well as in-country advice and what to expect when you get back. Tips for travellers is relevant to all travellers, whatever their age. We also cover the importance of getting the right kind of travel insurance and the questions you need answered in **Chapter 2 – Finance**.

But there are some other issues that perhaps might be more important for older travellers to consider. You almost certainly have more in the way of assets than someone straight from school or university – things like a house, insurance and pension schemes; valuable personal property.

In the unlikely event of something going wrong, it makes sense to ensure your affairs are in order and to have someone you trust authorised to take care of your affairs until you can do so for yourself. It will make things that much easier for those back home, who may be coping with the trauma of a loved one in hospital overseas, if they have some idea of how you want your affairs to be handled.

You should consider two things – making a will and possibly appointing someone with legal power of attorney.

Making a will

Points to remember when making a will:

· It doesn't have to be expensive.

· It can be amended later if your circumstances change.

· You can make it clear what you want to happen to your property.

· It prevents family squabbles.

· It allows you to choose executors you can trust.

You should:

· Give yourself time to think.

· Use a professional, preferably one experienced specifically with will preparation.

· Make sure you can update it without large additional charges.

· Make sure there's an opt out from executor or probate services if you don't need them – by the time the will is needed, which could be many years away, it may be that someone in the family, who was too young when you made it, who can deal with it.

Power of attorney

Many people choose to make an informal arrangement with a family member to take care of things at home while they're travelling, but if you were to need someone authorised to pay bills at home or liaise with your travel insurance company, it might make sense to have a proper, formal arrangement in place before you go to give them the authority to act on your behalf.

You might be able to arrange with your bank to add them as a signatory to your account, in case it should be necessary, as long as you feel comfortable that the person you choose will make the right decisions about your money if you can't.

A more secure way is to appoint a power of attorney, but be warned it's a lengthy process, which can take up to five months to process. Until the documents are properly registered, whoever you appoint cannot act for you.

There's no fast track procedure on compassionate grounds and the Public Guardians' Office website says: "If there are no problems with the LPA (Lasting Power of Attorney) or application, we are typically returning the registered LPA in around nine weeks from the date of receipt. If there are any problems with the LPA or application, we are currently informing the applicant within two weeks of receiving the application."

Getting it right when there are at least 30 pages of forms per person is no joke; and, if you're a couple, each one of you has to fill out a set. So to avoid delays and mistakes (with possible charging of repeat fees) it makes sense to get professional advice from a specialist.

The process is administered by the Office of the Public Guardian, which charges a fee of £150. But compare that with having someone professional look after your property and personal welfare. It can cost as much as £1500 for a couple. To find out more about the new legislation go to: **www.publicguardian.gov.uk**

Please see the directory pages starting on page 297 for information on companies and organisations offering trips and opportunities for career breakers and older gappers.

Travelling and accommodation

Travelling and accommodation

Getting about

Planes

Booking flights, transport and accommodation for your trip can be easy and straightforward. But when you are on your travels think about what season you're travelling in – is it low or high season? This will affect prices and also how far in advance you need to book everything.

The internet is invaluable when searching for ticket information, timetables, prices and special offers, whether you're travelling by air, sea, train or bus.

Because the internet gives customers so much information to choose from, travel companies have to compete harder to get your business. The internet shows you what flexibility is possible, so you could find more opportunities available.

When booking flights, have a look at special offers for round-the-world tickets first, find out how far in advance you can book, and then plan your destinations to fit. A fantastic website for looking up internal and external flights is **www.skyscanner.com**, which searches all the companies for you to get the best price, and you can look over a whole month if your dates aren't fixed.

If one of your destinations has a fixed arrival and departure date – for example if you're signed up for a voluntary project – you could try asking for a route tailor-made for you using the prices you find on the web. Travel agencies can often find better deals and it takes some of the hassle away from you. Like Round the World Experts (part of the Flight Centre) but there's also the likes of STA Travel.

Make sure you check out the company making an offer on the web before you use internet booking procedures (does it have a verifiable address and phone number?). Remember, under EU law companies must publish a contact address on their website. So, unless the company in question is a household name, or you are able to locate a legitimate address via another source, think twice before handing over your hard-earned cash.

It's important – as ever! – to read the Terms and Conditions to see what you're paying for and whether you can get your money back before you agree to buy – just as you would outside the virtual world.

Once you have made a booking now is the time to be taking out your travel insurance. See **Chapter 2 – Finance** for more information.

What to watch out for

Once you've booked a flight online, especially if you do it through an agent such as **www.lastminute.com**, rather than direct with the airline, you may have to pay extra fees for rescheduling, not to mention date restrictions if you need to change the date.

visit: www.gap-year.com

Unless you have a good, solid reason for cancelling – and most airlines define such reasons very narrowly – you also risk losing the money you've paid.

As we mention in **Chapter 1**, increasingly airlines are covering their additional fuel costs and taxes by adding charges for different services, like inflight baggage storage, airport duty, seats next to each other (if you're not travelling alone). You need to have your wits about you when you're going through the online booking forms as these extras can add a substantial amount to the final total, making that budget deal significantly more expensive than you originally thought (up to £100 at best and almost equalling the flight cost at worst).

Remember, the ads usually say 'flights *from* £XXX' and that's your clue to watch out for extras.

Bargain flights: scheduled airlines often offer discount fares for students under 26 so don't rule them out. Other cheap flights are advertised regularly in the newspapers and on the web. All sorts of travel agents can fix you up with multi-destination tickets, and student travel specialists often know where to find the best deals for gap-year students.

It's worth checking whether a particular flight is cheaper if you book direct with the airline – and if you are using a student travel card you may find that you have to do it this way to get the discount, rather than using one of the budget deal websites.

Above all, travel is an area where searching the internet for good deals should be top of your list – though it works best for single-destination trips rather than complex travel routes.

For example, make sure your tickets allow flexibility and what the costs would be if you decided to change your plans.

If you're thinking of travelling around Europe during your gap year, why not do it by train? Voyages-sncf.com gives you access to countless European destinations, from Paris to Vienna and Berlin to Madrid and above all, it's a fun and easy way to travel.

Voyages-sncf can get you from A to B throughout Europe, by high speed, overnight, regional and local trains - the choice is yours.

Rail travel is a very efficient way to explore Europe. Taking you into the heart of major cities, rural villages, seaside towns and mountain resorts, you'll arrive feeling refreshed and ready to explore. And you can relax in the knowledge that the train is also one of the greenest ways to travel.

Overnight trains let you make the most of your time in a destination and save on accommodation costs, while day trains travel at speeds of up to 320km per hour, whisking you through stunning scenery en-route. It's also a sociable way to travel and you'll soon find yourself swapping stories and practicing your language skills with the locals.

If you're considering a month long journey, then an Interrail adventure could be just what you're looking for. Whether you're planning on visiting as many countries as you can in one month, or you want to concentrate on one country, Voyages-sncf.com can help you to plan your Interail trip and we're also the only company in the UK able to book Interrail reservations online.

Get in touch today to start planning your European adventure!

To book, visit www.voyages-sncf.com or call 0844 848 5848

Trains

Travelling by train is one of the best ways to see a country – and if you travel on an overnight sleeper it can be as quick as a plane. India's train network is world-famous and an absolute must experience! But don't think you can't use trains in other parts of the world. What follows is just a taster.

Inter-railing – Europe and a bit beyond

If you want to visit a lot of countries, one of the best ways to travel is by train on an InterRail ticket. With InterRail you have the freedom of the rail networks of Europe (and a bit beyond), allowing you to go as you please in 28 countries.

From the northern lights of Sweden to the kasbahs of Morocco, you can call at all the stops. InterRail takes you from city centre to city centre – avoiding airport hassles, ticket queues and traffic jams, and giving you more time to make the most of your visit. Passes are available for all ages, but you need to have lived in Europe for at least six months.

Overnight trains are available on most of the major routes, saving on accommodation costs, allowing you to go to sleep in one country and wake up in another.

The InterRail ticket also includes some ferry crossings as a deck passenger, you may be travelling outside on the top deck in open air but at least it's covered in your ticket and will be no extra costs. For example, you can choose an overnight ferry crossing from Italy to main land Greece via lots of Greek islands for a spot of island-hopping on your ticket. You can also purchase a Thomas Cook InterRail timetable book republished every year to help plan your inter rail trip: **www.europeanrailtimetable.eu**

Supplements apply so ask when you book. You will have to pay extra to travel on some express intercity trains or the Eurostar. Most major stations such as Paris, Brussels, Amsterdam and Rome have washing facilities and left luggage.

117

The InterRail One Country Pass can be used for the following countries:

Austria, Belgium, Bulgaria, Croatia, Czech Republic, Denmark, Finland, France, Germany, Great Britain, Greece, Hungary, Italy, Luxembourg, Macedonia (FYR), Netherlands, Norway, Poland, Portugal, Republic of Ireland, Romania, Russia, Serbia, Slovakia, Slovenia, Spain, Sweden, Switzerland and Turkey.

The alternative choice is the InterRail Global Pass, which is valid in all participating InterRail countries. Available for several lengths of travel, it is ideal for gappers wanting to explore several, or even all, European countries in their year out.

One Country Pass prices

Second class prices vary by the country and range from £32 (under 26)/£43 (over 26) for three days in one month, to £82/£113 for eight days in one month in Bulgaria; to £177/£238 in France.

Belgium, The Netherlands and Luxembourg are combined as the InterRail Benelux Pass. For Greece you have the option to order a Greece Plus Pass, which includes ferry crossings to and from Italy.

Global Pass

For second class travel, over 22 continuous days, prices range from £274 (under 26) to £368 (over 26) and are valid from five days to one month. For further details on prices and how to buy an InterRail pass, visit their website: **www.interrail.eu**.

Eurostar

The Eurostar train is a quick, easy and relatively cheap way to get to Europe. You can get from London to Calais or London to Paris from £50, and the trains are comfortable and run frequently. Tickets can be purchased online at **www.eurostar.com**, in an approved travel agency, or at any Eurostar train station.

Trans-Siberian Express

If you're looking for a train adventure – and you have a generous budget to play with – what about the Trans-Siberian Express? You could do a 14-day Moscow-Beijing trip. Do this as a 'full-on' or a 'no-frills' package.

You can also choose from a range of other trips lasting from nine to 26 days. On top of this you will need some money for food and drink, visas, airfare *etc*.

For China, Russia and Mongolia you'll need to have a visa for your passport to allow you into each country. Contact each relevant embassy to find out what type of visa you will need (*ie* visitors or transit). It's probably easiest to arrange for all your train tickets, visas and hotel accommodation through a specialist agency, about six months before you leave. Your journey will be a lot easier if you have all your paperwork in order before you leave – although it will cost you more to do it this way.

The trains can be pretty basic, varying according to which line you're travelling on and which country owns the train. On some trains you can opt to upgrade to first class. This should give you your own cabin with shower, wash basin and more comfort – however, although you'll be more comfortable, you may find it more interesting back in second class with all the other backpackers and traders.

If you're travelling in autumn or winter make sure you take warm clothes – the trains have rather unreliable heating. If you travel in late November/December you may freeze into a solid block of ice, but it will be snowing by then and the views will be spectacular. Travelling in September will be warmer and a bit cheaper.

If you want to read about it before you go, try the *Trans-Siberian Handbook* by Bryn Thomas. It's updated frequently and it has details about the towns you'll be passing through, and includes the timetables.

There are several websites you can look up, but **www.trans-siberian.co.uk** is one of the best out there. For cheaper options you could also try Travel Nation, which has a useful page of FAQs on the Trans-Siberian Moscow to Beijing rail trip: **www.travelnation.co.uk/blog/moscow-to-beijing-on-the-trans-siberian-train**

India and the rest of the world

Tell anyone you're going to India and you'll invariably be told you must try a train journey. Indian trains are the most amazing adventure – with all sorts of extras - like a meal included in the price on the Shatabdi Express intercity commuter trains, or the vendors who wander the length of the train with their buckets of snacks, tea or coffee, calling their wares "chai, chai, chai" as they go.

But Indian trains get booked up weeks or months in advance, especially if you're planning to travel during any major public festival like Diwali, which is a national holiday. You need a seat or berth reservation for any long-distance journey on an Indian train; you cannot simply turn up and hop on. Bookings now open 90 days in advance. Reservations are now completely computerised and a tourist quota gives foreigners and IndRail pass holders preferential treatment. Go to: **www.irctc.co.in**

There's also a unique reservation system. After a train becomes fully booked, a set number of places in each class are sold as 'Reservation Against Cancellation' or RAC. After all RAC places have been allocated, further prospective passengers are 'wait-listed'. When passengers cancel, people on the RAC list are promoted to places on the train and wait-listed passengers are promoted to RAC.

If you want to try your hand at organising your own train travel in India you can get a copy of the famous Trains at a Glance from any railway station in India for Rs 35 (50p) or you can download it as a PDF from: **www.seat61.com/India.htm** But beware, it contains every train timetable (94 in all) for the sub-continent and it's very long.

Trains get booked up days, even weeks in advance so be sure to book ahead, **www. cleartrip.com** is an excellent, secure site to do this through.

Research the train network for your country as some countries have limited options, for example South America. However China has many great options. A great site to use for times there is: **www.china-diy-travel.com**. This site also shows you whether a train is selling out. It's pricey to book through the site so it's probably best to book at the train station itself. In China you always need to book in advance.

The Man in Seat 61 is possibly the most incredibly comprehensive train and ship travel website ever. It literally covers the world from India to Latin America, Africa and south-east Asia. It's not only about times, costs and booking, it goes into some detail about the kinds of conditions you can expect.

It's written by Mark Smith, an ex-British Rail employee and former stationmaster at Charing Cross. He has travelled the world by train and ship and it's a personal site run as a hobby, so he pledges it will always remain freely available: **www.seat61.com**

visit: www.gap-year.com

Buses and coaches

Getting on a bus or coach in a foreign country, especially if you don't speak the language, can be a voyage of discovery in itself. UK bus timetables can be indecipherable, but try one in Patagonia!

Get help from a local you trust, hotel/hostel staff, or the local police station if all else fails.

In developing countries, locals think nothing of transporting their livestock by public transport, so be prepared to sit next to a chicken! That said, some buses and coaches can be positively luxurious and they do tend to be cheaper than trains.

Be aware of the seasons when travelling; for example in South America, in low season (it's their winter) you can turn up a day before or on the day to buy bus tickets. There are lots of companies, so compare prices between each, and pick one. Most of the bus companies offer more or less the same, although there are luxury ones as well if you fancy being pampered.

Night buses are a favourite as they save you money on a nights accommodation. Look after your things when on buses – lock your bag up and tie it to your seat so you can sleep in peace. (Same advice for trains! Unfortunately sleeping travellers are a target for planned and opportunist theft.)

For buses that could be oversubscribed, book in advance either at the bus station (this gives you a good opportunity to familiarise yourself with the station), or through an agent/hostel in town. Usually there is an additional price for this.

The 'Old Grey Dog'

Greyhound buses have air conditioning, tinted windows and a loo on board, as well as a strict no smoking policy. Greyhound offers Hostelling International members a discount on regular one-way and round-trip fares. They have a Discovery Pass, which allows seven, 15, 30 and 60 days unlimited travel. There's the usual 10% discount for ISIC and Euro 26 ID cardholders (go to **www.discoverypass.com**).

The bus company operates outside America too, with Greyhound Pioneer Australia (**www.greyhound.com.au**) and for South Africa there's Greyhound Coach Lines Africa (**www.greyhound.co.za**). Check out their websites or contact them for information about their various ticket options.

See also: **www.yha.com.au** (Australia)
www.norcalhostels.org (USA)
Greyhound Lines, Inc
PO Box 660691, MS 470, Dallas, TX 75266-0691, USA
Tel: 214-849-8966;
www.greyhound.com

Student gappers could also check out **www.anyworkanywhere.com** for useful information and advice on special travel deals and discounts – planes, trains, coaches and ferries. Other useful sources of information are:

www.statravel.co.uk
www.thebigchoice.com

Oasis Overland, The Marsh, Henstridge, Templecombe BA8 0TF UK
T: +44 (0) 1963 363400
E: info@oasisoverland.co.uk   W: www.oasisoverland.co.uk

Come and join us on one of our overland adventure trips and we promise to take you to some of the most awesome and spectacular places in the world. We believe overlanding is one of the most inspirational and rewarding forms of travel that you will experience in your life!

If you dream of travelling through Africa, South America, Central Asia and the Middle East, then look no further than Oasis Overland. Our trips are always adventurous, sometimes unpredictable and not your average package holiday.

* Adventures range from 8 days to 39 weeks

* Travel by custom-built expedition truck

* Stay in campsites, hostels or out under the stars

* Get involved - campfire cooking, shop at local markets, collect the firewood

Along the way you can hike the Inca trail in Peru, come face to face with Mountain Gorillas in Uganda, trek the Tien Shan Mountains in Kyrgyzstan or bungy jump at Victoria Falls - to name just a few!

We have been specializing in providing overland adventure travel for more than 17 years and our reliable, friendly and personal service is why our travellers come back year after year!

Touring

Travelling as part of a tour – usually as part of a group of like-minded gappers, on a coach especially fitted out for the task – can prove a fun, action-packed adventure. It doesn't have to mean chugging around the tourist sights, staring at the wonders of the world passing by your window. A tour can mean anything from full-on adventure trips across the desert to smaller, more intimate tours along a specific theme, such as vineyards or culinary hotspots. It's worth knowing that volunteering organisations will often include and organize all your travel and accommodation with your trip.

Booking a place on a tour can be a great way to meet new people and shouldn't be dismissed just because some backpackers see it as 'the easy option'. If you do your research and book with the right company, you'll find yourself with a small bunch of like-minded people and a tour leader who should know your destination's history and culture inside out.

A good leader will also have contacts in the local community and can get you into local hotels and restaurants – leaving you to enjoy your travels rather than worrying about finding a place to sleep for the night.

Scout around for long enough and you'll find a tour to suit most tastes, from smaller groups of travellers who are serious about getting off the beaten track to meet the locals and experiencing their way of life, to younger, noisier groups looking for a fun, sociable way to explore a country or region.

Overlanding

Overlanding involves travelling in groups on a rough-and-ready truck. Vehicles come fully equipped with a kitchen and tents – perfect for both seasoned backpackers and first-timers. Companies such as Oasis Overland and Dragoman have vast experience in offering such trips.

We asked Oasis Overland to help us explain more:

"Overlanding is, not surprisingly, all about journeying overland and taking the time to experience the places you are passing through. These are adventurous trips that often go off the beaten track. It usually involves travelling in a truck that's been converted to carry passengers and along the way you camp or stay in hostels. Overland trucks are usually self-sufficient carrying tents, cooking equipment and food and everyone in the group mucks in with cooking, shopping at local markets, collecting firewood and setting up camp. There are overlanding opportunities around the world."

Why overlanding?

Some places can be difficult or expensive to get to under your own steam and an overland trip can provide a cheaper, hassle-free way of getting there. Being on a self-sufficient truck can mean that you get to stop and spend a night in the Sahara Desert or on the Altiplano, instead of passing through to the next town. Overlanding is a good option if you don't want to travel on your own or are apprehensive about being away from home for the first time as you're travelling in a group.

123

Benefits of overlanding

As well as the usual benefits of travel (broadening your horizons and your mind, learning self-sufficiency) by the time you finish your overland trip you will have gained great experience of team working as well as living with a group of people in close quarters and generally learning consideration for others. Overland trips are not hand-held holidays – you may have to organise your own flights and accommodation before joining the trip as well helping with the day-to-day running of the trip which will prove your organisational skills. Great stuff for your CV!

Practical skills you may pick up include camp craft (where not to pitch your tent, fire lighting *etc*, cooking for a large group of people) and languages in Spanish or French speaking parts of the world.

There are plenty of opportunities to step outside your comfort zone on an overland trip. For many, just travelling to a new country with a group of 20 strangers is an adventure in itself but if that isn't enough, on a longer expedition you may spend the day digging the truck out of a huge, muddy pothole or carrying sandmats for the truck to drive over in the desert and then camp out in the bush with only a bucket of water for a shower!

Car

Another popular option is to travel by car. It means you have somewhere to sleep if you get stuck for a bed for the night, you save money on train fares and you don't have to lug your rucksack into cafés.

If you are considering it, you need to know the motoring regulations of the countries you'll be visiting – they vary from country to country. Check that you are insured to drive abroad and that this is clearly shown on the documentation you carry with you.

The AA advises that you carry your vehicle insurance, vehicle registration documents and a current tax disc in the car and, of course, take your driving licence with you.

It is also advisable to take an International Driving Permit (IDP) as not all countries accept the British driving licence. In theory you don't need one in any of the EU member states, but the AA recommends having an IDP if you intend to drive in any country other than the UK – and it's better than getting into trouble and being fined for driving without a valid licence.

An IDP is valid for 12 months and can be applied for up to three months in advance. The AA and RAC issue the permits – you must be over 18 and hold a current, full, UK driving licence that has been valid for two years. You'll need to fill in a form and provide your UK driving licence, passport and a recent passport-sized photo of yourself, which you can take to a participating Post Office. Be warned, you need to allow at least ten working days for processing, so don't try and do this at the last minute.

The AA website has loads of information about the permit, and driving abroad in general here: **www.theaa.com/getaway/idp/**

It's a good idea to put your car in for a service a couple of weeks before you leave and, unless you're a mechanic, it's also worth getting breakdown cover specifically for your trip abroad. Any of the major recovery companies such as the AA, RAC or Green Flag offer this service. Remember, without cover, if you end up stuck on the side of the road it could be an expensive experience.

The RAC recommends taking a first aid kit, fire extinguisher, warning triangle, headlamp beam reflectors and spare lamp bulbs. These are all required by law in many countries and make sense anyway. **www.rac.co.uk**

The Foreign and Commonwealth Office has put together a handy road tool at **www. fcowidget.com**, which allows you to select your chosen country and be directed to the local regulations for your trip.

And here are the FCO's key tips for driving abroad:

1. Research – research the driving regulations for the country you will be driving through and check your insurance policy to ensure you are covered for breakdown recovery, medical expenses and driving overseas.

2. Prepare – prepare for driving abroad, research the regulations of what you are required to carry in your vehicle and ensure that your own or hired vehicle adheres to these. Remember these are often very different to the UK.

3. Once on the road – expect the unexpected, drive with confidence and always wear a seatbelt. Be safe, don't drink and drive, don't overload your vehicle, don't use your mobile, or get behind the wheel when tired.

Unless you're a very experienced driver, with some off-road experience, we wouldn't advise hiring a car and driving in many places in the developing world. South-east Asian, South Asian, South American and African roads are often little more than potholed tracks, and you really have to know what you're doing when faced with a pecking order decided purely by the size of your vehicle and the sound of your horn – not to mention negotiating wandering livestock, hand-pushed carts, overloaded local buses and trucks, and pedestrians with no road sense whatsoever.

But often you'll find you can hire a car and a driver pretty cheaply for a day or two and then you'll be an ethical traveller contributing to the local economy. In Australia, buying a cheap car to tour the country at your own leisure is a popular option. But attempting to drive around Australia in an old Ford Falcon or some clapped out old campervan is definitely a challenge.

Blue Ventures

the gap-year guidebook 2016

Ships and boats

If you want to get to the continent, taking a ferry across to France or Belgium can be cheap – but why not sail free as a working crew member on ships? Take a short course before hand to qualify as a deck hand or day skipper here, with a charity such as UKSA who offer professional maritime training courses alongside youth development programmes.

Or how about getting to grips with the rigging on a cruise yacht? There are numerous employers and private vessel owners out there on the ocean wave who take on amateur and novice crew. In this way you could gain valuable sailing experience and sea miles. You can also make some useful contacts on your way to becoming a professional crew member. And have the time of your life.

Hitch-hiking

Hitch-hiking more or less died out after its heyday in the late 1960s and 1970s – partly out of safety concerns and partly as more and more young people became car owners. But with the onset of the recession it's become a regular feature of the travel pages in many national newspapers.

It costs nothing, except being a friendly and courteous passenger, and losing a bit of time waiting around for a ride, but you need to know what you're doing – and you need to know that in some countries it's illegal and that the usual sticking-your-thumb-out signal used in the UK is considered extremely rude in some countries.

visit: www.gap-year.com

There are no hard and fast rules about getting a lift, but above all you do need to think about your safety if you're going to try it – we wouldn't advise hitching alone for either men or women but on the other hand, if there are more than two of you, you might have trouble persuading a driver to stop.

If you are going to try it, make sure you know the basics. There are two useful websites:

www.hitchwiki.org/en
www.hitching.it

Motorbike tours

If you're a keen biker and want to include your bike in gap travel plans, there aren't many places you couldn't go. There's an excellent website by UK couple Kevin and Julia Saunders who are double Guinness Book of Records winners for their bike expeditions around the planet. The site offers plenty of advice as well as the opportunity to join expeditions with guides and team leaders: **www.globebusters.com**

Bicycles

If you're feeling hyper-energetic, you could use your pedal-pushing power to get you around town and country. This is really popular in north Europe, especially Holland, where the ground tends to be flatter. Most travel agents would be able to point you in the right direction, or you can just rely on hiring bikes while you are out there – make sure you understand the rules of the road.

With a globally growing 'green awareness', there's been a real surge in promoting cycling in the UK and abroad. Weather and terrain permitting it's a wonderful way of seeing a city, or touring a region, be it Portugal, Sweden, Provence, Tuscany...

But why confine it to Europe? There are many places where bicycles can be hired and it's a great way of getting around. For example, you can hire bikes and a guide in Cambodia to visit the Angkor Wat Temple, you will see much more of the temples and surrounding forests and can pick your time to visit, thus avoiding the crowds.

You can also participate in some amazing gap-year programmes, such as cycling to raise sponsorship for worthwhile charities and community projects worldwide.

But charities aside, just get on your bike and enjoy a closer contact with nature and its vast range of spectacular scenery – getting ever fitter – for example, the USA's Pacific West Coast, Guatemala to Honduras, the Andes to the glaciers of Patagonia, Nairobi to Dar es Salaam, Chiang Mai to Bangkok, the South Island mountains of New Zealand...

Take a look at:

www.ride25.com offer a great way to see the world through their cycling holidays

www.responsibletravel.com for cycling and mountain biking holidays; also:

www.imba.com (the International Mountain Biking Association)

www.nzcycletours.com (independent cycle tours in New Zealand and worldwide links.)

Sustainable travel

Global warming, climate change and the world's depleting energy resources continue to be a serious concern, regardless of the economic climate, and increasingly people want to know how to be environmentally friendly on their gap travels. Nowhere is this likely to be more of an issue than in the types of transport you choose.

If you're hoping to travel to several destinations, time is inevitably an issue, so it may not be practical to avoid air travel altogether, but there are ways you can minimise your carbon footprint. If you're concerned about global warming, and want to do your bit, you can pay a small 'carbon offset' charge on your flight. If you want to know more try: **www.co2balance.com**

The site has a calculator so you can work out how much to pay for journeys by car, train or air. It also has some simpler options – for example £50 will offset one long-haul one-way flight from London to Australia. Your money goes towards sustainable development projects around the world and there's a complete list of all current projects on the website.

They are all managed by co2balance, but are also all independently validated and verified by international standards organisations. Projects include providing energy efficient woodstoves in east Africa, wind power in India and renewable energy projects in China.

The UK's Green Traveller website includes a list of the top ten fair trade holidays worldwide and lots more advice if you want your travel to be as environmentally friendly as possible: **www.greentraveller.co.uk**

To find out more about sustainable and responsible travel you could also look at the website of the International Ecotourism Society, which has a lot of tips for responsible travel both en route and in-country: **www.ecotourism.org**

Ethical travel

Thinking about the best way to get to and from your destination is one thing, but ethical travel means much more than that.

We asked Tourism Concern to explain further: "Tourism is an enormous industry and affects the lives of millions of people. Environments can be wrecked by irresponsible and unregulated diving, climbing and other outdoor activities.

"Communities have been forcibly removed from their land to make way for tourism developments across the world, from Africa to Australia. Water used for swimming pools, golf courses and twice daily power showers can dwindle supplies for the local populations. Exploitation of local workers is a problem usually invisible to a visitor's eyes. When you start to look more closely, the issues can seem overwhelming, but the good news is that with the decisions you make today and while you're away, you are taking big steps to ensure that your trip benefits everyone."

Here are Tourism Concern's ten tips for ethical travelling:

1) Be aware: start enjoying your travels before you leave. Think about what sort of clothing is appropriate for both men and women. If the locals are covered up, what sort of messages may you be sending out by exposing acres of flesh? But use your guidebook as a starting point, not the only source of information.

2) Be open: something may seem bizarre or odd to you, but it may be normal and just the way things are done to 'them'. Try not to assume that the western way is right or best.

3) Our holidays – their homes: Ask before taking pictures of people, especially children, and respect their wishes. Talk to local people. What do they think about our lifestyle, clothes and customs? Find out about theirs.

4) Giving constructively: giving sweets or pens to children encourages begging. A donation to a project, health centre or school is more constructive.

5) Be fair: try to put money into local hands. If you haggle for the lowest price, your bargain may be at the seller's expense. Even if you pay a little over the odds, does it really matter?

6) Buy local, behave local: look at the environment you're in, try to eat locally sourced foods and buy locally produced goods. Think about resources, don't shower for 20 minutes at a time in an arid zone, just because you might at home.

7) Ask questions: write a letter to your tour operator or venture manager about their responsible tourism policy.

8) Think before you fly: use alternative forms of transport where possible. The more and further you fly, the more you contribute to global warming and environmental destruction. Consider flying long-haul less often but staying longer when you're there.

9) Discover Tourism Concern: a charity that campaigns against exploitation in tourism and for fairly traded and ethical forms of tourism. Their website has a wealth of information on action you can take to avoid guilt trips. **www.tourismconcern.org.uk**

10) Be happy: by taking any, some or all of these actions you are personally fighting tourism exploitation. Enjoy your guilt-free trip!

Accommodation

Traditionally, hostels are the first option that springs to mind, whenever gappers or backpackers are looking for cheap accommodation.

Today there is a range of hostels available, which offer clean, safe and reasonably priced accommodation, some even have 'luxury' extras, such as internet connection, games rooms and laundry facilities.

There are a number of good apps available for booking accommodation, including booking.com, hostelworld.com and TripAdvisor.

Use your common sense and always check where the fire exits are when arriving at a hostel, because it's too late to look if there's already a fire and you're trying to get out of the building.

If you do find you're staying in a basic, no frills-style hostel, it's wise to make sure there's some ventilation when you have a bath or shower – faulty water heaters give off lethal and undetectable carbon monoxide fumes and will kill you without you realising it as you fall gently to sleep, never to wake up again. For this reason, do consider taking a small carbon monoxide reader.

Use your instincts – if you think the hostel's simply not up to scratch and too risky, go and find another one.

Camping

If you're on a budget camping or caravanning can be worth considering though they're not options for some parts of the world and, particularly with camping, you need to think about whether you really want to carry all that extra equipment.

Many campsites are replacing tents with huts; usually they're in places close to areas where you can hike. You'll get a bed in a hut and use of other facilities so you only need a sleeping bag or sheet sleeping bag – no need to carry a tent.

Caravans, campervans and places to park them

Renting a caravan or travelling under your own steam with a camper van is another possibility – they call them motorhomes in the USA and it's easy to see why. They do have the advantage of giving you a secure place to leave your stuff and of not having to carry it all on your back but they're plainly not an option everywhere in the world.

Check out these websites:

www.campingo.com/
www.internationalcampingclub.com
www.eurocampings.co.uk/en/europe
www.rentocamp.com
www.allstays.com/Campgrounds-Australia
www.familyparks.com.au
www.stayz.com.au

Temples and monasteries

Temples and monasteries are also an option worth exploring. The main consideration for deciding to stay in a monastery or temple guesthouse, should not be your budget, though there's no denying that it's affordable for the budget traveller. Indeed for anyone wanting some place to be able to relax and not be constantly on guard, or if you're seeking a peaceful sanctuary and simplicity, religious guesthouses are ideal.

Some places prefer that you have *some* link with their faith, even if only through a historic extended-family link, but there is a strong tradition of offering refuge, safety and peace in any religious community that isn't a closed order.

Historically, the religious communities and monasteries of many faiths have provided hospice and hospital services to their surrounding communities. Much of our early medical knowledge developed from here too.

Changing economics have also meant their costs have risen and many temples and monasteries have had to be practical about raising income for their communities and for the upkeep of buildings, whose antiquity makes them costly to maintain. Most are therefore open to guests regardless of faith.

Having said that, if you are considering this option, be prepared for rooms and meals to be simple, facilities to be austere and for the community to be quiet at certain times of the day. There will be daily rituals to the life of the community and, like anywhere else, it's only polite to respect their customs. Obviously it's not an option that would suit some gappers.

But a chance to think, to recharge the spiritual batteries, to learn more about oneself or a particular faith, maybe to learn yoga or meditation, is what some gappers are looking for and it can be worth considering this option as part of a gap programme. Respect traditions and be aware of your dress and manners as you could easily cause offence.

Hotels

If you've been on the move for several weeks and careful with the budget, you can find your spirits are flagging from coping with the often spartan conditions in budget hotels, hostels and the like.

A couple of days of comfort in a good hotel can be a worthwhile investment as a tonic, to give you time out to sort your stuff, get some laundry done, have a decent shower and sleep in a clean, comfortable bed before you set off again.

Most hotels around the world use the familiar one to five-star rating system, where five is luxury and one is likely to be a fleapit! But the symbols used can be anything from stars, diamonds and crowns to keys, suns, dots, rosettes and letters.

As with most things in life you get what you pay for, but prices will vary wildly depending on whether you're in peak tourism season or off-peak, currency rates and the costs of living in the country you're visiting, so you may be pleasantly surprised by the rates in some of the better hotels and find you can stretch your budget without reaching breaking point. (If you arrive late in the day don't forget to try to negotiate on fees. If rooms are empty you may get a discounted rate.)

But equally, hotel ratings are done by human beings, and they can vary wildly depending on who did them and which search engine you might have used. The best advice is to look for reviews or ratings from ordinary hotel guests who have actually stayed in the hotel – and slept in the beds!

There are several sources of independent information. Most of the travellers' guidebooks have lists of hotels within the different price ranges, but you have to bear in mind that, particularly in the tourism and hospitality industries, things can change between the time of printing and when you arrive.

If you want to check out a hotel while you're travelling, try **www.tripadvisor.com**

What makes this site special is that it's all written by travellers from their own experiences and it pulls no punches. There are millions of posts on just about every place or topic you can think of, covering destinations all over the world – including some that might surprise you, like the Middle East, (Saudi Arabia, Jordan, United Arab Emirates to name a few).

Useful websites for last-minute and affordable accommodation are:

'Bargain Rooms' – **www.roomauction.com** – you pay below the standard room rate by making the hotel a discreet offer, 'bidding' for the room.

www.laterooms.com – discount hotel rooms in UK and abroad; the low prices are genuine as they would rather see their rooms let out than not at all.

If you also have concerns about ethical tourism, whether it is the hotel's environmental impact or the conditions of its workers, the Ethical Consumer website has a report on these issues, which is downloadable as a PDF from: **www.ethicalconsumer.org/FreeBuyersGuides/traveltransport/hotels.aspx**

Lodging

Rental lodging has increased in popularity over the last few years due to the increase in websites such as (**www.airbnb.co.uk**). The website allows you to search rooms and whole properties that are available to rent around the world. You could find yourself lodging with nature in a tree house in Costa Rica's rainforest, or lodging in a room with a view of New York's Times Square - the possibilities are endless.

The online booking system is easy to use and the extent of information and inspiring images available on each rental lodging listed makes booking accommodation via a service such as this very appealing.

Couch Surfing

This is the ultimate in finding free accommodation and, although there were safety concerns when this service first started, it's now had more than a million satisfied customers. But this not-for-profit organisation has a philosophy that's about more than that – it's about creating friendships and networks across the world.

Here's what couchsurfing.com say on the safety issue:

"CouchSurfing has implemented several precautionary measures for the benefit of its surfers, hosts, and community. Every user is linked to the other users he or she knows in the system, through a network of references and friend links. In addition to the solid network with friend link-strength indicators and testimonials, we have our vouching and verification systems."

There's a lot more information on their website that should answer all your questions: **www.couchsurfing.com**

Please see the directory pages starting on page 301 for information on companies and organisations offering travel and accommodation services.

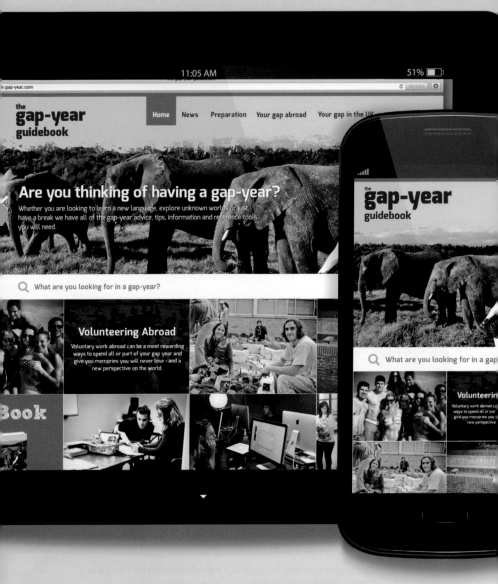

Working abroad

Sponsored by

Earn money overseas to help finance further travels on your gap-year

Oyster Worldwide are the experts in helping people to find work abroad on their gap-year. We have been working with employers overseas since 2000 and can secure you work in various industries, from working on a farm in Australia to working in a hotel (or even becoming a ski instructor) in Canada.

Working abroad looks fantastic on your CV and is a great way to spend part, or all, of your gap-year. Not only does it show that you can immerse yourself in a new country, make friends and live away from home, but it also demonstrates that you can hold down a paid job, get to work on time and live on a budget.

Canada, America, Australia and New Zealand are just a few of the countries that offer working holiday programmes to young people. All of these countries have exceptionally high standards when it comes to customer service, the need to be a hard worker and have a strong work ethic.

With Oyster, you can be sure that you will be well supported, both in the UK before your departure and by our local representatives when in-country. What's more, in Canada for example, the job and accommodation is organised before you even leave home so is ready and waiting for you on arrival.

Employers love working with us as they know you will have been interviewed by us, well prepared and fully briefed before arrival. When in country, they know that someone from Oyster will have helped you set up a bank account, and prepare for your new life. This means that on day one of work, you are ready to settle into your training right away and focus on your job.

Work abroad with Oyster – a couple of options:

Ski season

If you are a keen skier or boarder why not gain first rate experience and enjoy the season on your days off with our programmes working in Canada, or Romania? All are great jobs to enable to you earn good money and make friends for life. Examples include:

· Working as a ski instructor - if you love to ski, and have childcare experience to match, qualify as an instructor in Whistler and then have a job lined up teaching kids to ski for the rest of the season. Closer to home, secure a job working as an instructor for Romania's number one ski resort – Poiana Brasov – for the winter

· Work in a hotel, bar or restaurant in a full time entry-level position (housekeeping or kitchen assistant) in one of three top Canadian ski resorts – The Rockies, Whistler or French-speaking Tremblant. Have the guarantee of a paid job and accommodation ready for you before you leave home.

Earn money Down Under

For the true Aussie experience, sign up to our Outback training course where you'll learn to drive tractors, ride horses, herd cattle and become a farmer. At the end of your training week you'll have a guaranteed job lined up working on a farm.

Work Permits

Working abroad on your gap-year is becoming more and more popular each year. If you are considering this as a gap-year option, make sure you plan in advance. If you are planning to work outside Europe, you will most likely need to get a Work Permit. These are usually in limited supply and tend to run out quite quickly.

To be eligible for a Work Permit you generally need to be aged 18-30 at the time of application. If you are over 30, don't despair! You can still work in Europe with a British Passport.

Find out more – www.oysterworldwide.com

Working abroad

Working abroad is a great option if you desperately want to go overseas, can't really afford it and the bit you have managed to save won't cover much more than air fare.

It's one of the best ways to experience a different culture; you'll be meeting locals and experiencing what the country is really like in a way that you can't do as a traveller passing through. Most jobs give you enough spare time, in the evenings and at weekends, to enjoy yourself and make friends.

You don't have to be tied to one place for your whole gap-year – you can work for a bit and save up for your travels. That way you can learn more about the place and get the inside information from the locals about the best places to see before you set off.

You cover at least some of your costs, and, depending on what you do, the work experience will look good on your CV – but even if you're only doing unskilled seasonal work, prospective employers will be reassured that you at least know *something* about the basics like punctuality, fitting into an organisation and managing your time.

An internship with pay is a good way to get work experience if you already have an idea about your eventual career and will help in those early stages of the problem that affects many young people – when employers want experience but won't take you on so you can get it.

Jon Arnold, of Oyster Worldwide, told us: "Earning money on a gap-year is a very popular thing to do. A gap-year is a chance not just to flip burgers in your local burger restaurant or stack shelves in your local supermarket, you can go overseas and get a far more worthwhile experience.

"Paid work overseas looks fantastic on your CV. Good grades are simply not enough any more. Employers are looking for people who can demonstrate those 'soft skills' of teamwork, determination, leadership, confidence, independence and social skills. A well-spent gap-year is the perfect way to add these skills to your CV

Older gappers, too, may find that, despite the current global economic problems, their skills and experience are in demand, particularly in developing countries.

Key questions to get started

What kind of work do you want to do? There are some suggestions in this chapter but they're only a start.

· Is it to help pay your way on your gap?

· Is it to get work experience/enhance your CV?

· Where do you want to work? (Don't forget to check **www.fco.gov.uk** for country info.)

· What skills and experience do you have?

It doesn't have to be work experience or education, don't forget hobbies and interests. If you can ride a horse, dance, draw, paint, or are good at a particular sport, you could use any of those skills as a basis for finding work.

visit: www.oysterworldwide.com

PGL Travel Ltd

Planning ahead

Choosing your destination

There are some jobs that always need to be done, whatever the state of the world, and if you're just looking at ways of funding your travel you could look for seasonal farm work.

In most cases, gappers intending to do seasonal work outside the EU need to have a job offer in order to get a visa. If you should find that, when you get there the job is no longer available, you can try elsewhere – but we would advise you to have a back-up plan before you set off on your travels (*eg* contacts, an emergency fund, names of companies that specialise in work overseas).

If you are a UK citizen, or hold an EU (European Union) passport, you can work in any other EU member country without a visa or work permit and there are countless jobs available to students who can speak the right languages. Not all European countries are EU members – go to the European Union website to check: **www.europa.eu**

Speaking English is always an advantage for jobs in tourism at ski resorts, beach bars and hotel receptions and if you have a TEFL (Teaching English as a Foreign Language) certificate there's always the option of paid teaching.

You could try using message boards to find out what other gappers have done and what it was like. If you want to be more adventurous and venture outside Europe, then check the Foreign Office website – **www.fco.gov.uk** – for important advice on your possible destinations.

Raleigh International

Getting your paperwork sorted

Before you go, you should:

· Check whether you need to set up a job – you may need a confirmed work offer before you can get a work permit and visa – try **www.gap-year.com** for contact lists and more advice, or refer to the internship and graduate opportunities section in the directory of this guidebook.

· Check on the work permit and visa regulations for the country you plan to work in and make sure you have the right paperwork before you leave. Remember, you don't need a work permit or visa if you're an EU citizen and planning to work in an EU country.

· Check if there's any special equipment or clothing you'll need to take, *eg* sturdy boots and trousers for manual jobs, reasonably smart clothes for office internships *etc*.

· When you're getting your insurance, remember to check that you'll be covered if you're planning on working. Working can invalidate a claim for loss or damage to your belongings on some travel policies. If in doubt, ask.

· Make sure you understand all the regulations and restrictions. You can get into serious trouble if you work without the necessary documents – you don't want to be deported during your gap-year! The best place to get information is the relevant embassy in London - there's a link on **www.gap-year.com** to the Foreign and Commonwealth Office website, where you will find links to all embassies.

Finding a job

Finding a job may take time and effort. The more places you can send your CV to, the greater the chances of you getting a job. You can also register with international employment agencies but make sure you know what the agency fee will be if you get employment. To find short-term jobs try:

the gap-year guidebook 2016

Our 365 days programme include

Welcome and induction package
(No hassles when your arrive)

4 days at Noosa
(Top 3 backpacker beach destination)

5 days training course

Paid jobs in rural and outback Australia

Noosa

Springbrook farm

We will help you with all the paperwork required to work in Australia

Benefit from the training and preparation of an award winning organisation

Enjoy a flexible programme of work and travel (holiday breaks)

Year round support, 2nd and 3rd jobs

A little history – 24 years in the making

Visitoz was started in 1991 by Dan and Joanna Burnet who came to Springbrook Farm in South East Queensland from Scotland. Young people were asking to come to visit, and were put to work. Visitoz has been growing slowly and steadily ever since.

We now have a network of nearly 2,000 employers all over the country, from small family farms to some of the largest properties in Australia. They trust us and offer work to our participants. Over nearly 24 years we have welcomed, trained and found work for thousands of young people.

Visitoz is a family owned and run business.

An Australian working adventure

Learn more about us : Visitoz  www.visitoz.org

www.transitionsabroad.com
www.pickingjobs.com
www.anyworkanywhere.com
www.overseasjobcentre.co.uk

If you use an agency, always insist on talking to someone who has used it before – that way you'll really find out what the deal is.

Do a search to see if there's a website for a particular area you want to go to and then send or email your CV, with a short covering note, to any interesting local companies. Don't expect to be flooded with replies. Some companies are simply too busy to respond to every enquiry, though it always helps to enclose a stamped addressed envelope. It's also true that you may get lucky and have exactly the skills or qualifications they're looking for. Some companies will also advertise vacant posts on specialist employment websites, which often have an international section. You can register with the sites too, usually for free.

Tell everyone you know, including relatives and your parents' friends that you are looking for a job abroad – someone may know someone who has a company abroad who can help you.

Check the local papers and shop window notices. Lots of jobs are advertised in the local papers, or by 'staff wanted' notices put up in windows. So if you get there, and hate the job you've got, don't put up with it, or come running home – see if you can find something better. It's always easier to find employment when you're living locally.

Over the next few pages we've listed ideas on types of employment, and any companies we know about, that offer graduate opportunities or work experience, can be found in the directory. Always ask an employment company to put you in contact with someone they have placed before – if they say no then don't use them: they may have something to hide.

IST Plus

the gap-year guidebook 2016

my gap-year
Isabelle Bradshaw

I cannot express how glad I am that my journey led me to China, where I spent eight months au pairing in Beijing. Being an au pair in China is a strangely wonderful thing.

I spent my first few days getting to know my host family. There was forever an endless delight of dishes at meal times! The host child I was taking care of was just as quiet as I was in the beginning. We spent a while testing the water with each other until we both found we shared a love of Transformers. From there on, our evenings were spent running around the living room being chased by imaginary monsters, and being saved by our awesome kung fu moves. We became super heroes ourselves in those hours and I can't help but look back on those fond memories with a grin on my face.

There is a culture and an energy that just being in China brings like nowhere else. I found my niche in the city, my place among people with customs and behaviours very different to my own.

Through my Mandarin classes, I met other au pairs and made friends who I still keep in touch with now. Suddenly, Beijing expanded from my host family's flat to a wealth of new adventures to explore. Together we discovered the enthralling capital's wonders, and we shared endless hours of laughing and smiling, gossiping and groaning, but most of all they understood and helped with the ins and outs of fitting into this strange new world.

Though it saddened me when they left, I developed new found friendships as new au pairs arrived. To learn such a different language to your own is challenging and yet I found such ecstatic joy from being able to use it in a conversation that I'm glad it's a challenge I undertook. China has been the biggest adventure I ever undertook, I can't say it wasn't without difficulties, but each hurdle built me up stronger. I loved my time in China. I loved the people I met and the memories I shared. I loved it all.

However, my story doesn't stop there. After I returned home to England, my host family got in contact again, asking if I – with my family's help – would like to try and set up our own au pair company. We both knew how we should be treating the family and the au pair, and we were all dedicated to putting their best interests first. I want as many people as possible to have the same life changing experience as I did, to find their own adventure and that's why we have set up our own au pair company in China. I finally have a great excuse to visit China once again!

visit: www.oysterworldwide.com

Au pairing

Being an au pair is a good way to immerse yourself in a different culture, learn a new language and hopefully save some extra cash. You don't need any qualifications to be an au pair, although obviously some experience with children is a bonus. However, au pairing is a hard job and a big responsibility and you may well have to pass the equivalent of a Disclosure and Barring Service (DBS) check.

In return for board, lodgings and pocket money, you'll be expected to look after the children and do light domestic chores like ironing, cooking, tidying their bedrooms and doing their washing, for up to five hours a day (six hours in France or Germany), five days a week, as well as spending two or three evenings a week babysitting. If you are asked to work more than this then technically you are not doing the work of an au pair, but of a mother's help (which pays more).

Remember that an au pair is classified as 'non-experienced', and you should never be left in sole charge of a baby. If the family gives you more responsibility than you can handle say so. If they don't stop – quit.

Distant Shores, a new Au pair agency set up in Beijing, China comments on the opportunities China offers as an Au pair destination. "China is a large expanding market and we see it becoming a major gap-year destination in the years to come. There has never been a better time to visit and live in China: it is more accessible now than ever before; people are realising it's a safe country to visit and Mandarin lessons are growing in schools."

Finding an au pair agency

It may be safest to look for a placement through a UK-based au pair agency. It's also better for the prospective family abroad, since they will be dealing with an agency (possibly working together with an agency in the family's own country) that has met you, interviewed you and taken up references; they will want reassurance before they trust you with their children.

145

What you should check:

· Does the agency you use have connections with another agency in the country where you'll be working?

· Can they give you a list of other local au pairs so you'll have support when you're out there?

· Take time finding a suitable family. The fewer children the better, and you should expect your own room.

· What is there to do in your free time? You don't want to spend every weekend in your bedroom because you're stuck in the middle of nowhere.

· Do you get written confirmation of the hours, duties and pay agreed?

· The number and address of the local British Consulate – just in case.

Check that the au pair agency is a member of either the Recruitment and Employment Confederation (which has a website listing all its members and covering au pair employment in many countries) or of the International Au Pair Association (IAPA), which has a list of its registered agencies in 38 countries around the world:

International Au Pair Association
WYSE Travel Confederation
174 Keizersgracht
1016 DW, Amsterdam
The Netherlands
Tel: +31 (0)20 421 2800
Enquiry: inquiry@iapa.org
www.iapa.org

There are, of course, perfectly good agencies that do not belong to trade associations, either because they are too small to afford the membership fees, or because they are well-established and have a good independent reputation.

You can also find information on au pair work worldwide by using the internet. Registration is usually free and your details will be matched to the families around the world that have registered on the site and that meet your specifications (but make sure you talk to both the agents, here and abroad, and the prospective family before you make your final decision).

However, if you are considering organising an au pair placement independently, you should be aware of the risks:

· High probability of unsuitable au pair or host family candidates.

· Absence of a written contract.

· Little or no experience in the au pair industry.

· Lack of professionalism or financial stability.

· Non-existent standards or guidelines.

· Insufficient references and/or medical certification.

· Danger of document falsification.

· No rematch policy (secondary placement) if the initial placement is unsuccessful.

· No local support during the placement.

147

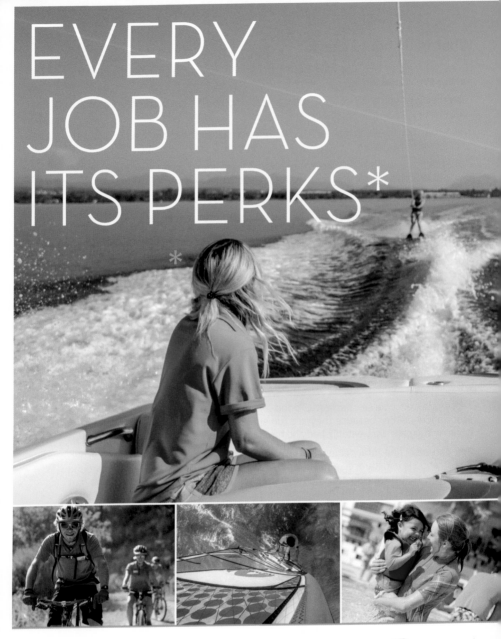

EVERY JOB HAS ITS PERKS*

Now recruiting for the coming summer season

We're recruiting now for the 2016 summer season. If you think you can match your love of watersports, cycling, tennis, fitness, food and childcare with the passion and personality needed to represent us, in one of a huge variety of roles across the Med, then we would love to hear from you.

Visit neilson.co.uk/recruitment/summer to see what's on offer.

drop us a line recruitment@neilson.com or call 01273 666130

neilson

RELAX AS HARD AS YOU LIK

· Limited understanding of national au pair and visa regulations.

Remember also that au pair agencies operating in the UK and sending au pairs abroad cannot, except under specified circumstances, charge for finding you a placement.

If you have a complaint against a UK agency it's best to take it up with the Department for Business, Innovation and Skills' Employment Agency Standards Helpline, Tel: +44 (0) 845 955 5105. It operates Monday-Friday 9.30am to 4.30pm.

Au pairing in Europe

There are EU laws governing the conditions in which au pairs can work:

· You must be 17 or over.

· You must provide a current medical certificate.

· You should have a written employment agreement signed by you and your host family; conditions of employment must be stated clearly.

· You should receive (tax exempt) pocket money.

· You should have enough free time to study.

· You should not be asked to work more than five hours a day.

· You must have one free day a week.

This is now the accepted definition for au pair jobs in the EU, but not necessarily in other countries. Some countries have different local rules.

Take a look at **www.conventions.coe.int/treaty/en/Treaties/Html/068.htm** for the details of the European Agreement and any local variations.

It's important to complete all the necessary paperwork for living and working in another country. Most agencies will organise this for you, and make sure the legal documents are in order before you leave.

You should listen to any legal advice you are given by the agency you use. Many also now require written references, police checks and other proof of suitability – which is as much a protection for you as it is for the parents of the children you might look after.

Here's an example. Most French agencies require a set of passport photos, a photocopy of your passport, two references (preferably translated into French), and your most recent academic qualifications, as well as a handwritten letter in French to your prospective family, which tells them something about you, your reasons for becoming an au pair and any future aspirations.

The agency may also ask for a medical certificate (showing you are free of deadly contagious diseases *etc*) dated less than three months before you leave, and translated into French. Au pairs also have to have a medical examination on arrival in France.

The French Consulate advises you to check that the family you stay with obtains a 'mother's help' work contract (*Accord de placement au pair d'un stagiaire aide-familiale*). If you are a non-EU citizen you are expected to do this before you leave for France, but British au pairs do not need to.

Au pairing in North America

Being an au pair in the USA is well paid. You'll receive $195 a week (£125 approximately), have your flight paid for, free health insurance, free food and lodging with your own room in the family house. You also get two weeks' holiday and a chance to travel for 30 days at the end of the year.

Many American families need childcare help because both parents work. Childcare is very expensive in the USA and so a highly effective network of agencies has developed to supply international au pairs to US families.

The US Government regulates the au pair programme and in order to obtain the required J-1 au pair visa you must go though a local UK agency. The requirements are quite strict:

· Be aged 18-26.

· Be educated to minimum GCSE standard.

· Speak English well.

· Have no criminal record (including cautions) and obtain an enhanced CRB check.

· Have a minimum 200 hours of babysitting experience with non-relatives.

· Be able to drive and swim.

· Have no visible tattoos!

You also receive a $500 credit towards the college course of your choice.

The US Department of State website has all the up-to-date legislation on au pairing in the US. See: **j1visa.state.gov/programs/au-pair**

If you enjoy being with children, this is a great option for a year. UK agencies include:

www.gap360.com
www.culturalcare.co.uk
www.aupairinamerica.com

If you want to combine au pairing with some study, the EduCare scheme in the US places people with families who have school-aged children and who need childcare before and after school hours. Au pairs on the EduCare scheme work no more than 30 hours per week in return for roughly two thirds of the rates paid to au pairs.

You must complete a minimum of 12 hours of academic credit or its equivalent during the programme year (financed by the host family for up to US$1000).

Internships and paid work placements

· Are you at university?

· Are you a new graduate?

· Are you looking for work experience to land your dream job?

· Want to spend a year in another country?

Taking an internship abroad – either as part of a university course or not – is a good way to boost your CV, as well as getting away for a year and doing something useful.

There is an increasing demand for paid work placements overseas and many gap-year companies now offer these. Paid work has always been popular as students seek to

IST Plus

top up funds for the next stage of their travels. But in the current economic climate gaining work experience has become an important consideration when planning a gap-year and many gap-year organisations are now in a position to help secure suitable placements.

Some careers, the media for example, are extremely tough to get into, so using your gap-year to get relevant work experience may be a good plan. You'll have the benefit of something to put on your CV and also get an idea of what the job is actually like. Internships are not usually open to people pre-university. Many international companies offer internships but if you're thinking of the USA you should know:

1. Internships in the USA can be difficult to get without paying for the privilege, unless you have personal contacts within the organisation you hope to work for.

2. The USA has a strict job-related work permit system and won't hand out these permits for jobs that American nationals can do themselves.

3. The USA authorities also need to be convinced that the work experience offered provides an opportunity to the UK student that he or she cannot get back home.

If the companies listed in our directory can't help you, try these websites:

www.cartercentre.org
www.summerjobs.com (enter internships in the search box)
www.internshipprograms.com
www.internabroad.com/search.cfm
www.transitionsabroad.com/listings/work/internships/index.shtml

Before you sign up, make sure you're clear just what your placement will involve. An internship should mean you are able to do interesting paid work related to your degree studies, current or future, for at least six months, but increasingly, even on some of the internship websites listed above, the distinction between a voluntary (unpaid) placement and an internship is becoming blurred so you may have to search for a while – or be creative and try a direct approach to companies in the fields that interest you.

Sport instructors

If you're already a qualified instructor in skiing, sailing, kayaking, diving, football, or any other sport for that matter, there are many places all around the world where you can use your skills – and many personal benefits.

Typical summer seasons run from the end of April to the beginning of November and winter seasons tend to run from the end of November until the end of April. That provides an opportunity for all-year round work, although it's worth noting that recruitment normally starts five months in advance. In some cases people can even get qualified and teach people to ski in the same season, such as in Oyster's Whistler Kids Instructor programme.

Here are a few websites worth having a look at:

Skiing:

www.oysterworldwide.com/gap-year/canada-whistler-blackcomb-ski-instructor-jobs
www.ifyouski.com/jobs/job/description/instructor
www.jobmonkey.com/ski/html/instructors.html

Football:
www.deltapublications.co.uk/soccer.htm – soccer coaching in the USA

General Sports:
www.adventurejobs.co.uk
www.campjobs.com

Skiing doesn't have to be in European resorts, don't forget there's the US and Canada, but there are also ski resorts in the foothills of the Himalayas! For diving jobs you can go pretty much go anywhere there's water and water sports. Football's popular throughout Africa and Latin America, and there are now several football academies in India looking for help to spread the message of the 'beautiful game'. But whichever sport is your passion, you can use it as part of your gap-year plan.

We have much more on the opportunities available for teaching and playing sport abroad in **Chapter 8**.

153

PGL, Alton Court, Penyard Lane, Ross-on-Wye HR9 5GL UK
T: 0844 3710 123
E: recruitment@pgl.co.uk   W: www.pgl.co.uk/jobs

Bring a little outdoor adventure to your gap year with PGL.

PGL is the UK's market leading provider of activity holidays and study courses for young people.

For over 400,000 children every year, a PGL holiday means the adventure of a lifetime. PGL employ a team of 2,500 vibrant, energetic staff each year to make that happen.

They have been offering young guests the experience of a lifetime since 1957 and now operate at 23 locations across the UK, France and Spain.

A job with PGL is an ideal way to spend your gap year. It is also a great way of saving money for a gap year whilst doing something different.

Capitalise job roles: PGL have an amazing range of positions to choose from watersports and land-based Activity Instructors, Group Leaders, Catering roles, Housekeeping roles, Drivers, French speaking Tour Leaders, Administrators, Reps and Group Co-ordinators; Operational support roles plus many more.

Working with PGL gives you the chance to work with people from around the globe, make new friends, enhance your CV and live in some stunning locations. At PGL the emphasis for guests and the staff team alike, is fun.

With positions available in the UK and Northern France from January to the end of November and Southern France and Spain operating from mid April to September, PGL have the flexibility to accommodate most requests, meaning you can get the contract length that suits your gap year needs.

Apply now and find your working adventure with PGL!

LoveTEFL

Teaching English as a Foreign Language (TEFL)

TEFL is one of the most popular ways of earning (and volunteering) when you travel, but you need to have a recognised qualification and it does help in getting a post abroad. It also has the advantage that, if you were thinking of teaching as a career, it's a good chance to find out if you like it before you begin your teacher training.

The two best-known British qualifications are:

· TESOL (a certificate from Trinity College, London).

· CELTA (Cambridge University certificate).

The USA has its own qualification and there are many private schools and colleges who offer their own certification. There are a great many colleges around the UK that offer TEFL courses but, ideally, you should check that the certificate you will be working for is one of these two.

It is worth doing your TEFL training within an accredited training centre, as most will help you find a placement once you qualify and face to face training can be more beneficial.

One word of warning, if you were hoping to get a job with one of the many well-known language schools around the world, some will insist that you undertake your TEFL training with them first. It's always worth checking this out, and deciding how you wish to use your training, before you sign up for a course. for more info, visit: **www.tefl.org.uk**.

my
gap-year
Alison Roxburgh

A year out between study and work can change your life. Interrailing, travels to Australia, South America, a summer in the US topped the charts for my peers keen to have some fun, expand horizons and obtain the all-important life experience demanded by prospective employers.

Sharing those goals, I applied for the Teach In Thailand programme with IST plus. Three months later, sweat dripping from nerves and intense heat, 30 pairs of eyes fixed on me as I began my first English lesson. For a year afterwards, the same eyes were smiling at me, shouting, "Hello, teacher!" as I walked to school every morning.

It was a completely different education to my formal studies at school and university. I contributed to school life and worked with Thai teachers and English-speaking teachers from around the globe. I could see the difference I made to the world I had entered; students got better at speaking English, reading, writing, listening - skills for life. I made friends and travelled at every opportunity, weekend trips to islands and beaches, navigating longer trips further afield; the idyllic becoming the norm.

Aside from good memories, what did I get from my year out? The skills I learned are still relevant when I go to job interviews now – communication skills such as delivering presentations or addressing particular groups of people, planning, organising and the ability to demonstrate my initiative and leadership. The courage it took to leave my comfort zone, the resulting sense of independence and much-sought-after life experience, these are the advantages I have when I approach a job interview.

Some years on from being a new graduate and completing my gap-year, I'm now the one sitting in the hiring chair. What do I look for when recruiting? See above.

For more information about IST Plus, see their advert on page 158

How to find TEFL work

The availability of work for people who can teach English can vary, particularly outside the EU. In most countries it is possible to give private lessons. As stated before, if you wish to work for a language school or academy, find out what their requirements are before you begin your training.

Most professional employers will expect you to have had some teaching practice before they will employ you. You should also find out more about the country you hope to find work in before you go. The contact details of the relevant embassies in the UK can be found on the FCO website – **www.fco.gov.uk** – and you should be able to obtain up-to-date details of visas, salaries, qualifications needed and a view about the availability of work in your chosen country. Rates of pay and conditions of employment will vary greatly from country to country and will most likely depend on your own education, training, experience and expertise.

In the UK, TEFL jobs are advertised in:
The Times Educational Supplement.
The Guardian.
In the education section of *The Independent.*
The EL Gazette.

www.oysterworldwide.com/projects/tefl
www.tefl.org.uk/tefl-jobs-centre
www.eslbase.com/jobs
www.cactustefl.com
www.eteach.com
www.esljobfeed.com

You could also check out the various 'blacklists' that have appeared on the internet in recent years. These list schools to avoid or watch out for. These are informal sites

ist plus

IST Plus, Crest House, 102-104 Church Lane, Teddington TW11 8PY UK
T: 020 7788 7877
E: info@istplus.com   W: www.istplus.com

IST Plus offers exciting and challenging paid work opportunities for Gap Year participants in Thailand, China and the USA.

Teach in Thailand/Teach in China

Graduates who want to widen their horizons and develop life skills before settling down with a job or career can teach English in schools or colleges in Thailand or China.

Participants must be graduates and native or near-native English speakers. No previous teaching experience or qualifications are needed at the time of application; participants undergo a week-long training and orientation session in Bangkok/Shanghai before they start their contracts.

Commit for 1 or 2 semesters (5 or 10 months), choose the age group preferred and a suitable placement will be found. There are two departures to each country per year.

A good local salary is provided as well as free accommodation. In-country support is provided by IST Plus' local partner in both Thailand and China.

Work in a US summer camp

Gap Year participants 18-30 years of age can spend the summer working in a US summer camp. General Counsellors look after groups of children or teenagers. Specialist Counsellors teach, coach or lead activities such as water sports, tennis, drama, arts and crafts. Support staff work behind the scenes at camp helping with administration, maintenance and other jobs.

Work and Travel USA

University students can spend the summer holidays working at seasonal jobs in the USA. Work and Travel USA is a flexible programme that helps participants work for up to 4 months in the summer in the USA.

run by people with experience of TEFL teaching. They should be a good place to find out about language schools around the world and whether or not it's worth your time pursuing a vacancy there.

The most popular destinations for TEFL teachers are China, Hong Kong, Japan, Thailand and, of course, Europe. As the EU grows, so does the demand for English teachers, and the advantage of securing a job within the EU is that the UK is a member. This will give you some protection and should involve far less paperwork than if you applied to work further afield.

In China, you are more likely to find work in a private school, rather than the state schools system, as the latter is controlled by the Department of Education in Beijing.

Hong Kong is an obvious choice as it was once a British Colony and English is a second language for nearly everyone there. The added advantage for those with no Chinese language skills is that all the road signs, public transport and government information are in English as well as Chinese and most of the shops, agencies and essential services (such as police, doctors *etc*) employ English speakers.

There is also a daily English language newspaper, *The South China Morning Post* and it may well be worth checking their online jobs section for vacancies: **www.cpjobs.com/hk/**

If you want to take your skills and use them in Japan you should check out **www.jet-uk.org**. This is the Japanese Government's website for promoting their scheme to improve foreign language teaching in schools. You do have to have a Bachelor's degree to qualify though. The *Japan Times* (which is online) also lists job vacancies in English: **www.jobs.japantimes.jp**

There is a great demand for English speakers in Thailand and so if you are taking your gap in that country, and wish to earn money whilst there, TEFL could well be the answer, particularly as you will be unable to find work in a country where foreigners are forbidden from taking most unskilled occupations. The *Bangkok Post* lists job vacancies, including those for English teachers, in their online jobs section: **www.bangkokpost.net**

Teaching English in private lessons

If you decide to supplement your income in-country by giving private lessons, you can put notices in schools, colleges, newspapers and local shops but there are some basic safety precautions you should take:

1. Be careful how you word your ad – *eg* 'Young English girl offering English lessons' is likely to draw the wrong kind of attention.

2. If you arrange one-to-one tuition, don't go to your student's home until you've checked out how safe it would be.

3. Equally, if you're living alone, don't give classes at home until you've got to know your student.

4. Arrange classes in public, well-populated locations, which will also help as teaching aids (coffee bars, restaurants, shops, markets *etc*).

5. Make sure you're both clear about your fee (per hour) and when it should be paid (preferably these should both be put in writing).

Usually, you'll be inundated by friends of friends as word gets round there's an English person willing to give private lessons.

IST Plus

Cookery

Cooking jobs are available abroad as well as in the UK, particularly during the summer months. Gaining some cooking skills is a great way to boost your CV and opens up new possibilities.

Families will often look for a young person to help *eg* during the long summer months – animal/child-friendly and an ability to drive are good skills combinations along with basic cooking skills to provide all-round household support. Some families have holiday homes abroad and in the traditional English holiday locations so there can be a chance to get to know a new area.

Seasonal work in Europe

Working in Europe offers endless possibilities – from fruit picking to hospitality and tourism, leading nature trips to teaching English (for more on this see our TEFL section on the previous pages). Some non-EU members need work permits so you should check the regulations in the country you want to go to.

Companies offer a variety of roles working with children at locations across the UK, France and Spain for as little as 12 weeks, to a maximum of ten months with the option to return the following year.

Jobs on offer include children's group leaders, activity or watersports Instructors, French-speaking tour leaders or administrators and Spanish-speaking roles. Non-guest-facing roles include support team positions: catering assistants, chefs, drivers, retail, housekeeping and maintenance. Some roles do not require qualifications or previous experience – in fact there are opportunities for a comprehensive training programme including apprenticeships and coaching awards so you may even have the opportunity to gain an additional qualification for life at no cost to yourself.

visit: www.oysterworldwide.com

Blue Ventures

To find other short-term jobs try:

www.oysterworldwide.com/projects/paid-work
www.transitionsabroad.com
www.pickingjobs.com

Seasonal work in North America

Probably the most popular seasonal job for gappers in the US is working on a summer camp. The US has strict regulations on visas and work permits but summer camps are a well-established way of working for a short time.

US work regulations are very complicated, and specific, and this is one time where it would help to use a placement organisation to help you through the paperwork, but make sure you check out the small print about pay, accommodation and expenses.

Each year thousands of young British and European students apply to join the summer camp programmes in the US as counsellors. Note, though, that programmes can only be arranged with specialist organisations.

If you don't fancy summer camp there are lots of other possibilities, from working on a ranch to cruise ship jobs. Have a look at: **www.jobmonkey.com**

It covers all sorts of work from fishing jobs in Alaska, to working on a ranch, to casino and gaming clubs and cruise work. But check with the US embassy to make sure you can get a visa or a work permit for the job you fancy. See: **www.usembassy.org.uk**

There are plenty of opportunities for working holidays in Canada, most commonly at hotels and restaurants, and ski and summer resorts.

Jon Arnold, of Oyster Worldwide, pointed out that Canada has a limited supply of work permits. These are released in batches and they tend to run out very fast, so it's very important to plan ahead. "The work permits in 2015 were released in March and

Canvas Holidays, East Port House, 12 East Port, Dunfermline KY12 7JG UK
T: +44 (0) 1383 629012
W: www.canvasholidays.co.uk/recruitment

At Canvas we ensure that our customers return home having had the best holiday they have ever had. We believe that our staff at Canvas play a big part in achieving this. We are looking for approachable, friendly, helpful and hardworking individuals to join our overseas team. Working for Canvas gives you an opportunity to see new places, create memories and make new friends.

Courier Roles: Individual, Couple and Team Sites

You will be the face of Canvas Holidays and your duties will include delivering exceptional customer service, cleaning, preparing and maintaining customer accommodation for customer's arrival, welcoming them on to the campsite and ensuring that customers' needs are attended to during their stay. You will need to have initiative and be a quick thinker and be able to resolve problems efficiently and effectively. You will be responsible for the operation of your site and delivering the Canvas product.

Senior Courier/Site Manager Roles

Our Team Leaders ensure that every aspect of our customers holidays is of the highest standard possible. All successful applicants must have previous management/supervisory experience, exceptional customer service, maintenance, problem solving, organisation and communication skills.

Area Manager

Our Area Managers ensure that our Staff on site have all the support they need to have a successful summer. All successful applicants must have previous multi-site management experience, display budgeting, maintenance and accounting skills. You should be able to lead and motivate a team and have excellent communication skills. You must have a full clean driving licence.

For all roles, language skills are preferred but not essential.

April and there were 5000 available for British Passport holders. The limited number in each batch were gone within 12 minutes of release. In 2014, the permits were released even earlier in the year so it is really important to start planning your trip to Canada at least 12 months in advance to stand a chance of getting a work permit."

Jon added: "Working in a country like Canada for up to 12 months is an excellent way to spend your gap-year. There is so much to get involved in all-year round and the experience certainly won't do your CV any harm."

Seasonal work in Australia and New Zealand

Periods of working and travelling in Australia and New Zealand are a very popular option and you can do everything from fruit picking to helping Amnesty International. However, you don't have to stick to the traditional backpacker temporary work – fruit picking, bar work or call centres. If you have a trade, IT skills or a nursing qualification they're also good for finding work.

Australia has a well worked-out system to allow you to work and travel. It's called the working holiday visa (subclass 417). You can qualify for any specified work and UK passport holders can apply online. Specified work is work, whether paid or unpaid, in certain specified industries or postcodes – for more details have a look at:

www.immi.gov.au/visitors/working-holiday/417/specified-work.htm

The main points are:

· You must be between 18 and 30.

· It costs around £210 (AU$440).

You will also be required to have a health certificate before you apply for your visa.

What you can do:

· Enter Australia within 12 months of the visa being issued.

· Stay up to 12 months.

· Leave and re-enter Australia any number of times while the visa is valid.

· Work in Australia for up to six months with each employer.

· Study or train for up to four months.

To find out more go to:
www.border.gov.au/Trav/Visa-1/417-

Or call the High Commission in the UK:
Australian High Commission,
Australia House, Strand, London WC2B 4LA
Tel: 020 7379 4334
uk.embassy.gov.au

To find seasonal work try:
www.visitoz.org
www.seasonalwork.com.au/index.bsp
www.workaboutaustralia.com.au

Successful applicants should allow about three weeks to find work, although it may well come quicker than that. The average rate of pay for temporary staff us at about A$15 to A$21 an hour, enabling a good standard of living that can help fund travels.

my
gap-year
Toby

Toby, 18, from the UK contacted Go Workabout in need of help. Like many gap-year travellers Toby was excited about taking a break after school and exploring the world but was nervous having never travelled before. Through a custom package we were able to completely set Toby up to legally work in Australia.

Toby came out to Australia in late November just before the summer peak season started which enabled us to place him at a resort in the beautiful South West WA region.

After completing his six months at the resort Toby was keen to complete his rural employment in order to get his second year visa. Toby had proven to be a hard, reliable worker so we were able to place Toby in agricultural work that enabled him to complete his 88 days for his second year visa. Toby continued to work for us with another one of our clients in the North West of WA during his second year visa.

At the end of Toby's Australian working holiday adventure we assisted him in completing his tax return and superannuation return. Toby comments "I would have been completely lost if it wasn't for the help Go Workabout gave me in setting up my tax file number, superannuation and bank account and guiding me through the Australian employment process." This refund gave Toby a decent fund to use for a two month trip through South East Asia before returning home to the UK.

Toby comments on his time working abroad in Australia. "It's safe to say that this trip has so far been the best experience of my life, especially in Dunsborough and at the lodge. I have made so many new friends and have done so many amazing things. I still can't believe I know how to surf!"

For more information about Go Workabout, see their advert on page 146

Joanna Burnet, of Visitoz, told us: "Our participants go to the job of their choice on their ninth day in Australia. Those searching for work in the cities should allow at least six weeks to find a job; those looking for fruit picking work should allow longer than that. A lot of people run out of money in these six or eight weeks and have to return home. It is always the best to book with an organisation that (a) guarantees you a soft landing in Australia and gets all your ready-to-work paperwork done for you and (b) guarantees a job."

New Zealand has a similar working visa scheme for either 12 or 23 months – and also a health certificate requirement. To qualify you must:

1. Usually be permanently living in the United Kingdom – this means you can be temporarily visiting another country when you lodge your application.

2. Have a British passport that's valid for at least three months after your planned departure from New Zealand.

3. Be at least 18 and not more than 30 years old.

4. Not bring children with you.

5. Hold a return ticket, or sufficient funds to purchase such a ticket.

6. Have a minimum of NZ$350 per month of stay in available funds (to meet your living costs while you're there).

7. Meet New Zealand's health and character requirements.

8. Satisfy the authorities that your main reason for going to New Zealand is to holiday, not work.

9. Not have been approved a visa permit under a Working Holiday Scheme before.

the gap-year guidebook 2016

Taking a

GAP YEAR

You're thinking about Australia..

So ask yourself

What do you want
TO ACHIEVE

Have a story
to tell ?

?

Open your
mind ?

Develop
skills ?

Earn
money ?

VISITOZ.
.ORG

An Australian
working adventure

The regulations for British subjects are very clearly laid out on the NZ Government website:

www.immigration.govt.nz/migrant/stream/work/workingholiday/
unitedkingdomworkingholidayscheme.htm

And here are a few websites to check for seasonal work in New Zealand:

www.picknz.co.nz
www.seasonaljobs.co.nz
www.backpackerboard.co.nz/work_jobs/seasonal_jobs_new_zealand.php

Help with applying for a working holiday visa

Individuals can apply for working holiday visas themselves or use an agency to prepare the paperwork for you. UK agencies for this include:

www.oysterworldwide.com
www.visabureau.com
www.realgap.com

If you are not British you should check the websites to see if your citizenships allows you to obtain the visa.

The sort of work that you can obtain is not restricted, but in most cases you are only allowed to work for the same employer for six months. The idea is that it is a holiday being supported by working, rather then work being the prime reason for travelling.

Please see the directory pages starting on page 317 for information on companies and organisations offering working abroad opportunities.

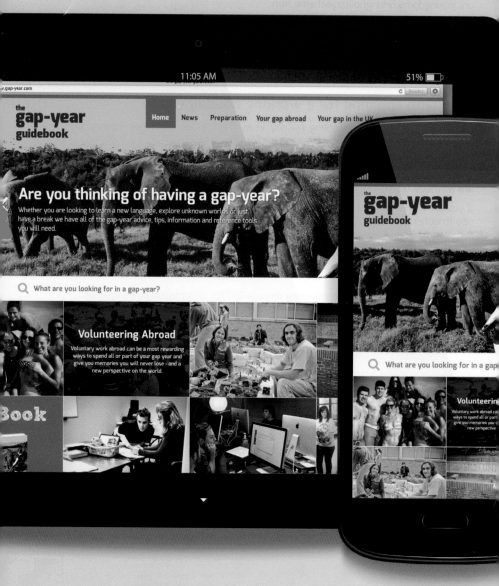

Welcome to the NEW gap-year website!

www.gap-year.com

6

Volunteering abroad

Sponsored by

theleap

Making The Leap to your gap-year!

Volunteering

Gratifying, humbling, life-changing... these are all words Leapers have used to describe the act of volunteering. But they're just a meaningless jumble of letters, until you experience it for yourself...

Reasons to volunteer?

It's a two-way exchange

Volunteering is not a one-way street. You'll learn just as much from being immersed in another culture as others will learn from you.

Put the pride back into voluntourism

'Voluntourism' is a term with a bit of a shaky rep after the famous (admittedly hilarious) 'gap yah' YouTube videos. Suggesting that gap-year volunteers are border-line alcoholics with nothing more than self-gratification in mind. Don't believe the hype - this is a stereotypical misconception, and far from the truth about most young people who choose to volunteer.

Organised in the right way, by a reputable and experienced company like The Leap, which carries out researched and well-led projects, volunteers can make a difference – even in a short period.

Get the feel-good factor

The act of making a positive impact, even in a small way, to someone else's day is a great thing and will stay with you long after your volunteer project has ended.

Boost your CV sky high

Your reasons for volunteering don't have to be purely altruistic. It's OK to consider how your gap-year and summer experiences at this age will reflect on you in the future when you come to apply for that dream job.

The competition for top jobs is tough; you need to start thinking about how you are going to stand out. Being a volunteer will equip you with a range of skills and experiences that will impress future employers and what's more, it gives you an exciting experience to talk about at an interview.

Get off that backpacker trail

Most independent backpackers barely scratch the surface of the country or culture they are visiting, merely passing through with a day or two in each place. Their memories may be fun, but it's very different to the authentic interaction with locals, understanding of a place and lasting impression that volunteering provides.

So, what to do next?

Research companies and don't be fooled by the cheap seats – look into the nitty gritty of what is being offered – where will you live, with who, doing what, extra costs?

To start the ball rolling head over to The Leap

We offer award-winning volunteering and intern projects in Africa, Asia and South America. Unlike other gap-year companies, all our programs include a mix of different projects in a mix of locations - with a team of like-minded people.

You'll travel to several different places across the country you've chosen to visit, and take part in all sorts of activities along the way.

You'll also do the whole thing as part of a team of 8-15 other guys and girls taking The Leap, who you'll meet before you go. Having them there will make a huge difference to what you can achieve and the fun you can have, and ensures that a great social life comes as standard.

Leap variety? How does it work?

A volunteer program in Ecuador is the ultimate South American experience: an epic adventure travelling through the heights of the Andes, down into the steamy Jungle and onto the white sands of the Galapagos and Pacific Coast.

All the while getting stuck into environmental conservation in the Galapagos, jungle reforestation, building community infrastructure, organic cocoa farming, leading kids on outward- bound adventures, building fresh water wells in remote villages, developing artisan markets, an adrenaline adventure week and Spanish lessons – all neatly packed into 10 weeks.

Or how about getting stuck into a law, business or teaching internship in Arusha, the safari capital of Tanzania, combining it with a safari and helping in an orphanage all before nipping over to the Indian ocean to volunteer in a local school and hanging out on the tropical island of Zanzibar...bliss...

The details

10 or 6 week programs.

Summer gaps of 6 weeks.

Cost: £1900 – £3000 includes accommodation, food, transport, project materials, donations to the community, in-country project leaders, 24/7 back-up.

Approximately 65% of the cost is spent overseas.

So if any of this seems like your metaphorical cup of tea, then check out the website **www.theleap.co.uk** and feel free to request one of our lovely brochures.

6 Volunteering abroad

Blue Ventures

Voluntary work abroad can be one of the most rewarding ways to spend all, or part, of your gap-year. You could find yourself working with people living in unbelievable poverty, disease or hunger. It can be a humbling and hugely enriching experience and it can make you question all the things you've taken for granted in your life. It's no exaggeration to say it can be life-changing.

Some people who have done it have ended up changing their planned course of study at university or even their whole career plan. Year Out Group's members, who are all gap providers, report that volunteering is the top gap choice among all age groups and had risen by 20% in the last full year for which they carried out research.

Teaching and working with children are the most popular options and interestingly women gappers outnumber men, and women are also more likely to choose volunteering and expeditions rather than courses or cultural exchanges.

Who goes volunteering?

It's clear from speaking to gap providers that students still make up most of the market, but the picture is changing.

Our friends at Kaya Responsible Travel, who offer volunteering opportunities in more than 20 countries, told us: "About a third of our volunteers are 18-to-21 years, another third are 22-to-26. Then about a quarter are 27-55 with another 5% being

visit: www.theleap.co.uk

55+ and an equal number under 18. So you can see that our programs have a wide reach. There are certain projects that we might direct younger volunteers towards, and a few projects that are specifically for those aged 30+, so getting advice from your placement advisor can give a better idea of the typical participant on a particular program – though in our experience a mix of ages often adds to everyone's learning and enjoyment, as we encourage full integration regardless of age, project or where you come from.

"In terms of trends, we see more students and college leavers volunteering as a way to get work experience in their fields, but we are also seeing professionals, empty-nesters and retirees wanting to travel in a more meaningful and immersive setting, and turning to volunteering as the perfect travel option."

Projects Abroad, who have been offering volunteering abroad placements for more than 20 years, agreed: "In the last 12 months we have seen an increase in the number of UK career breakers and retired people choosing to volunteer with us. We have even designed grown-up special group trips to welcome groups of adults aged 50+ on two week service trips designed for them to go abroad and give back."

Why volunteer?

We think Jon Arnold, of Oyster Worldwide, answers this question rather well:

"Volunteering overseas does not only help you, but hopefully it helps others as well. Whether you are on a traditional gap-year or a career break, there is so much you can achieve by volunteering overseas.

"You can't expect to eradicate Third World poverty in a three-month volunteer trip, but you can make a truly positive impact on at least a few people's lives. Whether it is teaching someone to read or inspiring a group of kids to learn English, you can leave knowing you have helped them.

"Volunteering abroad makes you more interesting to speak to. After overseas volunteering, you will be able to talk about times when you worked as part of team, showed leadership and determination. This will look really good on your CV, allow to stand out from the crowd and help you achieve your dream job."

Richard Nimmo from Blue ventures, who arrange marine conservation expeditions in some of the most pristine environments in the world, told us that many of their volunteers use the experience to flesh out academic knowledge with some real practical experience; "As well as all the soft skills that can be gained from a meaningful time away, a marine conservation expedition is the perfect way to get a head-start in a career in the field of marine biology and conservation by learning from top scientists."

There's no denying that the economic situation has also added to the need for volunteers, so volunteer help is likely to be even more needed and appreciated. Voluntary work abroad can also give you wonderful memories and a new perspective on the world.

On an organised voluntary project you often live amongst the local community and tend to get closer to daily life than you do as an independent traveller. By taking part in an organised voluntary work project you can learn about a different culture, meet new people and learn to communicate with people who may not understand your way of life, let alone your language.

173

DON'T JUST
WALK
THROUGH LIFE...

TAKE THE
LEAP!

MAKE YOUR GAP YEAR COUNT

Travel, Work & Volunteer

Africa, Asia, South America & Caribbean

- Teaching & Childcare
- Conservation Projects
- Horse Safari

- Community Building
- Law, Business & Media

www.theleap.co.uk

The Leap

You will come away with an amazing sense of achievement and (hopefully) pride in what you have done. Career breakers have also found that a volunteer gap has not only been a satisfying experience but given them new ideas and attitudes too. A structured volunteer placement can also give a new dimension to the skills you can highlight on your CV.

This is particularly important considering the current job market, say Projects Abroad, and something that many students think about before they choose their volunteer gap-year:

"As long as you are using the time to do something constructive then you will gain a huge amount from a gap-year. It can make you more employable by enhancing your CV, but it also improves what employers call 'soft skills' such as teamwork, leadership and responsibility.

"For students wanting to get onto competitive university courses like medicine or veterinary medicine for example, having spent time gaining work experience on a related project overseas can also help with university applications."

Our friends at the National Union of Students told us that they believe volunteering abroad can prove a life-changing experience for gappers.

"One way of using a year out is to see at as a break, a way to re-think your options, take some time to do the things you always wanted to do, or do things to open up doors and acquire skills you don't necessarily get in the classroom. Volunteering can be a rewarding and useful way to gain some skills and make beneficial contacts and you might want to get some valuable work experience in a field that interests you.

"If you do decide to volunteer abroad you should be careful about which organisations you support. Look for projects that emphasise learning and you can learn much from the communities in which you will live and work with. The most rewarding projects will not necessarily be most the glamorous but will be the ones where you really feel benefited a community in a way that simply sending money would not have."

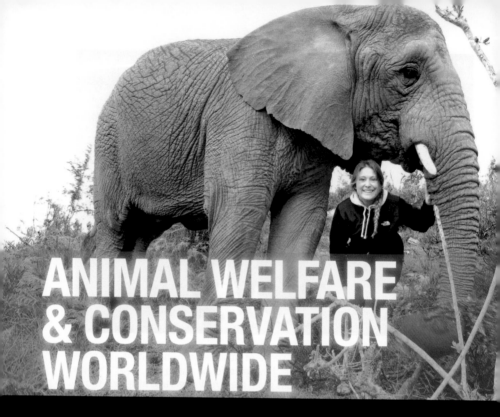

ANIMAL WELFARE & CONSERVATION WORLDWIDE

BEARS / ELEPHANTS / LIONS / MARINE LIFE / MONKEYS ORANGUTANS / SHARKS / TURTLES / WILDLIFE

- Hands-on animal care and rehabilitation
- Research and monitoring
- Preserve rescued animals in sanctuaries
- Land and marine conservation
- Veterinary internship
- Game Ranger course
- Diving internship

www.oysterworldwide.com

Speak to Anne for more information by calling her on **01892 771 975** or email her on **anne@oysterworldwide.com**

Blue Ventures

Distant Shores also commented: "If you do a gap-year right you not only grow as a person, but are able to tackle future challenges with a whole new range of skills you'll have learnt. Skills which cannot be taught in schools, such as demonstrating a long term commitment and being able to relate and adapt to a different culture."

Being realistic, voluntary work can be tough. You may be out in the middle of nowhere, with no western influence to be seen; food, language – the entire culture is likely to be totally different from what you're used to and there might not be many English speakers around: so you may have to cope with culture shock or feeling lonely, isolated and homesick at first, but if you stick with it you'll usually find those feelings will go as you get more involved in what you're doing.

Onaris Africa offer some advice on how to prepare yourself for a volunteer experience: "The most important advice we give is to embark on the journey with an open mind, particularly when taking part in volunteer experiences. It's so easy to have pre-conceived ideas about what developing communities are like and its only natural to feel passionate about wanting to do all you can to help. But it's important to try and look at things from an unbiased perspective, try to understand the community before you try to help them. There may be a certain way we do things in the West, but that doesn't necessarily make it the best way, or the right way for the host community."

177

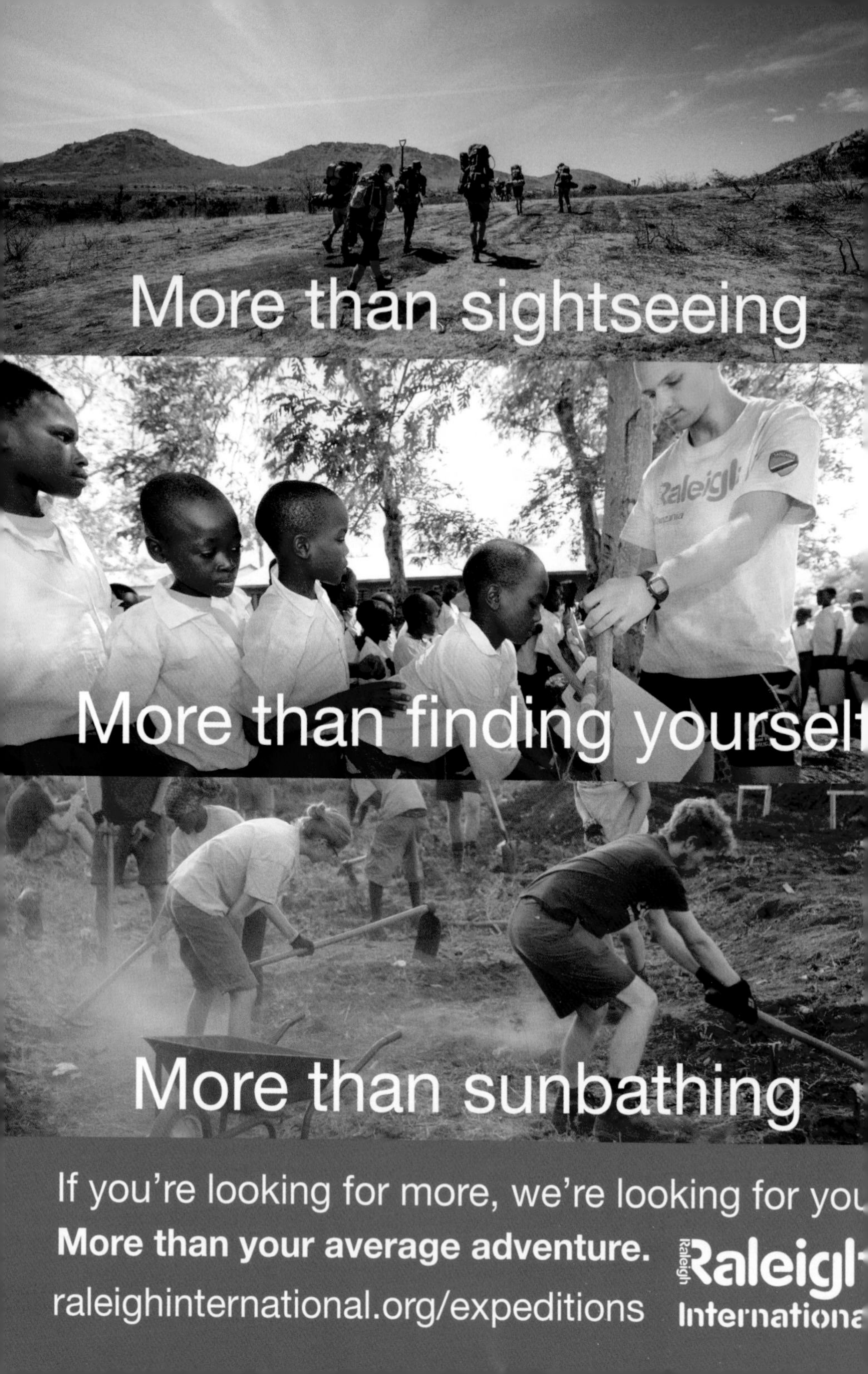

More than sightseeing
More than finding yoursel
More than sunbathing
If you're looking for more, we're looking for yo
More than your average adventure.
raleighinternational.org/expeditions

my gap-year
Sophie Gates

I knew when I applied to study veterinary medicine at university that getting in was going to be difficult, so it came as no surprise when on results day I narrowly missed the grades for my offer to study at Liverpool. I quickly decided to take a gap-year and reapply, but wanted to make the most of my year out and do something I may never get the chance to do again.

I started looking online for gap-year trips where I could work alongside vets in other countries. Deciding on Africa was easy - its wildlife and beautiful landscapes are second to none. I soon found the African Conservation Experience website and looked at all of the different projects they offered. I filled out their online application and was contacted the next day with the offer of a place on my first choice of project; the wildlife veterinary experience with Dr Rogers.

When we landed in South Africa we were met at the airport by members of the ACE team who took us to our different projects. I arrived at my project and was met by a member of the host family I would be living with for the next month. The whole family were lovely, so welcoming and accommodating - they even spent their weekends driving us around, taking us to different sites and on day trips. They went to great lengths to ensure we got the most out of our trip, whether it was driving us for two hours to see elephants or getting up at 4am with us to meet the vet for early rhino dehorning.

Working with Dr Rogers was an incredible honour, I got to see and do such a massive range of things I never dreamed I would. I was not sat 100 yards away in a truck watching from a 'safe' distance, I was stood right there with the vet monitoring the breathing of the sedated rhinos and leopards, and even got the chance to administer drugs to the animals. I learnt so much, Dr Rogers is an incredible teacher and always explained what he was doing and why, and never got annoyed at having to repeat the long names of the drugs I couldn't remember (just make sure you pronounce the 't' in warthog, that does annoy him!). He always encouraged us to get involved, take lots of pictures and even let me take a ride in the helicopter, he is a genuinely nice guy and it was a pleasure working with him.

Every second of the trip, without exception, was perfect. I would give anything to go back and do the month again and wouldn't change a thing - except maybe never coming home.

For more information about African Conservation Experience, see their advert on page 188

GLOBAL
VOLUNTEER
PROJECTS

GLOBAL
MEDICAL
PROJECTS

GLOBAL
MEDIA
PROJECTS

> Volunteer placements
> Pre-university medical experience
> Media and journalism internships

> Find out more: 0191 222 04
GlobalVolunteerProjects.co

Kanaama Interactive

Are you going for the right reasons?

Sounds like a silly question, doesn't it? But volunteering requires people who really want to make an impact and so something to help others, rather than those interested in a round-the-world jolly.

Our friends at Raleigh International told us: "Raleigh tends to attract people who want to make a real impact on sustainable projects whilst gaining a variety of transferable skills. We want volunteers with an open mind, commitment and a desire to change their world for the better. It's not for everyone so it's important that people understand what you're getting into before you sign up. Volunteers live and work in very basic conditions, collecting and purifying their own water, potentially digging their own toilet and living in close conditions with each other and local communities. All volunteers go through extensive training and are guided by a team of volunteer managers and our country staff."

Jon Arnold agrees the right attitude is very important: "It is not just about developing yourself but also helping others. You've got to make sure though that you are immersing yourself into the project and not seeing it just as something to tick off your 'bucket list'.

"We've noticed an increasing hedonism amongst some young people. They want to take a gap-year but they want to cram everything they can into the time, often to the detriment of the projects themselves. This has seen an increase in the number of organisations seizing on a money making idea and offering shorter and shorter volunteer programmes. There comes a point when people need to ask whether they are actually making a positive contribution or just getting involved to 'tick a box' to say they've 'taught in a school' on their gap-year and doing more harm than good.

"For people who really want to make a difference and learn about a whole new

181

culture, you have to stay on the project for a significant period of time, ideally 3-6 months. You can't expect to make as much of a positive impact in a short 2-4 week trip for example. These people understand and have the conviction to make a real difference on their gap-year by immersing themselves on the projects and their new life to truly get the most out of the whole experience."

What would you like to do?

There are a huge amount of options, as you'll see in this chapter and the directory section, so you need to make sure you find the best fit for you. All of the companies we speak to come back with the same advice: make sure you do your research!

Raleigh are a leading charity provider of expeditions and volunteer projects abroad. They believe there are a huge amount of skills to be learned on the wide number of projects available to the interested gapper. They told us:

"Once you've made the decision to volunteer abroad, it's important to always do your research. There are lots of organisations that you can volunteer abroad with but you need to find the right one for you. Find out what you'll be doing, where your money will go, what support you will get and make sure this fits in with your own goals.

"With most volunteering opportunities, you'll find that you are taken well out of your comfort zone into incredibly challenging environments. You could find yourself in charge of a team of young volunteers in a managerial, decision-making and problem-solving role. Or you could be working with grass roots NGOs, devising an environmental project plan and gaining valuable insights into the development sector. Whatever you choose, volunteering abroad can help you gain experience in team-building, coaching, logistics, operations, multimedia or middle-management.

"Before embarking on any trip, people should do their research, think about what they want to get out of their time out, ask lots of questions and go with the organisation that most suits them. People coming with us tend to want a structured programme, working together in a team, with set objectives and guidance from project managers. For us it's really important that volunteers, local communities and project partners all work together and that all projects have a genuine, positive, sustainable impact."

Global Volunteer Projects

the gap-year guidebook 2016

Forest Animal Rescue, 640 NE 170th Ct., Silver Springs FL 34488 USA
T: +1 352 625 7377
E: volunteer@forestanimalrescue.org   W: forestanimalrescue.org

The perfect opportunity to learn about the welfare of big cats, bears, wolves, monkeys, bats and more while helping the staff and interns of a wild animal sanctuary to provide them with lifetime care.

If you love animals and enjoy making a real difference in their lives, this is the gap-year for you!

Forest Animal Rescue is a fully accredited sanctuary, dedicated to rescuing wild animals from improper conditions in captivity and providing them with lifetime care.

Over 100 wild animals, all rescued from situations that required intervention. Most of them had been starved, mistreated or abandoned and were on the brink of being destroyed by authorities. They cannot be released into the wild – but you can help to provide them with the best care they can have.

There is nothing more rewarding that watching an animal that arrived malnourished and scared, begin to thrive once again, both physically and emotionally. They are provided with large, natural spaces and allowed to be themselves. As they learn to trust their caregivers, they are provided with excellent nutritional and veterinary care. They now enjoy lifelong sanctuary and companionship of others of their own kind in a non-breeding setting.

You would be part of a dedicated team of staff and volunteers that helps with all aspects of sanctuary operations. Activities range from preparing food and feeding the animals to providing enrichment, cleaning enclosures, washing food bowls, building and expanding habitats and important maintenance of the sanctuary.

Raleigh International

Current trends

The most popular voluntary work activity is working as a teacher or teaching assistant. Teaching placements may include sports coaching, teaching assistants, pastoral care outside the classroom or taking a class.

Voluntary work on community and conservation projects also remain popular. Community projects, such as building a school room or a dam, vary in type and length and tend to be done in teams and be of shorter duration than teaching or caring placements.

Conservation projects usually last a few weeks and should provide an excellent insight into aspects of conservation that only hands-on experience can provide.

The most popular destinations for volunteering include South Africa, Tanzania, Thailand, Cambodia, Madagascar, Nepal and India. You will have read a little more about these locations – and the Year Out Group's explanation of their popularity – in **Chapter 1**.

South Africa consistently proves popular, with wildlife volunteering a particular draw. "Within that, the more hands-on the involvement for the volunteers, the more popular the project," say African Conservation Experience. "Volunteers do not want to observe, they want to be involved."

Oyster Worldwide told us: "South Africa remains our most popular destination. The animal welfare and short-term programmes have been the most popular as they give people the chance to do something amazing and really help a project even if they can only commit to a two-week trip."

And here's what Projects Abroad had to say: "Our most popular destinations include Ghana, Tanzania, South Africa, Nepal and Peru. The most popular project types are care placements and medicine and healthcare placements. A lot of our volunteers are looking to either help local people in disadvantaged communities or to gain practical experience before starting a university degree in an area like nursing or

VOLUNTEER SPORTS COACHING, TEACHING & CHILDCARE

BRAZIL / CHILE / NEPAL / ROMANIA SOUTH AFRICA / TANZANIA

- Teach English while learning a language
- Bring fun and emotional support to children
- Coach sports in townships
- Bring laughter to children in hospital care
- Live as a local and help communities

www.oysterworldwide.com

Speak to Roger for more information by calling him on **01892 771 971** or email him on **roger@oysterworldwide.com**

dentistry for example. Our conservation projects are also very popular and will take you to some incredible places from working in the canopy of the Peruvian Amazon Rainforest to diving and tagging sharks in the tropical waters of Fiji."

One exciting new development – and one that comes highly recommended by the NUS – is the government-funded International Citizen Service (ICS) programme.

It seeks to put young people at the forefront of the fight against global poverty and over the next three years 7,000 young people from the UK will work in partnership with young people in developing countries, on projects to fight poverty where help is needed the most.

The scheme follows a hugely successful pilot year and aims to offer a transformative experience for 18-25 year olds. The programme is designed to deliver three outcomes: to have a real and lasting development impact on sustainable development projects; to help the volunteers both from the UK and from developing countries learn key life skills such as teamwork, leadership, communication and project planning: and to instil in these volunteers a life-long commitment to development and to becoming active citizens, engaged in their communities back in the UK.

Only you can decide what's most important to you, it depends on whether you're more into plants, animals and the environment, in which case you'd be happier on a conservation project. If you're a people person you might do something that helps disadvantaged people, whether they're children, adults, and disabled or able-bodied.

Whichever you feel is right for you there's a huge range of companies and types of voluntary placements to choose from.

Even if you are straight from school or university and haven't yet had much experience of work-related skills you shouldn't underestimate the skills and qualities you may have, and take for granted, that can be far less accessible to disadvantaged people in places where such things as access to education or to communications are not universally available.

International Volunteer HQ

AFRICAN CONSERVATION EXPERIENCE

Make a difference as a conservation volunteer

Have you dreamt of tracking predators through the bush, working alongside a wildlife vet, observing dolphins or hand rearing rhino?
Come and share our passion for Africa!

OUR PROJECTS

- Shadow an experienced **Wildlife Vet** in South Africa
- Care for injured and orphaned animals at a **Wildlife Rehabilitation Centre**
- Assist **Game Rangers** and **Field Researchers** with wildlife surveys, reserve patrols and game capture and relocation
- Study dolphins and whales on **Marine Conservation Projects**

HOW DOES IT WORK?

Placements are available throughout the year and our team will help you choose the right project. You can volunteer for only 2 weeks or up to 3 months - it's up to you. Placement costs start from £2,600, including return flights from London, transfers, accommodation, meals, in-country support and the financial contributions to the projects.

Info@ConservationAfrica.net

www.conservationafrica.net

T. +44 (0)1454 269 182

A.C.E RESPONSIBLE TRAVEL

WORK WITH THE WILDLIFE

Oyster Worldwide

How much time do you want to spend?

This is about how committed a volunteer you want to be. Would you feel more satisfied spending two weeks on a building project providing homes for people displaced by a natural disaster? Or are you the kind of person who wants to get stuck into a long-term project, where the results you see will be more gradual?

Because voluntary work is so popular with gappers, commercial companies offering volunteering packages exist alongside the more traditional not-for-profit organisations and the idealism associated with voluntary work, though still there, has come under some commercial pressure.

Some companies offer two to four-week holidays combined with some voluntary work, but equally there are many organisations still committed to the idealism of volunteering, offering placements from a few months to up a year or more.

However, you may not want (or be able) to offer more than a few weeks or months of your time, so the combined holiday/short volunteering option might be for you. There's no point in committing yourself to a whole year only to find that, after a few weeks, you hate it and want to go home early. The two-to four-week option may also be a good 'taster' experience to help you decide whether to commit to something more long-term.

So, it's a good idea to be honest with yourself about what you want – there's nothing wrong with wanting to travel and have a good time. But, whatever you choose, make sure you are clear about what you will be doing *before* you sign up and part with your money.

Maekok River Village Resort, Huay Nam Yen, Thaton, Mae Ai, PO Box 3,
Chiang Mai 50280 Thailand
T: +66 (0) 53 053 628
E: rosie@maekok-river-village-resort.com
W: www.maekok-river-village-resort.com

The Maekok River Village and Outdoor Centre has been hosting gap-year students since 2007. The resort and centre, co-owned and managed by two British ex- teachers, is located in the far North of Thailand and set amongst the mountains which form the border with Myanmar.

Most of the schools in the area are populated by ethnic minorities – from the various hilltribes and by children of Shan immigrants from Myanmar. We have worked with visiting international schools for many years to improve the facilities in some 30 schools, but we are also providing opportunities for gap-year/career breakers to spend time teaching English or indeed any other subjects, in these under-provided schools.

For details about spending 3 weeks to 3 months with us, contact Rosie on rosie@maekok-river-village-resort.com

www.maekok-river-village-resort.com   www.mrvproject.com

Raleigh International

When to start applying

Applications can close early, particularly for expeditions and conservation projects needing complex funding or for those tied in with international government programmes. If you'd like to go on one of these projects, planning should start about a year ahead, usually in the autumn term of the academic year.

Jon Arnold from Oyster Worldwide suggests booking early to avoid disappointment "We have limited places available on our animal welfare and paid work programmes. If you can, book at least 12 months before to secure the price and your place."

Others can be taken up at very short notice. In fact, some organisations can take in applications during the August period (when you are getting A level results or going through clearing), and book you on a project that starts in September. If you don't have much time before your gap starts (maybe you didn't get the grades you expected, or you've made a last-minute decision to defer university for a year, or your company has offered you a sabbatical or made you redundant) it is always worth contacting a voluntary organisation about a project you're interested in. They may have had a last-minute cancellation.

Stiff competition

As more people are becoming motivated by the almost daily media reports on poverty in the developing world and on various global threats to the planet's climate, ecology and environment, to go out and do something, the competition for places can be fierce. Companies can afford to be picky – you may find you have to prove to them that you should be selected to go before they will accept your money!

They have a point. Increasingly NGOs and volunteers are trying to make sure both sides benefit from the experience, so placement organisations put a lot of effort into checking and briefing as well as getting you out there and providing in-country support. If you can't stick it, everyone loses out – including the person who could have been chosen instead of you.

my gap-year
Dougie

I always wanted to do a gap-year and follow in the footsteps of my siblings but I also wanted to do something a bit different. When I heard about Raleigh International and what they did I knew it was the organisation for me. Raleigh gives you the chance to do things that you would never get to try at any other time in your life. I now feel like I have a global network, not just UK based friends. The memories that I will return with aren't just a photo album, it is what I have learnt and developed as a person.

The water project we worked on in the village of Matapalo in Nicaragua was amazing. It is very rare that you would get the chance to go somewhere so remote in a foreign country and be treated as one of their own. Living amongst a community who embraced us like family was overwhelming, they took me in like a son.

The village was one of the many communities in Nicaragua without access to a clean and sustainable water source. This meant that families, mostly women, spent hours every day collecting water from the river, which was contaminated and detrimental to their health. Often girls in the family are kept back to help their mothers with chores like this, which prevents them from attending school.

We worked hard on the project, together with the Matapalo community and to turn on the taps at the end and celebrate with them was very rewarding. To go from watching my host mum struggle in her daily life, carrying a 25 litre water can to the river numerous times a day to seeing her turn on the tap four metres away from her front door was incredible.

We also did a lot of work to raise awareness of gender equality issues which is a real issue in Nicaragua. We hosted children's activities which gave women time to get away and talk together, which sounds so simple but it's something they never get the time or opportunity to do. We also crossed language divides through shadow puppetry to show women's roles in the village which worked really well. I felt that this programme wasn't just about infrastructure, we had time to consider global issues and to help raise awareness and start discussions about other ways the community could find to strengthen its resources.

To be able to get that out of the project was amazing and I am really keen to stay involved with campaigning on International Women's Day and raising funds for Raleigh. All volunteers stayed in homestays. You stay with a family along with another volunteer, who you become close to as you are experiencing this unique thing together.

On the adventure phase of our expedition we did a trek which was so tough but so rewarding. We walked 250km, from one side of Costa Rica to the other. There was one day when we were stuck in the jungle, we had two compasses which were facing completely different directions, and we didn't know which one was right. It was about 4pm, dark was coming and we only had limited food and water as we were on our way to the next food drop. The decision was made that we had to stop, set up camp and get on with it and that is exactly what everyone did. It was the making of our group, no-one complained, everyone set up and looked after each other.

On our first day (16 days prior), we would have panicked, but we had been through so much already, everyone knew we could do it if we worked as a team. We slept it off and got moving again in the morning, we hadn't had breakfast and only had limited water. It was the lowest moment but on reflection was a moment of understanding of our capabilities as individuals and as a team too.

It really struck us that people across the world are constantly living within limited means and struggle to access food and water on a daily basis. We didn't realise that trek would give us this sense of understanding, however it really put things into perspective for all of us and made us think about the meaning of social justice.

All in all the trek was amazing, you fantasise about finishing it for 19 days and then you arrive on this beautiful deserted beach with the sun setting, it was pretty special. It was an unbelievable feeling of accomplishment and relief. It's the friends that you make, the views and the confidence you take from having completed an immensely challenging physical and mental challenge that make it all worthwhile.

Actually experiencing those things that you have watched documentaries on for years about a poor, rural community, to go there and live it and have an entire group of different nationalities all giving their opinions on the social issues was so interesting. It was a crucial part of the Raleigh experience, getting the volunteers to think about the wider influence of their actions. People from different parts of the world and from different backgrounds would also have different views on things, but to get people to understand those views and to give them the opportunity to speak up in an open forum was really beneficial.

Brilliant, fantastic, amazing, all adjectives which describe an unforgettable experience.

I will be going to Durham in September to study International Relations and I feel that through Raleigh I have had my eyes opened and it has definitely confirmed for me who I am and what I want to do. With my international relations degree I plan to either try and join the foreign office or to enter journalism.

For more information about Raleigh International, see their advert on page 178

Travellers Worldwide, 2A Caravelle House, 17-19 Goring Road, Worthing BN12 4AP UK
T: 01903 502 595
E: info@travellersworldwide.com   W: www.travellersworldwide.com

Travellers Worldwide is a Leading International Provider of Voluntary Placements & Work Experience Internships Overseas.

Established in 1994 and with a 20-year unparalleled record of safety, you can be confident that your placement will be the ideal environment to nurture your personal and professional development.

You will be following in the footsteps of thousands of like minded individuals to places where you will really make a difference and have an adventure of a lifetime.

Visit our site or contact us directly to discover our full range of opportunities (over 300 in 20 countries).

CONSERVATION | TEACHING | CARE | MUSIC | MARINE | SPORTS | LANGUAGES

International Volunteer HQ

What is the cost?

It varies hugely – some companies just expect you to pay for the air fare – others expect you to raise thousands of pounds for funding. It can be hard to combine raising money with studying for A levels or with work, but there are a lot of ways to do it.

As usual, the earlier you start, the easier it will be. The organisation that you go with should be able to give advice, but options include organising sponsored events, writing to companies or trusts asking for sponsorship, car boot sales, or even just getting a job and saving what you can.

If approached, many local newspapers will do a short article about your plan if it's interesting enough – but it's better to ask them during the quieter news spells, like the summer holiday months, when they'll be more likely to welcome an additional story.

The last resort is to go cap-in-hand to your parents, either for a loan or a gift, but this can be unsatisfying and they may simply not be able to afford it. If your parents or relatives do want to help, you could ask for useful items for Christmas or birthday presents – like a rucksack.

Career breakers will have different considerations. There's more on this in **Chapter 3 - Career breaks and older travellers**, but if you work for a large organisation it's worth asking whether they have any links to projects, or run their own charitable foundation, which might offer placements to employees.

What to expect

Placements range from a couple of weeks to a whole academic year, but most provide only free accommodation and food – a very few provide pocket money. You'll need to be resourceful, be able to teach, build, inspire confidence, communicate and share what you know. Physical and mental fitness, staying power and the ability to get on with people are essential.

blue ventures
beyond conservati

Join us on an unforgettable dive expedition in Madagascar or Belize!

As featured in:

Contribute to our rigorous marine conservation and community work and immerse yourself in stunning coral reefs whilst gaining scientific research skills, SCUBA diving qualifications, and knowledge of diverse cultures. You will be living in a beautiful tropical setting in eco huts overlooking the ocean and will come away with memories that last a lifetime.

For more details about our expeditions please visit www.blueventures.org, contact one of our team of advisers on +44 (0)20 7697 8598 or email info@blueventures.org

 facebook.com/blueventures

 @BlueVentures

> 66 Challenging, exciting, rewarding... an expeditio with Blue Ventures will change your life! 99
> **NICK HAYES**

> 66 My expedition was one of the most memorable and important experiences of my life. Your ideas are valued and your participation is appreciated. 99
> **MONIKA CALITZ**

Blue Ventures recent awards include:

 Member of

www.blueventures.org

my gap-year
Michaela

I went to Cambodia with The Leap for whom I now work, which is great as I get to keep on travelling! Travel is my passion and I love meeting new people from all over the world.

The day to day activities in Cambodia are pretty varied, from teaching English classes at a buddhist pagoda, to building classrooms at an orphanage, working with rescued elephants and building clean water wells for families who don't have access to clean drinking water. It's a really community based project, so a lot of the work is with the local people and kids, which is one thing I really loved about it.

I think the Cambodia project is really special because you are able to really immerse yourself in the local culture and although there's a language barrier with some of the locals, you're still able to forge friendships that you'll never forget. You work with local people on a daily basis from the ages of one right up to 60. The whole team are looked after by a wonderful Cambodian family, and if you are a foodie like me I think you'll find that part of the trip pretty special too.

Cambodia is a really interesting place and culturally its a world away from England, which is another reason why I love it, its exciting. Firstly I really love the way that people in Cambodia greet each other and say thank you, it's always done with your hands pressed together in a prayer position and with a bowed head - your hands are then lifted to a height depending on the amount of respect due to the person. For example if its a child, your hands are just in front of you but if its an elder, your hands will move more towards your face. Its important to remove your shoes before you enter any Cambodian home as a mark of respect. And if you meet a Buddhist monk you're not allowed to touch them. You should also try and point your feet away from them when sitting down to be polite.

In Cambodia they speak Khmer (pronounced Khmai), its a beautiful language which is written in symbols rather than letters. I found that some adults and teenagers spoke enough English to be able to have a great conversation. But its surprising how much you can get across with just hand actions and facial expressions. Actually when I was studying for my TEFL (Teaching English as a Foreign Language certificate) they said that it's sometimes easier to teach English in a classroom if you allow no local language to be spoken. But it's really fun to learn some Khmer and have a practice, if you manage to master it - tell me how!

For more information about The Leap, see their advert on page 174

my
gap-year
Emily Johnson

I spent five weeks volunteering on a medical project in the city of Guadalajara, Mexico with Global Volunteer Projects. I was working in the Green Cross, an emergency trauma clinic that provides urgent medical care ranging from cuts and scrapes to life threatening illnesses or injuries. I can honestly say my time spent there was probably one of the best experiences of my life.

On a regular basis I would take blood pressures, insert cannulas to start IV's, cast broken limbs, inject painkillers and clean, bandage and suture wounds. During my time there I literally saw everything including broken and dislocated bones, open wounds, heart attacks, burns, epileptic seizures and drug overdoses.

I would work Monday to Friday starting in the afternoons and leaving in the evening before it got dark. I would spend the day assisting the doctors and nurses treating any patients that came in. The great thing is that I would turn up to the start of my shift and have no idea what was going to come through the doors.

Easily the best thing about working at the Green Cross clinic was the opportunity of being able to do and achieve things that I would not be able to do in the UK. There are some moments that I will remember for a long time including a couple of occasions when we had patients that were so ill or injured that they required resuscitating and I assisted with their CPR.

If anyone is considering doing a medical project in Mexico, I cannot recommend it enough. You will gain invaluable experience, especially if you are considering a career in the medical world. Overall this project was exciting, interesting and challenging and I would do it all again in a heartbeat.

For more information about Global Volunteer Projects, see their advert on page 180

Blue Ventures

Are there ethical concerns?

The debate continues about the ethics of volunteering, and covers a variety of issues:

· Is it environmentally sustainable?

· Does it really benefit the people or is it creating a dependency culture?

· What's the 'benefit balance' between volunteer satisfaction and the community being helped?

Fair Trade Volunteering (**www.fairtradevolunteering.com**) has been created and established by leading volunteer organisations and advisors in the travel industry to enable volunteers to make a choice as to which volunteer experience they would like to have, and to give organisations wishing to provide FTV projects guidelines, help and support to be able to deliver them.

The 'volunteering industry' has in the past few years become just that – an industry, with different organisations giving different levels of importance to the benefit for the projects, the experience for the volunteer and the profit for the company. Just as the Fairtrade Foundation has helped the consumer to be able to make an informed decision when buying coffee, bananas and chocolate *etc*, Fair Trade Volunteering is looking to do the same for volunteering placements.

Here's what they told us: "Our belief is that short periods of volunteering can be positive, but only really if they are part of a longer partnership with the project, and combined with financial support above and beyond the volunteer's contribution, to ensure the work done can be continued throughout the year. Organisations that are approved by Fair Trade Volunteering not only ensure that the cost of the volunteer (and their work) is covered, but that there is also a financial premium given to the

OUTREACH
INTERNATIONAL

VOLUNTEER TO MAKE A DIFFERENCE AS PART OF YOUR GAP YEAR

FOR 17 YEARS WE HAVE BEEN PROVIDING RESPONSIBLE VOLUNTEERING PLACEMENTS IN COMMUNITY-LED PROJECTS.

- TEACHING
- WORKING WITH CHILDREN
- COMMUNITY SUPPORT
- WILDLIFE & CONSERVATION
- NGO SUPPORT
- HEALTHCARE

"IT'S AN ADVENTURE, A LEARNING EXPERIENCE AND FOR ME A ONCE IN A LIFETIME OPPORTUNITY. IF GIVEN THE CHANCE I WOULD GO BACK AND DO IT ALL AGAIN"

BETHANY, STUDENT, KENYA

WWW.OUTREACHINTERNATIONAL.CO.UK
VISIT OUR WEBSITE TO START YOUR MEANINGFUL ADVENTURE TODAY

CAMBODIA | COSTA RICA | ECUADOR | GALAPAGOS | KENYA | MEXICO | NEPAL | SRI LANKA | TANZANIA

Blue Ventures

project to ensure their work can be further supported above and beyond the work done by the volunteers.

"Added to this, they must also show a long-term partnership with their projects, ensuring that the work done by the volunteer and the funds being sent are part of a longer term set of objectives. This means a volunteer who is only able to commit to a short period at a project is able to see that their contribution, both financial and physical, is part of a bigger picture that is making a genuinely positive difference.

"At the end of the day, it is up to the consumer to decide. By buying non-Fairtrade coffee, you are not necessarily doing a bad thing, you are still helping to provide a living for the people who make it. If you do buy Fairtrade however, it is because you are willing to pay the premium which Fairtrade ensures for its workers. The same holds for Fair Trade Volunteering."

Tourism Concern, meanwhile, is an independent, non-industry based UK charity that fights exploitation in tourism. They believe that it is vitally important for volunteer organisations to demonstrate that they have attained a recognised level of responsibility in the way they recruit volunteers, find placements and manage the volunteering process, and they have developed the gap-year and International Volunteering Standard (GIVS). International Volunteering Organisations in the UK are now being assessed under GIVS and Tourism Concern advises you look for the GIVS kitemark in order to ensure that you sign up to worthwhile and rewarding placements.

ONARIS
AFRICA
PERSONAL. ETHICAL. MAGICAL.

Onaris Africa, 2 St Philip's Place, Birmingham B3 2RB UK
T: +44 (0)8438 866008
E: info@onarisafrica.org   W: www.onarisafrica.org

Onaris Africa is a not-for-profit social enterprise which began with one simple aim in mind, to create genuine and sustainable social change in Africa by facilitating high impact volunteer experiences.

We hold this at the core of everything we do. We believe that sharing time, skills and knowledge with communities in need, helps to balance inequalities, encourage understanding and makes a fairer world for everybody.

What makes Onaris special is that we deliver on our promise of impact and ensure that our volunteers have an ethical experience. Whilst volunteers often embark on their journey with the best intentions - lack of preparation, not understanding the host communities and unproductive management by their volunteer organisation can often lead to ineffective placements that lack sustainable impact.

Embarking on a volunteer experience is a big deal. Deciding on doing it right is an even bigger deal. We recognise that choosing the right organisation can make all the difference, not only to the host community, but also to your own sense of self-fulfilment.

That's why our placements in East Africa focus on development at a structural level. What use is it for you to spend weeks painting a school, if you have no experience as decorator and the locals could be paid to do a better job?

At Onaris Africa we do not see any value in cookie cutter-type volunteer experiences. We tailor make each placement, matching your skills and experience to the needs of the host organisation.

We do not find placements for volunteers, but find volunteers for placements. The community needs are at the heart of everything we do.

GIVS assesses organisations on eight key principles:

1. **Purpose**: achievable objectives that have been identified by host partners and communities.

2. Marketing: marketing and imagery that is consistent with good practice.

3. Recruitment: fair, consistent and transparent recruitment procedures.

4. Pre-placement Information: clear and accurate information on the sending organisation, their partners, programmes and volunteer placements.

5. Pre-placement training: appropriate preparation, training and induction.

6. Volunteer support: ongoing support appropriate to the placement and volunteer.

7. Risk Management: ensuring protection, safety and well being of volunteers and those they work with.

8. Monitoring & Evaluation: ongoing monitoring and evaluation in order to improve performance and ensure work remains relevant.

For more information go to **www.tourismconcern.org.uk**

Here are some easy steps to follow from Tourism Concern to help you be a more ethical traveller – and your experience will be richer as a result.

1. Your holiday, their home: your travel destination is a place where people live; people who may have different values and sensibilities to your own. Opening your mind to new cultures and traditions is part of the joy and adventure of travelling. Be respectful but don't be afraid to ask questions. Getting to know the local people is the best way of learning about a place.

2. Switch off and relax: whilst your visit may provide some economic benefits to local people, it can also use up scarce natural resources. Water is in short supply in many tourist destinations, and one tourist can use as much water in one day as 100 people in a developing country would in a year. Keep this in mind when using water or electricity on holiday.

3. Keep children smiling: it is best never to give anything directly to children (not even sweets) as they may think there is no need to go to school (and hassle other travellers). Donating to a local school, hospital or orphanage will have a lasting impact. Tragically more than one million children are sexually abused by tourists every year. Help protect children by telling your hotel manager if you see something suspicious.

4. Haggle with humour: try to keep your money in the local economy; eat in local restaurants, drink local beer or fruit juice rather than imported brands and pay a fair price when you're buying souvenirs and handicrafts. Bargaining can be great fun, so haggle with humour – but remember that if you bargain too hard, sheer poverty might make a craftsman accept a poor price just so that he can feed his family that day. Pay what something is worth to you.

5. Support Tourism Concern: Tourism Concern – 'the voice of ethical tourism' – is a UK charity that campaigns against exploitation in tourism and for fairly traded and ethical forms of tourism. The website has a wealth of information on action you can take to avoid guilt trips. **www.tourismconcern.org.uk**

kanaama interactive

Kanaama Interactive, 24a Princes Ave, N10 3LR UK
T: +44 (0)20 8883 9297
E: prue@kiuganda.org   W: www.kiuganda.org

Volunteers wanted! An opportunity awaits to explore life through a different lens and discover the difference you can make to a vibrant rural community.

KI is a committed, non-profit team facilitating volunteering in the sub-county of Kashare in south west Uganda. We particularly welcome experienced people on career breaks, sabbaticals or looking for a fresh challenge. You have an array of knowledge, life skills and experiences to pass on that are useful.

Staying in a comfortable house, volunteers enjoy a warm welcome and delicious food from family members of one of KI's directors, as well as first-hand insight into community life in the region.

KI works together with Kanaama Interactive Community Support (KICS), a small UK-registered charity (1132288) with its office in Kashare. Since 2008 KI volunteers have helped to build up work by KICS. This now reaches 2,000 beneficiaries and many more through women's microcredit, agricultural training, smokeless stoves and support for 60 orphans and vulnerable children. A literacy project has started, and plans are underway to make sanitary towels with girls to improve school attendance.

Volunteers have helped with teaching, IT skills and systems, documentation, case studies and scoping reports. The most requested volunteering is now in schools, especially with children from families without English – the gateway to secondary level. For unqualified vols, we offer a bank of materials for language work and activities, which we hope you will add to, guided and supported by an experienced local teacher. Ways you could help:

* Term-time in primary schools – English in small groups plus sports and social activities

* Holiday schemes in August and Dec/January – stories, plays, craft activities, sports, outings

* Classroom teaching in secondary schools – qualified teachers for at least a month

* KICS welcomes offers of capacity building for local staff and stakeholders by suitably qualified and experienced volunteers

You will find Kanaama heart-warming and transformative. Read our visitor blogs and reports! Week-end game-park and gorilla visits at a distance of four to five hours! Kanaama charges of £500 for a month negotiable for longer periods. For travel to Kanaama and local info see our Visitor's Guide under www.kiuganda.org/visit-kanaama/advice/.

International Volunteer HQ

Some other points worth emphasising

Big organisation or small specialist? You might feel safer going with a big voluntary organisation because they should be able to offer help in a nasty situation. Experience is certainly important where organisations are concerned. But often a small, specialist organisation is more knowledgeable about a country, a school or other destination.

Size and status have little bearing on competence. A charity can be more efficient than a commercial company. Conversely a commercial company can show more sensitivity than a charity.

There are few general rules – talk to someone who's been with the organisation you're interested in. Organisations vary as to how much back up they offer volunteers, from virtually holding your hand throughout your stay and even after you come back, to the 'sink or swim' method.

You need to know yourself if you're going to get the most out of your volunteering **gap**. If you feel patronised at the slightest hint of advice then you might get annoyed with too much interference from the organisation.

Though do bear in mind that they probably know more than you do about the placement, what sort of vaccinations you're going to need, what will be useful to take with you, and how to get the necessary visas and permits. Equally if you're shy or nervous it might be as well to go with an organisation that sends volunteers in pairs or groups. There's nothing wrong with either type of placement – it's about choosing what's right for you.

Talk to a few organisations before you decide which one to go with – and, probably even more useful, talk to some previous volunteers. They'll be able to tell you what it's really like; don't just ask them if they enjoyed it, get them to describe what they

did, what they liked and why, what they didn't like and what they'd do differently.

Remember, wherever you're sent, you can't count on much. Regardless of the organisation, you will be going to poor countries where the infrastructure and support services can be minimal – otherwise why would they need volunteers?

Expect to be adaptable. Regardless of the reputation of the voluntary work organisation you choose, or the competence of voluntary work coordinators in a particular country, it's about your skills and human qualities and those of the people you'll be with so there's bound to be an element of chance as to whether the school you are put in, for example, really values you or whether you get on with the family you stay with. It's worth checking first what training is given and what support there is in-country, but be aware that you may not get what you expect – you need to be adaptable and make the most of whatever situation you find yourself in.

Safety first

If you're going with a good organisation they shouldn't send you anywhere too dangerous – but situations change quickly and it's always worth finding out for yourself about where you're going.

Check out the Foreign Office's travel advice pages on **www.fco.gov.uk.** The Foreign Office site also has lots of advice on visas, insurance and other things that need to be sorted out before you go, and advice on what to do in an emergency abroad. There's much more on all this in **Chapter 1 – Tips For Travellers**.

Also, make sure you have proper insurance cover and that it is appropriate for where you're going, the length of time you'll be away and for any unexpected emergencies.

Please see the directory pages starting on page 325 for information on companies and organisations offering opportunities to volunteer abroad.

my gap-year
Toni Parker

When thinking about what travel I wanted to do as part of my gap-year I knew that wanted to help at a project with tigers. I spoke to Anne at Oyster Worldwide who recommended I go to LIONSROCK in South Africa, this really appealed to me. I was especially keen on this programme because it is run by a wildlife charity.

LIONSROCK is home to more than 100 rescued lions and tigers, as well as cheetah, leopards, wild dogs and caracals. As a volunteer I monitored the animals and made them enrichment activities every week. I helped with the feeding twice a week and cleared out the enclosures. I also witnessed some veterinary procedures and the transfer of lions to different enclosures within the sanctuary. As lions are social animals it is important to try and put them together into prides as many rescued lions arrive at LIONSROCK on their own, and many have been alone all their life.

Being so close to these magnificent creatures and knowing that you are contributing to their welfare and protection was the most rewarding part of my experience. They are all rescued animals and many have spent their entire lives in tiny, filthy, concrete floor cages, so LIONSROCK is a million times better for them. Most of the animals would not be able to survive in the wild due to their past circumstances so will live out the rest of their lives here.

This was the first time I had lived away from my parents, so I enjoyed the experience of cooking, shopping and travelling on my own for the first time. The experience allowed me to develop more confidence in my own abilities and be exposed to a different culture.

If you are thinking about doing something like this I would say just do it! I spent a lot of time dreaming of going on an adventure like this. Then one day I was enquiring about projects and the next day I was getting ready to pay the deposit and looking up flight times. Always be careful on the animal projects you choose to go to, especially ones that involve lions in South Africa. I was really happy with Oyster as I felt the projects were really focused on the welfare of the different animals.

For more information about Oyster Worldwide, see their advert on page 176

Learning abroad

Learning abroad

CESA Languages

While your gap-year will inevitably be about personal growth, because of all the new things you experience and see you could build on this by using it as an opportunity to combine living and studying abroad. This might not seem appealing if you've just 'escaped' from a period of intense study and exams, but consider this:

· The learning doesn't have to be goal-oriented or laden with exam stress, you could learn a new skill and gain a qualification.

· You could pursue an interest, hobby or passion you haven't had time for before.

· You'll be able to explore and enrich your knowledge in your own way, rather than following a curriculum.

· You could also find you've added another dimension to your CV.

· You'll meet like-minded folk and have a lot of fun.

These are some of the things you could do: learn a language in-country, do a sports instructor course, music or drama summer schools, explore art, music, culture and learn about conservation. If you're not jaded with study or are at a time of life when a postgraduate qualification would be useful, and a career break possible, you could go for an academic year abroad. Another option for those of you who want to try to earn while you travel is to do a TEFL course.

Here's a good link for courses abroad: **www.studyabroaddirectory.com**

visit: www.gap-year.com

An academic year abroad

A good way of getting to know a place and its people in depth is to spend a whole academic year at a foreign school, either in Europe, the USA, or further afield. One possibility is an academic year before university:

· French Lycée

· German Gymnasium

· School in Spain

· Spanish-speaking school in Argentina

The most relevant EU education and training programmes are Comenius, Erasmus and Leonardo. For more information see:

Comenius: **www.britishcouncil.org/comenius.htm**

Erasmus: **www.britishcouncil.org/erasmus**

Leonardo: **www.leonardo.org.uk**

A scheme called Europass provides trainees in any EU country with a 'Europewide record of achievement for periods of training undertaken outside the home member state'. So it's important to ask the school: "Is this course recognised for a Europass?"

University exchange

If you want to spend up to a year abroad at a European university as part of the European Union's Erasmus (European community Action Scheme for the Mobility of University Students) scheme, you'll need to have some working knowledge of the relevant language – so a gap-year could be the time to start, either studying overseas or in Britain. Information about Erasmus courses is usually given to students in their first year at university. To apply for Erasmus you must be an EU citizen. When you spend your time abroad, you continue to pay tuition fees or receive loans or grants as if you were at your university back home. For more information visit: **www.britishcouncil.org/erasmus**

The scheme is also open to teaching and non-teaching staff at higher education and HE/FE institutions, as long as your home higher education institution has a formal agreement with a partner in one of the eligible countries. It must also have an Erasmus University Charter awarded by the European Commission.

Postgraduate MA/visiting fellowship/exchange

Several universities in the UK have direct links to partnership programmes with others around the world, but if you want to widen your search, the Worldwide Universities Network (WUN) (**www.wun.ac.uk/about**) is a good place to start looking for exchange, overseas study and funding for research projects. It's a partnership of 16 research-led universities from Asia, Australia, Asia, Europe and North America.

WUN's Research Mobility Programme funds a period of study overseas, for senior postgraduates and junior faculty, to establish and cultivate research links at an institutional and individual level between the partners in Europe, North America, South-East Asia and Australia. It is also intended to encourage the personal and academic development of individuals early in their research careers.

American University, 4400 Massachusetts Avenue NW,
Washington DC 20016 USA
T: +1 202 885 1000
W: www.american.edu/spexs/augap

Spend a semester or summer learning and participating in community service in
Washington, DC and discover who you want to be. American University's International
Gap Program is designed for students who are ready to build a foundation for future
academic and career success and a better understanding of global issues.

"I decided to join the AU Gap Program because I wanted to combine a school that has
great academics, resources, and facilities, with a city teeming with bright minds and
exciting ideas. The AU Gap Program allowed me to take advantage of both."

-Howey Qiu, AU Gap student, Spring 2015

How it works: High school rising seniors or high school graduates can enroll in a
semester (either fall or spring) or a summer session. International students will have an
enriching service learning component in their gap plan all the while gaining the tools to
succeed in a college or university - in the U.S. or elsewhere.

Our Gap Program seminar classes are learning laboratories - taking full advantage
of Washington, DC. The classes are interactive sessions led by a professor who will
introduce you to local, national, and global experts. You will participate in site visits to
area nonprofit organizations, government agencies, and businesses.

The AU Gap experience will impact your understanding of world issues and possibly
guide your decision of what to study later at college.

You will live on the AU campus and have access to AU campus resources. In addition,
since this is an academic experiential learning program, you will have an AU transcript to
take with you for possible transfer to another college program.

SACI Florence

Arts and culture

Art

If you want to go to art school, or have already been, no matter which art form interests you, travelling and soaking up the atmosphere is a good way to learn more and give you ideas for your own work. It's also a great opportunity to add to your portfolio.

You don't have to be an art student or graduate to enjoy the beauty of art and artefacts produced by different cultures. Most courses listed in this guidebook are open to anyone who wants to explore the arts in a bit more depth.

For example, have a look at the courses offered by the following organisations:

Art History Abroad: **www.arthistoryabroad.com**

SACI Florence: **www.saci-florence.edu**

Culture

It's a cliché, but also true, that travel broadens the mind and you'll absorb much about the culture of the places you visit just by being there. However, if you want to develop your understanding in more depth, maybe learn a bit of the language and discover some of your chosen country's history, then you could go for the cultural component of some of the language courses listed in the directory.

Alternatively, you might like to try something like The John Hall Venice Course, which gives an insight into Western culture and achievements and features time spent in London, Venice, Florence and Rome. To find out more visit **www.johnhallvenice.com**.

Discover Civilisation with AHA

'Incomparable to any other gap year'

What? Inspiring journeys in Italy with expert tutors, seeing and discussing many of the world's greatest achievements in art, architecture and sculpture.

When? 6 week courses throughout the year and 2–4 week courses in the summer.

Where? Naples, Venice, Rome, Siena, Florence, Sicily and much more ...

Why? "I've just spoken to Rosie and I have never spoken to a happier girl. She gains so much from AHA and your life culture. I don't know how you do it, but you clearly have a magical way of finding the very best of tutors. Bravo!" Angela 2014

"I know that AHA has inspired me more in such a short time than my 14 years at school and I will be making every effort to return to Italy for many year and to try and recapture the magic and glory of our time. I feel incredibly lucky to have had such a breathtaking experience and made such firm frien both students and tutors. I really feel that AHA is incomparable to any other gap year and I genuine can't think of a better way to have spent mine."

Rosie, Early Summer Course 2014

ART HISTORY ABROAD
Tel: 01379 871800

www.arthistoryabroad.co

Design and fashion

Every year, when the new season's collections are shown on the world's fashion catwalks, it's clear that the designers have 'discovered' the fabrics, or decoration or style, of one region or another.

So for those with a passion for fashion a gap-year is a great opportunity to experience the originals for themselves. Wandering the streets in other countries, and absorbing the street style can be an inspiration.

Then there's the opportunity to snap up, at bargain prices, all kinds of beautiful fabrics that would cost a fortune back home.

But if you wanted to use part of your gap to find out more about fashion and design you could also join a fashion summer school in one of Europe's capitals, take a look at a few we've listed below:

IFA Paris Fashion School: **www.ifaparis.com**

Ecole supérieure d'art Françoise Conte: **www.fconte.com**

Paris American Academy: **www.saiprograms.com/paris/paa**

Pauline Fraisse Art & Culture: **www.paulinefraisse.com**

Or why not India? The country's National Institute of Fashion Technology in Delhi runs summer schools for fashion stylists – here's the link: **www.nift.ac.in**

215

MET Film School

Film, theatre and drama

If you're thinking of a short course in performing arts, the USA is one of the most obvious places to go – most famously the New York Film Academy, which has a very useful page for international students:

www.nyfa.edu/admissions/international_student.php

The Academy runs summer schools in London, Paris, Florence, Colombia, China, Japan and South Korea.

We also recommend Met Film School who run courses at their studios in Berlin, incorporating writing, producing, directing and editing.

You can find out more at: **www.metfilmschool.de**

For a wider search try: **www.filmschools.com**

Or how about New Zealand? Try: **www.drama.org.nz**

If you want dance as well, the world is your oyster. You can learn salsa in Delhi (as well as in South America) and the traditional Indian Kathak dance in the USA.

And then, of course, there's Bollywood. There are courses in film direction, cinematography, sound production and editing at the Film and Television Institutes of India, in Pune (south-west of Mumbai), which runs a number of courses for overseas students: **www.ftiindia.com**

John Hall Venice, c/o 9 Smeaton Road, SW18 5JJ UK
T: +44 (0)20 8871 4747
E: info@johnhallvenice.com   W: www.johnhallvenice.com

The John Hall Venice Course is an epic gap year experience and one that you will never forget. It is a nine-week introduction to some of the finest and most thought-provoking achievements in the Western world, from the classical past to today.

There are lectures and visits by a team of world-class experts and the course includes painting, sculpture, architecture, music, world cinema, literature and global issues. There are practical classes in studio life drawing and portraiture, as well as classes in photography, Italian language and cookery.

The course consists of a week in London, six weeks in Venice, a week in Florence and a week in Rome. The heart of the experience is Venice - to be in the historic and uniquely beautiful city of Venice, living more like a resident than a tourist, is a life-changing experience.

Students come from around the world - UK, America, Africa, Europe and Asia, creating a cosmopolitan collegiate atmosphere that leads to friendships and connections for life.

There are many privileged private visits throughout the course, including an unforgettable night visit to St.Mark's in Venice.

The John Hall Venice Course gives a foretaste of a university style of living and learning. It will leave you with not only some lifelong friendships, but also a totally new awareness of what European civilization is about, and with a seriously improved CV.

July 2016 sees the launch of the John Hall **New York** Course. Covering the art and culture of Manhattan especially modern and contemporary art, but also film, music and literature. Lectures, presentations and on-site visits with top quality experts; artists, collectors, curators and critics who will expose the history and cultural artistic output of those who lived and worked and still live and work in New York.

Music

Whether you're into classical or pop, world music or traditional, there are vibrant music scenes all over the world.

From the studios that have sprung up in Dakar, the West African capital of Senegal, to the club scenes of Europe, to more formal schools, check out the opportunities to combine your interest with travel and maybe learn to play an instrument, if you don't already, or another one if you do.

We've checked online for short music courses, since the UNESCO site no longer offers a directory, and although there are plenty out there, it's a case of searching by location.

Here's one for all UK summer schools, including music: **www.summer-schools.info**

Media and journalism

Although the print media has been suffering from the global recession there are, of course, other options.

You may want to get into media/journalism but you're not the only one, so do thousands of others and the competition is intense.

The skills you'll need could include media law, shorthand, knowledge of how local and national government works and, not least, the ability to construct an attention-grabbing story!

To get a job you may need to do more than gain a media studies degree or have on-the-job training in a newsroom. It's therefore, always a good idea to demonstrate your commitment and a gap is a good time to do this. You can try contacting your local paper for a work experience placement, though don't expect to be paid!

Plus, if you search the internet there are plenty of internships in newsrooms – many of them in India, where there's still a lot of attachment to local and national newspapers. We Googled 'journalism placements and internships' and found possibilities around the world. These websites may also be useful:

www.gorkanajobs.co.uk
www.tigweb.org/resources/opps
www.internews.org

Many large media organisations have Twitter pages specifically for jobs and internships, following those that interest you and keeping an eye out may be a good way to discover placements.

Photography

Travelling offers you the chance to develop your skills as a photographer – after all almost everyone takes pictures to remember their travels. But if you've always dreamed of turning professional, it's a chance to practice.

You could be innovative by contacting a local newspaper or magazine and asking if they'll let you accompany one of their photographers on assignments. You won't be paid but you'll learn a lot and it might give you pictures to add to your portfolio.

the gap-year guidebook 2016

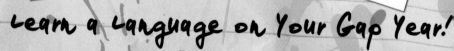

CESA Languages

Languages

You learn a language much more easily and quickly if you're living in the country where it's spoken, but there's more than one reason to learn a new language. There's more to a language than just words: most language courses will include local culture, history, geography, religion, customs and current affairs – as well as food and drink.

Gemma Rescorla, director of Live Languages Abroad, told us: "Learning a language abroad is a life skill by which you can reap so many rewards. Not only is it an amazing feeling to be able to communicate with someone in their own language, it also: improves your cultural awareness; enhances your learning ability, increases your confidence; helps your career prospects; gives you a taste for travel; and the opportunity to make life-long friends from all around the world."

Think laterally about where you want to study. Spanish is spoken in many countries around the world, so you could opt for a Spanish course in South America, rather than Spain, and then go travelling around the country, or learn Portuguese in Brazil, where it's the main language, or perhaps French in Canada.

Be aware though that if you learn a language outside its original country you may learn a particular dialect that is only spoken in a specific region of the country as a whole. It may even be considered inferior by some people (or not understood) elsewhere in the country.

CESA Languages offer some advice for gappers thinking about learning a language abroad: "Students have to be honest with themselves. What do they want from their time on a course? Just wanting to improve your language skills is too vague. Do you need to achieve a certain language level, in order to reach a specified goal? Is there a university course place you can obtain or career plan that you would be better suited for because of your language tuition and experience of living abroad? Make sure you concentrate on being able to prove your achievements when abroad. Knowing the outcomes you want from the course in advance will enhance your chances of onward success and maximise your opportunities once you've finished the programme."

Finding the right place to learn

Universities often have international summer school centres or courses for foreign students, or there's the popular network of British Institutes abroad. And there are hundreds (probably thousands) of independent language colleges to choose from, either directly or through a language course organiser or agency in the UK.

The advantage in dealing with a UK-based organisation is that, if something goes wrong, it is easier to get it sorted out under UK law.

Choosing a course provider

There are a number of companies that you can choose to take your language course with. Do make sure you get as much information from them as possible before making your choice.

Live Languages Abroad offer some excellent options. Their website can be found at: www.livelanguagesabroad.co.uk

These pages are also worth at look:

www.cesalanguages.com
www.esl.co.uk
www.europa-pages.co.uk – for language courses in European countries.
www.ialc.org (International Association of Language Centres)

Living with a family

If enrolling on a language course sounds too much like school, another way of learning a language is staying with a family as an au pair or tutor (giving, say, English or music lessons to children) and going to part-time classes locally.

John Hall Venice

SACI®
Studio
Art
Centers
International
Florence

SACI Florence, Palazzo dei Cartelloni, Via Sant'Antonino, 11, Firenze 50123 Italy
T: +1 (212) 248 7225
E: admissions@saci-florence.edu   W: www.saci-florence.edu

MAKE ART IN ITALY AT SACI!

SACI is a US accredited university program in Florence, Italy, for undergraduate and graduate students seeking studio art, design, and liberal arts instruction. Gap year students are welcome in **SACI**'s Academic Year Abroad, Academic Semester Abroad, and Summer Studies programs. Founded in 1975, **SACI** also offers MFA in Studio Art, MFA in Photography, MA in Art History, and Post-Baccalaureate Certificate Programs in Conservation or Studio Art. Classes meet in two Renaissance palazzi in the heart of Florence's historic center. **SACI** offers a wide range of studio and academic courses, all taught in English, as well as Italian language courses at all levels.

SACI's mission is to provide undergraduate and graduate students with a challenging, life-enhancing experience in the center of Florence in traditional and contemporary studio arts, design, conservation, and art history. Students directly access centuries of Italian culture through a wide range of courses of academic excellence. **SACI** engages in leading areas of research and exploration, interacts with the community through artistic and social programs, and prepares students to excel in their chosen field.

Alumni artists from many US partner schools, and from around the world, credit the supportive environment of the school and instructors with having a profound impact on their art careers.

Says one alumna, "SACI simultaneously created an environment of creativity while also providing excellent resources for me to make art. They established a situation that enabled critical developments in my art to manifest and grow."

Visit **www.saci-florence.edu** for a photo tour, application deadlines, scholarship details, alumni success stories, an online application, and more.

Blue Ventures

Language courses

Courses at language schools abroad can be divided into as many as ten different levels, ranging from tuition for the complete beginner to highly technical or specialised courses at postgraduate level. The usual classification of language classes, however, into 'beginner' or 'basic', 'intermediate' and 'advanced', works well. Within each of these levels there are usually subdivisions, especially in schools large enough to move students from one class to another with ease.

When you first phone a school from abroad or send in an application form, you should indicate how good your knowledge of the language is. You may be tested before being allocated your class, or you may be transferred from your original class to a lower or higher one, as soon as they find you are worse or better than expected.

Different schools will use different methods of teaching: if you know that you respond well to one style, check that is what your course offers. Foreign language lessons are often attended by a variety of nationalities, so they are almost always conducted in the language you are learning, forcing you to understand and respond without using English. In practice, however, most teachers can revert to English to explain a principle of grammar if a student is really stuck.

The smaller the class the better, though the quality of the teaching is most important – at more advanced levels, well-qualified graduate teachers should be available. Language schools and institutes show a mass of information, photographs and maps on their websites, so it's easy to find out if the school is near to places that interest you, whether it's in a city centre or near a coastal resort. The admissions staff should be happy to give you references from previous students.

In the directory, you'll find some of the organisations offering language opportunities to gappers, from formal tuition to 'soaking it up' while you live with a family. We've split the organisations according to the languages they offer: Arabic, Chinese, French, German, Greek, Indonesian, Italian, Japanese, Portuguese, Russian and Spanish. Here's a quick look at each:

225

BOOST
UBIS UNIVERSITY
YOUR INTERNATIONAL CAREER
IN EMERGING MARKETS

"Targeting a job in emerging markets is probably the best decision a young talented motived individual should take in today's challenging world"

Mike Johnson, Author of The WorldWide WorkPlace
: Solving the Global Talent Equation

The University of Business and International Studies (UBIS) is a Swiss Boutique University . Our goal is to prepare our graduates to advance forward in the international job market.

MBA EMERGING MARKET
(15 months)

The MBA Emerging Countries program is a perfect combination of highly experienced Faculty members from different regions of the world with an extensive blended learning approach (on-ground interactive sessions and online curriculum permanent access, short-track seminars from experts and company visits).

▸6 months in Geneva, headquarters of many multinationals and international organizations

▸6 months in Bangkok, the center of Asian Business.

▸4 months in an emerging market

ASEAN BUSINESS EXPERIENCE
(3 months)

This 3 months program intend to promote regional and global understanding about ASEAN countries from the perspective of ASEAN along with increasing the international community's awareness about ASEAN common historical, cultural, and regional identity, consequently providing a well balanced perspective in ASEAN studies

▸3 months program in Bangkok

▸International Faculty with extensive exposure to ASEAN

▸Field Visits and relevant experiential learning opportunities

▸Networking opportunities

6 ENTRY DATES PER YEAR
APPLY NOW
More details on www.ubis-geneva.ch

UBIS University of Business and International Studies
46 avenue Blanc - 1202 Geneva-Switzerland
info@ubis-geneva.ch - www.ubis-geneva.ch - +41(0)22 732 62 82

Astana - Baku - Bangkok - Cairo - Dubai - Geneva - Hangzhou - Ho Chi Minh City
Hong Kong - Libreville - London - Macau - Moscow - Paris - San Diego - Shanghai - Tbilisi
Tunis - Warsaw - Washington - Yangon

Arabic

Arabic is the language in which the *Qur'an* is written and, although there are translations into the local languages of Muslims around the world, there's also a lot of argument about the way they're translated. This has led to differences about what Islam means.

It's all a matter of interpretation of the roots of words and what's more there are two main versions of Arabic: Fousha – Modern Standard Arabic; and Aameya – Egyptian Colloquial Arabic.

Chinese

As Chinese enterprises become global, the language is becoming a popular choice in UK schools, with as many as 400 state schools now offering lessons.

There are two main dialects. Cantonese is the language of most Chinese people living abroad, from Singapore to Europe and the USA. Cantonese is also spoken widely in the Guangdong and Guangxi provinces of mainland China and in Hong Kong and Macau.

Mandarin is the official language of government, international relations and much education in China is undertaken in Mandarin. It is the more formal language and most students are advised to learn it.

Both languages are tonal (the same sound said in a different tone will change the meaning of a word) and therefore can be quite difficult for English speakers to learn. The different tonal pronunciation, vowels and consonants effectively turn Mandarin and Cantonese into two different languages, although both use the same written characters. There are many, many other Chinese dialects, including Hokkien, Hakka, Wu and Hui.

You can find course information at: **www.mandarinhouse.cn/chinesecourses.htm**

It has a choice of 12 different courses in Chinese, including one for expatriates, in Beijing or Shanghai.

the gap-year guidebook 2016

LoveTEFL

LoveTEFL, Woodside House, 261 Low Lane, Leeds LS18 5NY UK
T: +44 (0)113 829 3300
E: info@lovetefl.com   W: www.lovetefl.com

Travelling the world is obviously amazing, but travelling with TEFL is even better. TEFL or Teaching English as a Foreign Language is all about exploring the world whilst learning new skills and getting experience for real life. So while you're exploring ancient temples in Cambodia, walking the Great Wall in China or simply relaxing at the local beach, you'll also contribute to your career!

Who can teach English abroad?
...Anyone! If you can speak English, you can teach English. You don't even need any teaching experience!

So where do I start?
Our range of online TEFL courses give you all the skills and knowledge you need to teach English abroad. Each section covers the main TEFL essentials like classroom confidence building, lesson planning, employment advice and more.

Once you're TEFL qualified, it's time to start teaching and travelling! TEFL Internships offer you an immersive journey up to 6 months long, living, exploring and teaching in amazing bucket-list destinations. If you're look for something more travel focused, our adventure tours offer action-packed travel giving you up to 3 months of exploring, teaching and living to the max.

You'll join a group of like-minded travellers and take on the adventure with them. We offer in-country orientations and excursions, so you'll get a proper sense of the country you're in from the people know it best – the locals – and all the support you need.

What are you waiting for?
It's really easy to get started – all you need is the passion for travel and a taste for adventure.
Visit us online or give us a call on **+44 (0)113 829 3300** to find out more.

French

Languages have changed over time as they have been introduced to other parts of the world from their home countries and then developed in their own directions. Then there are the local dialects. French covers French as it's spoken in France, but then there's also Swiss French, Belgian French and Canadian French.

There's a busy French community in the UK, a large French Lycée in London and more than one teaching institute run by French nationals, so there are plenty of opportunities to carry on developing your French language skills when you return to the UK.

German

German has many very strong dialects (particularly in Austria, Switzerland and much of South Germany), and it is important to bear this in mind if you want to study German academically, or use it for business, in which case you may need to be learning and practising *Hochdeutsch* (standard German).

Many universities in Germany, Austria and Switzerland run summer language schools for foreign students.

Contact:

German Embassy
23 Belgrave Square
Cultural Department
London SW1X 8PZ
Tel: +44 (0) 20 7824 1300.

Their website has a section on studying in Germany: **www.london.diplo.de** There's also a lively German community in the UK and many courses run by the Goethe Institut (**www.goethe.de/ins/gb/lon/enindex.htm**). So, there are plenty of opportunities to carry on practising your German when you get back.

Greek

The thoughts of the great philosophers such as Socrates and Aristotle, upon whose ideas the foundations of western values were built, were written in ancient Greek.

Democracy, aristocracy, philosophy, pedagogy and psychology are just some of the many Greek terms that are part of our culture and language.

Modern Greek is spoken by ten million Greek citizens and by about seven million others spread around the world.

Indonesian

Based on the Malay trade dialect, Bahasa Indonesia is the national language of the Republic of Indonesia. In a country of more than 230 million people, who speak over 580 different dialects, having a national language makes communication easier, in much the same way as Hindi does in India.

There's no general greeting in Indonesian; there are different words specific to the time of day. But it's said to be an easy language to learn and Indonesia is such a popular backpacker destination it's likely to be worth making the effort. Here's a web link to get you started: **www.expat.or.id**

my gap-year
Rafaela Schoffman

My gap-year at SACI turned out to be far greater than I had ever expected. As an Israeli, after high school I went straight into the army and focused on my military service for the next two years. By the time I completed my service, I was eager to see the world and spent the following year and a half travelling.

It was during my three month stay in New Zealand that I began to explore options for what I would do after my travels. I didn't know what I wanted to study, where I wanted to live or what I wanted to do with the rest of my life. I remembered that someone had mentioned an international art school in Florence, and decided to look into it. Having studied at a high school for the arts in Jerusalem, I knew I was interested in this field, but I didn't know which medium or how to pursue it. Applying for a four year degree seemed like a huge commitment that I wasn't ready for.

The gap-year at SACI was the perfect solution. It gave me the opportunity to be exposed to different disciplines in fine arts, photography and design. There was an extremely rich array of classes to choose from, and outstanding and engaged teachers, my overall experience was both challenging and rewarding. This year prepared me in the best way possible, both personally and academically, to have the confidence to now pursue a higher degree in photography.

Thanks to this program, I had the time to explore the arts in a way I hadn't done before and to take a deeper look at myself. This year was crucial in helping me to discover the direction I really wanted in my life, to understand what truly motivated me, and with the tremendous support of my teachers to make the best decision for my professional future. I cannot express how much value I place on my gap-year experience.

For more information about SACI Florence, see their advert on page 224

Italian

Schools vary from the very large to very small, each with its own character and range of courses in Italian, Italian culture, history, art, cooking and other subjects. As in language schools across most of Europe, the language is often taught in the morning with extracurricular activities in the afternoon. If you want to do a course from March onwards it is advisable to get in touch with them at least two months in advance, as courses and accommodation get booked up early.

Most schools can fix you up with accommodation before your trip, either with a family, bed and breakfast, half-board, or even renting a studio or flat. If you're part of a small group, you might prefer to arrange accommodation yourself through a local property-letting agent, but this can be tricky unless you have someone on the spot to help.

Japanese

If you can get to the Japanese Embassy in London you can look up a comprehensive guide in its large library called Japanese Language Institutes (based in Japan). The library also has material on learning Japanese and stocks Japanese newspapers including the English-language *Japan Times*, which runs information on jobs in Japan.

There's information about studying in Japan on the embassy website, with guidance on the type of visa you will need if you want to teach English as a foreign language or do other types of work there.

Japanese Embassy, 101-104 Piccadilly, London W1J 7JT
Tel: +44 (0) 20 7465 6500
www.uk.emb-japan.go.jp/en/embassy

Portuguese

You don't have to go to Portugal to learn Portuguese – it's the main language of Brazil too, so if you're heading for Latin America on your gap, try:
www.esl.co.uk/en/learn-portuguese-in-brazil.htm

Russian

We suggest you check with the Foreign & Commonwealth Office before making any plans to travel to Russia to study.

That said, both ESL and Live Languages Abroad offers Russian language lessons in Russia:
www.livelanguagesabroad.co.uk/category/russian/russian-in-russia
www.esl.co.uk/en/learn-russian-in-russia.htm

Spanish

Spanish is the third most widespread language in the world after English and Mandarin Chinese. Over 400 million people in 23 countries are Spanish speakers – Mexico and all of Central and South America (except Brazil) designate Spanish as their official language.

Forms of Spanish can also be heard in Guinea, the Philippines and in Ceuta and Melilla in North Africa. But if you go to a language school inside or outside of Spain, you will

my gap-year
Ed Hands

Ed Hands set off to Italy on a six week trip with Art History Abroad.

With Art History Abroad your classroom is Italy and it couldn't be better: the food, the people, the nightlife, the attractions – the list is endless. It's amazing how every session reveals new ideas and ways of looking so that you never tire of travelling and learning about the country and all it has to offer.

Breath-taking moments become the norm with Art History Abroad. Going in spring and off-season, we were able to see the Sistine Chapel with barely anyone else there. A private night-time viewing of St Mark's Basilica, a guided visit of the Golden House of Nero and an evening of wine, champagne and olive oil tasting are just a few more examples of unique experiences we enjoyed. The timetable was balanced with ample free time, giving us the chance to explore on our own or simply relax and take advantage of being in Italy.

I loved how we were able to learn without the pressure of exams looming over us. This meant that each of us could take what we wanted from the course. Some, like me, had studied history of art at school; others were new to the subject. For me, Art History Abroad provided a foundation in aesthetics, art history, and a vast knowledge bank. I learnt more in six weeks with Art History Abroad than I did in two years studying art history at school.

The tutors are particularly special, not only are they super knowledgeable but they are young-hearted and become friends to all. They also make the whole trip run smoothly by organising our tickets, travel, accommodation, supper and queue jumping tickets; this allowed us to spend more time having fun.

On returning from a six week adventure, our group of 14 students all agreed that our time in Italy was the highlight of our gap-years. My words do not do justice to what a great time we had - it was perfect.

Perhaps this video captures it better than I can: www.youtube.com/watch?v=QnNCvGJ7THo

For more information about Art History Abroad, see their advert on page 214

John Hall Venice

probably be learning formal Castilian.

For information about universities and language courses, try:

Spanish Embassy, Education Department, 20 Draycott Place, London SW3 2RZ
Tel: +44 (0) 20 7727 2462
If you want to learn it in Latin America try:
www.expanish.com
www.spanish-language.org

Multi languages

There are companies offering courses in many different languages. When you're getting references, make sure they're not just for the company – but specifically for the country/course you're interested in.

TEFL

Recent research has revealed that within the next ten years roughly half the world will be using English, so there's never been a better time to do a TEFL course. Like having a sports instructors' certificate, a TEFL qualification is useful if you want to earn a little money for expenses on a gap and it's a passport that will get you into many countries around the world and in close contact with the people. For more information on getting a TEFL qualification go to **Chapter 5 - Working Abroad**.

Please see the directory pages starting on page 347 for information on companies and organisations offering opportunities for learning abroad.

233

my
gap-year
Trevor Biggs

When researching gap-year programmes, I realised that there are a lot of options out there. I searched the web for hours last summer, trying to find a program right for me; beneficially and financially. I knew I wanted to go to Berlin, Germany for about nine weeks, but given the choices, it was hard to settle on one. I found

CESA Languages Abroad through one of my many searches and within minutes of scanning their website I knew they were a top candidate. Not only could they set me up with a course in Berlin learning German, but I also found the option of indulging another passion of mine: snowboarding in the Austrian alps! I sent many questions to the staff at CESA and they always responded promptly, despite the six hour time difference. With the time for my trip fast approaching, I knew the right choice to make. CESA registered me in Berlin for six weeks and another two weeks in Kitzbühel, Austria.

I arrived in Berlin at the beginning of October for the first course. It took me a few weeks to get used to the language; speaking in German and thinking in English do not go hand in hand. But there is no better way to learn a language than to immerse oneself in it. CESA, at my request, set me up with a host mother in an apartment near the school, which happened to be in a trendy district of Berlin. Per our arrangement, I had my own room, and she provided breakfast. She was very helpful in describing things to do in the area and giving me tips about the city, but my host mother did not speak any English, which was helpful for me to really immerse myself in German! The only downside to learning German in a major city with millions of people is that English is heard and spoken almost anywhere. I found it best to try to speak German as much as possible and when a native asked me, "Is English better?", I resisted giving in. The more I pushed myself, the more I learned.

The classes are very helpful in the process. Regardless of one's German ability, the instructors speak their native language at all times. It may seem daunting at first, but after a week, I caught on very quickly and found it even more exciting to advance my knowledge of this language. In-class activities often included watching a German film, doing group projects, lots of conversation, researching German history and much more.

It was easy to make friends at the school. On my first full day, there was definitely the feeling of, "What am I doing here?" It was a little scary to be there alone. But, within my first week, I had met dozens of other students, my age or older, from all over the world, many of whom I still am in touch with. The school also organized weekend trips to German cities and sometimes outside the country, such as one trip I took, to Szczecin, Poland.

My stay in Kitzbühel was a contrasting experience but just as beneficial. The vibe in Kitzbühel is very much of a ski town, very relaxed, and felt completely different to Berlin (in a good way). The classes were based on conversation and we learned a lot about the history of Austria, and Kitzbühel as a medieval city. Our learning also expanded outside the classroom onto the ski slopes, which was my favorite part! There is nothing more beautiful and dramatic to see than the Alps covered in white, powdery snow. By the end of my stay, I had accumulated so much knowledge in this complicated language. The school in Berlin guarantees success in German, and CESA will help you get there. As I sat on the plane heading home to Boston, I relived my experiences and travels in the previous nine weeks. All of it went flawlessly, with much thanks and appreciation to CESA Languages Abroad. My time abroad was life changing; I believe every student should take a gap-year in another country after high school. The folks at CESA worked hard to make sure my experience was without worry and enjoyable. Bis nächstes mal!

For more information about CESA Languages Abroad, see their advert on page 216

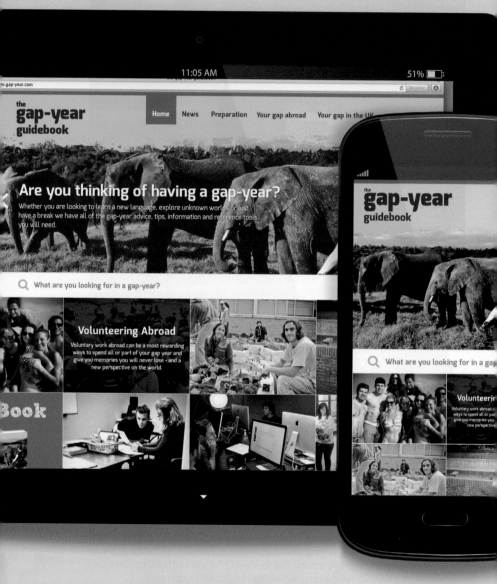

Welcome to the NEW gap-year website!

www.gap-year.com

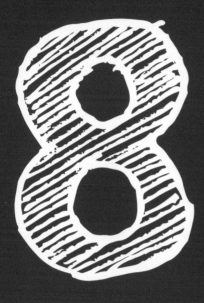

Sport

Sport

Travelling abroad doesn't mean that you have to stop playing the sports that you love – sports coaching projects are also a great way to give something back to a community on a gap-year or career break abroad. If you are looking to join a sports volunteer project, there are many different projects and destinations available.

Lots of companies offer you the chance to live, play, train and coach many different sports all over the world. Whether your chosen sport is football, cricket, rugby, netball, tennis, sailing or even polo, you can use your skills to enrich the lives of others by becoming a volunteer coach or use your time to improve your own skills for a career in your chosen sport.

And a sporting placement abroad can seriously boost your personal development – showing your commitment, teamwork and leadership skills to prospective employers. So whether you want to use your football skills to become a coach teaching children in South Africa, join a cricket club for the season in Australia, experience the challenge of playing rugby in New Zealand or learn how to sail and dive in Thailand, there is definitely a placement out there for you.

Anne Smellie, of Oyster Worldwide, told us: "Many people are involved in sports as part of their daily lifestyles, and this passion is increasingly becoming an important part of the gap-year.

"Making a difference and doing something important on a gap-year has always been key, and this is ever more so the case.

"Making a genuine contribution to lives of young kids in poorer countries, all whilst playing the sports that you love, is an experience that is second to none. It looks fantastic on your CV, gives you some real employability skills, surrounds you in another culture – and is a lot of fun."

Training to be an instructor

There are many options to consider, but three of the most popular and well-established areas for gap-year students are skiing, snowboarding and scuba diving

There are well-established routes for training as a professional and choices of courses tailored to gap-years. Specialist gap-year training companies will take care of all organisation and train you through national governing body sports coaching qualifications.

There are lots of options out there, with all the northern hemisphere courses running from December to March and the southern hemisphere's winter season, June to October.

The British Association of Snowsport Instructors (BASI) is the official UK organisation with responsibility for the training and grading of snowsports instructors and provides official BASI Gap 10-week courses through its licensed ski school providers, ICE and New Generation, that operate in the world's premier ski resorts – Val d'Isere, Courchevel, Meribel and La Tania.

238

visit: www.gap-year.com

Flying Fish

Once qualified as a level 2 ski instructor, your most likely first job would be teaching at a resort ski school. There is plenty of employment for newly qualified instructors, as long as you arrange your work visa in advance.

With a season's experience you are likely to be more in demand as an employee. Italy, Switzerland, Germany, Austria, Croatia, Spain, Andorra, USA, Canada and Japan are among the countries with established ski industries in the northern hemisphere.

Your opportunities in France can still be limited, though. The French snowsports authorities have traditionally made it difficult for non-French nationals to work in the Alps.

The biggest problem for a new instructor looking for a job is the lack of experience – and so any opportunity to gain experience should be grabbed with both hands.

A good idea may be to apply to ski schools for part-time work during the busy holiday weeks of Christmas/New Year, half-term and Easter. It may well lead to more work.

In the southern hemisphere New Zealand is famous for its mountains, but don't overlook Australia, which has several winter resorts too. Some schools in Australia and New Zealand employ new instructors from early season hiring clinics: you are expected to attend a short period of in-house training and if you measure up you get a job.

The instructor lifestyle is hard work but a lot of fun, although entry-level jobs are not too highly paid. On the plus side, you work on the sea or the slopes and have plenty of time to improve your own skills and enjoy your favourite sport.

Watersports instructor courses are also amongst the most popular for those interested in learning a new sport on their gap-year. In addition to diving, you will also find plenty of courses to qualify you to teach windsurfing, yachting and sailing, canoeing, kite surfing, kayaking – any activity on or around water, you can teach!

the gap-year guidebook 2016

my gap-year
Lucy

Whilst researching gap year options I came across the Oyster Worldwide ski instructor programme in Whistler Blackcomb and knew this was the perfect programme for me. I managed to convince my friend to come with me and it wasn't a problem that she wasn't a great skier as Oyster also run a childcare programme. This meant she could work in the ski school 'den' rather than out on the slopes.

Before embarking on our first independent adventure we had a pre-departure course in September where we got to meet everyone else coming to Whistler with us, find out tonnes of information and have an interview with the manager of Whistler Kids. This was a fantastic day to ask all of our questions and get us more excited for our season, if that was even possible!

After saying goodbye to our parents and Jon from Oyster at Heathrow we all flew to Vancouver, where we were met by Tory the local representative. She took us to our accommodation and helped us get set up for our life and work in Canada. We had monthly meet-ups with Tory for continued support throughout the season.

The first few weeks were all about training. We took our Level 1 instructor qualification which was tough but extremely helpful and boosted my skiing immensely. We then moved on to Whistler Kids training where we leant how to apply our new teaching knowledge to young children and how life in the ski school works. We covered all the essentials like the best games to play and where the cookies were kept!

My typical working day involved being assigned my class of up to five children aged 3 or 4 years old, normally who had never skied before. We spent our days on the magic carpet learning how to stop and turn. It is a long day for the kids which sometimes made for challenging work but frequent hot chocolate and story breaks kept them happy. Teaching the same class all week meant I got to see incredible improvements in their skiing; nothing beats the feeling of being able to ski down the mountain at the end of the week to the proud parents waiting in the village.

Living in such a spectacular ski resort for five months meant I spent most of my time off exploring the mountain with my new friends. We tried snowmobiling, zip-wiring and even a bungee jump – terrifying but brilliant fun!

Since my time in Whistler I have completed my degree at university and I still look back with such fond memories; I will never forget my amazing season in Whistler. The continued support from Oyster was fantastic and made the process run so smoothly and easily. I would highly recommend this programme to anyone with a passion for skiing and working with children.

For more information about Oyster Worldwide, see Chapter 6 - Volunteering Abroad

Blue Ventures

Getting a job

Once you have earned your qualification, the world is your oyster for potential jobs.

We asked Colin Tanner, from SITCo, for his advice. He told us: "In order to get a job then employers (ski schools) will be looking for a number of things – a qualification, personal skills and experience.

"Taking part in a course will help you towards the qualification. The personal skills are an important part of instructing, and your own personal skills will get developed through any course from experienced trainers. Actual teaching experience is the hard part to get, but once you get your foot in the door you will be away. Sometimes you just need to look to some of the smaller resorts for your first job, gain some experience and then apply to the big glamour resorts.

"When writing your CV, adapt it to the business; your people skills and your presentation will be as important as the number of A levels. Such things as previous experience of teaching the local kids football team *etc* will be good to show you are a 'people person'."

Make sure you write a good covering letter with your CV. This is particularly important for jobs overseas where an interview might not be practical.

If you do have an interview, make sure you ask about the things that matter to you – terms and conditions of service, accommodation, feeding arrangements, insurance and equipment requirements, days off, daily routine, annual leave, flights home, *etc*. And don't forget about money – how do you get paid? And what are the career opportunities? Is there a job specification available?

Our friends at Oyster point out that there are some ski instructor courses that you can sign up for, safe in the knowledge that you will have a guaranteed job for the rest of the season, such as their course in the Canadian resort of Whistler.

"On arrival, you take a four-week course to gain your CSIA Level 1 instructor qualification and then begin working for Whistler Kids as an instructor for the rest of the season," they told us.

"This is not any old job, it's a job that comes with enormous responsibility – looking after other people's children on a mountain! This not helps with your own personal development but also shows future employers a lot about you as well."

For more information on this course, have a look at:

www.oysterworldwide.com/projects/ski-season/

Work permits are snapped up very quickly though, so make sure you apply 12 months in advance!

Volunteering as a sports coach

There are hundreds of sports-based volunteer programmes available, from coaching cricket to underprivileged children in India to coaching football in inner cities in the UK.

Gap-years can be spent doing practically every sport you can think of, from hockey to netball and from basketball to football. There's also a range of countries you can go to. The benefits are obvious, says Anne Smellie of Oyster Worldwide:

"You can coach your favourite sports, from football to rugby, from netball to hockey and from cricket to swimming to deserving kids in some of the world's poorest areas. We all saw the documentaries on television during the 2014 World Cup about the amazing sports ventures that people are involved in in the favelas in Brazil - and how much sport can make a difference.

243

my
gap-year
Hannah Rowley

Arriving in Belfast for the tall ships festival was truly amazing, 52 ships moored around the docks and 20,000 well-wishers make such a fantastic sight! I was there to board Lord Nelson, one of the Jubilee Sailing Trust's unique tall ships that enables people of all physical abilities to experience a sailing adventure.

We were headed for Aalesund in Norway for an exciting voyage across the North Sea. Leaving was hard for me as I hadn't been away from home for so long before, but I couldn't wait for the adventure we were embarking on.

During the voyage I was really pushed out of my comfort zone and did things I never imagined I could do. From going on watch with people I'd never met before, to climbing aloft (I'm terrified of heights!). I was amazed by the challenges I overcame. I couldn't have done it without my friends and the crew. And not forgetting my buddy Nicola who inspired me so much; despite living with chronic pain she's achieved so much and also climbed aloft during the voyage, a dream she'd had for many years but never been able to do.

Arriving in Norway was amazing, especially taking part in the crew party and parade! Although it was somewhat bittersweet as I knew I'd soon have to leave my new friends and new home, and not forgetting the fantastic food we were treated to everyday!

It really was an experience I'd never forget. It enabled me to grow my confidence and I learnt so much about people from different backgrounds. I'd developed such strong bonds with everyone, and knew I'd come away missing them very much. So much in fact, that I'm already looking to book my next voyage!

For more information about Jubilee Sailing Trust, see their advert on page 246

"These kids do not have the opportunity to enjoy sports in an environment that we are used to here – and they are desperate for your help. As well as giving them an environment in which to play and learn games, they also learn motivation, team work and enthusiasm which is tough to get elsewhere."

As a sports-coaching volunteer, you will have the opportunity to help build communities through sport. For example, in working with a local football academy in Ghana, you will be able to establish relationships with young players who often have a fantastic talent and profound love of the game – but have been unable to progress because of a lack of physical training, emotional guidance and financial support. Giving them the opportunity to develop both their skills and their character can be a life-changing experience. Even without formal coaching qualifications, you can offer them constructive advice and new ideas on tactics, skills and their mental approach to training and competition, simply by arriving with enthusiasm, imagination and a general understanding of the game.

Development may not simply be about coaching. It may also involve education to understand how and why their ideas count, perhaps even some time as an English language teacher. On the best placements, you'll find yourself contributing to community development, in sport and beyond.

"It is hard to put into words how moving it is to teach these kids, who have so very little, the enjoyment of sports," Anne says.

"To see them progress with each session is an amazing experience, and you will work through that with them; from the frustration of not understanding something the first time, to the joy of being able to learn a new trick or a skill. These sports sessions give each child a moment of happiness and release, which is one of the greatest things that you could give someone."

The attributes you need depend on the activity you go for. If it involves teaching kids, you'll obviously need to have empathy with children, and if it involves a lot of hardcore activity, you'll need to be reasonably fit and resilient.

Oyster Worldwide

245

Experience a life-changing gap year experience on-board our tall ships!

We're a unique international charity with a mission to provide lifechanging experiences to people of all abilities, ages and backgrounds through the challenge and adventure of tall ship sailing. Over the last 35 years, we've welcomed over 45,000 crew members aboard our two globally unique, custom built tall ships with over half having some form of physical disability, including 5,000 wheelchair users. We change lives by improving self-esteem, building confidence, and providing fantastic leadership and life skills.

See the world
Dip your toes into the crystal blue waters of Fiji or enjoy an epic voyage through the Panama Canal!

Meet new people
Join one of our voyages and meet lots of new people from all over the world, of all ages, backgrounds and abilities.

Learn key skills
Life on-board our tall ships can be tough, but it'll give you skills you can use for life!

Boost your C.V
Travelling the world whilst on-board a Jubilee Sailing Trust tall ship is sure to shine bright on your C.V!

JUBILEE SAILING TRUST
changing lives

See the world on-board our unique tall ships

Discover more at www.jst.org.uk or call our team on +44 (0)23 8042 6849

Even if the sport has nothing to do with your future career path, it will boost your CV. Better still, if in an interview you can make an energetic case for why you did it, it will make you stand out above others who have sat around on their bums in the summer. It can only impress a future employer.

In the developing world, sport is often more than just competition or idle pastime. Often sport can have a real impact at the heart of communities, and play a pivotal role in the health and prosperity of the people.

Playing sport

More and more people are looking to take a sports gap-year with a purpose, so they are using their time out to play a season of sport abroad: for example cricket in Australia, or rugby in New Zealand or South Africa.

Placements on these 'academy programmes' will usually mean you are matched with a club abroad at a suitable level for your standard, for whom you play at the weekends whilst perfecting your game throughout the week with coaching, fitness training and sports psychology from local coaches.

You may be set a specific training regime to stick to, which might include things like:

· Gym fitness work and flexibility training.

· Sport-specific fitness training.

· One-on-one sessions to develop specific skills.

· Video analysis.

· Group training sessions with other academy players.

· Club practice sessions.

· Sessions with players of a higher standard, perhaps even professionals.

247

my gap-year
James Furnell

19-year-old James Furnell from Chepstow spent his gap year on the beach, getting paid to windsurf.

After windsurfing on holiday I thought it would be fun to become an instructor during my gap year. The Flying Fish course in Sydney was particularly appealing as it gave me the chance to do much more than just windsurf.

I had about four weeks' windsurfing experience when I joined the course, although several people in my group had never windsurfed before and still passed. It doesn't matter if you don't have any experience, although I would recommend you try the sport first to make sure you like it!

Windsurfing around Sydney Harbour was amazing. Learning to drive a powerboat past the Sydney Opera House and under Sydney Harbour Bridge and then having lunch opposite the Opera House on our own beach are moments I don't think I will ever forget.

Obviously the qualification was valuable to my CV and employability but the experience of windsurfing and surfing every day with a brilliant group of people in one of the greatest cities in the world has to really be the most valuable thing I gained.

After I qualified, I applied for a job through the Flying Fish website, and immediately received an email from Mark Warner asking me to come to an interview. I was offered the job as a windsurfing instructor and given a choice of where I wanted to go.

Having spent a brilliant summer in Greece, I have come back to the UK to read Economics at the University of Birmingham.

Next summer I plan to work in Egypt or Vass as a windsurfing instructor - or start an internship in the city. I think the internship may have to wait for another year!

For more information about Flying Fish, see their advert on page 242

Of course, you don't have to be looking at improving your skills to a semi-professional standard. You can also use your gap-year to take up a completely new sport. Perhaps you are interested in learning jiu-jitsu in Brazil, or polo in Argentina – you can certainly find placements to cover most sports in a huge range of countries.

Xtreme sport

Taking a gap-year gives you a once in a lifetime opportunity to do something amazing – the things that you just can't do at home and are likely to never forget. To some adventurous types, this means really exciting stuff, activities and adventures that get the butterflies going and gives you very sweaty palms.

There are companies that organise adrenaline-pumping activities in various locations around the world. These include adventures that really test your metal on a gap-year can have positive consequences when you return home.

That could mean bungee jumping or skydiving, scuba diving, swimming with whalesharks in Thailand or learning to surf in Australia. It would certainly pay to book before you go – you can organise things in-country but why take the chance of missing out? Also bear in mind that such activities are expensive - so make sure you have planned your budget in advance.

There is also merit in the idea of taking a qualification in an extreme sport – which might even help you stay for longer in certain countries.

See the directory pages starting on page 365 for information on companies and organisations offering gap-year opportunities

my
gap-year
Sean Francis

Having had no experience as a scuba diver, I was concerned I would be a slow learner and be of little use to Blue Ventures and their conservation work in Madagascar. Blue Ventures' well trained and patient dive instructors made me feel at ease taking my first breaths underwater. Even if I felt a little shaky in the beginning, I ended up diving an average of twice a day, five days a week. Partway through my expedition, I felt like I had been born to live in the water. As for the field scientists, they were remarkable in their ability to help me memorize and identify the corals, fish, and invertebrates in the ocean. By the end of my expedition, I could comfortably and confidently identify the vast majority of the marine life.

It is not all work and no play while on the expedition; there was plenty of time to explore the village and see the unique Vezo people. These genial people greeted me with smiles and their welcome 'Salama'. Children run through the streets and jump in the water, laughing and playing without a care in the world. Adults dutifully work and sell their wares on the main street but are eager to share their world with volunteers. There were also many opportunities to sail to nearby islands, explore Baobab forests, and visit other villages along the coast. Rarely would other volunteers find me resting in the hammock.

Blue Ventures attracts a full spectrum of people. However, within a few hours of meeting, we all had become colleagues, days later we were friends, and by that sad day at end of the journey we were family. This is a trip of a lifetime that you will not want to miss.

For more information about Blue Ventures, see Chapter 6 - Volunteering Abroad

Working in
the UK

Working in the UK

Why work on a year out?

If you're not working to raise money for gap travel and you've just finished school or university, you might want a break from study and take a deep breath or two for a while. But even though work doesn't seem too appealing, just try going through the complex claiming procedure for the Jobseekers' Allowance and then living on it for a few weeks, and you'll soon see that working has its advantages.

But there are plenty of much better reasons to use a gap for work:

Saving money for university

Going to university is an expensive thing to do. Today, the vast majority of graduates are heavily in debt and this burden will be with them for many years to come.

Graduate debt is rising sharply as temporary jobs dry up and tuition fees, rent and travel costs increase.

Studies suggest students typically spend £5000 a year on living expenses, including nearly £2000 on rent, £750 on bills, £700 on groceries, £700 on socialising, £400 on travel and £500 on books, equipment and field trips.

With tuition fees at £9000 a year, total debt for a three-year course could break the £50,000 barrier.

Even so, earning just a little bit now could really help your bank balance in the future.

Showing commitment

If you're attracted to a career in popular professions like the media, medicine and law, which are incredibly competitive and hard to get into, it could well prove necessary to grab any experience you can, paid or unpaid. It might make all the difference down the line when you have to prove to a potential employer that you really are committed.

Work experience

Another consideration is the frequency with which people applying for jobs report being rejected at interview 'because of a lack of work experience'. A gap is a great time to build up an initial experience of work culture as well as getting a foot in the door and getting recognised; in fact many students go back to the same firms after graduation.

Not sure what you want to do?

If your degree left you with several possible options and you couldn't face the university final year/graduate 'milk round' or you're undecided what career direction you want to head in, then a gap could be a great time to try out different jobs and to get a feel for what you might want to do in the future.

Whatever your reasons for working during a gap, you should start looking early to avoid disappointment.

visit: www.gap-year.com

Writing a CV

Fashions change in laying out a CV and in which order you arrange the various sections.

The advice is that a CV should be no more than two A4 pages and also that it should be tailored to the sector you're applying for.

The thing to remember is that employers are busy people, so they won't have time to read many pages, especially if they're trying to create a shortlist of maybe six interviewees from more than 100 applications for just one job.

If you're at the start of your working life, there's a limit to how much tailoring you can do. A good tip is to put a short summary of your skills, and experience to date, at the top so the recruiter knows what you can do. It can either be a bullet point list or a short paragraph, but remember that it's essentially your sales pitch explaining why you're useful to the company. It should only be a short summary of what's contained in the sections that follow.

There are a number of online CV-writing advice sites and templates that can help you, but do check for any fees before you start.

Here's a selection:
https://nationalcareersservice.direct.gov.uk/advice/getajob/cvs/Pages/default.aspx
www.alec.co.uk/cvtips
www.soon.org.uk/cvpage.htm

Here's a list of headings for the details your CV should include:

· Personal details: name, address, phone and email. You do not have to include gender, age, date of birth, marital details or nationality nor send a photograph, in fact some employers actively discourage photos for fear of being accused of bias in selecting people for interview.

253

DO YOU LOVE THE OUTDOORS, HAVE A PASSION FOR ADVENTURE AND WANT TO TRAIN AS AN INSTRUCTO

Rock UK is a Christian charity, passionate about developing young people, bringing adventure into learning & using the outdoors to transform lives

- Learn new skills whilst working with children & young people in the outdoors
- 3 months of intensive, action-packed training, developing your skills, knowlec & understanding in the core areas of Faith, Learning & Adventure at our Scottish Centre
- A further 9 - 10 month placement at one of our 4 centres across the UK
- Training, accommodation and a weekly allowance provided
- Develop your own support network
- Train for nationally recognised qualifications in outdoor activities
- Huge opportunities for personal development within a supportive team

The Rock UK Gap Year trainee instructor role is subject to an Occupational Requirem that successful applicants should be practising Christians

FIND OUT MORE:

Call - 01933 654103   Email - job.enquiry@rockuk.org   www.rockuk.org

 RockUKAdventures   @rockukadventure

Faith - Learning - Adventure - Instructing - Team - Servi

- Short skills paragraph or key skills bullet points (see above).

- Work experience and skills: in order with most recent first. You can include part-time working that you've combined with education, as well as any voluntary work you've done, but if neither is directly within the job sector you're applying for, you need to focus on the transferable skills you got from it *eg* familiarity with office routines, record keeping, filing, if you've been in an office, or people skills if you worked in a shop.

- Achievements: have you been on any committees? (student council?), organised any events or fundraisers? Again, concentrate on what you learned from it, such as organisational skills, persuading companies to donate prizes for a raffle, planning catering and refreshments.

- Other skills: such as the Duke of Edinburgh's Award Scheme, workshops you've attended, hobbies *etc*.

- Education: again most recent first, with subjects studied and grades.

- References: you usually need two, one of them a recent employer, the other from school or university, though on a CV you only need to say 'references can be supplied'.

Getting the job

How do you get that first job with no prior experience? What can you offer?

The key is creativity. Show the company you're applying to that you can offer them something that nobody else can and do this by giving them an example. Be creative: If you're applying to an advertising firm, for instance, then mock up some adverts to show them.

Want to go into journalism? Write some sample articles and send them to local newspapers. Write to the editor and ask whether you could volunteer to help out in the newsroom to get a feel for the environment and the skills you'll need – a kind of

my gap-year
Shanee Wise

Shanee Wise travelled to the UK from Australia and joined PGL as an outdoor activity instructor.

I found out about PGL while working at a hotel in Scotland. The people I was travelling with told me that PGL was an amazing experience. I wanted to work in the outdoors with kids, learn new skills and meet new people.

At PGL I have learned how to work with kids, run activity sessions, including climbing and abseiling, and how to speak in front of groups of children. I have gained so much confidence since starting my job as an activity instructor.

As well as the job itself, one of the best things about living at a PGL centre is the social life, and in my free time I get to exercise, research my future travels, and see the surrounding area.

Working for PGL is a great experience and I would recommend it to anyone. I'm going back to Australia in a few months time and am thinking about applying to work for PGL in Australia!

For more information about PGL Travel Ltd, see Chapter 5 - Working Abroad

extended work experience to add to what you should have had via school.

You could try this with companies in other fields you're interested in. Be proactive and persevere. It will show you have initiative and commitment and whatever your eventual career it will also help you to learn the basics of acting professionally in a professional environment.

Do the research: Whatever your chosen field, find out about the company and show your knowledge about the industry. If you are going for an industry, such as medicine or law, then showing that you are more than competent and willing is all that you can really do. Saying this, you have to make sure that you stick out from other applicants.

Contacts

In the directory of this guidebook we list some companies that specifically employ gap-year students or offer graduate opportunities. But take this as a starting point – the tip of the iceberg – there are hundreds of other companies out there waiting to be impressed by you.

Research is crucial. Tailor your approach towards that specific company and never just expect to get a job; you have to work at it. The general rule is that nobody will call you back – be the one who gets in contact with them.

Job surfing

You don't get the personal touch from a website that you do by going into a local branch and getting advice, or registering face-to-face, but recruitment websites are really useful if you know what you want to do and you have a 'skills profile' that one of their customers is looking for. Some of them are aimed at graduates and students, others at a general audience, others at specific areas of work (IT, for example).

Here are a few to start with:

Student summer jobs

www.activate.co.uk

(This one contains gap-jobs, summer jobs, internships and jobs for new graduates.)

Graduate careers:

www.milkround.com

jobs.guardian.co.uk

General vacancies:

www.reed.co.uk
www.jobsite.co.uk
www.monster.com
www.fish4jobs.co.uk
www.gumtree.com

Technology specialists:

www.agencycentral.co.uk/jobsites/IT.htm

Finance:

www.exec-appointments.com

On spec

If you can't find what you're looking for by using contacts, advertisements, agencies or the internet there is always DIY job hunting. You can walk into shops and restaurants to ask about casual work or use a phone directory (*eg Yellow Pages*) to phone businesses (art galleries, department stores, zoos...) and ask what is available.

Ring up, ask to speak to the personnel or HR manager and ask if and when they might have jobs available and how you should apply. If they ask you to write in, you can do so after the call. If you go in, make sure you look smart.

Remember, opportunities in the big professional firms are not always well publicised.

Temporary jobs (except agency-filled ones) are often filled by personal contact. If you have a burning desire to work for an architects' or lawyers' firm, for example, and you find nothing advertised, you could try making a list and phoning to ask if work is available.

Think about people you might already know in different work environments and ask around for what's available.

Banking: approach local branches for work experience. Also, try: **www.hays.com**

Education: most educational work experience is tied in with travelling abroad, to places like Africa or Asia, mostly to teach English. However, there are ways of gaining experience back home in England.

A very popular way is to see if the school that you have just left would like classroom helpers, or perhaps they need help in teaching a younger sports team. The key to this is to ask around and see what might be available.

But remember, for any work with children you will have to have a DBS (Disclosure and Barring Service) check. These were previously known as CRB (Criminal Records Bureau) checks. For more information, see: **www.gov.uk/disclosure-barring-service-check**

As well as straight teaching, any experience with children can be very useful, so try looking at camps and sports teams that may need help – there are a few contacts for camps within the Seasonal Work section.

Legal and medical: it's well known that studying for these two professions is lengthy and rigorous, so any amount of work experience could prove very useful. There's plenty available, but lots of competition for the places so you need to start looking early.

Nearly all NHS hospitals look for volunteer staff. So, if you can't find a worthwhile paid job, just contact the HR manager at your local hospital.

Try also: **www.jobs.nhs.uk** (for all NHS jobs)
www.lawgazettejobs.co.uk (for law jobs, including trainee positions)

Media, publishing and advertising: working on television or the radio is a favourite and it is no surprise that, because of this, the media is one of the hardest industries to break into.

Work experience is highly recommended. Many companies are very willing to try out gap-year students as trainees, as raw talent is such a limited commodity they want to nurture it as much as possible – plus it's cheap.

There are many websites dedicated to media jobs, but a good place to look for publishing vacancies is **www.thebookseller.com**

Theatre: many theatres provide work experience for gap-year students, so it's definitely worthwhile contacting your nearby production company. This industry recognises creativity and application probably more than any other, so starting out early and fiercely is the only way to do it.

Try also: **www.thestage.co.uk/recruitment**

Internships

Graduates cannot rely on the safety net of the traditional internship or graduate job this year. A survey by the Higher Education Statistics Agency last year found that nearly one in 10 students were believed to be unemployed six months after graduating from UK universities. Applicants for jobs are expected to have more skills, better grades and some form of industry experience as a minimum. In such turbulent times it is essential to make your CV stand out and rise above the competition of the near 400,000 graduates leaving the UK's 168 universities every year.

Check out **www.enternships.com** for ideas about some of the opportunities that are out there.

There's also some good information at: **www.allaboutcareers.com/careers-advice/internships**

Interviews

Once your persistence has got you an interview, you need to impress your potential employers.

Attitude – confidence and knowledge are probably top of the list for employers, so that is what you must portray, even if you're a bag of nerves and haven't got a clue. They want to know you're committed.

the gap-year guidebook 2016

Dress – make sure you are dressed appropriately (cover tattoos, remove nose piercings *etc*, don't show too much flesh, have clean and brushed hair – all the stuff that your teachers/parents tell you and really annoys you). If you're going for a creative job (advertising, art, *etc*) then you can probably be a little more casual – when you phone the secretary to confirm your interview time and venue, you can ask whether you'll be expected to dress formally. Alternatively, you could go to the company's offices around lunchtime (usually 1pm) and have a look at how people coming out are dressed.

Manner – stand straight; keep eye contact with the interviewer and smile. Be positive about yourself – don't lie, but focus on your good points rather than your bad ones.

Be well prepared to answer the question: "So, why do you want this job?" Remember they'll want to know you're keen, interested in what they do and what benefit you think you can bring to their company.

Gap-year specialists

If you would like to get a work placement from a gap-year specialist, the contacts listed in the directory sections in this guidebook are a good starting point for organisations to approach.

Another option is the Year Out Group, the voluntary association of gap specialists formed to promote the concept and benefits of well-structured year out programmes and to help people select suitable and worthwhile projects. The group's member organisations are listed on their website and provide a wide range of year out placements in the UK and overseas, including structured work placements.

Year Out Group members are expected to put potential clients and their parents in contact with those who have recently returned. They consider it important that these references are taken up at least by telephone and, where possible, by meeting face-to-face. See **www.yearoutgroup.org**

Gap-year employers

In the directory we've listed companies that either have specific gap-year employment policies or ones that we think are worth contacting. We've split them into three groups: festivals, seasonal work and graduate opportunities and work experience.

This isn't a comprehensive list, so it's still worth checking the internet and your local companies (in the *Yellow Pages*, for example).

Festivals

Whether musical, literary or dramatic, there are all kinds of festivals taking place up and down the country every year. You need to apply as early as possible, as there aren't that many placements. Satellite organisations spring up around core festivals; so if you are unsuccessful at first, try to be transferred to another department. The work can be paid or on a voluntary basis. Short-term work, including catering and stewarding, is available mainly during the summer. Recruitment often starts on a local level, so check the local papers and recruitment agencies.

It's also worth having a look at this site: **www.festaff.co.uk/jobs-at-festivals**

visit: www.gap-year.com

Seasonal and temporary work

A great way to make some quick cash, either to save up for travelling or to spend at home, is seasonal work. There are always extra short-term jobs going at Christmas: in the Post Office sorting office or in local shops. In the summer there's fruit or vegetable picking for example. There's a website that links farms in the UK and worldwide with students looking for holiday work: **www.pickingjobs.com**

Another option, if you have reasonable IT skills, is to temp in an office. July and August are good months for this too, when permanent staff are on holiday. You can register with local job agencies, which will almost certainly want to do a simple test of your skills. Temping is also a great idea if you're not at all sure what sector you want to work in – it's a good chance to find out about different types of work.

Pay, tax and National Insurance

You can expect to be paid in cash for casual labour, by cheque (weekly or monthly) in a small company and by bank transfer in a large one. Always keep the payslip that goes with your pay, along with your own records of what you earn (including payments for casual labour) during the tax year: from 6 April one year to 5 April the next. You need to ask your employer for a P46 form when you start your first job and a P45 form when you leave (which you take to your next employer). If you are out of education for a year you are not treated as a normal taxpayer.

Personal allowances – that is the amount you can earn before paying tax – are reviewed in the budget each year in April. To find out the current tax-free personal allowance rate call the Inland Revenue helpline or go to: **www.hmrc.gov.uk/nic**

the gap-year guidebook 2016

Minimum wages, maximum hours

In the UK, workers aged 16 and 17 should get a 'development rate' of £3.87 an hour; 18-to 20-year-old workers should receive £5.30 an hour; and workers aged 21 and over should get £6.70 per hour.

To check on how the National Minimum Wage applies to you, go to the Department for Business, Enterprise and Regulatory Reform (formerly called the DTI) website: **www.gov.uk/national-minimum-wage**

Alternatively, phone the National Minimum Wage Helpline on 0845 6000 678.

If you think you are not being paid the national minimum wage you can call this helpline number: 0800 917 2368.

All complaints about underpayment of the National Minimum Wage are treated in the strictest confidence.

The UK also has a law on working hours to comply with European Union legislation. This says that (with some exemptions for specific professions) no employee should be expected to work more than 48 hours a week. Good employers do give you time off in lieu if you occasionally have to work more than this. Others take no notice, piling a 60-hour-a-week workload on you. This is against the law and, unless you like working a 12-hour day, they must stop.

Please see the directory pages starting on page 379 for information on companies and organisations offering opportunities to work in the UK on your gap-year.

10

Volunteering
in the UK

10 Volunteering in the UK

Volunteering doesn't have to be done in a developing country, amongst the poorest on the planet, to bring a sense of satisfaction. There are many deserving cases right on your doorstep. You might also find that, if you do voluntary work close to home, it will make you more involved in your own community.

What's more, the global recession has prompted a greater need for volunteers, as charities have had to cut back on paid staff in the wake of reduced donations.

Some charities have also reported a huge increase in the numbers of potential volunteers. Arguably this reflects the numbers of graduates coming out of university unable to find work as well as high numbers of reported redundancies.

Volunteering Matters, who have been placing volunteers in community projects for more than 50 years, focus on the needs of four groups of people: disabled people, older people, young people and families. They believe that appointing volunteers to projects in their local community powers effective change as well as boosting CVs.

"Full-time volunteering with us offers young people an alternative to the traditional gap-year, giving them a new experience and enabling them to gain valuable skills for their future career or further education.

It is a unique opportunity for people aged 18 to 25 to assist on social care projects across the UK – it helps develop skills and improves self-confidence, allowing volunteers to meet new people and change lives."

Benefits of UK volunteering

You can:

· Do some things you couldn't do abroad. Good examples are counselling, befriending and fundraising, all of which need at least some local knowledge.

· Have more flexibility: you can do a variety of things rather than opting for one programme or project.

· Combine volunteering with a study course or part-time job.

· Get to know more about your own community.

· Get experience before committing to a project abroad.

· Develop career options – a now well-accepted route into radio for example is to do a volunteer stint on hospital radio.

If you choose to spend at least some of your gap doing something for the benefit of others here in the UK, you'll get the same satisfying sense of achievement as volunteers who have been on programmes elsewhere.

To get the most out of volunteering during your gap-year, you must consider what you would like to achieve. Try asking yourself about your interests, skills and experience to define what type of volunteering role you are looking for.

Volunteering England (**www.volunteering.org.uk**) is a volunteer development agency

committed to supporting, enabling and celebrating volunteering in all its diversity. Their work links research, policy innovation, good practice and grant making in the involvement of volunteers.

Here's what they told us: "There are literally thousands of exiting gap-year projects going on in exotic locations all around the globe; but if you are serious about building skills and improving your employability, a job specific placement in the UK may be more useful.

If you would like a career in the media, three months at a local hospital radio station may not sound as exciting as counting bottle-nosed dolphins in Costa Rica but it is a lot more relevant to prospective employers.

If you are considering a competitive career such as law or media, bear in mind internships can be difficult to get, but even a day's work shadowing or working more hours at your part-time job can help demonstrate those all-important employability skills such as team working and motivation. If you are interested in law, see if you can help out at your local citizen's advice bureau. If you would like to be a doctor, see if you can help out at your local hospital. They often need volunteers to run the hospital shop and to befriend patients and it will also give you a good idea of what working in a hospital will be like.

Volunteering in the UK has other benefits too: it is usually cheaper and it can provide a tangible benefit to your local community. For example student volunteers contribute over £42million to the economy each year through their activities (*National Student Volunteering Survey*) and many people go on to find jobs as a direct result of their volunteering.

Research has also proved that those who do voluntary work, or are helped by volunteers, adopt healthier lifestyles, can cope better with their own ill-health, have greater confidence and self-esteem, have an improved diet and even have a higher level of physical activity."

my gap-year
Christina Pacitto

Christina, 24, from Stockton-on-Tees, spent eight months on a Volunteering Matters Choices placement in London, caring for Emma Sarre, who has Down's Syndrome

Before starting my volunteering placement, I was unemployed. Following my graduation from Durham University in the summer of 2013, where I achieved an undergraduate degree in Modern Languages and Cultures, I spent several months travelling and on my return to the UK I found it very difficult to get a job. I had done some volunteering at university that had sparked my interest in the social care field, but I had very little idea of what I wanted to do career wise and felt lost.

I discovered Volunteering Matters by chance. I was doing a general internet search into volunteering opportunities and stumbled across the webpage for full-time volunteering placements with Volunteering Matters. I was inspired to volunteer in order to further explore the field of social care, to experience something completely new, to face different challenges and to gain new skills.

When I started my volunteering placement, I found myself in a completely alien situation where I had to learn and adapt quickly. I had no experience of supporting people with learning disabilities or working with people who display challenging behaviours so moving across the country to volunteer as a live-in carer for a young woman with Down's Syndrome seemed like a daunting prospect. The biggest challenge I had when starting my volunteering was that I had to quickly build a relationship with my service user so that I would be able to support her to live independently. I had to mould my communication skills and use tact, patience and empathy to gain her trust. I initially found it difficult when Emma displayed difficult behaviour. I would find myself not really knowing what to do for the best but over time I have become much more confident in my ability to work with her and communicate effectively to solve problems that arise.

Through volunteering, my listening and communication skills have improved massively - I have more empathy and have become more confident and assertive, and feel that I know the best ways to resolve conflict.

The stable presence of me as a volunteer who has Emma's best interests at heart, has really helped her and allowed her to continue to live as independent a life as possible, something that I think everyone deserves to have. I implemented routines, chore lists and rewards charts with Emma to give structure to her day and gave her something to look forward to.

Volunteering is a great chance to do something for someone else and to boost your CV at the same time. Volunteering matters because it puts you in a position where you are dealing with some of the more isolated members of society and gives you the chance to contribute to reducing that isolation.

Volunteering has changed my life in ways I couldn't ever have imagined, and led me to pursue a further education and career that I feel passionate about.

To find out more about volunteering you can visit Volunteering England's website www.volunteering.org.uk, where you can find your nearest volunteer centre.

www.do-it.org.uk or www.vinspired.com also list volunteering opportunities online.

Wherever you are, volunteering is an opportunity to learn about other people and about yourself.

If you're just starting out on a career path and are unsure what you want to do, volunteering can be an opportunity to gain relevant work experience. If you know, for example, that you want a career in retail, a stint with Oxfam will teach you a surprising amount. Many charity shops recognise this and offer training. Careers in the charity sector are also extremely popular and can be quite hard to get into, so a period of voluntary work will demonstrate your commitment and willingness to learn.

Volunteering for a while can also be useful for those who are maybe thinking of a career change or development. For example you could use your skills to develop a charity's website, or perhaps you have experience of marketing or campaigning.

While you're volunteering your services you can also use the time to find out more about the organisation's work, whom to talk to about training or qualifications and about work opportunities within the organisation.

What can you do?

Before contacting organisations it is a good idea to think about what you would like to do in terms of the activity and type of organisation you would like to work for. There's good advice on this at: www.volunteering.org.uk/IWantToVolunteer

The UK has its share of threatened environments and species, homeless people and the economically disadvantaged, and those with physical disabilities or mental health problems. In some ways, therefore, the choices for projects to join are no different in the UK from the ones you'd be making if you were planning to join a project abroad.

Cash-strapped hospitals are always in need of volunteers – Great Ormond Street Children's Hospital in London is a good example. They look after seriously ill children and need volunteers to play with the children and make their stay less frightening. It also runs a hospital radio station – Radio Lollipop – in the evenings and on Sundays, for which it needs volunteers.

Or you could help with a youth sports team, get involved in a street art project, or with a holiday camp for deprived inner-city youngsters – there are many options and there are any number of inner-city organisations working to improve relations between, and provide/identify opportunities for, people from different ethnic groups, faiths and cultures.

Remember, though, that any volunteer work you do that puts you directly in contact with young people and other vulnerable groups, such as people with mental health problems, or care of the elderly, is likely to mean you'll need a CRB (Criminal Records Bureau) check for both their protection and yours. In some cases, you'll have to pay for this yourself.

Where to start?

Your own home town will have its share of charity shops on the high street, and they're always in need of volunteers. But you could also try local churches or sports groups. Check your local paper for stories on campaigns, special conservation days and other stories about good causes close to home that you might be able to support.

visit: www.gap-year.com

What qualities does a good volunteer need?

The Samaritans is one organisation that's reported an upsurge in calls to its confidential helpline as a result of the recession – and if you've been in the position of losing your job, and are maybe thinking of volunteering to help others, it would be a good idea to think hard about whether you're able to offer what's needed.

Here's what the Samaritans have to say: "Samaritans volunteers need to be able to listen. They are not professional counsellors. They can also:

· question gently, tactfully – without intruding;

· encourage people to tell their own story in their own time and space;

· refrain from offering advice and instead offer confidential emotional support; and

· always try to see the other point of view, regardless of their own religious or political beliefs."

Go to this section on the Samaritans website: **www.samaritans.org/volunteer-us**

You can find out more here on the training and support you will be given before you are taken on.

ChildLine too has good advice for volunteers on its website and sees them as the essential basis of ChildLine's service. They need volunteers to speak to children and young people on their helpline, to work with them in schools, and to support fundraising, administration and management.

The charity provides full training and support, and has centres in London, Nottingham, Glasgow, Aberdeen, Manchester, Swansea, Rhyl, Leeds, Belfast, Exeter and Birmingham. Follow this link for more information:
www.nspcc.org.uk/what-you-can-do/volunteer-or-work-for-us/

There's a need for volunteers to help with disadvantaged people of all ages and if you're older, and considering volunteering, your work skills could come in handy. Many charities may need professional advice from time to time. If you have expertise in accountancy, administration, construction and maintenance, the law, psychiatry or treasury you might be able to help.

Helping refugees

The International Red Cross has a long history of helping traumatised and displaced people around the world, from being the first port of call in an emergency to monitoring the treatment of political prisoners, it is often trusted as the only impartial authority allowed access to detainees.

The British Red Cross has a specific scheme dedicated to helping refugees adjust to life in the UK. Trained volunteers provide much needed support to thousands of people every year, helping them to access local services and adjust to life in a new country. The Red Cross's services provide practical/emotional help to vulnerable asylum seekers and refugees. This includes offering orientation services to help refugees adapt to life in the UK, providing emergency support for large-scale arrivals, providing emergency provisions for those in crisis and offering peer-befriending support to young refugees.

You can volunteer to help out in charity shops or with fundraising. To find out more about volunteering with the Red Cross go to: **www.redcross.org.uk**

my
gap-year
Leonard Gethin

Leonard, 18, from Bristol, is on a Volunteering Matters full-time volunteering placement at the University of Warwick, supporting a psychology student, Tarandeep, who has cerebral palsy and is in a wheelchair

I help Tarandeep to live as independently as possible, along with two other Volunteering Matters full-time volunteers.

I was inspired to volunteer because I'd just finished my A Levels and was originally planning to go straight to University but then I hesitated and wasn't that sure that I wanted to go straight away; I wanted to have some other kind of experience first. Friends had done volunteering abroad, travelling, and having a year off, and Full Time Volunteering with Volunteering Matters seemed more special than that, and more interesting.

My client was very nervous at the beginning. Coming to University and moving away from home for the first time was a really big thing for him, and then he had new carers looking after his personal routine on top of that. It was the first time that I'd lived away from home as well. We got beyond the nervousness quite quickly though. I adjusted to the personal care aspect faster than anything else; after a day it really didn't bother me in the slightest. It only took a few weeks to settle into a routine and become really comfortable.

There can be a danger of thinking of volunteering as a selfless, charitable act, which can put you in a superior position. I give Tarandeep personal care, but he gives back in other ways, there's definitely an equality.

I've gained maturity with personal care and have proved to myself that I have the ability to simply do what I need to do, and not be too worried or bothered by it. I've also developed my ability to give emotional support; to have patience with a person and to listen more, which is a really valuable skill to have.

What appealed to me about Full Time Volunteering is that it isn't very sexy or glamorous on the surface of it, but that's actually what I really liked about it. It's more genuine and honest than a gap year abroad, which is like taking a holiday, which wasn't really what I wanted. Obviously doing this is not a completely selfless act of charity - there's an element of doing it because it makes me feel good, and I'm gaining from it, but it's a quiet way of doing something nice and kind, which feels more rewarding and less in-your-face than other volunteering opportunities.

I think it should be mentioned to more people of my age as an interesting alternative, a volunteering opportunity that's a bit different. There are a lot of teenagers who feel lost and don't really know what they want to do with their lives, and I know I was definitely a bit like that. If you're that kind of person then something practical and meaningful like Full Time Volunteering is a really good thing to do.

Conservation

Perhaps you're more interested in conservation work? The British Trust for Conservation Volunteers is a good place to start. It offers short (and longer) training courses that are informal and designed to be fun – including practical skills such as building a dry stone wall, creating a pond or a wildlife garden. It also has a number of options for volunteer schemes you can join: **www.tcv.org.uk/volunteering**

Animals

Volunteer jobs with animal welfare organisations can vary from helping with kennel duties, assisting with fundraising events, carrying out wildlife surveys, to working on specific projects.

Animal Jobs Direct has information on paid work with animals but it also has a section for volunteers.

The web address below gives direct links to animal welfare and rescue charities that offer a variety of different and interesting volunteering opportunities –there are an amazing range of voluntary jobs available. Remember, many animal charities exist on limited funds and therefore voluntary workers are much needed and appreciated.

To find out more, visit: **www.animal-job.co.uk/animal-volunteer-work-uk.html**

Help with expenses

While giving your time for free is part of the definition of volunteering, financial help is often available and organisations shouldn't leave you out of pocket. Many charities will reimburse your expenses such as travel tickets and lunch costs.

For some long term volunteering placements, different rules apply and as well as having

271

your basic expenses covered, you may be given a 'subsistence allowance' to cover living costs like heat, light, laundry and food. You may also be given free accommodation – for example if you are volunteering for several months in a care home.

If you are interested in volunteering with an organisation, ask whether they cover volunteer expenses and find out what they will reimburse.

In the directory we list the contact details of a number of charities and organisations that are grateful for volunteers. If you can't find anything that interests you there, then there are a number of organisations that place people with other charities or that have a wide national network of their own – an internet search should give you a good list.

The following websites provide useful links and information about volunteering:
www.do-it.org.uk
www.ncvo-vol.org.uk
timebank.org.uk

Please see the directory pages starting on page 385 for information on companies and organisations offering volunteering opportunities in the UK.

11

Learning
in the UK

Learning in the UK

You don't have to spend your gap-year travelling the globe if that doesn't appeal to you. The point about taking a gap is to try out new experiences that leave you feeling refreshed and stimulated, to learn something new and possibly come up with some new ideas about where you want your life to head next.

So if you're frustrated that hardly anything you were taught at school seems relevant to your life, why not use your gap-year to learn new skills that you choose yourself? You can make them as useful as you want.

There are plenty of evening classes available at local colleges, though usually only in term time, and, if you're thinking of training that doesn't involve university or are looking for ways to expand your skill set as part of a change of career direction, check out the Skills Funding Agency and the Young People's , which exists to promote lifelong learning, with the aim of young people and adults having skills to match the best in the world. There's lots of information on what's available, including financial help, on: **www.gov.uk/government/organisations/skills-funding-agency**.

A gap is also a good opportunity to explore interests that may, up to now, have been hobbies; here are some suggestions:

Archaeology

Do relics from the past fascinate you? Would you love to find one? You could get yourself on an actual archaeological dig. One good place to start is with your local county council's archaeology department, which may know of local digs you could join. Nowadays, whenever a major building development is going through the planning application process, permission to build often includes a condition allowing for archaeological surveys to be done before any work can begin; so another source of information could be the planning departments of local district councils.

Art

If you're seriously interested in painting, sculpting or other artistic subjects, but don't know if you want to carry it through to a full degree, there is the useful option of a one-year art foundation course. These are available from a wide variety of art colleges.

A foundation course at art college doesn't count towards an art degree, in the sense that you can then skip the first year of your three-year degree course, but it can help you find out whether you are interested in becoming a practising artist, maybe an illustrator, an animator, a graphic designer, or are more interested in things like art history, or perhaps working in a gallery or a museum or in a field like interior design.

If you do want to go on to the three-year art school degree, competition for undergraduate places is based on the volume and standard of work in a candidate's entry portfolio. Having a portfolio from your foundation course puts you at a natural advantage.

visit: www.gap-year.com

National Apprentice Service

Cookery

A cookery course is a great way of learning a fundamental skill that can change your life, whether it leads to professional cooking jobs in your time off allowing you to pay your way while travelling, or simply sets you up with skills to cook for yourself and friends throughout university and beyond.

With just a few tips and tricks, sharp knife skills and plenty of ingredient know-how, learning basic cooking skills can transform the way you eat, shop and cook.

Offering four, six or ten-week courses in which students learn through demonstration and practical sessions, certificate cookery courses generally comprise a thorough understanding of basic cooking skills and techniques, a certificate in health and hygiene, as well as a basic grounding in pairing food with wine.

Cookery schools tell us that the majority of those who want to work after doing a cookery course do find cooking work. What's involved in being a chalet cook depends on what a ski company or employer wants. Usually the day starts with a cooked breakfast for the ski party, then possibly a packed lunch, tea and cake when hungry skiers get back, possibly canapés later, and a three or four-course supper. The food does need more than the usual amount of carbohydrates.

275

LEARN TO COOK
PROFESSIONALLY

ASHBURTON
CHEFS
ACADEMY
★ ★ ★

Learning to cook will not only greatly enrich your life and enjoyment of food, but ca
provide a wealth of opportunities during a gap year and beyond.

The **Ashburton Chefs Academy** is an award-winning, private culinary school offerir
inspirational cookery training designed to give home cooks the skills and confidence require
to cook professionally.

Our intensive, 4 week **Certificate in Professional Cookery** is an exciting chef foundation cours
that will teach you to how to cook to a professional standard, giving you the skills you need t
be a successful cook in ski chalets, on yachts, in cafés or just for your own pleasure.

Courses run monthly at our world-class training centres in Devon and West Yorkshire, whe
students learn from experienced, professional chef tutors using the best local ingredients. W
also offer an affordable residential option for the duration of your course.

To find out about this course, and over 40 other cookery courses, visit our website today.

Ski companies expect high standards and may ask for sample menus when you apply for chalet cooking jobs. Sometimes the menus are decided in advance and the shopping done locally by someone else; sometimes the cook has to do the shopping.

Perhaps surprisingly, ski companies and agencies rarely ask about language skills – the cooks seem to manage without.

Here's a list of highly recommended cookery schools for you to check out:

www.ashburtonchefsacademy.co.uk
www.cookeryschool.co.uk
www.cookeryatthegrange.co.uk
www.leiths.com
www.tantemarie.co.uk

Drama

There are plenty of amateur dramatic and operatic societies in small towns across the UK. If you've always had a hankering to tread the boards, they're a great way to find out more about all the elements of putting on a production. You may be able to volunteer at your local theatre and gain valuable experience that way. Ring them up or check out their website to see if they have a bank of volunteers.

Then there are short courses and summer schools. This site lists a wide range of programmes available over the summer holidays: **www.summer-schools.info**

the gap-year guidebook 2016

ROYAL CENTRAL
SCHOOL OF SPEECH & DRAMA

UNIVERSITY OF LONDON

Royal Central School of Speech and Drama, Embassy Theatre,
Eton Avenue, NW3 3HY UK
T: +44 (0) 20 7722 8183
E: enquiries@cssd.ac.uk   W: www.cssd.ac.uk/gapyear

The Gap Year Diploma is a one year, part-time course to develop your acting skills. It is designed for those aged 18-25 who are interested in preparing to apply for an acting course at higher education level.

The course develops career skills, audition techniques and acting skills, and you will perform extracts from plays in a studio-based performance. This may be an ideal course if you feel you want a year to hone your skills before applying to a full-time course, or to increase skills if you have not been successful at auditions.

You will develop your skills as an actor by taking specific classes in movement, voice and text realisation. This work will be underpinned and linked with audition technique for those wanting to apply to an undergraduate course. There will also be career development sessions offering guidance through the Higher Education/drama school process, and on prospective careers in the performing arts.

In the final term you will rehearse and perform a performance showcase. Although we do not invite agents to this, all students on this course will be seen by an undergraduate course tutor and will be offered guidance on applying to higher education courses.

National Apprentice Service

Driving

There may be a lot of pressure to minimise car use in an effort to reduce carbon emissions and tackle global warming, but there are still plenty of good reasons for learning to drive.

First, unless you're intending to live in an inner city indefinitely, you may need a driver's licence to get a job; secondly, it will give you independence and you won't have to rely on everyone else to give you lifts everywhere. Even though you might not be able to afford the insurance right now, let alone an actual car, your gap-year is an ideal time to take driving lessons.

The test comes in two parts, theory and practical: and you need to pass the theory test before you apply for the practical one. However, you can start learning practical driving before you take the theory part, but to do that you need a provisional driving licence. You need to complete a driving licence application form and a photocard application form D1 – available from most post offices. Send the forms, the fee and original documentation confirming your identity such as your passport or birth certificate (make sure you keep a photocopy) and a passport-sized colour photograph to the DVLA.

my gap-year
Fritha Lambert

Fritha Lambert is packing her bags once again. She's used to jetting off across Europe at a moment's notice, arriving at a city apartment where she'll stay for a few weeks at a time, cooking beautiful dishes which are then transported across town to wherever her boss happens to be working. "I never thought I'd end up doing something like this!" she says. She can't reveal the identity of her employer, suffice to say she's high up in the fashion industry, but getting this job was a dream come true—a dream that began at Ashburton.

Fritha joined the Professional Culinary Diploma course after deciding to follow her lifelong love of cookery instead of taking up a place at university. "I loved the course and especially the mixed age range and different backgrounds they came from – we had an accountant, an IT consultant, and an ex-police officer" she says. "I also have so much respect for our tutors; they are amazing at what they do. At the end of the course we had a lot of free rein, but we started by learning what they do and how they do it."

"We also learned practical advice about being in a big kitchen – like making sure you get all your equipment out the night before and hide it somewhere in your area so you can get going first thing. It really made the difference when I started work, especially coming in at 7.30am when everyone would be crammed around the equipment cupboards."

After graduating from Ashburton, Fritha went straight into the heart of the London restaurant scene as a pastry chef at the famous West-end restaurant, The Ivy. It was tough, she says, with long hours and every chef competing for their place in the kitchen. "It might seem glam, but it's hot, and tiring work and burns become second nature." When she moved on to Gordon Ramsay's Maze Restaurant in London as a pastry chef, she found her arrival coincided with the London Olympics. "I ended up working from 7.45am to 2am in the morning, then back the next day to do it all again."

Despite the hardships, Fritha's passion for cooking continued and eventually she made the decision to set up her own catering business. All was great, but it was about to get even better, after Ashburton contacted her about an intriguing private chef position. "Someone had approached the school about a private chef position and they sent the details on to me." Fritha had to jump through several hoops including cooking for the potential employer's personal assistant, then making specific dishes for sampling. "When I found out I'd got the job I put the phone down and danced around the house screaming with excitement. And of course I called my mum."

"I like being able to give pleasure from my cooking. It's about giving people the opportunity to slow down and to take time to savour what they're eating. And of course it's always nice to get some recognition as well."

You also need to check that you are insured for damage to yourself, other cars or other people, and if you are practising in the family car, your parents will have to add cover for you on their insurance.

The DSA (Driving Standards Authority) is responsible for driving tests. However, to avoid duplication, all information on learning to drive, including fees, advice on preparing for the test and booking one has been moved to the Government services website: **www.gov.uk/browse/driving/learning-to-drive**

Theory

The theory test is in two parts: a multiple-choice part and a hazard perception section. You have to pass both. If you pass one and fail the other, you have to do both again.

The multiple-choice is a touch-screen test where you have to get at least 43 out of 50 questions right. You don't have to answer the questions in turn and the computer shows how much time you have left. You can have 15 minutes' practice before you start the test properly. If you have special needs you can get extra time for the test – ask for this when you book it.

In the hazard test, you are shown 14 video clips filmed from a car, each containing one or more developing hazards. You have to indicate as soon as you see a hazard developing, which may necessitate the driver taking some action, such as changing speed or direction. The sooner a response is made the higher the score. Test results and feedback information are given within half an hour of finishing. The fee for the standard theory test is currently £23.

Your driving school, instructor or local test centre should have an application form, although you can book your test over the phone (0300 200 1122) or online at: **www.gov.uk/book-a-driving-theory-test**

Practical test

You have two years to pass the practical test once you have passed the theory part. The practical test for a car will cost £62, unless you choose to take it in the evening or on Saturday, in which case the cost will increase to £75.

It's more expensive for a motorbike and the test is now in two modules – module 1 is £10 for both evenings and weekends, module 2 is £70 for weekday and £82 for weekend and evening tests.

You can book the practical test in the same way as the theory test. The bad news is that the tests are tough and it's quite common to fail twice or more before a pass. The practical test requires candidates to drive on faster roads than before – you'll need to negotiate a dual carriageway as well as a suburban road. You'll fail if you commit more than 15 driving faults.

Once you pass your practical test, you can exchange your provisional licence for a full licence.

Instructors

Of course some unqualified instructors (including parents) are experienced and competent, as are many small driving schools – but some checking out is a good idea if a driving school is not a well-known name. You can make sure that it is registered with the Driving Standards Agency and that the instructor is qualified. AA and BSM charges can be used as a benchmark if you're trying other schools. There's information about choosing an instructor and what qualifications they must have if they're charging you here: **www.gov.uk/find-driving-schools-and-lessons**

Film

For those wanting to forge a career in the filmmaking industry it can be difficult to navigate the world of film school and to decide whether it is the right option for you.

To gain access to the industry it is important to have as much practical experience on your CV as possible. There are many options available, from working as a runner and camera trainee to gaining experience in post-production houses and internships in feature film production companies.

You can also spend your gap-year making your own films and learning from industry professionals to develop the skills needed for a career in filmmaking.

Met Film School, who are based at Ealing Studios in London, told us:

"We're part of the Met Film group consisting of the school, Met Film Production and Met Film Post. Unlike any other film school we are completely integrated within the film industry. Met Film Production develops and produces a number of feature films each year and Met Film Post is a leading post-production business, specialising in end-to-end sound and picture post.

"On most of our courses, students write, produce, direct and edit their own short films – benefiting from hands-on experience via numerous shooting and directing exercises, tailored coaching through one-to-one and group sessions with our tutors and access to state-of-the-art digital technology.

"It's worth remembering that it only takes one piece of work to kick-start your career and every time you get behind a camera you have a chance to make that film."

Language courses

Even if the job you are applying for doesn't require them, employers are often impressed by language skills. With the growth of global business, most companies like to think of themselves as having international potential at the very least.

If you didn't enjoy language classes at school, that shouldn't necessarily put you off. College courses and evening classes are totally different – or at least they should be. If in doubt, ask to speak to the tutor, or to someone who has already been on the course, before you sign up.

And even if you don't aspire to learn enough to be able to use your linguistic skills in a job, you could still take conversation classes so you can speak a bit of the language when you go abroad on your holidays. It is amazing what a sense of achievement and self-confidence you can get when you manage to communicate the simplest things to a local in their own language: such as ordering a meal or buying stamps for your postcards home.

The best way to improve your language skills is to practice speaking; preferably to a native speaker in their own country. But if you don't have the time or the money to go abroad yet, don't worry. There are plenty of places in the UK to learn a wide variety of languages, from Spanish to Somali. We've listed some language institutions in the directory, but also find out what language courses your local college offers, and what evening classes there are locally.

Music

Perhaps you always wanted to learn the saxophone, but never quite got round to it? Now would be an ideal time to start. If you're interested, your best bet is to find a good private tutor. Word of mouth is the best recommendation, but some teachers advertise in local papers, and you could also try an online search engine like **www.musicteachers.co.uk**

If you already play an instrument, you could broaden your experience by going on a residential course or summer school. These are available for many different ability levels, although they tend to be quite pricey. There's no central info source on the net, as there is for drama courses, but we searched the internet for residential summer music schools and found loads of individual schools offering courses, so there are bound to be some near you. See the directory for more information.

Online learning

There are plenty of online language learning courses for those who are welded semi-permanently to their computers.

You can now get very comprehensive language courses on CD-ROM, which include booklets or pages that can be printed off. The better ones use voice recognition as well, so you can practise your pronunciation. These can also be found in bookstores.

The internet itself is also a good source of language material. There are many courses, some with free access, some that need a very healthy credit card. If all you want is a basic start, then take a look at: **www.bbc.co.uk/languages**

This site offers you the choice of beginner's French, German, Italian, Mandarin, Portuguese, Greek, Spanish, Japanese, Urdu and some other languages, complete with vocabulary lists to download, all for free.

the gap-year guidebook 2016

As well as courses, there are translation services, vocabulary lists and topical forums – just do a web search and see how many sites come up. Many are free but some are extremely expensive so check before you sign up.

Practice makes perfect

When you need to practise, find out if there are any native speakers living in your town – you could arrange your own language and cultural evenings.

Terrestrial TV stations run some language learning programmes, usually late at night. If you have satellite or cable TV you can also watch foreign shows though this can be a bit frustrating if you're a beginner. It's best to record the programmes so you can replay any bits that you didn't understand the first time round.

Once you get a bit more advanced then you can try tuning your radio into foreign speech-based shows from the relevant countries. This is also a good way to keep up-to-date with current affairs in your chosen country, as well as keeping up your listening and understanding skills. Subjects are wide-ranging, and there's something to interest everyone.

Most self-teach language tapes have been well received by teachers and reviewers, but can be a bit expensive for the average gap-year student. So, you might be glad to hear that, if you have iTunes, you can download language podcasts from the store. Most of these are free and you have the option of subscribing so that new podcasts are automatically downloaded next time you log on.

Photography

There are lots of photography courses available, from landscape photography to studio work. Don't kid yourself that a photography course is going to get you a job and earn you pots of money, but there's nothing to stop you enjoying photography as a hobby or sideline.

visit: www.gap-year.com

If you do want to find out more about professional photography you could try contacting local studios and asking about the possibility of spending some time with them as a studio assistant. Another option is to contact your local paper and ask if you can shadow a photographer, so you can get a feel for how they work and perhaps start building a portfolio of your own.

Sport

After all that studying maybe all you want to do is get out there and do something. The same applies if you've been stuck in an office at a computer for most of your working life. If you're the energetic type and hate the thought of spending your gap-year stuck behind a desk, why not get active and do some sport?

There are sports courses for all types at all levels, from scuba diving for beginners to advanced ski instructor qualification courses. Of course if you manage to get an instructor's qualification you may be able to use it to get a job (see **Chapter 8 – Sport**).

TEFL

Teaching English as a Foreign Language qualifications are always useful for earning money wherever you travel abroad. The important thing to check is that the qualification you will be gaining is recognised by employers. Most courses should also lead on to help with finding employment. There's more on TEFL courses in **Chapter 5 – Working abroad**.

X-rated

For a real adrenalin rush, go for one of the extreme sports like sky boarding, basically a combination of skydiving and snowboarding – you throw yourself out of a plane wearing a parachute and perform acrobatic stunts on a board.

Or, if you like company when you're battling against the elements, then you could get involved in adventure racing: teams race each other across rugged terrain without using anything with a motor, *eg* skiing, hiking, sea kayaking. Team members have to stay together throughout the race. Raid Gauloises (five person teams, two weeks, five stages, half the teams don't finish!) and Eco-Challenge (ten days, 600km, several stages and an environmental project) are the two most well-known adventure race events.

If you want to get wet, then try diving, kayaking, sailing, surfing, water polo, windsurfing, or white-water rafting.

And if those don't appeal then there's always abseiling, baseball, basketball, bungee jumping, cave diving, cricket, fencing, football, golf, gymnastics, hang gliding, hockey, horse riding, ice hockey, ice skating, jet skiing, motor racing, mountain biking, mountain boarding, parachuting, polo, rock climbing, rowing, rugby, running, skateboarding, skating, ski jumping, skiing, skydiving, sky surfing, snowmobiling, snowboarding, squash, stock car racing, tennis or trampolining! If the sport you are interested in isn't listed in our directory then try contacting the relevant national association (*eg* the LTA for tennis) and asking them for a list of course providers.

Please see the directory pages starting on page 393 for information on companies and organisations offering learning opportunities in the UK.

my gap-year
Polly Waldron

How much performing experience did you have before applying for The Central School of Speech and Drama gap year diploma?

Before the gap year diploma most of my experience came from acting in school, in a community theatre group and a drama class every Saturday.

What made you decide to apply for the course?

I'd planned to go to university to study English Literature. But I realised I wasn't sure and wasn't happy; but the idea of taking a year out with no reason scared me because I know I like working. So I googled the drama schools I'd heard of and had a look for their short courses. I liked the gap year diploma because it left me time to go and do other things.

Did you have time between classes to pursue other projects or work?

Yes, I did a couple of TIE projects with a community centre up the road from Central, which was really enjoyable. I could easily have gone for more professional acting work. I know a lot of others on my course continued to work on getting agents etc. I was sure that I wanted to train further; mostly because the classes just made me so happy that I thought it was a good idea to spend three years of my life doing that. I had to work as well - temporary jobs and waitressing. I got a lot of material through that!

Who would you recommend applies to the gap year diploma, and why?

I would recommend applying if you want to go on to a full BA course, or if you're not quite sure. It's a good glimpse into drama school life without the full-on intensity. For me it was a perfect first step on the ladder.

Being Safe

Adventure Expeditions
UK +44 (0) 1305 813107
info@adventure-expeditions.net
www.adventure-expeditions.net
Outdoor First Aid training with ITC Certification - a nationally recognised qualification that fulfils training requirements for insurance purposes and those stipulated by training bodies.

Adventure First Aid
UK 0800 999 2716
info@adventurefirstaid.co.uk
www.adventurefirstaid.co.uk
Travel first aid and crisis management courses, delivered by experienced professional trainers.

British Red Cross
UK 0844 871 1111
information@redcross.org.uk
www.redcross.org.uk
The Red Cross (Charity No. 220949) offers first aid courses around the UK lasting from one to four days depending on your experience and the level you want to achieve.

DU Insure
UK +44 (0) 800 393 908
travel@duinsure.com
www.duinsure.com
Save up to 60% on High Street prices plus a further 10% discount if you book online. Comprehensive travel insurance for the adventurous traveller. Working holidays covered plus over 80 adventurous sports or activities. Medical emergency and money back guarantee.
For further information see pages 12-13

Free European Health Insurance Card
UK 0191 218 1999
www.nhs.uk
The European Health Insurance Card (EHIC) enables access to state-provided healthcare in all European Economic Area countries at a reduced cost or sometimes free of charge.

Healthy Travel
UK
enquiries@healthy-travel.co.uk
www.travelwithcare.com
Healthy Travel stock a range of health products and travel products suitable for all types of outdoor activities, from a walk in the country to trekking in the jungle.

InterHealth Worldwide
UK +44 (0)20 7902 9000
info@interhealth.org.uk
www.interhealth.org.uk
InterHealth provide clinics and travel health advice, *eg* on immunisations.

Intrepid Expeditions
UK 0800 043 2509
nigel@intrepid-expeditions.co.uk
www.intrepid-expeditions.co.uk
Runs many different survival courses, including a first aid course, ranging from two to 14 days.

MASTA
UK 020 7291 9333
enquiries@masta.org
www.masta-travel-health.com
MASTA healthcare provide travel clinics across the UK offering professional advice to travellers about their specific travel health needs including anti-malarials, vaccinations and disease prevention.

287

Objective Travel Safety Ltd

UK 01788 899 029

office@objectiveteam.com

www.objectivegapyear.com

A fun one-day safety course or personalised safety courses for travellers, designed to teach them how to think safe and prepare for challenges they may face.

Pacsafe

China +852 3664 8300

info@pacsafe.com

www.pacsafe.com

Pacsafe® offers a range of travel security products to keep travellers one step ahead of the game and their gear secure from opportunistic thieves. Pacsafe® gives travellers the peace of mind they need to get on and get out there on the road less travelled.

RYA

UK 023 8060 4100

admin@rya.org.uk

www.rya.org.uk

The RYA is the national body for all forms of boating and offers courses specialising in the technique of sea survival at training centres across the UK.

Safe Gap Year

UK 0845 602 55 95

Info@safegapyear.co.uk

www.safegapyear.co.uk

Safe Gap Year is a training and consultancy company specialising in Independent Travel Safety and Cultural Awareness.

St John Ambulance

UK +44 (0)8700 104950

www.sja.org.uk

The St John Ambulance Association runs first aid courses throughout the year around the country. Courses last a day and are suitable for all levels of experience.

Taurus Insurance Services

Gibraltar +350 0207 183 6081

team@taurus.agency

www.taurus.gi

Taurus Insurance Services provides gap year and working holiday travel insurance.

The Royal Life Saving Society

UK +44 (0) 1789 773 994

info@rlss.org.uk

www.rlss.org.uk

Contact The Royal Life Saving Society for information about qualifications in life saving, lifeguarding and life support.

TravelPharm

UK +44 (0)115 951 2092

info@travelpharm.com

www.travelpharm.com

Provides travellers with a range of medication and equipment at very competitive prices to make your journey both healthier and safer!

TripTogether

UK

support@triptogether.com

www.triptogether.com

Find a travel companion for any trip you have planned – from a city break to a month of backpacking.

Ultimate Gap Year

UK

info@ultimategapyear.co.uk

www.ultimategapyear.co.uk

Personalised safety training suitable for anyone embarking on a gap-year. Training held at homes throughout south-east England.

Communication

0044 Ltd
UK +44 (0)1926 332153
www.0044.co.uk
Their global SIM card could save you money on international calls.

Aether Mobile Ltd
UK
customersupport@aether-mobile.com
www.aether-mobile.com
Get your SIM now and cut your mobile phone calls by up to 90% when abroad and get free incoming texts and calls in all countries.

EE
UK 07953 966 502
www.ee.co.uk
Provider of international broadband dongles enabling travellers to connect to the internet by simply plugging their broadband dongle into their laptop.

ekit
UK 0800 028 2402/0800 376 2370
shout@ekit.com
www.ekit.com
ekit is a global provider of integrated communications, mobile, VOIP and Internet services, designed to keep travelers in touch.

EuroCallingCards.com
UK +44 (0) 208 099 5899
contactus@eurocallingcards.com
www.eurocallingcards.com
Leading online supplier of international phone cards.

Go Sim
UK 0800 376 2370
www.gosim.com
Supplier of pre-paid international mobile SIM cards for travellers wishing to make phone calls abroad.

Internet Outpost
Australia +61 7 4051 3966
info@internet-outpost.com
www.internet-outpost.com
Provide internet outpost retail stores throughout Australia, New Zealand and Indonesia. Some of the facilities you have access to are: CD Burning, Printing, Microsoft Word, Microsoft Excel, Faxing, Scanning, Photocopying and more.

My UK Mail
UK 0845 838 1815
contact@my-uk-mail.co.uk
www.my-uk-mail.co.uk
UK based company providing a mail holding and forwarding service to international destinations including permaneant and temporary addresses.

NobelCom
Bermuda 0800 652 1979
help@NobelCom.co.uk
www.nobelcom.co.uk
Supplier of pre-paid phone cards for international long distance calling that can be tailored to travellers needs.

O2
UK 0800 230 0202
www.o2.co.uk
Provider of international broadband dongles enabling travellers to connect to the internet by simply plugging their broadband dongle into their laptop.

PocketComms Ltd
UK +44 (0)1635 799484
sales@pocketcomms.co.uk
www.pocketcomms.co.uk
A manual pocket sized universal language system in pictorial form to help travellers communicate through language barriers.

Talkmobile
UK 0870 071 5888

www.talkmobile.co.uk

Talkmobile provides monthly or pay as you go international mobile SIM cards for travellers wishing to make phone calls abroad.

Virgin Broadband
UK 0845 650 4500

www.virginmedia.com

Provider of international broadband dongles enabling travellers to connect to the internet by simply plugging their broadband dongle into their laptop.

Planning the route

Gap Advice
UK 07973 548316

info@gapadvice.org

www.gapadvice.org

Independent gap year travel advice, information, help and ideas on projects and placements.

iGapyear
UK +44 (0)845 643 9338

info@igapyear.com

www.igapyear.com

iGapyear.com helps you do your prep work and make sure you arrange your perfect gap year. Choose from jobs, courses, placements and trips.

Working Holiday Store
UK +44 (0) 1737 887556

www.workingholidaystore.com

An independent company that aims to provide travellers with an online resource, enhancing their planning and prep for the adventure of a lifetime.

YearOutWork
UK

www.yearoutwork.co.uk

YearOutWork is dedicated to helping you plan your time out... whatever you choose to do.

What to take

Ardern Healthcare Ltd
UK 01584 781777

info@ardernhealthcare.com

www.ardernhealthcare.com

Ardern Healthcare Ltd specialise in offering travellers a suitable insect repellent, in the form of sprays, wipes and creams, whatever their age or destination.

Blacks
UK 0844 257 2078

customercare@blacks.co.uk

www.blacks.co.uk

Blacks has 90 UK stores and provides a wide range of outdoor equipment and clothing from leading brands including The North Face, Berghaus and Craghoppers.

Brunton Outdoor
USA +44 (0) 2392528711

support@bruntongroup.com

www.bruntonoutdoor.com

Compact personal power device, from the brunton freedom range, which recharges devices like MP3 players, smart phones, digital cameras and more via car or sun ray.

Cotswold Outdoor Ltd
UK +44 (0) 844 557 7755

customer.services@cotswoldoutdoor.com

www.cotswoldoutdoor.com

Cotswold Outdoor Limited have stores across the UK and provide camping equipment, clothes, maps, climbing gear and footwear from brands such as Osprey, Scarpa and Solomon.

Craigdon Mountain Sports
UK +44 (0)1467 629394
sales@craigdon.com
www.craigdonmountainsports.com
Craigdon Mountain Sports is Scotland's premier independent outdoor retailer and has 4 retail stores which stock a wide range of clothing and equipment.

Field and Trek
UK
www.fieldandtrek.com
Field & Trek has stores all over the UK and supplies outdoor equipment and performance clothing ranges from brands such as Berghaus, The North Face, Mountain Equipment, Merrell, and Lowe Alpine.

Gap Year Travel Store
UK 0843 886 2242
gy-support@gapyeartravelstore.com
www.gapyeartravelstore.com
Online store selling quality travel kit and equipment to backpackers and independent travellers.

For further information see page 38

Go Outdoors
UK +44 (0)844 387 6800
enquiries@gooutdoors.co.uk
www.gooutdoors.co.uk
Go Outdoors operates from 41 retail stores across the UK and offers a wide choice of outdoor accessories and equipment from brands such as Hi Gear, Ragatta, North Ridge and Outwell.

Lifesaver Systems
UK 0808 1782799/+44 (0) 1206 580999
info@lifesaversystems.com
www.lifesaversystems.com
All-in-one filtration system, in a bottle, which will turn the foulest water into safe drinking water without the use of chemicals, allowing for much lighter packing.

Millets
UK 0161 393 7060
customercare@millets.co.uk
www.millets.co.uk
Millets, with over 150 stores, is one of the UK's largest travel and outdoor retailer. Brands include Berghaus, Eurohike, Merrell, North Face and Peter Storm.

Nikwax Ltd
UK +44 (0)1892 786400
info@nikwax.com
www.nikwax.com
To clean and waterproof all your gear, extend its life and maintain high performance with low environmental impact - Nikwax it!

Nomad Travel & Outdoor
UK +44 (0) 845 260 0044
orders@nomadtravel.co.uk
www.nomadtravel.co.uk
As well as the usual stock of clothing, equipment, books and maps their 8 travel stores also hold medical supplies.

Outdoor Megastore
UK 0151 944 2202
admin@outdoormegastore.co.uk
www.outdoormegastore.co.uk
Online store for all your outdoor equipment.

Outdoor Spirit
UK +44.1387 252891
info@outdoor-spirit.co.uk
www.outdoor-spirit.co.uk
Online shop offering a rangre of out door clothing, including Dr Martens shoes and boots.

Simply Hike
UK 0844 567 7070
info@simplyhike.co.uk
www.simplyhike.co.uk
Simply Hike - dor camping gear, outdoor clothing and accessories.

Snow and Rock
UK 01483 445335

manager.direct@snowandrock.com

www.snowandrock.com

Snow & Ice have stores across the UK offering a wide choice of outdoor clothing and equipment including Arc'teryx, Merrell, The North Face and Salomon.

Steri Pen
USA +1 207 374 5800

support@steripen.com

www.steripen.com

Steripen is a portable, fast and easy way to ensure water is safe to drink through harnessing the power of ultraviolet light.

Travelbagsize.com
UK

info@travelbagsize.com

www.travelbagsize.com

Travel size toiletries, cosmetics, fragrance and accessories.

Trespass
UK +44 (0) 141 568 8089

www.trespass.com

Trespass is an outdoor clothing, footwear and equipment manufacturer and retailer with over 200 stores throughout the UK. It also operates an e-commerce website for purchasing online.

Vango
UK 01475 744122

info@vango.co.uk

www.vango.co.uk

Evergrowing range of tents, sleeping bags, rucsacks and outdoor accessories.

Yeomans Outdoors
UK 01246 477 513

www.yeomansoutdoors.co.uk

With over 90 stores across the UK, Yeomans Outdoors stocks a wide range of tents, camping equipment and outdoor clothing from brands such as Vango, Trekmates, Easycamp and Karrimor.

Credit Cards

Advanced Payment Solutions Ltd
UK 0871 277 5599

www.mycashplus.co.uk

Produce the Cashplus Card, a pre-paid card which ensures you do not go overdrawn, incure interest or fall prey to credit card fraud.

Escape Prepaid
UK 0871 220 6420

customerservices@escapeprepaid.co.uk

www.escapeprepaid.co.uk

With the 'Escape Travel Money Prepaid MasterCard' you can withdraw cash from over 1.5 million ATMs worldwide, usually without having to pay a fee.

my Travel Cash
UK 0845 867 6496

www.mytravelcash.com

my Travel money offer the pre-paid multi currency card which allows travellers to withdraw cash in any currency without ATM fees.

Virgin Money
UK 0845 089 6278

info@virginmoney.com

uk.virginmoney.com

Offers a 'Pre-paid Travel Money Card' enabling travellers to budget more easiliy and spend abroad with greater security.

Insurance

ACE European Group Ltd
UK 0800 028 2396

ace.traveluk@acegroup.com

www.aceinsure.com/backpacker

Offers gap year/backpacker/student traveller insurance to anyone aged 14-44 and traveller plus insurance for those aged 45-55 years.

American Express
UK 0800 028 7573

www.americanexpress.com

Provide cover 18-49 year olds wishing to take a gap year, sabbatical, or career break up to 24 months.

Blue Insurance
Ireland +353 0818 444449

info@blueinsurance.ie

www.blueinsurance.ie

Multitrip.com is a domain name of Blue Insurances, offering competitive prices to anyone less than 45 years of age on back-packer insurance for trips up to 12 months in length .

Boots UK Limited
UK +44 (0) 845 125 3810

www.bootstravelinsurance.com

The Boots UK Limited website has an area dedicated to gap-year insurance and offers policies to 18-34 year olds for 3-12 months.

BUPA Travel Services
UK 0800 030 4687

www.bupa.co.uk/travel

BUPA Explorer Travel Insurance offers three levels of cover to travellers aged 18-45 for up to an 18 month insurance period.

Columbus Direct

UK 0845 888 8893

admin@columbusdirect.com

www.columbusdirect.com

Columbus Direct offer backpacker insurance for anywhere in the world for 2-12 months. Also offer sports and activities cover.

Dogtag Ltd

UK +44 (0) 8700 364824

enquiries@dogtag.co.uk

www.dogtag.co.uk

Dogtag Ltd offer insurance cover for 'action minded' travellers aged 18-55 for up to 18 months.

DU Insure

UK +44 (0) 800 393 908

travel@duinsure.com

www.duinsure.com

Save up to 60% on High Street prices plus a further 10% discount if you book online. Comprehensive travel insurance for the adventurous traveller. Working holidays covered plus over 80 adventurous sports or activities. Medical emergency and money back guarantee.

For further information see page 82

Endsleigh Insurance Services Ltd

UK +44 (0) 800 028 3571

www.endsleigh.co.uk

Endsleigh has tailored gap-year cover to suit travellers for up to 12 months, with over 100 sports and activities covered as standard.

Essential Travel Ltd

UK 08713602720

customerservices@essentialtravel.co.uk

www.essentialtravel.co.uk

Special backpacker travel insurance for anyone aged betwen 19-45 years old.

Globelink International

UK +44 (0)1353 699082

globelink@globelink.co.uk

www.globelink.co.uk

Globelink provides coverage for almost any type of journey and age group (up to 84). Our Globetrekkers travel insurance provides excellent cover for student, gap year travellers, backpackers and over 65 travel insurance.

Holidaysafe

UK 0845 658 0570

website@holidaysafe.co.uk

www.holidaysafe.co.uk

Holidaysafe is a travel insurance provider based in Kent, UK. They have a range of cover options such as backpacking, sports, and long stay.

Insure and Go

UK +44 (0) 844 888 2787

www.insureandgo.com

Insure and Go provide backpacker travel insurance for up to 18 months. Free cover for many sports and activities.

Mind The Gap Year

UK +44 (0) 845 180 0059

www.mindthegapyear.com

Mind The Gap Year offers a low cost economy package or the fully inclusive standard package back packer insurance cover.

Navigator Travel Insurance Services Ltd

UK 0161 973 6435

sales@navigatortravel.co.uk

www.navigatortravel.co.uk

Navigator Travel Insurance Services Ltd offer specialist policies for long-stay overseas trips with an emphasis on covering adventure sports. These policies also cover casual working.

Post Office Travel Insurance

UK 0800 294 2292
www.postoffice.co.uk/travel
Provides cover to 18-35 year olds wishing to take a career or study break.

Round the World Insurance

UK +44 (0)1273 320 580
info@roundtheworldinsurance.co.uk
www.roundtheworldinsurance.co.uk
Round the World Insurance provide specialist travel insurance designed for people on round-the-world or multi-stop trips.

Sainsbury's Travel Insurance

UK 0800 316 1453
www.sainsburysbank.co.uk/insuring/ins_extendedtrip_trv_skip.shtml
Sainsbury's Extended Trip Travel Insurance have a policy tailored to those between 16 and 45, providing cover for up to 12 months.

Snowcard Insurance Services Limited

UK 0844 826 2699
enquiries@snowcard.co.uk
www.snowcard.co.uk
An all-round activities insurance covering winter, general mountain and water sports as well as the standard travel risks. The unique 'Snowcard' gives 24 hour access to Assistance International.

Taurus Insurance Services

Gibraltar +350 0207 183 6081
team@taurus.agency
www.taurus.gi
Taurus Insurance Services provides worldwide travel insurance.

Top Dog Insurance

UK 0800 093 6686
info@topdoginsurance.co.uk
www.topdoginsurance.co.uk
Providing gap year travel insurance which covers many extreme sports and activities, including bungee jumping, scuba diving etc. The flexible policy allows you to return home for short periods of time.

Travel Insurance Direct

UK 0800 652 9944
info@travel-insurance.net
www.travel-insurance.net
The Discovery policy is designed for anyone travelling on a budget, backpacking or travelling light. Whilst being a low cost option it still maintains excellent levels of medical insurance, including vital medical emergency repatriation cover.

Travelinsurance.co.uk

UK 0844 888 2757
Information@travelinsurance.co.uk
www.travelinsurance.co.uk
Provides cover for up to 18 months travelling. Cover can be arranged for medical expenses, personal accident to repayment of student loan.

True Traveller Insurance

UK 0800 840 8098
sales@truetraveller.com
www.truetraveller.com
True Traveller offer Single Trip and Backpacker Insurance from 1 day to 2 years, as well as Multi-Trip Insurance, and you can take out cover if you're already travelling.
For further information see page 84

World Nomads Ltd

UK +44 (0) 1543 432 872
www.worldnomads.com
World Nomads Ltd offer an insurance package specifically targeted at independent travellers under the age of 60 for up to 18 months.

Worldtrekker Travel Insurance

UK 0843 208 1928
info@preferential.co.uk
www.preferential.co.uk/worldtrekker

World Trekker Travel Insurance offers four levels of cover from Standard to Ultra to UK resident travellers up to the age of 45 years.

Career Breaks

Africa in Focus
UK 01803 770 956
info@africa-in-focus.com
www.africa-in-focus.com
A travel agency which offers overland travel tours throughout East and Southern Africa with more comfort and innovative facilities.

African Conservation Experience
UK +44 (0) 1454 269182
info@conservationafrica.net
www.conservationafrica.net
African Conservation Experience offer volunteering opportunities at wildlife conservation projects in Southern Africa. You can count on our full support and more than 10 years experience.
For further information see page 188

Audley Travel
UK 01993 838 020
careers.audleytravel.com
Audley Travel offers a wide range or holidays and destinations for every traveller. From luxury hotels to wildlife safaris and city tours, Audley Travel can offer a tailor-made experience.

Experience Travel
UK 020 3468 3029
info@experiencetravelgroup.com
www.experiencetravelgroup.com
Travel agent specialists which can arrange tailor made travel to Vietnam, Thailand, Cambodia, Sri Lanka, The Maldives and Laos.

Globalteer
UK 0117 2309998
www.globalteer.org
Globalteer is a registered UK charity offering career breakers affordable, sustainable volunteer placements within community and conservation projects overseas.

Inspire
UK 0800 032 3350
info@inspirevolunteer.co.uk
www.inspirevolunteer.co.uk
Inspire offers meaningful volunteer opportunities in Africa, Asia, South America & Europe. Share skills and change lives on teaching, childcare, conservation & business programmes overseas.

Inspired Breaks
UK 01892 701881
info@inspiredbreaks.co.uk
www.inspiredbreaks.co.uk
Company specialising in career breaks and volunteer work for the over 30s, hundreds of programmes in over 20 countries from two weeks to 12 months.

JET - Japan Exchange and Teaching Programme UK
UK +44 (0)20 7465 6668
ukjet@ld.mofa.go.jp
www.jet-uk.org
The JET Programme, the official Japanese government scheme, sends UK graduates to promote international understanding and to improve foreign language teaching in schools for a minimum of 12 months.

Nonstop Adventure
UK +44 (0)1225 632 165
info@nonstopadventure.com
www.nonstopadventure.com
Nonstop Adventure provide action sport instructor courses and improvement camps around the world. Their courses are ideal for a gap year, career break or career change.

PoD
UK 01242 250 901
info@podvolunteer.org
www.podvolunteer.org
PoD (Personal Overseas Development) is a leading non-profit organisation arranging ethical, inspiring and supported volunteering opportunities around the world.

Projects Abroad Pro
UK 01903 708300
info@projects-abroad-pro.org
www.projects-abroad-pro.org
Projects Abroad Pro is an arm of Projects Abroad, designed to encourage professionals on a career break and retired seniors to take part in voluntary work in a developing country.

For further information see page 182

Raleigh International
UK 0207 183 1286
info@raleighinternational.org
www.raleighinternational.org
Develop new skills, meet people from all backgrounds and make a difference on sustainable community and environmental projects around the world.

For further information see page 96

Secret Compass
UK: +44 (0)20 3239 8038; USA: +1 347 8900182
info@secretcompass.com
www.secretcompass.com
Secret Compass is a pioneering exploration, expedition and adventure travel company. Its teams aim to achieve the extraordinary in the world's wildest places.

It was founded in 2010 by two former commanders in the UK Army's Parachute Regiment, Tom Bodkin and Levison Wood (who is currently 'Walking the Nile'). Secret Compass is based in Bristol and London.

Sunvil Traveller
UK 020 8758 4774
www.sunvil.co.uk/traveller
A travel agency which can arrange long stay travel across Latin America.

The AfriCat Foundation
Namibia +264 (0)67 304566
africat@mweb.com.na
www.africat.org
P.A.W.S offer career breakers volunteer project work, in association with the world renowned AfriCat Foundation, aimed at restoring the Okonjima's reserve back into a Game Reserve.

The Book Bus Foundation
UK +44 (0) 208 0999 280
info@thebookbus.org
www.thebookbus.org
The Book Bus provides a mobile service and actively promotes literacy to underpriviledged communities in Zambia and Ecuador.

Undiscovered Destinations Ltd

UK 0191 296 2674
info@undiscovered-destinations.com
www.undiscovered-destinations.com
An adventure travel agency dedicated to providing truly authentic experiences, through small group tours or tailormade trips, to some of the world's most exciting regions.

VentureCo Worldwide

UK 01822 616 191
www.ventureco-worldwide.com
VentureCo provides the ideal combination for career break travellers who want to explore off the beaten track, learn about the host country and give something back to the communities they stay with.

Visitoz

Australia +61 741 686 106
info@visitoz.org
www.visitoz.org
Visitoz provides training and guarantees work for young people between the ages of 18 and 30 in agriculture, hospitality, child care and teaching all over Australia.

For further information see page 142

Welcome to the NEW gap-year website!

www.gap-year.com

Travelling and accommodation

Accommodation

An Óige - Irish Youth Hostel Association
Ireland +353 01 830 4555
info@anoige.ie
www.anoige.ie
The Irish YHA consists of more than 20 hostels throughout Ireland. They have a range of hostels, from large city centre buildings to small hostels in rural settings. Online booking available.

Gap Year Hostel
Singapore +65 6297 1055
info@gapyearhostel.com
www.gapyearhostel.com
Inspired, designed and managed by backpackers, Gap Year hostel is a well-equipped modern hostel offering easy access to the heart of Singapore. Features include CCTV and key-cards for security, air-con and high-speed fibre optic wifi for leisure, and complimentary breakfast and tea/coffee for comfort.

Hostelbookers.com
UK +44 (0) 207 406 1800
support@hostelbookers.com
www.hostelbookers.com
Youth hostels and cheap accommodation in over 3500 destinations worldwide, with no booking fees.

Hostelling International
UK 01707 324 170
info@hihostels.com
www.hihostels.com
Research, plan and book your trip online with Hostelling International. HI hostels are a great way to travel the world safely - explore new cultures and meet friends.

Hostelling International - Canada
Canada +1 613 237 7884
info@hihostels.ca
www.hihostels.ca
Contact details for the Canadian branch of this worldwide hostel service.

Hostelling International - Iceland
Iceland +354 575 6700
info@hostel.is
www.hostel.is
Hostelling International Iceland has 36 hostels all around the country, offering comfortable, budget accommodation which is open to all ages.

Hostelling International - USA
USA +1 240 650 2100
www.hiusa.org
Hostelling International USA has a network of hostels throughout the United States that are inexpensive, safe and clean.

Hostelworld.com
USA +353 1 524 5800
customerservice@hostelworld.com
www.hostelworld.com
Online booking site which operates a network of over 27,000 hostels in more than 180 countries. Provides confirmed reservations at a selection of youth hostels, independent hostels and international hostels.

KAYAK
USA
www.kayak.co.uk
KAYAK provides a price comparison site for hotels and flights all around the world, helping you to easily compare hundreds of travel sites with one search.

Scottish Youth Hostel Association

UK 01786 891400

info@syha.org.uk

www.syha.org.uk

There are over 70 SYHA hostels throughout Scotland. You can book online but you must be a member - you can join at the time of booking. Registered Charity No. SC013138.

Swiss Youth Hostels

Switzerland +41 (0) 44 360 1414

contact@youthhostel.ch

www.youthhostel.ch

They have 52 hostels, ranging from traditional Swiss chalets, to modern buildings, large historic houses and even one or two castles.

Uxlabil Eco Hoteles

Guatemala +502 2366 9555; +1 305 677 3107

www.uxlabil.com

Experience Guatemala at affordable prices. Uxlabil offers three unique hotels in Atitlán, Antigua and Guatemala City, each fully equipped with modern facilities and providing breathtaking views.

VIP Backpackers

Australia +61 (0) 2 9211 0766

info@vipbackpackers.com

www.vipbackpackers.com

VIP Backpackers is the largest independent backpacker accommodation network in the world, with over 1,200 hostels across 80+ countries, and counting.

Youth Hostel Association New Zealand

New Zealand +64 (0)3 379 9970

www.yha.co.nz

Budget accommodation in New Zealand. Hostels open to all ages. Book online before you go.

Youth Hostels Association of India

India +91 (011) 2611 0250

contact@yhaindia.org

www.yhaindia.org

Youth Hostel Association in India, with hostels which can be booked online through their website.

Car Hire

Auto Europe

UK 0800 358 1229

customerservice@auto-europe.co.uk

www.auto-europe.co.uk

Auto Europe can provide travellers with a vast selection of vehicles for hire in over 8,000 locations around the world.

AVIS

UK 0844 581 0147

www.avis.co.uk

AVIS worldwide can provide travellers with car hire from 4,000 locations in 114 countries.

Budget International

UK 0844 444 0002

www.budgetinternational.com

Budget International can provide travellers with car hire from 3,400 locations in 128 countries.

Europcar UK Ltd

UK 0371 384 1087

reservationsuk@europcar.com

www.europcar.co.uk

Europcar and its alliance partner Enterprise can provide travellers with car hire from more than 13,000 locations in about 150 countries.

Hertz
USA 0843 309 3099
www.hertz.co.uk
Hertz Global Holdings is an American car rental company providing a wide range of options for car hire around the world.

International Motorhome Hire
UK 01780 482 565
enquiry@rv-network.com
www.international-motorhome-hire.com
International Motor Home are an agency that organises the hire of motor homes, on behalf of travellers, throughout the world.

Motorhome International
USA +1 847 531 1454
info@motorhome-international.com
www.motorhome-international.com
Motorhome International provide RV Rentals and Motorhome Hire in the USA, Canada, Europe, New Zealand Australia & South Africa.

Spaceships
New Zealand +64 9 526 2130
info@spaceshipsrentals.co.nz
www.spaceshipsrentals.co.nz
Company offering campervan rentals in New Zealand and Australia.

Travellers Auto Barn
Australia +61 2 9360 1500 (outside Australia) 1800 674 374 (within Aus
info@travellers-autobarn.com.au
www.travellers-autobarn.com.au
No cheaper way to travel around Australia than in any of our campervans or stationwagons - we have offices all around Australia and all our rentals come with unlimited KM, free insurance, special discounts.

Adagio
UK 01707 386700
info@adagio.co.uk
www.adagio.co.uk
Adagio offers holidays with character. Whether your interest is in culture, cuisine, history or sightseeing, Adagio will help you have a calm, stress-free holiday where you can move at your own pace.

ATG Oxford
UK +44 (0)1865 315678
trip-enquiry@atg-oxford.com
www.atg-oxford.co.uk
ATG organises escorted and independent walking trips for trekkers of all abilities. Keep fit whilst enjoying the beautiful scenery and breathtaking views of Europe. Relax in comfortable accommodation, enjoy tasty food and good company.

Aurora Expeditions
Australia +61 2 9252 1033
www.auroraexpeditions.com.au
Aurora Expeditions offer cruise expeditions to all corners of the globe. From the frozen Arctic and Antarctica to the hot savannahs of Africa, explore new landscapes and participate in exciting activities that will make your trip one to remember.

Bamboo Travel
UK +44 (0)20 7720 9285
info@bambootravel.co.uk
www.bambootravel.co.uk
Discover Asia with Bamboo Travel. Explore the local culture and see the sights with a classic holiday, or enjoy a more action-packed trip with an active and adventure holiday. Special interest trips are available for those with a particular passion, and bespoke trips can be arranged to personalise your experience. Whether you're an individual adventurer seeking new experiences, a couple looking for a romantic honeymoon or a family wanting a trip which everyone can enjoy, Bamboo has you covered.

Buffalo Tours

Vietnam +84 4 3828 0702
info@buffalotours.com
www.buffalotours.com

Choose from a range of holidays, focusing on local culture, adventure or luxury trips, or opt for something different with a variety of day trips and short breaks, or even a cruise holiday.

Chameleon Worldwide

UK +44 (0)1962 737647
www.chameleonworldwide.co.uk

Discover new cultures, explore new landscapes, adventure into new areas or admire the local wildlife with Chameleon Worldwide's tailor-made holidays. Perfect for young explorers, adventurous couples and families alike.

Classic Journeys

UK +44 (0)1773 873497
info@classicjourneys.co.uk
www.classicjourneys.co.uk

Classic Journeys operates tailor-made, quality adventure holidays. Specialising in the area of Asia, a friendly, informal and relaxed trip will provide travellers with memorable and meaningful travel experiences, in addition to supporting educational, healthcare and environmental projects in local communities.

Country Walks

UK +44 (0)207 233 6563
info@country-walks.com
www.country-walks.com

Country Walks offers high-quality walking experiences through both guided and self-guided walking holidays. Trips provide beautiful landscapes and natural environments, cultural interest, accommodation, food and will give you an enhanced sense of wellbeing, leaving you re-energised and rejuvenated.

Cox & Kings

UK 020 7873 5000
cox.kings@coxandkings.co.uk
www.coxandkings.co.uk

Cox & Kings offer a variety of holidays to a number of destinations all around the world, whilst also promoting responsible tourism.

Expert Africa

UK +44 (0)20 8232 9777
www.expertafrica.com

Expert Africa is a travel company which organises safaris and holidays for all types of travellers. Team members have travelled extensively in Africa, providing advice and guidance from first hand experience to offer you the best possible trip.

Gapwork.com

UK +44 (0)1133 230759
info@gapwork.com
www.gapwork.com

Gapwork is an independent information provider specialising in gap years, gap year jobs, gap year vacancies, activities and voluntary work either in the UK or abroad.

Goa Way

UK 0207 258 7800
sales@goaway.co.uk
www.goaway.co.uk

Goaway specialises in organising travel to Goa and Kerala. You can book flights, hostels or even package tours.

Greyhound Lines Inc

USA +1 214 849 8966
ifsr@greyhound.com
www.greyhound.com

The most famous and largest bus company in America. Book online and join the millions of others who travel across America on the 'old grey dog'.

Invasion

UK 01613 123459
info@invasion.com
www.invasion.com

Invasion offers a variety of travel experiences whilst providing security to help ensure that every trip runs smoothly. Go on a city break across Europe, visiting Paris, Rome, Berlin, Barcelona and more, or attend lively festivals such as Oktoberfest, St. Patrick's Day or Pamplona. Whether you want to immerse yourself in culture or just go somewhere new and have fun, Invasion provides a memorable experience.

Journey Latin America

UK 0208 747 3108
sales@journeylatinamerica.co.uk
www.journeylatinamerica.co.uk

Journey Latin America is the UK's major specialist in travel to Central and South America. Learn a new skill with their 'Learn to ... ' holidays.

KE Adventure Travel

UK +44 (0)17687 73966
info@keadventure.com
www.keadventure.com

KE Adventure Travel is one of the world's leading independent adventure travel specialists. Whether you seek to walk amongst the world's highest peaks, explore untamed wilderness areas, or witness first hand the wildlife or culture of far-off lands, we have the perfect adventure for you.

Llama Travel

UK 020 7263 3000
mail@llamatravel.com
www.llamatravel.com

One of the UK's leading tour operators to Latin America, Llama Travel provides high quality holidays at the lowest possible prices. All of our staff have either lived in Latin America or know the countries well. Choose from 63 itineraries or design your own holiday by choosing where you would like to visit.

Oasis Overland

UK +44 (0) 1963 363400
info@oasisoverland.co.uk
www.oasisoverland.co.uk

Oasis Overland provide exciting and adventurous tours and expeditions in Africa, South America and Central Asia. You'll take an active involvement in the day to day running of the trip with like-minded travellers as you explore different cultures and regions.

For further information see page 122

Outward Bound Costa Rica

Costa Rica +506 2278 6058
info@outwardboundcr.org
www.outwardboundcostarica.org

Outward Bound Costa Rica challenges participants to live bigger, bolder lives. Embark on a life-changing journey through our rigorous programs in Costa Rica and Panama, expanding capacity in leadership, intercultural competence, Spanish language, self-awareness, and life skills.

Peter Sommer Travels

UK +44 (0)1600 888220
info@petersommer.com
www.petersommer.com

Peter Sommer Travels provide inspirational trips, stimulating & enlightening expert-led tours and relaxing & beautiful gulet cruises. On offer are a range of archaeology tours, food tours and walking holidays by land and sea. Our escorted tours in Turkey, Greece and Italy will take you to some of the world's best preserved ancient and historic sites.

Rainforest Expeditions

Peru +51 9935 12265
sales@rainforest.com.pe
www.perunature.com

Rainforest Expedition is a Peruvian Ecotourism company. Since 1989 our guests and lodges, have added value to standing tropical rain forest turning it into a competitive alternative to unsustainable economic uses.

Smaller Earth UK
UK +(44) 0151 702 6808
uk@smallerearth.com
www.smallerearth.com
Smaller Earth is one of the UK's leading gap year travel providers, sending thousands of travellers abroad every year. Whether you're looking to volunteer in Africa, earn money in Australia or party in Bangkok, we've got the perfect collection of travel programmes for you.

STA Travel
UK 0333 321 0099
www.statravel.co.uk
This company has branches or agents worldwide and a Help Desk telephone service, which provides essential backup for travellers on the move.

ThaIntro
UK +44 (0)845 3700 499
enquiries@thaintro.com
www.thaintro.com
Travel to Thailand and meet like-minded travellers. Explore wondrous Thai temples and beautiful national parks, relax on the warm beaches or try your hand at snorkelling in the sparkling clear waters, and enjoy an up-close experience with elephants in the jungle. Thaintro offers a great stepping stone into Thailand.

Tourdust Ltd
UK +44 (0)203 291 2907
help@tourdust.com
www.tourdust.com
Tourdust specialises in adventurous holidays for independent minded travellers, combining down-to-earth adventures with carefully selected boutique hotels. They partner closely with local guides and hotels to offer high quality and great value holidays.

Travel Talk
UK +44 (0)20 8099 9596
info@traveltalktours.com
www.traveltalktours.com
UK adventure and cultural tour operator, whom design tours especially for fun-loving and motivated people aged between 18 and 39.

Travelbag Ltd
UK 0871 703 4698
www.travelbag.co.uk
Book flights, hotel, holidays and even find insurance on their website.

TrekAmerica
UK 0208 682 8920
www.trekamerica.co.uk
With year round departures and over 50 unique itineraries from 3 to 64 days in length TrekAmerica tours are the ideal way to explore North America.

USIT
Ireland +353 (0)1602 1906
info@usit.ie
www.usit.ie
Irish travel agents offering cheap flights from Dublin, Cork and Shannon specifically aimed at students.

Warriors
South Africa +27 82 802 0880
marketing@warriors.co.za
www.warriors.co.za
Warriors offers a variety of programs to participate in a range of experiences that are designed around the 5 core values of emotional fitness, social skills development, adventure & eco-tourism, entrepreneurship and work readiness and health & fitness to support the transition of entering adulthood.

Wildlife Worldwide

UK 01962 302 088

sales@wildlifeworldwide.com

www.wildlifeworldwide.com

Wildlife Worldwide has been organising tailor-made wildlife tours since 1992. We provide tailor-made Indian & African safari holidays, whale watching holidays, wildlife cruising and Antarctic & Arctic voyages.

Getting about

Cheap Flights

UK

www.cheapflights.co.uk

This useful website does not sell tickets but can point you in the right direction to get the best deal.

EasyJet Plc

UK

www.easyjet.com

Offers cheap flights to European destinations with further reductions if you book over the internet.

ebookers.com

UK

www.ebookers.com

Cheap flights can be booked through their website.

Florence by Bike

Italy +39 055 488992

info@florencebybike.it

www.florencebybike.it

Scooter, motorbike and bike rental company in Florence. Also sells clothing and accessories as well as bike parts.

International Rail

UK +44 (0)871 231 0790

sales@internationalrail.com

www.internationalrail.com

InterRail Pass provides unlimited travel on the sophisticated European Rail network. The pass is very flexible allowing you to choose either one country or all 30 countries.

Kiwi Experience

New Zealand +64 9 336 4286

www.kiwiexperience.com

Extensive bus network covering the whole of New Zealand. Passes valid for 12 months.

Ryanair

UK

www.ryanair.com

Low cost airline to European destinations.

Stray Ltd

New Zealand

enquiries@straytravel.co.nz

www.straytravel.co.nz

Stray is New Zealand's fastest growing backpacker bus network - designed for travellers who want to get off the beaten track.

Thomas Cook

UK

www.thomascook.com

General travel agent with high street branches offering flights and late deals.

Travellers Contact Point

Australia +61 2 9211 7900

www.travellers.com.au

A specialist travel agency for independent and working holiday travellers. We have shops in Australia, New Zealand and the UK.

Voyages-sncf.com
UK 0844 848 5848

www.voyages-sncf.com

Specializes in selling tickets and passes for travel throughout Europe by train. Available to buy online, at their London Travel Centre or via their call centre.

For further information see page 116

Tours

Acacia Adventure Holidays
UK +44 (0) 20 7706 4700

info@acacia-africa.com

www.acacia-africa.com

Acacia offers exciting and affordable overland tours and small group safaris across Africa. Enjoy game viewing, desert adventures, beach breaks, dive courses or trekking!

Adventure Tours Australia
Australia +61 (0)3 8102 7800

admin@adventuretours.com.au

www.adventuretours.com.au

Adventure Tours Australia is an award winning company specialising in small group nature-based tours for the active traveller.

Adventure Tours NZ
New Zealand +64 9 526 2149

reservations@adventuretoursnz.co.nz

www.adventuretours.com.au

Adventure Tours NZ offer specialised small group nature-based tours for the active traveller on a budget. Go off the beaten track, see unique scenery and wildlife.

Adventure Travellers Club P Ltd
Nepal

info@nepaltravellers.com

www.nepaltravellers.com

Offers trekking and adventure tours in Nepal, Tibet, Bhutan and Indian regions. Includes peak climbing, jungle safaris, river rafting and much more.

Afreco Tours Ltd
UK +44 (0) 845 812 8222

info@afrecotours.com

www.afrecotours.com

Afreco Tours specialises in African safari ranger training and wildlife adventures - from seven days to one year.

Africa Travel Co
South Africa +27 21 3851530

cpt@africatravelco.com

www.africatravelco.com

Specialists in trips around Africa ranging from three to 56 days.

African Horizons
Zambia +877 256 1074

safariplans@gmail.com

www.africanhorizons.com

Provides quality African travel not only to the savvy globetrotters among us but also to those who have never experienced the thrill of an African safari or wildlife tour.

AITO – Association of Independent Tour operators
UK +44 (0) 208 744 9280

info@aito.com

www.aito.com

Expert, independent tour operator specialising in offering an unrivalled collection of affordable holidays to every corner of the globe.

Alaska Heritage Tours
USA +1 907 777 2805

info@AlaskaHeritageTours.com

www.alaskaheritagetours.com

At Alaska Heritage Tours we strive to give you the best of Alaska, the way you want it - with pre-packaged Alaska vacations and itineraries. Explore Alaska's top destinations.

visit: www.gap-year.com

Alpine Exploratory

UK +44 (0) 1729 823197

info@alpineexploratory.com

www.alpineexploratory.com

Alpine Exploratory specialises in self-guided walking and trekking tours in Europe. Full programme of guided tours also offered, as well as bespoke holidays.

Andean Trails

UK +44 (0) 131 467 7086

info@andeantrails.co.uk

www.andeantrails.co.uk

Andean Trails is an owner run specialist adventure travel company organising small group tours to Peru, Bolivia, Ecuador, Cuba, Guyana and Patagonia.

Backpacker Travel Auctions

Australia

info@safaripete.com

www.safaripete.com

Safari Pete can offer you directions to the best deals on tours around Australia and New Zealand.

Bicycling Empowerment Network

South Africa +27 21 788 4174

andrew@benbikes.org.za

www.benbikes.org.za

BEN, a non-profit organisation, promotes the use and sale of refurbished bicycles. They conduct Bicycle Township Tours empowering local people and winning International Responsible Tourism Awards.

Black Feather - The Wilderness Adventure Company

Canada +1 705 746 1372

info@blackfeather.com

www.blackfeather.com

Company offering canoeing and kayaking trips and expeditions to remote artic locations. Offer women only trips and will do a customized trip for groups of four or more.

Borderlands Travel

UK +44 (0)1913 082201

info@borderlandstravel.com

www.borderlandstravel.com

Borderlands offer escorted group tours in beautiful destinations in Europe and tailor-made itineraries for individuals and small groups. Take a cultural journey through cities steeped in history, visit UNESCO World Heritage Sites and travel through some dramatic scenery, all whilst under the guidance of an expert escort.

Borneo Anchor Travel & Tours/ Sabah Divers

Malaysia +60 88 256 483

sabahdivers2u@yahoo.com

www.borneoanchortours.com

They offer various wildlife, nature and adventure packages all over Sabah, Malaysian Borneo.

BridgeClimb Sydney

Australia +61 (0) 2 8274 7777

admin@bridgeclimb.com

www.bridgeclimb.com

BridgeClimb provides the ultimate experience of Sydney, with guided climbs to the top of the world famous Sydney Harbour Bridge. Climbers can choose between The Express Climb, The Bridge Climb or The Discovery Climb.

Cape York Motorcycle Adventures

Australia +61 (07) 4059 0220

adventures@capeyorkmotorcycles.com.au

www.capeyorkmotorcycles.com.au

Motorcycle tours in north Queensland from one to eight days duration. Private charter also available. They have their own motorbikes and a support vehicle that accompanies the longer excursions.

Cordillera Blanca Trek
Peru +51 (0) 43 427 635
info@cordillerablancatrek.com
www.cordillerablancatrek.com
Offers treks in Machu Picchu, a volcanco tour and more.

Do Something Different
UK +44 (0)208 090 3890
contact-us@dosomethingdifferent.com
www.dosomethingdifferent.com
Want to dog sled in the Rockies? Take a Hong Kong Island or helicopter tour? Or climb Auckland Harbour Bridge?

Dolphin Encounter
New Zealand +64 3 319 6777
info@dolphin.co.nz
www.dolphinencounter.co.nz
Swim or watch dolphins in Kaikoura. You do need to book in advance as there is a limit to how many swimmers are allowed per trip.

Dorset Expeditionary Society/ Leading Edge Expeditions
UK
dorsetexp@gmail.com
www.dorsetexp.org.uk
Dorset Expeditionary Society promotes adventurous expeditions to remote parts of the world. Open to all. May qualify for two sections of the Duke of Edinburgh's Gold Award.

Dragoman
UK +44 (0)1728 861133
info@dragoman.co.uk
www.dragoman.com
Overlanding is stil the most authentic and accessible way of discovering new countries, their people and culture. Join us in Africa, America and Asia.

Eco Trails Kerala
India +91 48125 24447
mail@ecotourskerala.com
www.ecotourskerala.com
This tour company provides budget holiday tour packages in the Kumarakom and Alleppey Backwater areas.

Equitours - Worldwide Horseback Riding Adventures
USA +1 307 455 3363
www.ridingtours.com
With over 30 years experience, Equitours offer tested and tried horseback tours on six continents. Rides from three to eight days (or longer) for riders of all experience.

Explore Worldwide Ltd
UK 01252 884223
res@explore.co.uk
www.explore.co.uk
Company organising special tours in small groups. Types of worldwide tours available are walking holidays, dog-sledding, wildlife and railway tours amongst others.

Fair Dinkum Bike Tours
Australia +61 0()7 4053 6999
dave@fairdinkumbiketours.com.au
www.fairdinkumbiketours.com.au
Offer a range of tours using local guides to cater for all levels.

Flying Kiwi
New Zealand +64 3 547 0171
info@flyingkiwi.com
www.flyingkiwi.com
Flying Kiwi bus tours around New Zealand offer a unique and fun experience. Camping or cabin options are available in exciting locations and usually meals are included.

Fräulein Maria's Bicycle Tours
Austria +43 650 3426297
biketour@aon.at
www.mariasbicycletours.com
Maria's Bicycle tours take you to the main attractions from the film The Sound Of Music! The tour lasts three hours with stop points along the way and operates between May and September.

G Adventures
Canada +1 416 260 0999
travel@gadventures.com
www.gadventures.com
G Adventures offers one of the widest selection of affordable small-group tours, safaris and expeditions across the world.

Go Differently Ltd
UK +44 (0) 1273 732236
info@godifferently.com
www.godifferently.com
Company offering small-group, short-term volunteering and tailor-made holidays based on the appreciation and respect of the local environment and people.

Grand American Adventures
UK 03339 997965; +44 208 682 8921
www.grandamericanadventures.com
Grand American Adventures specialises in tours to the Americas, with unrivalled knowledge and experience we are committed to bringing you the finest small group adventures available. Enjoy spectacular natural sights, challenging and rewarding activities and encounters with some of the world's most colourful cultures and wildlife.

Grayline Tours of Hong Kong
China +852 2368 7111
sales@grayline.com.hk
www.grayline.com.hk
Special sightseeing day tours around Hong Kong and Macau.

Haka Tours
New Zealand +64 3 980 4252
info@hakatours.com
www.hakatours.com
Haka Tours represents the ultimate in New Zealand adventure holidays, from small group adventures to New Zealand snow tours exploring the impressive Southern Alps and the active volcanoes of the North.

High Places Ltd
UK +44 (0)845 257 75
holidays@highplaces.co.uk
www.highplaces.co.uk
Independent specialist trekking company organising tours to 22 countries.

Highland Experience Tours
UK +44 (0)131 226 1414
info@highlandexperience.com
www.highlandexperience.com
Travel company offering one day and private tours around Scotland, such as a two day highland tour, a whisky tasting tour, or a tour of Scotland personalised to your own requirements.

In the Saddle Ltd
UK +44 01299 272 997
rides@inthesaddle.com
www.inthesaddle.com
Specializes in horse riding holidays all over the world, catering for all levels of experience. From ranches in the Rocky Mountain states of Montana and Wyoming, to expeditions in remote and unexplored parts of the world.

Inside Japan Tours
UK +44 (0)117 370 9751
info@insidejapantours.com
www.insidejapantours.com
Specialist company offering tours of Japan, including small group tours and individual, self-guiding tours. You can also book a Japan Rail Pass online here.

International Wilderness Leadership School

USA +1 800 985 (4957)/ +1 907 766 3366
info@iwls.com
iwls.com

An outdoor school specialising in the highest quality guide training, outdoor leadership training, wilderness education and technical instruction.

Intrepid Travel

UK 0800 781 1660
islington@intrepidtravel.com
www.intrepidtravel.com

For travellers with a yearning to get off the beaten track, Intrepid opens up a whole new world of adventure travel.

Jungle Surfing Canopy Tours

Australia +61 7 4098 0043
info@junglesurfing.com.au
www.junglesurfing.com.au

Night walks in a tropical rainforest or jungle surf through the Daintree Rainforest.

Kande Horse Trails

Malawi +265 (0) 8500416
info@kandehorse.com
www.kandehorse.com

Experience the Malawi bush on horseback. All ages and riding abilities catered for.

Killary Adventure Company

Ireland 00 353 (0) 95 43411
adventure@killary.com
www.killaryadventure.com

We specialise in adventure activities that range from bungee jumping to kayaking on Irelands only fjord and much more in between. Whether you are a soft adventurer or after the extreme adrenaline thrill we have something for you.

KT Adventure

Vietnam +84 4 36740486
info@vivutravel.com
www.vivutravel.com

KT Adventure, part of Vivu Travel, offer specialised tours in Vietnam, from adventure tours to motorbiking.

Live Travel

UK +44 (0) 208 894 6104
phil.haines@live-travel.com
www.live-travel.com

Personalised travel plans offered as well as group tours.

M. Trek and Tour

Morocco 00212 524330597
info@moroccotrek.co.uk
www.mtrekandtour.com

Trekking trips, tailormade tours, group holidays and specialised activity weeks in Morocco.

Melbourne Street Art Tour

Australia +61 (03) 9328 5556
booking@melbournestreettours.com
www.melbournestreettours.com

Melbourne Street Art Tours, led by one of Melbourne's elite street art stars, gives you an overview of the Melbourne underground street art scene.

Mountain Kingdoms Ltd

UK +44 (0)1453 844400
info@mountainkingdoms.com
www.mountainkingdoms.com

Himalayan Kingdoms is the UK's foremost quality trekking company, running treks and tours to the great mountain ranges of the world.

Olympic Bike Travel
Greece +30 283 1072 383
info@olympicbike.com
www.olympicbike.com
A variety of bike tours available for all ages. From a ride down the highest mountain in Greece, to bike and hiking tours.

On The Go Tours
UK 0207 371 1113
info@onthegotours.com
www.onthegotours.com
Special tours such as solar eclipse tours and railways of the Raj can be arranged.

Oyster Trekking
UK
trek@oystertrekking.com
www.oystertrekking.com
Take the trek of a lifetime in the stunning Himalayas, with full Oyster support and a fair price. Adventurous treks include Everest Base Camp. The Langtang, Ghale Guan and Annapurna Base Camp.

Oyster Worldwide Limited
UK +44 (0) 1892 770 771
anne@oysterworldwide.com
www.oysterworldwide.com
Take the trek of a lifetime in the stunning Himalayas, with full Oyster support and a fair price. Adventurous treks include Everest Base Camp. The Langtang, Ghale Guan and Annapurna Base Camp.
For further information see pages 136-137

Palmar Voyages
Ecuador +593(9) 9 480 2268
gerencia@palmarvoyages.com
www.palmarvoyages.com
Tailor-made programmes for tours in Ecuador, Peru, South America, the Andes and the Galapagos Islands.

Pathfinders Africa
Zimbabwe +263 4 870 573
info@pathfindersafrica.com
www.pathfindersafrica.com
Pathfinders Africa is an African-based expedition company that operates from Zimbabwe. Developed to meet the needs of the adventurous traveller, Pathfinders' over-riding philosophy is of friendliness and individuality.

Peregrine Adventures Ltd
UK +44 0844 736 0170
travel@peregrineadventures.co.uk
www.peregrineadventures.com
Peregrine offer small group adventure tours worldwide. They offer a vast range of tours from polar expeditions to trekking the Himalayas.

Peru Trip Advisors
Peru +51 1 241 7429
info@peru-tripadvisors.com
www.peru-tripadvisors.com
Explore Peru, from the Inca Trail to Machu Picchu with an inclusive and personalised tour.

Pioneer Expeditions Worldwide
UK 01202 798922
info@pioneerexpeditions.com
www.pioneerexpeditions.com
High and Wild plan some of the most unusual and exciting adventures to destinations worldwide.

Pura Aventura
UK 01273 961928 / +44 1273 961 921
info@pura-aventura.com
www.pura-aventura.com
Various beautiful tailor-made tours in exotic locations. Career break to fulfil a long held dream or a special diversion on your gap-year perhaps?

Pure Australia Travel Guide

UK

info@pure-australia.co.uk

www.pure-australia.co.uk

Pure Australia - everything you need to know before travelling or working in Australia.

Rickshaw Travel

UK +44 (0) 1273 322 399

info@rickshawtravel.co.uk

www.rickshawtravel.co.uk

Rickshaw Travel is a UK based ABTA/ATOL bonded travel operator, that uses locally owned accommodation with an authentic feel that is a cut above the usual backpacker haunts.

Rickshaw Travel

UK 01273 322390

hello@rickshawtravel.co.uk

www.rickshawtravel.co.uk

A friendly Brighton based travel company who believe in creating personal and meaningful travel experiences, taking you to the heart of a destination.

Our style of travel is unique – using our destination expertise, we've carefully created a choice of bite-size trips typically 3-4 days long. These usually include local excursions, charming authentic accommodation and all connecting transport. Build your own travel experience by piecing these trips together to create your perfect itinerary.

Ride With Us

UK (+44) 0870 850 4136

sales@ridewithustours.co.uk

www.ridewithustours.co.uk

Organised motorcycle holidays around western and eastern Europe that offer something for everyone regardless of their touring experience.

Saddle Skedaddle

UK +44 (0)191 265 1110

info@skedaddle.co.uk

www.skedaddle.co.uk

Some say there is no better way to see a country, its culture, its wildlife and its people, than by bike! This company offers off-road, road or leisure cycling.

Safari Par Excellence

UK +44 (0) 1548 830 059

www.zambezi.co.uk

Safari company with a 'no fuss or frills' ethos. They cover Zimbabwe, Zambia, Botswana, Namibia and other countries in Africa.

Scenic Air

Namibia +264 61 249 268

windhoek@scenic-air.com

www.scenic-air.com

Scenic Air caters for individual travellers, families as well as groups. They offer flights to all of the popular tourist destinations in Namibia.

Selective Asia

UK +44 (0) 1273 670001

contact@selectiveasia.com

www.selectiveasia.com

Selective Asia offers a range of unique, privately guided tours and adventure holidays in Cambodia, Laos, Vietnam and Thailand.

Specialtours Ltd

UK +44 (0) 20 7386 4690

info@specialtours.co.uk

www.specialtours.co.uk

International art and cultural tours. Access wonderful private houses, art collections and gardens. Most tours are accompanied by an expert lecturer.

Suntrek

UK 0800 781 1660

www.intrepidsuntrek.com

Adventure tours arranged in the USA, Mexico, Alaska, Canada, Central and South America and Australia.

Sunvil

UK +44 (0) 20 8568 4499

www.sunvil.co.uk

A range of active holidays/trips available including sailing holidays around the world.

The adventure company

UK 0845 287 6541

www.adventurecompany.co.uk

Offers inspirational holidays and trips worldwide that venture off the well trodden tourist trails.

The Bundu Safari Company

UK 0800 781 1660

www.intrepidbundu.com

The Bundu Safari Company has teamed up with Intrepid Travel to offer exciting safari adventures.

The Dragon Trip Pte Ltd

UK +44 (0)207 936 4884

info@thedragontrip.com

thedragontrip.com

The Dragon Trip is a provider of affordable holidays in China in the form of backpacking trips.

The Imaginative Traveller

UK 0845 287 2908

online@imtrav.net

www.imaginative-traveller.com

Individual, escape and volunteering tours available.

The Oriental Caravan

UK +44 (0)1424 883 570

info@theorientalcaravan.com

www.theorientalcaravan.com

The Oriental Caravan is a truly independent adventure tour operator specialising in escorted small group travel in the Far East.

The Russia Experience

UK 0845 521 2910

expert@trans-siberian.co.uk

www.trans-siberian.co.uk

The Trans-Siberian is a working train covering 9,000 km, 10 time zones, 16 rivers and some 80 towns and cities. A once in a lifetime experience.

The Unique Travel Company

UK 01264 889 644

info@theuniquetravel.co.uk

www.theuniquetravel.co.uk

We provide a personal, affordable Sri Lankan experience that gives you a truly unique experience knowing that you are also putting money back into the island to help it grow and prosper - we feel this is what responsible tourism is about.

Timberline Adventures

USA +1 800 417 2453

timber@earthnet.net

www.timbertours.com

Hiking and cycling tours in the USA.

Top Deck

UK 0845 257 5212

info@topdecktravel.co.uk

www.topdeck.travel

Providing unforgettable travel experiences for 18 to 30 somethings. Extended trips, festivals, ski and sailing in Europe, holidays in Egypt, Morocco, Jordan and Israel, safaris in Africa, adventures in Australia and New Zealand.

Tour Bus

Australia

questions@tourbus.com.au

www.tourbus.com.au

If you are looking for Tour Bus options within Australia or around the world you will likely find some great resources here.

Tourism Queensland

UK 44 20 7367 0981

www.experiencequeensland.com

Explore the many beautiful destinations Queensland has to offer.

Travel Nation

UK +44 (0)1273 320580

www.travelnation.co.uk

Independent specialist travel company providing expert advice and the best deals on round-the-world trips, multi-stop itineraries, overland/adventure tours and Trans-Siberian rail journeys.

Travellers Connected.com

UK

info@travellersconnected.com

www.travellersconnected.com

A totally free community site for gap-year travellers. Register and contact travellers around the world for to-the-minute advice on the best places to go and best things to do.

Tribes Travel

UK +44 (0)1473 890499

enquiries@tribes.co.uk

www.tribes.co.uk

A Fair Trade Travel company with lots of exciting tours for you to choose from, such as budget priced walking safaris to the more expensive once in a lifetime trips.

Tucan Travel

UK +44 (0)800 804 8435

www.tucantravel.com

Tucan Travel are an adventure tour operator, specialising in group tours in South and Central America, Asia, Europe and Africa

Vodkatrain

UK +44 (0) 20 8877 7650

www.vodkatrain.com

Experience the Trans-Mongolian railway and the Silk Road, travelling with local people, sampling local food and travel at local prices.

Walks Worldwide

UK 0845 301 4737

sales@walksworldwide.com

www.walksworldwide.com

Walks Worldwide is a leading independent specialist for trekking and walking holidays, offering a wide choice of walking holidays to all the world's great trekking and walking destinations, many of which are unique to Walks Worldwide.

World Expeditions

UK +44 (0)20 8545 9030

enquiries@worldexpeditions.co.uk

www.worldexpeditions.com

Adventure travel company offering ground breaking itineraries on every continent. They offer exciting all inclusive adventures and challenges worldwide.

Working abroad

Au Pairing

Au Pair Ecosse
UK +44 (0) 1786 474573
ruth@aupairecosse.com
www.aupairecosse.com
Au Pair Ecosse places au pairs with families in Scotland and sends British au pairs to families in Europe and America using established, reputable agent partners.

Au Pair in America (APIA)
UK 0207 581 7322
info@aupairamerica.co.uk
www.aupairamerica.co.uk
Whether you're looking for a year out or a legal cultural exchange opportunity, APIA's au pair programs give you plenty of free time to explore, study, travel and make new friends, complete with support throughout your stay.

Bunters Au Pair Agency
UK +44 (0)1327 831144
office@aupairsnannies.com
www.aupairsnannies.com
Bunters offers various au pair positions in the UK and Europe.

Childcare International Ltd
UK +44 (0)20 8731 4551
office@childint.co.uk
www.childint.co.uk
Childcare International, together with their partner agencies abroad, arrange au pair placements across Europe, Australia, New Zealand, Canada and the US.

Distant Shores
UK +44 15242 73722
www.dsaupairs.com
Distant Shores offers 3-9 month au pair placements in China to 18-29 year-olds wanting to share and learn language and culture.

Gap 360
UK 01892 527392
info@gap360.com
www.gap360.com
Gap 360 is an exciting travel company offering an amazing range of affordable gap year adventures.

Planet Au Pair
Spain +34 91 546 6605
info@planetaupair.com
www.planetaupair.com
Company placing au pairs throughout Europe and the USA.

Total Nannies
UK +44 (0)207 0601213
www.totalnannies.com
This company places nannies and au pairs worldwide.

Internships & Paid Work Placements

African Conservation Experience
UK +44 (0) 1454 269182
info@conservationafrica.net
www.conservationafrica.net
African Conservation Experience offer volunteering opportunities at wildlife conservation projects in southern Africa. You can count on our full support and more than 10 years experience. See our main advert in Conservation

For further information see page 188

317

AgriVenture

UK +44 (0)1664 560044

clare@agriventure.com; judy@agriventure.com

www.agriventure.com

Spend your gap year getting fantastic work experience in South Pacific/North America/Japan/Europe. Work in agriculture or horticulture. Get paid for the work you do whilst living and working with one of our fully approved hosting enterprises.

Flying Fish UK Ltd

UK +44 (0)1983 280641

mail@flyingfishonline.com

www.flyingfishonline.com

Flying Fish trains and recruits over 1000 people each year to work worldwide as yacht skippers and as sailing, diving, surfing, windsurfing, ski and snowboard instructors.

For further information see page 152

Gap 360

UK 01892 527392

info@gap360.com

www.gap360.com

Gap 360 is an exciting travel company offering an amazing range of affordable gap year adventures.

Global Choices

UK +44 (0) 20 8533 2777

www.globalchoices.co.uk

Offers internships and working holidays in USA, Australia, Canada, UK, Ireland, Brazil, Argentina, Spain, Greece and Italy.

Graduate Gap Year

UK

enquiries@graduategapyear.com

www.graduategapyear.com

Graduate Gap Year offers unrivaled opportunities to gain substantial work experience, through a placement overseas - in Africa, China, India and South-East Asia.

InterExchange

USA +1 212 924 0446

info@interexchange.org

www.interexchange.org

InterExchange offers J-1 & H-2B visa programs throughout the US. Options include au pair, internship, seasonal work and travel and summer camp positions.

International Exchange Programme UK (IEPUK)

UK +44(0)1572 823 934

ws@iepuk.com

www.iepuk.com

Based in the United Kingdom IEPUK is offering a wide range of international exchange programmes and educational packages to support study and work experience abroad.

Invasion

UK 01613 123459

info@invasion.com

www.invasion.com

Invasion offers a variety of work placements abroad, from the USA to Australia, including Canada, South Africa, Thailand and China. Earn money whilst travelling across the country and exploring the area, making new friends and discovering new cultures.

IST Plus

UK 020 7788 7877

info@istplus.com

www.istplus.com

Internships in the USA, Australia, New Zealand. Summer work in the USA. Summer camp in the USA. Gap-year work in Australia, New Zealand. Volunteer in Thailand. Teach in Thailand, China (for graduates).

For further information see page 158

visit: www.gap-year.com

Lucasfilm
USA

jobs.lucasfilm.com

As you can imagine, internships with Lucasfilm are few and far between. They are also quickly filled. See their website for further details.

Mountbatten Institute
UK 0845 370 3535

info-uk@mountbatten.org

www.mountbatten.org

Grab a whole year's worth of paid work experience through the Mountbatten Programme and enhance your CV.

PGL
UK 0844 3710 123

recruitment@pgl.co.uk

www.pgl.co.uk/jobs

As the UK's market-leading provider of residential activity holidays and educational courses for children, PGL have an immense variety of Gap Year Jobs to offer for your Gap Year: and we pay you!

For further information see page 154

The New England Wild Flower Society & Garden in the Woods
USA +1 508 877 7630

information@newenglandwild.org

www.newfs.org

The oldest plant conservation organization in the USA and a leader in regional plant conservation programmes and native plant studies. They have volunteering and internship opportunities.

Twin Work & Volunteer
UK 0208 297 3278

www.workandvolunteer.com

Work and volunteer programmes listed. Also offers a travel insurance package.

Up with People
USA +1 303 460 7100

www.upwithpeople.org

A global education organization which aims to bring the world together through service and music. The unique combination of international travel, service learning, leadership development and performing arts offers students an unparalleled experience and a pathway to make a difference in the world, one community at a time.

Visitoz
Australia +61 741 686 106

info@visitoz.org

www.visitoz.org

Visitoz provides training and guarantees work for young people between the ages of 18 and 30 in agriculture, hospitality, child care and teaching all over Australia.

For further information see page 166

Work the World Ltd
UK +44 (0) 1273 974 634

info@worktheworld.co.uk

www.worktheworld.co.uk

Organises healthcare and community development projects that provide maximum benefit to both the participants and the overseas communities they support.

WYSE Work & Volunteer Abroad
Netherlands +31 (0)20 421 2800

www.wyseworkandvolunteer.org

WYSE Work & Volunteer Abroad is the leading global forum for organisations involved in all aspects of work abroad, volunteer, internship, and work & travel.

Seasonal work

Acorn Adventure

UK +44 (0)1384 398870
info@acornadventure.co.uk
www.acornadventure.co.uk

Acorn Adventure specialises in trips for schools and youth groups nationwide, inspiring a love of the great outdoors in young people so that they go on to lead active lives and develop a special connection with nature. A wide range of adventurous activities are available at natural outdoor environments such as mountains, lakes, rivers and caves in France, Italy, Spain and South Wales.

AmeriCamp

UK +44 (0)1613 123640
info@americamp.co.uk
www.americamp.co.uk

We offer people around the world the chance to work in the USA at a summer camp and become an AmeriCamper. We pay at least $1500 and you make memories that last a lifetime! Join the AmeriCamp Revolution!

BUNAC

UK +44 (0) 333 999 7516
info@bunacusa.org
www.bunac.org

BUNAC the work and travel expert offers exciting work abroad, volunteering abroad programmes and gap year opportunities.

Camp America

UK 0207 581 7373
enquiries@campamerica.co.uk
www.campamerica.co.uk

Camp America sends over 7,500 people to work on summer camps in the USA every year with up to 4 weeks independent travel after camp!

Camp Leaders In America

UK +44 (0) 151 708 6868
uk@campleaders.com
www.campleaders.com

For those aged between 18 and 25 who love fun, adventure and are passionate about a sport, hobby or interest and want to get paid for enjoying it, look no further than Camp Leaders. Combine life-changing cultural experiences with the perfect summer job abroad.

Canvas Holidays

UK +44 (0) 1383 629012
www.canvasholidays.co.uk/recruitment

We have paid positions at over 100 campsites across Europe. We require a minimum of eight weeks commitment for July and August.

For further information see page 162

Castaway Resorts

Thailand +66 (0)831 387 472 / +66 (0)811 707 605
www.castaway-resorts.com

Castaway Resorts invite enthusiastic active young people on a gap year to join our friendly teams at one of our tropical beach resorts in Thailand.

CCUSA

UK 0208 874 6325
info@ccusa.co.uk
www.ccusa.com

Work in summer camps in beautiful locations in America. You don't need any experience or qualifications but you do need to be at least 18 years old. Also available, a range of worldwide programs including winter seasons in Canada.

Changing Worlds
UK +44 (0)2081 238702
info@changing-worlds.com; media@
changing-worlds.com
www.changingworlds.co.uk
We offer a range of gap year placements in: Australia, China, Fiji, Ghana, India, Indonesia, South Africa, Thailand and many more. So, if you like the idea of travel, meeting like-minded people and don't mind working hard, then this is for you!

Château Beaumont
UK +44 (0)1388 741370
holidays@chateau-beaumont.co.uk
www.chateau-beaumont.co.uk
Chateau Beaumont is a small friendly language and activity centre based in the Normandy region of France.

Gap 360
UK 01892 527392
info@gap360.com
www.gap360.com
Gap 360 is an exciting travel company offering an amazing range of affordable gap year adventures.

Go Workabout
Australia +61 (0)8 6226 9979
info@goworkabout.com
www.goworkabout.com
Arranges work in Australia for working holiday makers before they travel.
For further information see page 146

Immigration New Zealand
UK 09069 100 100 (premium rate number)
www.immigration.govt.nz/branch/
londonbranchhome
New Zealand government website offering details on working holidays for visitors to the country.

Leiths List, Agency for Cooks
UK +44 (0) 1225 722983
info@leithslist.com
www.leithslist.com
Find short term cookery jobs such as chalet and holiday home work Once qualified (see cookery section), you can earn money in your gap year or university holidays.

Mark Warner Ltd
UK 0844 273 7332
newbookings@markwarner.co.uk
www.markwarner.co.uk
Leading independent tour operator with opportunities all year round in ski and beach resorts. Variety of hotel positions and fully inclusive benefits package on offer.

Natives.co.uk
UK +44 (0)1772 639604
info@natives.co.uk
www.natives.co.uk
Seasonal recruitment website for ski or summer resorts.

Neilson Holidays
UK 0844 879 8155 / 8817
sales@neilson.com
www.neilson.co.uk
This company offers a selection of worldwide sporting holidays, all year round.
For further information see page 148

Oyster Worldwide Limited
UK +44 (0) 1892 770 771
anne@oysterworldwide.com
www.oysterworldwide.com
Oyster is the specialist gap-year provider offering paid work projects abroad. Whether you're a ski nut or budding jackaroo, you'll get excellent, personal support throughout.
For further information see page 140

PlayaWay

Spain UK: 0871 288 4412; Non UK: +34 922 79 31 93
info@playawayabroad.com
www.playawayabroad.com

Offering seasonal bar and club work at resorts such as Ibiza, Malia, Zante and Magaluf.

Season Workers

UK 0845 6439338
info@seasonworkers.com
www.seasonworkers.com

A free resource featuring information on destinations and itineraries, as well as a searchable database of paid and voluntary opportunities.

The Travel Visa Company Ltd

UK +44 (0) 1270 250 590
info@thetravelvisacompany.co.uk
www.thetravelvisacompany.co.uk

The Travel Visa Company Ltd specialises in obtaining all types of visas for destinations right across the world including Australia, USA, India, Russia, China and Sri Lanka.

Visas Australia Ltd

UK +44 (0)1270 250 590
sales@visas-australia.com
www.visas-australia.com

Visas Australia Ltd specialises in processing and issuing all types of visas, particularly suited to gap-year travellers. Their service is approved by both the Australian Tourist Board and Australian High Commission.

Visitoz

Australia +61 741 686 106
info@visitoz.org
www.visitoz.org

Visitoz provides training and guarantees work for young people between the ages of 18 and 30 in agriculture, hospitality, child care and teaching all over Australia.

For further information see page 142

Xtreme Gap

Netherlands +44 (0)20 32867065
info@xtremegapyear.co.uk
www.xtremegapyear.co.uk

Gap company offering extreme sporting adventures.

TEFL

Adventure Alternative

UK +44 (0) 28 708 31258
office@adventurealternative.com
www.adventurealternative.com

Teaching and volunteering in needy schools and orphanages in Kenya and in schools in Kathmandu (includes Himalayan trek).

Link Ethiopia

UK +44 (0)20 8045 4558
chris@linkethiopia.org
www.linkethiopia.org

Experience Ethiopia and teach basic English to small groups on a very inexpensive three-month placement with us. Registered Charity No. 1112390.

LoveTEFL

UK +44 (0)113 829 3300
info@lovetefl.com
www.lovetefl.com

TEFL (Teaching English as a Foreign Language) is all about exploring the world while learning new skills and getting useful experience for 'real life'. LoveTEFL offer internationally recognised TEFL training, and unique teaching/travel adventures and internship.

For further information see page 228

Oyster Worldwide Limited

UK +44 (0) 1892 770 771
anne@oysterworldwide.com
www.oysterworldwide.com

Highly motivated university graduate? We can organise a top quality TEFL course followed by a well-paid job teaching English in China or Thailand.

For further information see page 140

Shane Global Language Centres

UK +44 (0) 20 7499 8533 (option 1)
marketing@shaneglobal.com
www.shaneglobal.com

If you don't yet have your TEFL qualification, Saxoncourt runs full time four-week courses in London and Oxford, leading to either the Trinity TESOL diploma or the Cambridge CELTA qualification.

Syndicat Mixte Montaigu-Rocheservière

France +33 (0) 2 51 46 45 45
anglais@sm-montaigu-rocheserviere.fr
www.gapyear-france.com

Receives local government funding to teach English in primary schools, offering five posts annually - and it also employs a sixth person to work as a language assistant in a local college and lycée.

The Language House

France +33 (0)6 84 83 85 59
info@teflanguagehouse.com
www.teflanguagehouse.com

TEFL/TESOL programme available. Also courses in French, Arabic, Spanish or Italian. Small classes.

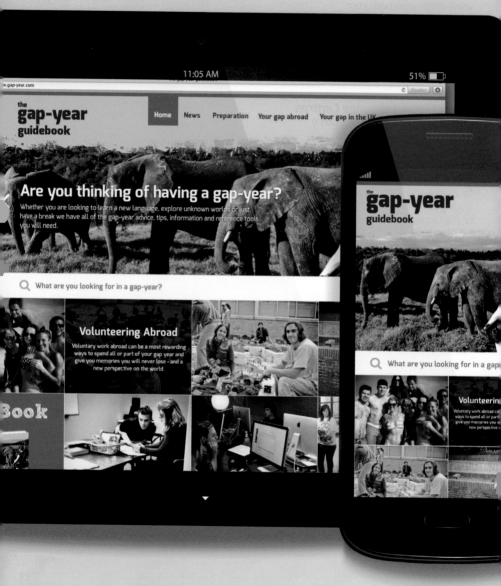

Conservation

Adventure Under Sail

UK +44 (0)1305 858274
enquiries@adventureundersail.com
www.adventureundersail.com

TS Pelican of London is a unique square rigger that sails thousands of miles each year with a voyage crew of young people and the young at heart!

African Conservation Experience

UK +44 (0) 1454 269182
info@conservationafrica.net
www.conservationafrica.net

African Conservation Experience offer volunteering opportunities at wildlife conservation projects in southern Africa. You can count on our full support and more than 10 years experience. See our main advert in Conservation

For further information see page 188

African Conservation Trust

South Africa +27 33 342 2844
talk@projectafrica.com
www.projectafrica.com

The mission of ACT is to provide a means for conservation projects to become self funding through active participation by the public.

African Wildlife Protection Fund Leadership (AWPF)

South Africa +27 (0)23 004 0074
info@awpf.co.za
www.awpfleadership.co.za

AWPF offers learners the opportunity to develop leadership and survival skills such as team work, community work & development, animal tracking, self-reliance skills and survival/bush craft skills whilst visiting some of the largest private game reserves in South Africa, providing great sight-seeing experiences.

All Out Africa

Swaziland +268 2416 2260
info@alloutafrica.com
www.alloutafrica.com

All Out Africa offers various volunteering opportunities in Africa, from marine conservation to studying the savannah and its native species. Make a difference whilst absorbing the beauty and culture of Africa.

Amanzi Travel

UK +44 (0) 117 253 0888
info@amanzitravel.co.uk
www.amanzitravel.co.uk

Amanzi Travel offers tailor-made volunteer opportunities in Africa or Asia. Perfect for a career break, gap year or holiday, get involved with wildlife conservation, marine, medical, teaching, orphan care and sustainable community programmes. There are also opportunities to join world famous courses where you will learn to be a game ranger as well as adventure overland tours - a great way to explore more of these beautiful continents.

Andaman Discoveries
Thailand +66 (0) 87 917 7165
info@andamandiscoveries.com
www.andamandiscoveries.com
Tours allow visitors to experience the traditional culture and ecology of rural coastal Thailand. Volunteer, stay with a family or partake in an eco-project.

Azafady
UK 0208 960 6629
info@azafady.org
www.madagascar.co.uk
Pioneer Madagascar is a 2-10 week volunteer scheme that offers first-hand experience of frontline development and conservation work in beautiful and remote areas.

Biosphere Expeditions
UK 0870-4460801
uk@biosphere-expeditions.org
www.biosphere-expeditions.org
Biosphere Expeditions is an international non-profit wildlife volunteer organisation, founded in 1999, that runs conservation expeditions for environmental volunteers all across the globe.

Blue Ventures
UK +44 (0) 20 7697 8598
info@blueventures.org
www.blueventures.org
Blue Ventures runs award-winning marine research projects for conservation, education and sustainable development. Volunteers participate in diving and terrestrial activities in partnership with local communities.

For further information see page 196

Camps International Limited
UK +44 (0)1425 485390
info@campsinternational.com
www.campsinternational.com
Gap-year volunteer holidays available. Spend time in community and wildlife camps and still have the time and opportunity to trek mountains and dive in the ocean.

Comunidad Inti Wara Yassi
Bolivia +591 4 413 6572
info@intiwarayassi.org
www.intiwarayassi.org
CIWY is always looking for volunteers to help care for rescued wildlife and the day-to-day running of their three reserves in Bolivia. Volunteers help care for and interact with numerous animals including pumas, jaguars, monkeys, tapirs, tortoises, exotic birds and more, whilst helping to improve their lives and raise awareness of poaching and illegal animal trade.

Concordia International Volunteers
UK 01273 422 218
info@concordiavolunteers.org.uk
www.concordiavolunteers.org.uk
Concordia offers the opportunity to join international teams of volunteers working on short-term projects in 60 countries in Europe, North America, Latin-America, Africa and Asia.

Conservation Volunteers Australia
Australia +61 (0) 3 5330 2600
info@conservationvolunteers.com.au
www.conservationvolunteers.com.au
Conservation Volunteers Australia offers projects across Australia, including tree planting, wildlife surveys, track building, year-round. Contribution for meals, accommodation and travel applies.

Conservation Volunteers New Zealand

Australia +61 (0) 3 5330 2600

info@conservationvolunteers.com.au

www.conservationvolunteers.com.au

Conservation Volunteers New Zealand offers projects year-round, including habitat restoration, tree planting, track building. Contribution for meals, accommodation and travel applies.

Coral Cay Conservation

UK 0207 620 1411

info@coralcay.org

www.coralcay.org

Volunteer with award-winning specialists in coral reef and rainforest conservation expeditions. Scuba dive or trek in tropical climes and work with local communities to aid long-term conservation efforts.

Crees Foundation

Peru: +51 (0)84 262 433 /
UK: +44 (0)20 7581 2932

www.crees-manu.org

Crees Foundation offers various volunteering opportunities in Peru, ranging from 1 week to 12 weeks duration. Live and work in the heart of the Amazon rainforest. Help support sustainable development and conduct conservation research.

Discover Nepal

Nepal +977 1 4413690

stt@mos.com.np

www.discovernepal.org.np

The aim of Discover Nepal is to provide opportunities for the involvement in the development process, and to practically contribute towards the socio-economic development of the country.

Dyer Island Cruises

South Africa +27 (0)82 801 8014

bookings@whalewatchsa.com

www.whalewatchsa.com

Dyer Island Cruises offer volunteering opportunities, in addition to activities such as shark cage diving, boat-based whale and bird watching and plane-based wildlife viewing.

Earthwatch Institute

UK 01865 318 838

info@earthwatch.org.uk

www.earthwatch.org.uk

Work alongside leading scientists around the world and help solve pressing environmental problems. With expeditions on over 25 research projects to choose from, conduct hands-on conservation research in stunning locations whilst having an experience of a lifetime.

Ecoteer

UK +44 (0)1752 426285

contact@ecoteer.com

www.ecoteer.com

Community-based placements in countries around the world and most are free! Volunteer with us and make everlasting friends across the whole world!

Ecoteer (Malaysia)

Malaysia +6 012 217 3208 (Malaysia)

explore@ecoteer.com

www.ecoteerresponsibletravel.com

With Ecoteer Responsible Travel you will help communities and wildlife at our various projects across Asia.

Edge of Africa

South Africa +27 (0) 443820122

info@edgeofafrica.com

www.edgeofafrica.com

Edge of Africa offer volunteer programmes to suit your personality, preference and budget. Give the edge and volunteer in Africa.

Essential Croatia
UK
info@essentialcroatia.com
www.essentialcroatia.com

Join the Griffon Vulture and nature protection programme. Volunteer opportunities available year round on the beautiful and upsoilt island of Cres-Croatia.

Fauna Forever Tambopata
Peru
www.faunaforever.org

Volunteer researchers needed for wildlife project in the Peruvian Amazon. Fauna Forever Tambopata is a wildlife monitoring project based in the Amazon rainforest of Tambopata in south-eastern Peru.

FirstStep.me
South Africa
contact@firststep.me
www.firststep.me

FirstStep.me is an information and reference based online magazine.

Forest Animal Rescue
USA +1 352 625 7377
volunteer@forestanimalrescue.org
forestanimalrescue.org

The perfect opportunity to learn about the welfare of big cats, bears, wolves, monkeys, bats and more while helping the staff and interns of a wild animal sanctuary to provide them with lifetime care.

For further information see page 184

Friends of Conservation
UK +44 (0) 20 7348 3408
focinfo@aol.com
www.foc-uk.com

There are some opportunities to volunteer on overseas projects such as the Namibian based Cheetah Conservation Fund. Volunteers are also needed in the UK and at their head office in London. Registered Charity No. 328176.

Fronteering
Canada +1 604-831 7725
fronteering.com

Fronteering takes you off the beaten path to volunteer with wildlife, conservation, communities or internships.

Frontier
UK +44 (0) 20 7613 2422
info@frontier.ac.uk
www.frontier.ac.uk

With 250 projects around the world Frontier offers volunteers the chance to get involved in an array of activities from wildlife and marine conservation to trekking and biodiversity research, teaching and community development.

Galapagos Conservation Trust
UK 0207 399 7440
gct@gct.org
www.savegalapagos.org

The Galapagos Conservation Trust has two aims: to raise funds to support the expanding conservation work and to raise awareness of the current issues the islands face. Registered Charity No. 1043470.

Gapforce
UK 0207 384 3028
info@gapforce.org
www.gapforce.org
Gapforce has established itself as a leading provider for enjoyable gap adventures worldwide including volunteering. It is the parent company of Trekforce and Greenforce.

Global Action Nepal
UK +44 (0) 7941 044063
info@gannepal.org.np
www.gannepal.org.np
Global Action Nepal projects are always closely in harness with grass roots level needs, focusing on community-led, participatory development. Registered Charity No. 1090773.

Global Vision International (GVI)
UK 01727 250 250
info@gviworld.com
www.gvi.co.uk
With unparalled in-country support, GVI volunteers benefit from exceptional training and a Careers Abroad job placement scheme.

Global Volunteer Network
New Zealand +64 0800 032 5035
info@volunteer.org.nz
www.globalvolunteernetwork.org
Volunteer through the Global Volunteer Network to support communities in need around the world. Volunteer placements include schools, refugee camps, wildlife sanctuaries and nature reserves.

Greenforce
UK +44 (0) 20 7384 3028
info@greenforce.org
www.greenforce.org
Greenforce is a not-for-profit organisation offering voluntary and paid work overseas. With ten years experience and a range of opportunities, Greenforce will have a programe to suit you.

International Volunteer HQ (IVHQ)
New Zealand: +64 6 758 7949;
UK: 0808 234 1621
info@volunteerhq.org
www.volunteerhq.org
IVHQ offers volunteer programs in more than 30 different locations worldwide including: Africa, Asia, Central & South America, The Pacific and Europe. Programs have many different start dates and a wide range of volunteer work opportunities including: Medical & Healthcare, Arts & Music, Education, Conservation and Construction.
For further information see page 206

Intrax/ProWorld
USA +1 877 429 6753
info@globalinternships.com
www.globalinternships.com/us/social-development-internships
Projects offered: conservation, health care, education, human rights, journalism, and business projects. Programmes start every month of the year.

InvAID
UK 01612121051
info@invasion.com
www.invasion.com
We offer people around the world the opportunity to volunteer in countries such as Brazil, The Maldives and Thailand. Not only do you get the Invasion experience, but you get to make a real difference in people's lives whilst being based in some of the most rewarding locations in the world.

6 Volunteering abroad

Kaya Responsible Travel
UK +44 (0) 161 870 6212
info@kayavolunteer.com
www.kayavolunteer.com
Kaya offer over 200 volunteer projects worldwide working with local communities and conservation initiatives from 2 weeks to 12 months. Placements are tailored to specific needs and skills of students, career breakers', retirees, families or groups.

Local Ocean Trust : Watamu Turtle Watch
Kenya +254 717 57 87 23
www.watamuturtles.com
There's so much at the Local Ocean Trust for you to get involved in, with programmes such as turtle nest protection, turtle rehabilitation centre, turtle net release and research and data entry. There is also an education and community outreach programme for those interested in giving humanitarian aid.

N/a'an ku se Foundation
Namibia +264 (0)81 261 2709
volunteer@naankuse.com
www.naankuse.com
Help to preserve and conserve the Namibian ecosystem by volunteering with N/a'an ku se. With projects ranging from 2 weeks to 3 months and no experience or qualifications necessary, there is something for everyone.

Nature Guide Training
South Africa 27 734689267 / +27 836677586
sarah@natureguidetraining.com
www.natureguidetraining.co.za
Situated on a private game reserve three hours drive from Johannesburg, Nature Guide Training offer a series of programmes in nature guiding and other tailor-made courses.

On African Soil
South Africa +27 78 820 3353
julia@onafricansoil.com
www.onafricansoil.com
Become an On African Soil Volunteer and take part in wildlife conservation and social upliftment projects.

On Track Safaris (Ingwe Leopard Research Program)
UK
carol@ontracksafaris.co.uk
www.ontracksafaris.co.uk/styled-28/vol.html
Our project allows volunteers to join us in our own private research reserve in South Africa in which they will learn the different concepts of conservation such as wildlife identification, bush senses, bush craft, data input and analysis, tracking ect.

Orangutan Foundation
UK +44 (0) 20 7724 2912
www.orangutan.org.uk
Participate in hands on conservation fieldwork that really makes a difference and see orangutans in their natural habitat.

Outreach International
UK +44 (0) 1458 274957
info@outreachinternational.co.uk
www.outreachinternational.co.uk
Outreach International places committed volunteers in carefully selected projects on the Pacific coast of Mexico, Sri Lanka, Kenya, Cambodia, Nepal, Costa Rica, Ecuador and the Galapagos Islands.
For further information see page 200

Oyster Worldwide Limited

UK +44 (0) 1892 770 771

anne@oysterworldwide.com

www.oysterworldwide.com

Oyster is a specialist gap-year provider offering genuine opportunities with endangered or abused animals. Vets, zoologists and animal lovers all welcome. Excellent, personal support throughout.

For further information see page 176

Pacific Discovery

New Zealand +64 3 5467667

info@pacificdiscovery.org

www.pacificdiscovery.org

With programmes blending meaningful and challenging travel, cultural immersion, volunteer and community service project, Pacific Discovery offers inspiring summer, semester and gap-year educational travel programs abroad.

Rangers Survivalcraft

South Africa +27 (0)23 004 0074

info@rangerssurvivalcraft.com

www.rangerssurvivalcraft.com

A non profit organisation based in the Western Cape of South Africa, Rangers Survivalcraft offers a 2 week or up to 5 week mini-gap programme for young people. Visit some of the largest private game reserves in South Africa and help work on building a private nature reserve. Develop leadership skills, survival skills and be part of the conservation and educational development programme. Additionally, help make a difference in the lives of people by working with disadvantaged youth and communities through the Young Rangers programme.

Real Gap Experience

UK +44 (0)1273 647220

info@realgap.co.uk

www.realgap.co.uk

Real Gap offers a wide and diverse range of programmes. These include: volunteering, conservation, adventure travel and expeditions, sports, teaching English, round the world, paid working holidays and learning.

ReefDoctor Org Ltd

UK +44 (0)208 788 6908

volunteer@reefdoctor.org

www.reefdoctor.org

Become a volunteer ReefDoctor and contribute to marine research, education, conservation and sustainable community development alongside our team of local and international scientists.

Rempart

France +33 (0)1 42 71 96 55

contact@rempart.com

www.rempart.com

Rempart, a union of conservation associations organises short voluntary work in France. The projects are all based around restoration and maintenance of historic sites and buildings.

Shumba Experience

UK +44 (0)845 257 3205

info@shumbaexperience.co.uk

www.shumbaexperience.co.uk

Join our exciting wildlife and marine conservation projects in Africa. You'll be volunteering on game reserves to help conserve lions, elephants, leopards and rhinos.

Starfish Ventures Ltd
UK +44 (0)3300 010807
info@starfishvolunteers.com
www.starfishvolunteers.com
Starfish has a volunteer placement for you, whatever your skills, they can be put to good use in our various projects in Thailand.

Sumatran Orangutan Society
UK +44 (0)1235 530825
www.orangutans-sos.org
SOS is looking for committed, energetic volunteers to support our small team. The roles will involve fundraising, campaigning, and raising awareness about orangutans and the work we do in Sumatra.

Sunrise Volunteer Programmes
UK +44 (0) 121 5722795
info@sunrint.com
en.sunrint.com
Specialist for volunteer projects in China, offering volunteer opportunities in social, environment, education, medical, journalism and community areas around China.

The British Exploring Society (BSES Expeditions)
UK +44 (0)20 7591 3141
info@britishexploring.org
www.britishexploring.org
BSES Expeditions organises challenging scientific expeditions to remote, wild environments. Study climate change whilst mountaineering or kayaking in the Arctic, measure biodiversity in the Amazon or investigate human interaction with the environment in the Himalayas.

The Great Projects
UK +44 (0)208 885 4987
info@thegreatprojects.com
www.thegreatprojects.com
We, The Great Projects, specialise in wildlife volunteering projects and currently have 38 projects and 17 Tours throughout Africa, Asia, Europe and South America.

The Leap Overseas Ltd
UK 01672 519922
info@theleap.co.uk
www.theleap.co.uk
Team or solo placements in Africa, Asia or South America. Volunteer to get stuck into our unique mix of eco-tourism, community and conservation projects. Connect with local people.

For further information see pages 170-171

TrekFORCE
UK +44 (0) 207 384 3028
info@trekforce.org.uk
www.trekforce.org.uk
TrekFORCE offers expeditions in Bornea, Central America, Nepal and Papua New Guinea. Learn survival skills, jungle training and work on conservation and community projects. Expedition leadership training also available.

Tropical Adventures Foundation
Costa Rica +506 8868-0296
info@tropicaladventures.com
www.tropicaladventures.com
Provides volunteer tour packages for individuals, families and groups interested in exploring the culture, language and natural beauty of Costa Rica.

UNA Exchange
UK 02920 223 088
info@unaexchange.org
www.unaexchange.org
Registered charity that supports people to take part in international volunteer projects in over 50 countries across the world. Each project is organised by one of our international partner organisations, based in the country of the project. Projects cover a large range of themes including; social, environmental, construction and cultural projects.

Volunteer Latin America
UK +44 (0)20 7193 9163
info@volunteerlatinamerica.com
www.volunteerlatinamerica.com
Volunteer abroad for free or at low-cost in Central and South America via the greenest volunteer advisor on the planet.

Voluntour South Africa
South Africa +27 (0)82 416 6066
info@voluntoursouthafrica.com
www.voluntoursouthafrica.com
VSA offers you a chance to make a lasting difference to the lives of others. If you have a sense of adventure and feel the urge to experience new cultures and make a difference then VSA is the right place for you

Wilderness Awareness School
USA +1 425 788 1301
wasnet@wildernessawareness.org
www.wildernessawareness.org
The school, a not for profit environmental organisation, offers courses for adults in tracking, wilderness survival skills and a stewardship programme.

Wildlife PACT
India +91 99 10 586006
wildlifepact@gmail.com
www.wildlifepact.org
Wildlife PACT offers volunteering opportunities to students of wildlife, ethnology, anthropology, conservation and environment studies. Short and long term projects available.

WorkingAbroad
UK +44 (0)1273 479047
victoria.mcneil@workingabroad.com
www.workingabroad.com
Choose from a range of volunteering opportunities, including marine and terrestrial wildlife conservation, environmental education, language teaching, childcare and healthcare. Caters for all ages, gap years up to seniors, professionals taking sabbaticals and students wanting to gain field experience.

Worldwide Experience
UK +44 (0) 1483 860 560
www.worldwideexperience.com
Worldwide Experience specialises in volunteer gap-year placements in conservation, marine and community projects throughout Africa.

WWOOF (World Wide Opportunities on Organic Farms)
UK
www.wwoof.org.uk
Join WWOOF and participate in meaningful work that reconnects with nature, share the lives of people who have taken practical steps towards alternative, sustainable lifestyles.

2Way Development

UK +44 (0) 20 7148 6110
volunteer@2waydevelopment.com
www.2waydevelopment.com

2Way offer a support service to people looking for volunteering experiences worldwide.

Action Aid

UK +44 (0)1460 238000
supportercare@actionaid.org
www.actionaid.org.uk/experiences

Take part in ActionAid's First Hand Experience and change lives, including your own. ActionAid is offering volunteering opportunities in South Africa and Nepal, working alongside local people to build homes and centres to benefit whole communities for the better.

Africa & Asia Venture

UK +44 (0)1380 729009
av@aventure.co.uk
www.aventure.co.uk

Established in 1993 AV specialises in community, sports coaching and teaching volunteer projects in Africa, Asia and Latin America. We offer group based projects from 3 weeks to 5 months, including designated travel time.

African Impact

South Africa 0800 098 8440
info@africanimpact.com
www.africanimpact.com

African Impact is a volunteer travel organisation providing meaningful interactive volunteer programs throughout Africa for a positive and measurable impact on local communities and conservation efforts.

All Out Africa

Swaziland +268 2416 2260
info@alloutafrica.com
www.alloutafrica.com

All Out Africa offers various volunteering opportunities in Africa, from caring for orphans to teaching the disadvantaged. Make a difference whilst absorbing the beauty and culture of Africa.

Alliance Abroad Group

USA +1 (512) 457 8062
www.allianceabroad.com

Alliance Abroad is a non-profit organisation that provides international teaching, work and volunteer placements. Our services include guaranteed placement and 24/7 personal assistance.

ATD Fourth World

UK 0207 703 3231
atd@atd-uk.org
www.atd-uk.org

ATD Fourth World is an international voluntary organisation working in partnership with people living in poverty worldwide.

BERUDA

Cameroon +237 67760 1407;
+237 67732 3407
berudepservices@gmail.com
www.berudep.org

BERUDA's vision is 'to eradicate poverty and raise the living standards of the rural population of Cameroon's North West province'. They rely on volunteers to help them achieve this.

BMS World Mission

UK +44 (0) 1235 517700
www.bmsworldmission.org

BMS World Mission is a Christian organisation which sends people in teams and as individuals or families to 34 countries worldwide.

Brathay Exploration Trust
UK 01539 433 942
www.brathayexploration.org.uk
BET has taken around 10,000 people on over 700 expeditions designed to broaden knowledge and help the planet. We are an environmental and cultural education charity that builds partnerships to provide UK and worldwide exploration opportunities to young people. From measuring the depths of Lake District tarns to glacial surveying in Norway, BET specialises in going the extra distance.

Bruce Organisation
Peru
info@bruceorg.org
www.bruceperu.org
Our mission is to help as many of the poorest children in the third world as we can to receive as good an education as their circumstances permit.

Cameroon Association for the Protection and Education of the Child (CAPEC)
Cameroon +237 22 03 01 63
info@capecam.org
www.capecam.org
Volunteer to teach children in Cameroon. See website for vacancies and details of programmes available.

Camphill Association of North America
USA +1 802 472 1102
info@camphill.org
www.camphill.org
Each year many people come to live and work in one of our Camphill Communities in North America for a Gap Year experience. Whether you are taking a break after high school, during your college studies or you are just looking for a new perspectives your life and your work, Camphill has plenty of gap year opportunities for you.

Camphill Communities of Ireland
Ireland +353 045 483 735
info@camphill.ie
www.camphill.ie
Camphill Communities of Ireland is part of an international charitable trust working with people with intellectual disabilities and other kinds of special needs.

Volunteers live, work and share their lives with the community for periods of time between 3 months and two years, helping to make a difference.

Challenges Worldwide
UK +44 (0)131 225 9549
info@challengesworldwide.com
www.challengesworldwide.com
Volunteers with professional skills and experience are needed to work on Challenges Worldwide's many projects.

Changing Worlds
UK +44 (0)2081 238702
info@changing-worlds.com;
media@changing-worlds.com
www.changingworlds.co.uk
We offer a range of gap year placements in: Australia, China, Fiji, Ghana, India, Indonesia, South Africa, Thailand and many more. So, if you like the idea of travel, meeting like-minded people and don't mind working hard, then this is for you!

Cicerones de Buenos Aires Asociación Civil
Argentina +54 11 5258 0909
contacto@cicerones.org.ar
www.cicerones.org.ar
Volunteering in Argentina: Cicerones in Buenos Aires works in a friendly atmosphere ensuring contact with local people, experiencing the city the way it should be!

335

City Year

USA +1 617 927 2500

www.cityyear.org

City Year unites young people of all backgrounds for a demanding year of community service and leadership development throughout the US. This organisation recruits from US only.

Cosmic Volunteers

USA +1 215 609 4196

info@cosmicvolunteers.org

www.cosmicvolunteers.org

American non-profit organisation offering volunteer and internship programmes in China, Ecuador, Ghana, Guatemala, India, Kenya, Nepal, Peru, the Philippines, and Vietnam.

Cross-Cultural Solutions

UK 0845 458 2781

www.crossculturalsolutions.org

Cross-Cultural Solutions operates volunteer programmes in 12 countries in partnership with sustainable community initiatives. CCS brings people together to work side-by-side with members of the local community while sharing perspectives and cultural understanding.

Cultural Canvas Thailand

USA

info@culturalcanvas.com

www.culturalcanvas.com

Cultural Canvas Thailand offers unique and meaningful volunteer experiences in Chiang Mai, Thailand. Placements are available in the following areas: hill tribe education, women's empowerment and Burmese refugee education and assistance.

Development in Action

UK

info@developmentinaction.org

www.developmentinaction.org

Development in Action is a youth and volunteer led development education charity, whose main aim is to engage young people in global issues and promote global citizenship.

Discover Adventure Ltd.

UK 01722 718444

www.discoveradventure.com

Discover Adventure Fundraising Challenges are trips that are designed to be challenging, to push your limits. They are not holidays! They involve preparation in terms of fundraising and improving fitness.

Dragonfly Community Foundation

Thailand +66 087 963 0056

martin@thai-dragonfly.com

www.dragonflycommunity.org

Volunteering programs are currently arranged through Dragonfly Volunteer Projects.

Ecuador Volunteer

Ecuador +593 2 255 7749

www.ecuadorvolunteer.org

Ecuador Volunteer Foundation, is a non-profit organization that offers volunteer work opportunities abroad.

EIL (Experiment for International Living)

UK 01684 562 577

info@eiluk.org

www.eiluk.org

Offers a diverse range of programmes in the UK and worldwide, including volunteering, individual homestays and group learning.

Embrace Tanzania

Tanzania +255 772744588
info@embracetanzania.org
embracetanzania.org

Embrace Tanzania was established under two very simple premises; to support and assist East African communities in need of basic services and to provide placements for people in search of ethically minded volunteer projects within this truly wondrous part of the world.

Volunteers will assist with teaching and caring for young children in selected schools in Zanzibar.

Gap Medics

UK +44 (0)191 230 8080
info@gapmedics.com
www.gapmedics.co.uk

Gap Medics organise medical and nursing placements and projects in Africa and Asia.

Gap Year South Africa

UK +27 71 383 7155
info@gapyearsouthafrica.com
www.gapyearsouthafrica.com

Specialises in sports coaching, teaching, health awareness projects in South Africa. Our project duration is between three weeks and three months.

Glencree Centre for Peace and Reconciliation

Ireland +353 (0) 1 282 9711
info@glencree.ie
www.glencree.ie

Glencree welcomes international volunteers who provide practical help in exchange for a unique experience of working with those building peace in Ireland, Britain and beyond.

Global Media Projects

UK +44 (0) 191 222 0404
info@globalmediaprojects.co.uk
www.globalmediaprojects.co.uk

Offers print/online and broadcast media projects in China, India, Ghana, Mexico, Romania and Tanzania.

Global Volunteer Projects

UK 0191 222 0404
info@globalvolunteerprojects.org
www.globalvolunteerprojects.org

With Global Volunteer Projects you can teach conversational English in schools, help in orphanages or work with animals on conservation projects.

For further information see page 180

Global Volunteers

USA (800) 487 1074
email@globalvolunteers.org
www.globalvolunteers.org

Join a team of short-term volunteers contributing to long-term, comprehensive community projects on a volunteer vacation abroad or a USA volunteer program.

Great Aves

UK 01832 275 038
www.greataves.org

Great Aves is a Gap Year Charity that runs volunteer projects in South America. Volunteers work on the Arajuno Road Project teaching English or working on community based conservation and development projects.

Habitat for Humanity Great Britain

UK 01295 264 240
supporterservices@
habitatforhumanity.org.uk
www.habitatforhumanity.org.uk

Habitat for Humanity aims to eliminate poverty housing and homelessness. Volunteers travel to their chosen country to spend 8-16 days living and working alongside the local community.

i volunteer

India +91 11 65672160
dehli@ivolunteer.in
www.ivolunteer.in

Volunteering opportunites are shown on their website. You could end up working in an orphanage, on a helpline, on relief effort or in a school.

ICYE UK (Inter Cultural Youth Exchange)

UK +44 (0) 20 7681 0983
info@icye.org.uk
www.icye.org.uk

Sends people aged between 18 and 30 to work in voluntary projects overseas in including counselling centres, human rights NGOs, farms, orphanages and schools for the disabled. Registered Charity No. 1081907.

International Volunteer HQ (IVHQ)

New Zealand NZ: +64 6 758 7949; UK: 0808 234 1621
info@volunteerhq.org
www.volunteerhq.org

IVHQ offers volunteer programs in more than 30 different locations worldwide including: Africa, Asia, Central & South America, The Pacific and Europe. Programs have many different start dates and a wide range of volunteer work opportunities including: Medical & Healthcare, Arts & Music, Education, Conservation and Construction.

i-to-i Volunteering

UK +44 (0)1273 647 210
enquiries@i-to-itravel.com
www.i-to-i.com

At i-to-i, we work in partnership with locally run projects in over 20 countries offering you the chance to make a difference on your next trip in a safe, supported, and sustainable manner.

IVS (International Voluntary Service)

UK +44 (0) 131 243 2745
info@ivsgb.org
www.ivsgb.org/info

IVS brings volunteers together from many different countries, cultures and backgrounds to live and work on projects of benefit to local communities.

Josephite Community Aid

Australia +61 (0) 2 9838 8802
help@jcaid.com
www.jcaid.com

Australian organisation committed to helping poor and underprivileged with the aid of volunteers.

Kanaama Interactive

UK +44 (0)20 8883 9297
prue@kiuganda.org
www.kiuganda.org

An opportunity awaits to import your skills to Uganda, explore life through a different lens and discover the huge differences you can make to a vibrant rural community. KI is a committed, non-profit team facilitating volunteering in a rural community of south west Uganda, the sub-county of Kashare. We particularly welcome experienced people on career breaks, sabbaticals or looking for a fresh challenge.

For further information see page 204

Karen Hilltribes Trust

UK +44 (0) 1904 612 829

www.karenhilltribes.org.uk

The Karen Hilltribes Trust (Registered Charity No. 1093548) sends volunteers to teach English in Thailand. You will live with a Karen Hilltribe family and your placement can be between 2 and 5 months teaching 5 days a week.

Kaya Responsible Travel

UK +44 (0) 161 870 6212

info@kayavolunteer.com

www.kayavolunteer.com

Kaya offer over 200 volunteer projects worldwide working with local communities and conservation initiatives from 2 weeks to 12 months. Placements are tailored to specific needs and skills of students, career breakers', retirees, families or groups.

Khaya Volunteer

South Africa +27 (0) 41 582 1512

info@khayavolunteer.com

www.khayavolunteer.com

Khaya Volunteer offers affordable and unique volunteering projects and programs in South Africa, Tanzania, Uganda and more.

Kings World Trust for Children

UK +44 (0)1428 653504

annemarie@kingschildren.org

www.kingschildren.org

The Kings World Trust for Children aims to provide a caring home, an education and skills training for orphaned and homeless children and young people in south India.

L'Arche UK

UK +44 (0) 800 917 1337

info@larche.org.uk

www.larche.org.uk

L'Arche is an international movement where people with and without learning difficulties share life together. There are Communities in 34 countries. Volunteers are involved in all aspects of community life, are trained and supported, have free board and accommodation, a modest income and other benefits.

Lattitude Global Volunteering

UK +44 (0) 118 959 4914

volunteer@lattitude.org.uk

www.lattitude.org.uk

Lattitude Global Volunteering is a youth development and volunteering charity that send young people to a huge range of challenging and rewarding placements worldwide.

Madventurer

UK +44 (0)191 645 2014

volunteer@madventurer.com

www.madventurer.com

Offer group community projects in towns and villages in Ghana, Kenya, Uganda, Tanzania, South Africa, Fiji and Thailand.

Maekok River Village Resort

Thailand +66 (0) 53 053 628

rosie@maekok-river-village-resort.com

www.maekok-river-village-resort.com

The Maekok River Village Resort offers opportunities for those on gap years or career breaks to spend time teaching and helping to improve the facilities in schools in Thailand.

For further information see page 190

Onaris Africa

UK +44 (0)8438 866008
info@onarisafrica.org
www.onarisafrica.org

Onaris Africa specialise in student and graduate skills-matched volunteer experiences. Our group tours are built around your skillset. Experience Africa and make an impact!

For further information see page 202

Otra Cosa Network

UK 01926 730 029
info@otracosa.org
www.otracosa.org

Based in Huanchaco, northern Peru, Otra Cosa Network offers a wide variety of affordable and satisfying volunteering opportunities to well-motivated volunteers from around the world.

Outreach International

UK +44 (0) 1458 274957
info@outreachinternational.co.uk
www.outreachinternational.co.uk

Outreach International places committed volunteers in carefully selected projects on the Pacific coast of Mexico, Sri Lanka, Cambodia, Nepal, Costa Rica, Ecuador and the Galapagos Islands.

For further information see page 200

Oyster Worldwide Limited

UK +44 (0) 1892 770 771
anne@oysterworldwide.com
www.oysterworldwide.com

Oyster is a specialist gap-year provider with teaching and childcare projects around the world. We offer a personal approach with experienced managers supporting you throughout your trip.

For further information see page 186

Pepper

UK +44 (0)20 3514 5390
hello@pepperexperience.com
www.pepperexperience.com

Pepper is a unique gap-year and adventure travel company offering tailor-made experiences, as well as custom trips, in South Africa.

Peru's Challenge

Peru +51 84 272 508
volunteer@peruschallenge.com
www.peruschallenge.com

Join a volunteer and travel programme and assist the work of charity organisation, Peru's Challenge, in rural communities in Peru.

Plan My Gap Year

UK 01892 890473
info@planmygapyear.co.uk
www.planmygapyear.co.uk

Award winning international volunteer placement organisation offering affordable short-term volunteer programmes from two weeks up to six months.

Project Trust

UK 01879 230 444
info@projecttrust.org.uk
www.projecttrust.org.uk

Project Trust (charity no. SC025668) offers long term structured volunteering placements for school leavers (between ages of 17-19) in over twenty countries in Africa, Asia and Central and South America. Projects, lasting 8 or 12 months, include teaching, social care, journalism and outward bound.

Projects Abroad

UK +44 (0) 1903 708300
info@projects-abroad.co.uk
www.projects-abroad.co.uk

Overseas placements. Teach English, gain invaluable experience in Medicine, Conservation, Journalism, Business, Care and Community, Sports, Law and Human Rights, Veterinary and more.

For further information see page 182

Quest Overseas

UK 01273 777 206
info@questoverseas.com
www.questoverseas.com

Quest Overseas specializes in gap-year adventures into the very heart and soul of South America and Africa. We offer volunteers the chance to understand life far removed from home.

Raleigh International

UK 0207 183 1286
info@raleighinternational.org
www.raleighinternational.org

Sustainable development charity. We are powered by young people that want to make the world a better place. We work with communities living in poverty around the world in Borneo, Costa Rica and Nicaragua and Tanzania.

For further information see page 178

Reaching Out to Cambodian Communities (ROCC)

UK
roccuk@gmail.com
www.roccuk.com

ROCC is a charitable organisation which sends volunteers out to rural Cambodia to help create sustainable communities by teaching health and English as well as implementing vital community interventions such as building water wells and health centres. They work with a local NGO called CoDeC who have worked with numerous charities such as SKIP and UNICEF

Restless Development

UK 0207 976 8070
info@restlessdevelopment.org
www.restlessdevelopment.org

Restless Development run Health Education and Community Resource Programmes in South Asia and Africa. Volunteers are asked to fundraise a donation to the charity.

Serenje Orphans School Home

Switzerland
contactsoa@yahoo.com
www.serenjeorphansappeal.com

Our Zambian orphanage offers a rewarding and safe experience in rural Zambia for committed volunteers.

Skillshare International UK

UK 0116 2541862
info@skillshare.org
www.skillshare.org

Skillshare International recruits professionals from different sectors to share their skills, experience and knowledge with local partner organisations in Africa and Asia as volunteers.

Smile Society

India
www.smilengo.org

SMILE Society invite international volunteers and students to join us in our welfare projects, international work camps, summer camps, internship programmes and volunteer projects in India.

Spirit of Adventure Trust

New Zealand +64 (0) 9 373 2060
info@spiritofadventure.org.nz
www.spiritofadventure.org.nz

Become part of the volunteer crew on one of the Trust's youth development voyages around New Zealand each year.

341

Tanzed
UK 01270 214 779
tanzeduk@yahoo.co.uk
www.tanzed.org.uk
Working alongside Tanzanian nursery teachers as a classroom assistant you will be living in a rural village with plenty of opportunity to contribute to the community using your energy and enthusiasm.

Task Brasil Trust
UK
www.taskbrasil.org.uk
Task Brasil Trust is a charity helping impoverished children in Brazil. Volunteers always needed. Registered Charity No. 1030929.

The Book Bus Foundation
UK +44 (0) 208 0999 280
info@thebookbus.org
www.thebookbus.org
The Book Bus provides a mobile service and actively promotes literacy to underpriviledged communities in Zambia and Ecuador.

The Dragon Trip Pte Ltd
UK +44 (0)207 936 4884
info@thedragontrip.com
thedragontrip.com
The Dragon Volunteer Trips offer the chance to learn Mandarian, change children's lives and travel in breathtaking scenery.

The Humanity Exchange
USA +1 778 300 2466
admin@thehumanityexchange.org
www.thehumanityexchange.org
The Humanity Exchange provides grassroots Volunteer Abroad programs in communities across Ghana, Cameroon, Benin and Columbia, and unique opportunities to volunteer and Learn French in Africa.

The Worldwrite Volunteer Centre
UK +44 (0) 20 8985 5435
world.write@btconnect.com
www.worldwrite.org.uk
Join WORLDwrite's campaign for young volunteers who feel strongly about global inequality, want to make an impact and use film to do it. Registered charity No. 1060869.

The Year Out Group
UK
info@yearoutgroup.org
www.yearoutgroup.org
The Year Out Group is an association of the UK's leading Year Out organisations, promoting the concepts and benefits of well-structured year out programmes and helping young people and their advisers in selecting suitable and worthwhile projects.

Think Pacific
UK 0113 253 8684
info@thinkpacific.com
www.thinkpacific.com
Think Pacific offer you the chance to make a difference to the communities and places you visit, guiding you on a meaningful adventure through the glorious islands of Fiji.

Travellers Worldwide
UK 01903 502 595
info@travellersworldwide.com
www.travellersworldwide.com
Travellers is a leading international provider of voluntary placements and work experience internships overseas.
For further information see page 194

Uganda Lodge Volunteer Centre
Uganda Uganda: +256 774768090; UK: +44 1932 562757
info@ugandalodge.com
www.ugandalodge.com
Rural Project offering affordable short/long volunteer placements (all ages) in school, clinic, sports coaching, community or building work etc. Safaris/Gorilla-Treks organised. British on-site coordinators.

Unipal
UK
info@unipal.org.uk
www.unipal.org.uk
Unipal (A Universities' Trust for Educational Exchange with Palestinians) seeks to facilitate a two-way process of education; providing English-language teaching in Palestinian refugee camps in the West Bank, Gaza and Lebanon and introducing British students to a knowledge and understanding of the situation and daily lives of refugees.

VAP (Volunteer Action for Peace)
UK 0844 209 0927
action@vap.org.uk
www.vap.org.uk
Organises international voluntary work projects in the UK each summer and recruits volunteers to take part in affordable placements abroad that range between two weeks and 12 months.

Volunteer for Africa
UK
info@volunteer4africa.org
www.volunteer4africa.org
Non-profit organisation that helps volunteers and responsible travellers truly make a difference. Search the site for volunteer work or organisations needing supplies in the area you plan to visit.

Volunteer Maldives PVT Ltd
Republic of Maldives +94 77 394 1309
info@volunteermaldives.com
www.volunteermaldives.com
Volunteer Maldives is committed to making a real and tangible difference to these warm and friendly communities. When you travel with us you can rest assured that the work you do will directly benefit the islanders that have been identified by these local communities and the NGO's we work with.

Volunteer Vacations
UK 01483 331551
info@volunteervacations.co.uk
www.volunteervacations.co.uk
Voluntary sports coaching, teaching and orphange work abroad helping disadvantaged children.

Volunteer Work Thailand
UK
info@volunteerworkthailand.org
www.volunteerworkthailand.org
Non-profit organisation that helps people find volunteer work in Thailand including many opportunities to volunteer for free.

Volunteering India
India IN: +91 9716 235 166; UK: +44 (0)20 8133 9939
info@volunteeringindia.com
www.volunteeringindia.com
Volunteering India provides safe, affordable and meaningful volunteer programs in India to individuals, groups or families. A variety of programs are offered, including cultural exchange programs, internships and gap year programs in New Delhi, Palampur/Dharamsala and South India including Bangalore, Mysore and more.

A choice of programs includes working with orphans, women empowerment programs, health/HIV programs, teaching English, summer volunteer programs, street children programs and more.

Volunteering Solutions
India +91 9871371009
info@volunteeringsolutions.com
www.volunteeringsolutions.com

A safe and affordable volunteer program offering the oppurtunity to volunteer in hospitals, orphanages and clinics around the world. Volunteers will be immersed into the culture and live with local families.

Volunteers for International Partnership
USA +1-802-246-1154
info@partnershipvolunteers.org
www.partnershipvolunteers.org

VIP offers volunteer opportunities for individuals or groups to do international community service in health, social services, environment and education.

VRI
UK +44 (0) 20 8864 4740
enquiries@vri-online.org.uk
www.vri-online.org.uk

VRI is a small UK registered charity (No. 285872) supporting sustainable development projects in rural India, and offering opportunities to stay in one.

WaterAid
UK +44 (0) 20 7793 4594
www.wateraid.org

WaterAid is an international charity enabling the world's poorest people access to safe water and sanitation. You can volunteer to help them in the UK.

Whipalong Volunteer Program
South Africa +27 (0) 83 626 6324
info@whipalong.co.za
www.whipalong.co.za

The Whipalong Volunteer Program invites volunteers to be a part of the on-going rehabilitation and re-schooling of abused and neglected horses in South Africa. Volunteers' responsibilities include lunging, backing of young horses, feeding, grooming, tack maintenance and general care of the horses and yard, in addition to regular riding.

Willing Workers in South Africa (WWISA)
South Africa +27 (0)44 534 8958
www.wwisa.co.za

The core aim of WWISA is to help bring desperately needed community development services to poorly provisioned and frequently overlooked historically disadvantaged rural townships.

WLS International Ltd
UK 0203 384 7024
info@gapyearinasia.com
www.gapyearinasia.com

WLS International is one of the leading volunteer organizations with programs in Cambodia, China, Nepal, India, Indonesia, Sri Lanka, Thailand and Vietnam.

Work & Volunteer Abroad (WAVA)
UK 0800 80 483 80
www.workandvolunteer.com

Experience the world on one of WAVA's Gap Year programmes. Choose from a range of volunteer and work Gap Year travel projects around the world, and let WAVA help you See more & Do more around the world.

WorldTeach

USA (857) 259-6646
info@worldteach.org
www.worldteach.org

WorldTeach partners with governments and other organizations in developing countries to provide volunteer teachers to meet local needs and promote responsible global citizenship.

WWV - WorldWide Volunteering

UK +44(0) 117 955 9042
wwv@wwv.org.uk
www.wwv.org.uk

Registered charity (No. 1038253), set up to help people of all ages to find their ideal volunteering project either in the UK or in any country in the world.

Medical

Global Medical Projects

UK +44 (0)191 222 0404
info@globalmedicalprojects.co.uk
www.globalmedicalprojects.co.uk

Global Medical Projects are specialists in arranging worthwhile medical work experience placements for Pre-university students, students on their vacation, students on their electives and qualified medical personel.

International Volunteer HQ (IVHQ)

New Zealand NZ: +64 6 758 7949; UK: 0808 234 1621
info@volunteerhq.org
www.volunteerhq.org

IVHQ offers volunteer programs in more than 30 different locations worldwide including: Africa, Asia, Central & South America, The Pacific and Europe. Programs have many different start dates and a wide range of volunteer work opportunities including: Medical & Healthcare, Arts & Music, Education, Conservation and Construction.

For further information see page 206

Kaya Responsible Travel

UK +44 (0) 161 870 6212
info@kayavolunteer.com
www.kayavolunteer.com

Kaya offer over 200 volunteer projects worldwide working with local communities and conservation initiatives from 2 weeks to 12 months. Placements are tailored to specific needs and skills of students, career breakers', retirees, families or groups .

Medical Projects

UK
info@medicalprojects.co.uk
www.medicalprojects.co.uk

For aspiring doctors, midwives and nurses aged 16-19 who are looking for real-life experiences to help kickstart their medical careers. Placements include working in partner hospitals in India, Ghana and Europe and are excellent for providing both UCAS points towards university applications and practical work experiences in medical care.

Outreach International

UK +44 (0) 1458 274957
info@outreachinternational.co.uk
www.outreachinternational.co.uk

Outreach International places committed volunteers in carefully selected projects on the Pacific coast of Mexico, Sri Lanka, Cambodia, Nepal, Costa Rica, Ecuador and the Galapagos Islands.

For further information see page 200

Learning abroad

Academic year abroad

A Real China (ARC)
China +86 21 61557932
info@arc-ce.com
en.arc-ce.com
ARC offers a 'cultural ambassador' programme, matching young people with families based in or around Shanghai. Participants provide the family with valuable English interaction and access to Western culture, whilst receiving an immersive experience if Chinese life, accompanies by professional Chinese classes.

Although no salary is available, a financial support package of up to US$1,500 is offered to cover flights, visa costs, etc.

African Leadership Academy
South Africa
info@africanleadershipacademy.org
www.africanleadershipacademy.org
African Leadership Academy offers high school students worldwide the opportunity for an unparalleled African experience, by studying abroad or spending a gap-year with them.

Aidan College
Switzerland +41 (0)24 485 11 23
info@aidan.ch
www.aidan-college-switzerland.ch
Aidan College provides a unique environment where you can combine a wide range of challenging pursuits, both intellectual and physical, to make the most of your gap year.

American University
USA +1 202 885 1000
www.american.edu/spexs/augap
Spend a semester or summer learning and participating in community service in Washington, DC and discover who you want to be. American University's International Gap Program is designed for students who are ready to build a foundation for future academic and career success and a better understanding of global issues.
For further information see page 212

For further information see page 212

Class Afloat
Canada +1 902 634 1895
admissions@classafloat.com
www.classafloat.com
Sail on a tall ship to exotic ports around the world and earn university credits. Also offers Duke of Edinburgh's Award Scheme.

College for International Co-operation and Development (CICD)
UK +44 (0)1964 631 826
www.cicd-volunteerinafrica.org
CICD offers programmes from 5 or 12 months or longer, consisting of 5 months training, studies and preparation, followed by 6 months volunteer work at a development project in Africa or India and a one month follow-up period back at the college afterwards. Ideal for those looking to do volunteer work abroad and who would prefer to have more preparation before going out there.

Council on International Educational Exchange (CIEE)

USA 1-207-553-4000
contact@ciee.org
www.ciee.org
CIEE offer a wide range of international study programs such as study abroad programs for US students, gap-year abroad programs and seasonal work in the USA for international students.

Diablo Valley College

USA +1 925 685 1230
www.dvc.edu
Diablo Valley College offers a varity of programmes to international students, available as day, evening, summer, online or hybrid classes.

Education in Ireland

Ireland +353 1 7272967
educationinireland@enterprise-ireland.com
www.educationinireland.com
Live and study in Ireland, earning degrees at ordinary and Honours Bachelors, Masters and Doctorate levels and undergraduate and postgraduate diplomas over a full range of disciplines.

Graduate Prospects

UK +44 (0) 161 277 5200
enquiries@prospects.ac.uk
www.prospects.ac.uk
Prospects - the UK's official graduate careers website.

IE University

Spain +34 921 412 410
university@ie.edu
www.ie.edu/university
IE University is an international university which takes a humanistic approach to higher education: a university of entrepreneurs whose education and research model integrates knowledge and enables students to specialize flexibly.

Institute of International Education

USA
iiedirectories@eircom.net
www.iiepassport.org
Search for international education opportunities by country, city, subject and many other criteria.

John Cabot University

Italy +39 06 681 9121
admissions@johncabot.edu
www.johncabot.edu
John Cabot University - an American university in the heart of Rome.

Leiden University

Netherlands +31 (0) 71 527 4024
www.leiden.edu
Leiden University is one of Europe's foremost research universities. This prominent position gives our graduates a leading edge in applying for academic posts and for functions outside academia.

Minds Abroad

China +86 (871) 532 5089
info@mindsabroad.com
www.mindsabroad.com
Minds Abroad is a US-based organization that conducts study abroad programs in China and India for both individual students and also customized faculty-led groups from college and universities across the US and Europe.

Office of International Education, Iceland

Iceland +354 525 4311
ask@hi.is
www.ask.hi.is
Find information on all the higher education institutions in Iceland, as well as practical things to do before arriving, visas, admissions, residence permits, etc.

Queenstown Resort College

New Zealand +64 3 409 0500

www.queenstownresortcollege.com

Offers a diverse range of world class courses and programmes including diplomas, internships, a range of English language courses, leadership development programmes, and short courses for visitors.

Scuola Leonardo da Vinci

Italy

scuolaleonardo@scuolaleonardo.com

www.scuolaleonardo.com

One of Italy's largest provider of in-country Italian courses in Italy, for students who wish to experience living and studying in Italy.

The English-Speaking Union

UK +44 (0)20 7529 1561

jacqueline.finch@esu.org

www.esu.org

The English-Speaking Union organises educational exchanges in high schools (mostly boarding) in the US and Canada, awarding up to 30 scholarships a year to gap-year students.

The US-UK Fulbright Commission

UK 0845 894 9524

advising@fulbright.co.uk

www.fulbright.co.uk

EAS is the UK's only official source of information on the US education system, providing objective advice through in-house advising and a variety of outreach events.

University of Business & International Studies

Switzerland +41 (0)22 732 6282

info@ubis-geneva.ch

www.ubis-geneva.ch

UBIS is a Swiss Boutique University that prepares graduates to advance forward in the international jobs market.

For further information see page 226

University of New South Wales

Australia

summerdownunder@unsw.edu.au

www.summerdownunder.unsw.edu.au

UNSW's Summer Down Under program gives students the opportunity to sample courses and experience university life alongside local and international UNSW students during the Australian summer.

Where There Be Dragons

USA +1 303 413 0822

info@wheretherebedragons.com

www.wheretherebedragons.com

Runs semester, gap-year and college-accredited programmes in the Andes, China, Himalayas and more.

Art

Aegean Center for the Fine Arts

Greece +30 22840 23 287

studyart@aegeancenter.org

www.aegeancenter.org

The Aegean Center offers small group and individualized study in the visual arts, creative writing and music. Facilities are located in two stunning locations: the Aegean islands of Greece and Italy's Tuscany.

ARTIS - Art Research Tours

USA +1 800 232 6893

david@artis.info

www.artis-tours.org

ARTIS (Art Research Tours and International Studios) provide high quality international art and cultural study abroad programmes at affordable prices, located in beautiful art capitals throughout the world.

349

SACI Florence

Italy +1 (212) 248 7225

admissions@saci-florence.edu

www.saci-florence.edu

A non-profit educational institution for students seeking fully accredited studio art, design, and liberal arts instruction.

For further information see page 224

SAI - Study Abroad Italy

USA +1 (707) 824 8965

mail@saiprograms.com

www.studyabroadflorence.com

In conjunction with Florence University SAI offer the chance for international students to live in the heart of this bustling Renaissance city while experiencing modern Florentine life.

Studio Escalier

USA +1 718 228 4109

info@studioescalier.com

www.studioescalier.com

Admission to their three month intensive courses in painting and drawing is by advance application only. Anyone is welcome to apply who has a dedicated interest in working from the human figure.

The British Institute of Florence

Italy +39 (0) 55 2677 81

www.britishinstitute.it

Located in the historic centre of Florence within minutes of the main galleries, museums and churches, the British Institute offers courses in history of art, Italian language and life drawing.

The Marchutz School

France +33 442 966 013

www.marchutz-school.org

Offers artists a unique opportunity to live, learn and grow in the incomparable Provencal setting of Aix-en-Provence, France.

Culture

Alderleaf Wilderness College

USA +1 360 793 8709

www.wildernesscollege.com

A centre for traditional ecological knowledge offering innovative wilderness survival, animal tracking and nature courses in the Pacific Northwest of the United States.

American Institute for Foreign Study (AIFS)

USA (203) 399 5000

info@aifs.com

www.aifs.com

One of the oldest, largest and most respected cultural exchange organizations in the world. Their programmes include college study abroad, au pair placement, camp counselors and staff.

Art History Abroad (AHA)

UK +44 (0) 1379 871 800

info@arthistoryabroad.com

www.arthistoryabroad.com

Travel through stylish Italy with a group of people just like you. Study beautiful art and architecture with brilliant tutors. Have fun and make friends for life.

For further information see page 214

Cultural Experiences Abroad (CEA)

USA +1 800 266 4441

info@gowithcea.com

www.gowithcea.com

CEA sends thousands of students on study abroad programmes at multiple universities in 15 countries including Argentina, China, Costa Rica, Czech Republic, England, France, Germany, Ireland, Italy, South Africa and Spain.

Eastern Institute of Technology
New Zealand +64 6 974 8000
info@eit.ac.nz
www.eit.ac.nz
Te Manga Mâori - EIT in Hawke's Bay offers the opportunity to study the Maori language and culture from beginners through to advanced level.

El Casal
Spain +34 93 217 90 38
john@elcasalbarcelona.com
www.elcasalbarcelona.com
Based in Barcelona, El Casal offers the chance to soak in Catalan culture through a programme specifically for gappers who want to learn Spanish.

Istituto di Lingua e Cultura Italiana Michelangelo
Italy +39 055 240 975
www.michelangelo-edu.it
The Michelangelo Institute offers cultural courses on art history, Italian language, literature, commerce and commercial correspondence, and 'L'Italia oggi'.

John Hall Venice
UK +44 (0)20 8871 4747
info@johnhallvenice.com
www.johnhallvenice.com
Courses based in Venice, London, Florence and Rome with a sensational combination of lectures, visits and classes in art, music, world cinema, literature, global issues, Italian, cookery and photography.
For further information see page 218

Knowledge Exchange Institute (KEI)
USA 1 212 931 9953
info@keiabroad.org
www.keiabroad.org
Study abroad and intern abroad programmes designed to meet your academic, professional and personal interests.

Lexia Study Abroad
USA +1 800 775 3942
info@lexiaintl.org
www.lexiaintl.org
Cultural study programmes that encourage students to connect with their community while pursuing academic research. Participate in the daily life and work of a community in countries worldwide.

Road2Argentina
Argentina +54 114 833 9653
info@road2argentina.com
www.road2argentina.com
Study abroad in Argentina and learn all about the country and its culture.

scenns
Thailand +66 (0)806 023 184
scenn@scenns.com
www.scenns.com
Scenns offers accommodation and various culture related tutorials for individuals and small groups. We also offer advice for exploring the Thai-Burma border region, potential volunteer placings, and are always ready to help with any queries.

SIT Study Abroad
USA +1 888 272 7881
studyabroad@sit.edu
www.sit.edu/studyabroad/
Offers undergraduate study abroad programmes in Africa, Asia and the Pacific, Europe, Latin America and the Middle East.

The Pimenta - Kerala Spice Garden Bungalows

India +91 485 2260216
harithafarms@gmail.com
www.thepimenta.in

Experience of what it's like to be part of a typical Kerala homestead. Stay in a tropical spice forest garden using Indian Permaculture and bio-organic techniques. See the spices growing. Explore neighbouring villages, enjoy picnics to waterfalls, visit an elephant training centre, tea gardens, old temples, churches and temple festivals.

Design & Fashion

Blanche Macdonald Centre

Canada +1 604 685 0347
info@blanchemacdonald.com
www.blanchemacdonald.com

If you are looking for a career in design & fashion, the Blanche Macdonald Centre offers numerous courses in Makeup Artistry, Fashion Design, Fashion Merchandising, Hair Design, Esthetics/Spa Therapy and Nail Technology. Considered to be the premium industry leader, the college graduates over one thousand students per year and has three campuses in Vancouver, British Columbia, Canada.

Domus Academy

Italy
info@domusacademy.it
www.domusacademy.com

In 2009 Domus Academy joined the Laureate International Universities Network, an international high-level education network for art and design. The Academy offers 10 masters courses, attended by students from all over the world.

Florence Institute of Design International

Italy +39 055 23 02 481
registrar@florence-institute.com
www.florence-institute.com

The Florence Institute is an international design school specialising in design courses for students from around the world, with all classes taught in English.

Istituto di Moda Burgo

Italy (+39) 02783753
imb@imb.it
www.imb.it

International fashion design school Istituto di Moda Burgo offers high-quality courses in fashion design, fashion stylist and pattern making.

Metallo Nobile

Italy +39 055 2396966
school@metallo-nobile.com
www.metallo-nobile.com

Metallo Nobile offers courses in jewellery making and jewellery design, located in the heart of Florence.

NABA - Nuova Accademia de Belle Arti

Italy +39 02 973721
www.design-summer-courses.com

NABA summer courses are divided into three levels: introduction, workshop and advanced. They have courses in design, fashion, graphic design and visual arts.

Polimoda Institute of Fashion Design and Marketing

Italy +39 055 275061
info@polimoda.com
www.polimoda.com

Based in Florence, Polimoda Fashion School offers a variety of summer courses for those interested in all aspects of fashion.

RMIT Training

Australia +61 (0) 3 9925 8111

enquiries@rmit.edu.au

www.shortcourses.rmit.edu.au

Has a Career Discovery Short Course in fashion. An intensive programme which includes lectures by experienced industry professionals alongside studio workshops.

Film, Theatre & Drama

Actors College of Theatre and Television

Australia +61 (0) 2 9213 4500

info@actt.edu.au

www.actt.edu.au

ACTT is Australia 's leading independent college for the performing arts and the only acting school in Sydney offering an extensive range of accredited acting courses and technical production courses for overseas students.

EICAR - The International Film & Television School Paris

France (+33) 01 49 98 11 11

inquiries@eicar.fr

www.eicar-international.com

Offers short summer workshops taught in English during July and September in the following areas: filmmaking, script writing, editing, HD Video and sound.

European Film College

Denmark 0045 86 34 00 55

info@europeanfilmcollege.com

www.europeanfilmcollege.com

Offering students a unique experience, an international learning environment offering young filmmakers and actors an intense eight-month course.

Full Sail University

USA +1 407 679 6333

www.fullsail.edu

If you're after a career in music, film, video games, design, animation, entertainment business, or internet marketing, Full Sail is the right place for you.

Hollywood Film & Acting Academy

USA

www.hwfaa.com

The traditional film school alternative, offering shorter more intense programme in feature films, movie making and acting.

Met Film School

UK +44 (0)20 8832 1933

info@metfilmschool.co.uk

www.metfilmschool.co.uk

Are you passionate about film and want to spend your year doing something creative and fun? Take the plunge and study filmmaking at Met Film School Berlin, where your gap year leads to a qualification and new practical skills.

For further information see page 222

NYFA (New York Film Academy)

USA +1 212 674 4300

film@nyfa.edu

www.nyfa.com

The New York Film Academy runs programmes all year round in New York City and at Universal Studios in Hollywood.

PCFE Film School

Czech Republic +420 257 534 013

info@filmstudies.cz

www.filmstudies.cz

Offers workshops, semester and year programmes in filmmaking including directing, screenwriting, cinematography, editing and film history and theory.

353

The Acting Center
USA +1 818 386 9099
www.theactingcenterla.com
No audition is necessary but an interview is required. Classes are available in evenings during the week and on weekends.

The Los Angeles Film School
USA 323 860 0789
www.lafilm.com
Has degree programmes in filmmaking, game production and animation. International students must acquire a student visa before studying in the United States.

Tribeca Flashpoint College
USA +1 312 332 0707
info@tribecaflashpoint.edu
www.tribecaflashpoint.edu
Tribeca Flashpoint College is a two-year, direct-to-industry college focusing exclusively on the following disciplines: film/broadcast, recording arts, visual effects and animation and game development.

TVI Actors Studio - Los Angeles
USA +1 818 784 6500
www.tvistudios.com
TVI Actors Studio offers acting classes, workshops, and seminars for aspiring and professional actors.

Vancouver Film School
Canada +1 604 685 5808
www.vfs.com
Centre for both training and higher learning in all areas related to media and entertainment production.

Music

Backbeat Tours
USA +1 901-272-BEAT (2328)
tours@backbeattours.com
www.backbeattours.com
Backbeat Tours provide numerous tours around Mephis, from an Elvis-themed Hound Dog Tour to the Historic Memphis Walking Tour, and even a chilling Memphis Ghost Tour. All tours are available as a step-on service or as custom private tours for tour operators, conventions, corporate groups or any party of 15 or more.

Brooks Institute
USA +1 805 585 8000
www.brooks.edu
Brooks Institute offers training in filmmaking, graphic design and photojournalism. The courses are designed for anyone who aspires to a career in photography, filmmaking, visual journalism, or graphic design.

Country Music Travel
USA
mail@countrymusictravel.com
www.countrymusictravel.com
Country music-themed vacations and escorted tours, from trips to Dollywood entertainment park, to music cities tours in Nashville and Memphis.

Jazz Summer School
UK +44 (0) 208 989 8129
www.jazzsummerschool.com
Jazz Summer School offering places at the French jazz summer school in the South of France or The Cuban music school in Havana.

Scoil Acla - Irish Music Summer School
Ireland +353 (0)85 881 9548
info@scoilacla.com
www.scoilacla.com
Summer school established to teach Irish Piping (Irish War Pipes), tin whistle, accordian, banjo, flute and harp.

Songwriter Girl Camps
USA +1 615 323 2915
info@songwritergirl.com
www.songwritergirl.com
Songwriter Girl Camps offer weekend songwriting camps for girls and women of all ages and ability.

SummerKeys
USA +1 207 733 2316
www.summerkeys.com
Music vacations for adults in Lubec, Maine. Open to all 'musical people' regardless of ability with workshops and private tuition in a variety of instruments.

SummerSongs Inc.
USA +1 845 594 1867
info@summersongs.com
www.summersongs.com
SummerSongs is a not-for-profit corporation dedicated to the art and craft of songwriting. It offer seasonal songwriting camps (summer and winter) on both the East and West coasts of the United States.

Taller Flamenco
Spain (+34) 954 56 42 34
info@tallerflamenco.com
www.tallerflamenco.com
Taller Flamenco is a learning centre for Flamenco and Spanish Language in Seville. Courses include flamenco dance, flamenco guitar, singing and percussion.

United DJ Mixing School
Australia +61 (03) 9639 9990
admin@djsunited.com.au
www.djsunited.com.au
Offer an introductory course over two weekends, which gives the basics of DJ-ing and a longer comprehensive course that runs over twelve weeks.

World Rhythms Arts Program (WRAP)
USA
www.drum2dance.com
Classes develop your working knowledge of instruments, rhythms, dances, songs, styles, methods and applications.

Photography

c4 Images & Safaris
South Africa +27 (0) 12 993 1946
shem@c4images-safaris.co.za
www.c4images-safaris.co.za
Offers short photography workshops and wildlife safaris in South Africa with emphasis on helping you to improve your photography skills.

Europa Photogenica
USA
FraPhoto@aol.com
www.europaphotogenica.com
This company provides carefully planned, high quality, small group photo tours designed for photographers of all levels who wish to improve their photographic skills using Europe as their classroom.

Joseph Van Os Photo Safaris
USA (206) 463-5383
info@photosafaris.com
www.photosafaris.com
Joseph Van Os Photo Safaris guide you to some of the world's finest wild and scenic locations with the main purpose of making great photographs.

Keith Moss Street Photography Courses
UK +44 (0) 1287 679 655
www.
photographycoursesandworkshops.co.uk
Specialising in black and white street photography, Keith Moss offers courses in Europe's most inspiring cities. The courses provide an insight into what it takes to capture the essence of the street.

London Photo Tours & Workshops
UK +44 (0)7738 942 099
www.londonphototours.co.uk
London Photo Tours and Workshops specialise in short courses, tours, and small-group photography workshops, offering experienced and friendly tuition.

Nigel Turner Landscape Photography
USA +1 702 7695110
npturner@cox.net
www.nigelturnerphotography.com
Nigel Turner Landscape Photography offers landscape photography workshops in the American West. Improve your technique with friendly and relaxed tuition and explore some of the most beautiful places in the United States.

Photo Holidays France
UK
aw@andrewwhittuck.co.uk
www.photoholidaysfrance.co.uk
A private photography school in the south of France offering one to one photography tuition specialising in landscape and portrait photography.

Photographers on Safari
UK +44 (0(1664 474040
info@photographersonsafari.com
www.photographersonsafari.com
Photographers on Safari offer UK and International Photography Trips and Safaris. Photograph animals in their natural environment with expert Photography Tuition.

Steve Outram Crete Photo Tours & Workshops
Greece +30 28210 32201
steveoutram@gmail.com
www.steveoutram.com
Professional photographer Steve Outram uses his local knowledge of Zanzibar, Lesvos and western Crete to show you how to make the most of photographic opportunities and develop your skill as a photographer.

Chinese

Bridging the Gap China
China +86 777 562 8765
enquiries@bridgingthegapchina.co.uk
www.bridgingthegapchina.co.uk
Bridging the Gap offers courses which combine learning Mandarin Chinese with sightseeing and cultural activities in the Yunnan province, China.

Hong Kong Institute of Languages
China +852 2877 6160
info@hklanguages.com
www.hklanguages.com
Regardless of your goal, to become fluent in a new language for interest, to travel abroad, or to sharpen your global business acumen, the HK Institute of Languages provides the best teachers, the best experience, the most fexible hours and the best locations at your own choice!

Hong Kong Language Learning Centre

China +852 2572 6488
hkllc@netvigator.com
www.hkllc.com
Language school in Hong Kong which specialises in Cantonese and Mandarin conversation and Chinese reading and writing for expatriates, locals and overseas Chinese.

Live the Language (LTL) Mandarin School

China +86 10 5100 1269
info@livethelanguage.cn
www.livethelanguage.cn
Live the language of Mandarin by studying in China. Immerse yourself in the language and the culture as you participate in individual or group classes and explore the streets of China. Gap year programmes are also available, with opportunities for work experience and earning money teaching English.

WorldLink Education US Office

USA
www.worldlinkedu.com
WorldLink Education's Chinese language programme immerses you in Mandarin Chinese through class instruction, after-class tutoring, language exchanges with native speakers and a range of optional extra activities.

French

Accent Français

France +33 (0) 467 58 12 68
contact@accentfrancais.com
www.accentfrancais.com
This school runs intensive French courses in Montpellier particularly for non-French speakers. They last between one week and several months.

Alliance Française de Londres

UK +44 (0) 20 7723 6439
info@alliancefrancaise.org.uk
www.alliancefrancaise.org.uk
Alliance Française is a non-profit-making organisation whose goal is to teach French and bring cultures together (group classes and bespoke tuition available).

BWS Germanlingua

Germany +49 (0) 89 599 892 00
info@bws-germanlingua.de
www.bws-germanlingua.de
BWS Germanlingua is based in Munich and Berlin; all staff are experienced teachers, and classes have a maximum of 12 students.

CESA Languages Abroad

UK +44 (0) 1209 211 800
info@cesalanguages.com
www.cesalanguages.com
Perfect your language skills, experience the culture first-hand and have an amazing gap-year with CESA.
For further information see page 216

CMEF, Centre Méditerranéen d'Etudes Françaises

France +33 (0)4 93 78 21 59
centremed@monte-carlo.mc
www.centremed.monte-carlo.mc
Located in the South of France between Nice and Monaco - Monte Carlo. An international language school with a long tradition on French language courses.

En Famille Overseas

UK +44 (0)1273 588636
info@enfamilleoverseas.co.uk
www.enfamilleoverseas.co.uk
En Famille organises tailor-made homestays in France, Spain and Italy, for individuals and groups. Travellers stay in a host family and learn the language, as well as joining in the life of the family.

France Langue (BLS)
France +33 (0)5 56 06 99 83
bordeaux@france-langue.fr
www.france-langue.com
Based in Bordeaux and Biarritz, BLS offer a wide range of French courses to suit your exact requirements.

Institut Français
UK +44 (0)20 7871 3515
box.office@institutfrancais.org.uk
www.institut-francais.org.uk
The Institut Français is the official French Government centre of language and culture in London.

Institut Savoisien d'Etudes Françaises pour Etrangers
France +33 (0) 4 79 75 84 14
isefe@univ-savoie.fr
www.isefe.univ-savoie.fr
An institute which specialises in teaching French as a foreign language to adults from non-Francophone countries.

Live Languages Abroad
UK +44 (0)1736 740000
info@livelanguagesabroad.co.uk
www.livelanguagesabroad.com
At Live Languages Abroad we believe that the best way to learn a language is to live the language abroad. With our experience of providing language courses abroad, we will be able to provide you with the best course, accommodation and location.
For further information see page 220

Lyon Bleu International
France +33 (0) 437 480 026
learnfrenchinlyon@lyon-bleu.fr
www.lyon-bleu.fr
Lyon Bleu International, in Lyon, is dedicated to teaching the French language and culture.

TASIS, The American School in Switzerland
Switzerland +41 91 960 5151
admissions@tasis.ch
www.tasis.ch
Each year, the TASIS schools and summer programmes attracts students from around the world who share in a caring, family-style international community.

Vis-à-Vis
UK +44 (0) 20 8786 8021
www.visavis.org
French courses offered in France. Various accommodation options are available, and there is the usual range of course length, level and intensity.

German

German Academic Exchange Service (DAAD)
UK +44 (0)20 7831 9511
info@daad.org.uk
www.daad.org.uk
The German Academic Exchange Service is the German National Agency for the support of international academic cooperation.

Goethe Institut
UK 0207 596 4000
info@london.goethe.org
www.goethe.de/enindex.htm
The Goethe Institut is probably the best-known international German language school network.

Live Languages Abroad

UK +44 (0)1736 740000

info@livelanguagesabroad.co.uk

www.livelanguagesabroad.com

At Live Languages Abroad we believe that the best way to learn a language is to live the language abroad. With our experience of providing language courses abroad, we will be able to provide you with the best course, accommodation and location.

For further information see page 220

Greek

College Year in Athens

Greece +30 210 7560-749

programs@dikemes.edu.gr

www.cyathens.org

College Year in Athens offers unparalleled learning opportunities for English-speaking students seeking a programme of study in Greece.

Live Languages Abroad

UK +44 (0)1736 740000

info@livelanguagesabroad.co.uk

www.livelanguagesabroad.com

At Live Languages Abroad we believe that the best way to learn a language is to live the language abroad. With our experience of providing language courses abroad, we will be able to provide you with the best course, accommodation and location.

For further information see page 220

Italian

Accademia del Giglio

Italy +39 055 23 02 467

info@adg.it

www.adg.it

This quiet, small school takes about 30 students, taught in small classes. As well as Italian language courses, they offer classes in drawing and painting.

Accademia Italiana

Italy +39 055 284 616

study@accademiaitaliana.com

www.accademiaitaliana.com

An international design, art and language school, the Accademia Italiana puts on summer language courses as well as full-year and longer academic and Masters courses.

Centro Machiavelli

Italy +39 0 55 2396 966

school@centromachiavelli.it

www.centromachiavelli.it

A small language school in the Santo Spirito district of Florence, Centro Machiavelli teaches Italian to those who want to use the language creatively and who are interested in the culture of Italy. Explore Florence in between lessons for a truly cultural experience.

Europass

Italy 0039 055 2345802

europass@europass.it

www.europass.it

Europass has offered individual and varied Italian language courses in the heart of Florence since 1992.

Il Sillabo

Italy +39 347 9779531

info@ilsillabo.it

www.ilsillabo.it

Il Sillabo is a small, family-run language school in San Giovanni Valdarno, Italy.

Istituto Europeo

Italy +39 05523 81071

info@istitutoeuropeo.it

www.istitutoeuropeo.it

The Italian Language Music Art School in Florence. Enjoy yourself learning a beautiful language: come study Italian, music, art with us.

Live Languages Abroad

UK +44 (0)1736 740000

info@livelanguagesabroad.co.uk

www.livelanguagesabroad.com

At Live Languages Abroad we believe that the best way to learn a language is to live the language abroad. With our experience of providing language courses abroad, we will be able to provide you with the best course, accommodation and location.

For further information see page 220

Lorenzo de' Medici

Italy +39 055 287 203

info@lorenzodemedici.it

www.ldminstitute.com

Istituto Lorenzo de' Medici is committed to delivering a high-quality international learning experience through which students advance along their formal educational paths, develop their creativity, realize their own potential, and empower themselves to impact the world around them.

Japanese

Kichijoji Language School

Japan +81 (0) 422 47 7390

www.klschool.com

At Kichijoji Language School you will have the opportunity not only to learn Japanese; but, also to live the culture and to explore, for yourself, Tokyo, the exciting city we call home.

The Yamasa Institute

Japan +81 (0) 564 55 8111

info@yamasa.org

www.yamasa.org

The Yamasa Institute is an independent teaching and research centre under the governance of the Hattori Foundation. It is APJLE accredited.

Multi-languages

Caledonia Languages Abroad

UK +44 (0)1316 217721

info@caledoniaworldwide.com

www.caledoniaworldwide.com

Short courses in French, Italian, German, Russian, Spanish and Portuguese in Europe and Latin America, for all levels, start all year round, most for a minimum of two weeks.

CERAN Lingua International

Belgium +32 (0) 87 79 11 22

customer@ceran.com

www.ceran.com

CERAN runs weekly intensive residential language programmes in Dutch, French, German and Spanish.

EF Education First

UK +44 (0)207 341 8500

www.ef.edu/pg/gap-year

EF Gap Year Programs offer you the opportunity to learn a foreign language, while also experiencing a new culture and facilitating personal growth.

ESL - Language Travel

UK +44 (0) 20 7451 0943

info@esl.co.uk

www.esl.co.uk

ESL Language Travel offers immersion language courses abroad in over 20 languages in more than 300 inspirational destinations. The start dates and durations of our courses are very flexible allowing you to easily fit language learning abroad into your Gap Year.

Eurolingua Institute

UK

www.eurolingua.com

Eurolingua is a network of institutes teaching 12 languages in 37 countries. Group programmes give 15 hours of tuition a week, according to your level.

Inlingua International
Switzerland
www.inlingua.com

Inlingua is one of the world's leading language training organizations with 309 language centers in 35 countries across Europe, Africa, Asia, North and South America.

Language Courses Abroad
UK +44 (0) 1509 211612
info@languagesabroad.co.uk
www.languagesabroad.co.uk

Languages courses available in French, German, Greek, Italian, Portuguese, Russian, Spanish and others.

Learn Languages Abroad
Ireland +353 (0)1451 1674
info@languages.ie
www.learn-languages-abroad.co.uk

Learn Languages Abroad will help you find the course best suited to your needs.

Live Languages Abroad
UK +44 (0)1736 740000
info@livelanguagesabroad.co.uk
www.livelanguagesabroad.com

At Live Languages Abroad we believe that the best way to learn a language is to live the language abroad. With our experience of providing language courses abroad, we will be able to provide you with the best course, accommodation and location.

For further information see page 220

Modern Language Studies Abroad (MLSA)
USA (815) 464-1800
info@mlsa.com
www.mlsa.com

Offers language study abroad programmes in the following countries: Spain, Italy, France and Costa Rica.

OISE Oxford
UK 01865 247 272
oxford@oise.com
www.oise.com

Have their own unique teaching philosophy which leads students to gain confidence, fluency and accuracy when speaking another language taught by a native-speaker.

Portuguese

CIAL Centro de Linguas
Portugal +351 217 940 448
portuguese@cial.pt
www.cial.pt

With schools in Lisbon and Faro, CIAL organises courses in Portuguese for foreign students.

Live Languages Abroad
UK +44 (0)1736 740000
info@livelanguagesabroad.co.uk
www.livelanguagesabroad.com

At Live Languages Abroad we believe that the best way to learn a language is to live the language abroad. With our experience of providing language courses abroad, we will be able to provide you with the best course, accommodation and location.

For further information see page 220

Russian

Live Languages Abroad
UK +44 (0)1736 740000
info@livelanguagesabroad.co.uk
www.livelanguagesabroad.com

At Live Languages Abroad we believe that the best way to learn a language is to live the language abroad. With our experience of providing language courses abroad, we will be able to provide you with the best course, accommodation and location.

For further information see page 220

Obninsk Humanities Centre
Russian Federation +44 (0) 208 858 0614 (UK number)
lara.bushell@btinternet.com
www.dubravushka.ru
Learn Russian in Russia, with qualified English-speaking Russian teachers and students, at Dubravushka, Russia's leading independent boarding school.

The Russian Language Centre
UK +44 (0) 20 7831 5330
info@russiancentre.co.uk
www.russiancentre.co.uk
The Russian Language Centre in London offers a range of courses for groups and individuals: intensive, accelerated and private.

Spanish

Academia Hispánica Córdoba
Spain +34 957 488 002
info@academiahispanica.com
www.academiahispanica.com
Academia Hispánica Córdoba offers small-group language tuition to suit all levels. Learn Spanish in Spain, whilst immersing yourself in the wonderful culture.

AES Cabin Crew
Spain +34 622 910856
contact@aescabincrew.com
www.aescabincrew.com
AES Cabin Crew offer 3-month courses in Spain for learners to achieve the official European cabin crew (or flight attendant) qualification, in addition to daily Spanish Classes.

An additional month of only Spanish is also available for any students who wish to improve their language skills even further, and there is plenty of opportunity to immerse yourself in Spanish culture and explore the best sights Spain has to offer.

AIL Madrid Spanish Language School
Spain +34 91 725 6350
www.ailmadrid.com/gap-year/home
AIL Madrid offers a gap year (or bridge year) program directed to high school graduates and University undergraduates, graduates and postgraduates wanting a break from their studies or career. Use your language skills for practical work experience or for meeting new people.

Amigos Spanish School
Peru +51 (84) 24 22 92
amigos@spanishcusco.com
www.spanishcusco.com
Non-profit Spanish school. With every hour of your Spanish classes, you pay for the basic care of a group of underprivileged children at their foundation.

Apple Languages
UK +44 (0) 1509 211 612
info@applelanguages.com
www.applelanguages.com
The best place to learn Spanish, French, Italian or German is in a country where the language is spoken, and Apple Languages offers a variety of courses in a number of countries. They also offer courses specifically for under 18's and over 50's, so there's something for everyone.

CAPS - Home to Home
Spain +34 93 864 88 86
caps@hometohome.es
www.hometohome.es/caps/eng/assistants.html
CAPS is a programme designed for young people who would like to spend a year in Spain helping in a School as Conversation Teaching Assistant.

CESA Languages Abroad
UK +44 (0) 1209 211 800
info@cesalanguages.com
www.cesalanguages.com
Perfect your language skills, experience the culture first-hand and have an amazing gap-year with CESA.

For further information see page 216

Comunicacion Language School
Spain +34 950 33 34 15
info@comunicacionee.com
www.comunicacionee.com
Come and enjoy professional Spanish classes, a great beach and lots of outdoor and cultural activities in Almería province, Spain. Stay in an apartment, a hostel or with a Spanish host family.

Don Quijote
UK +44 (0)20 8786 8081
www.donquijote.org
Don Quijote is a leading network of schools teaching Spanish in Spain and Latin America.

Enforex
Spain +34 91 594 3776
info@enforex.es
www.enforex.com
Learn to speak Spanish in Spain or Latin America. Over 30 centres all in Spanish speaking countries. Summer camps also available.

Expanish
Argentina +54 11 5252 3040
contact@expanish.com
www.expanish.com
Learn Spanish in Buenos Aires located in the city centre, home to some of the oldest historical sites in the city.

International House Madrid
Spain +34 913 197 224
info@ihmadrid.com
www.ihspanishinmadrid.com
Learning Spanish in Madrid allows you to bask in the culture of the Spanish people, converse first hand with Spanish native speakers, and enjoy the full beauty of this beautiful vibrant city.

Live Languages Abroad
UK +44 (0)1736 740000
info@livelanguagesabroad.co.uk
www.livelanguagesabroad.com
At Live Languages Abroad we believe that the best way to learn a language is to live the language abroad. With our experience of providing language courses abroad, we will be able to provide you with the best course, accommodation and location.

For further information see page 220

Mente Argentina
Argentina +44 (0)20 3286 3438
info@menteargentina.com
www.menteargentina.com
Mente Argentina provides two different options for learning Spanish in Buenos Aires. Learn in top Universities in Argentina or, alternatively, learn at Mente's private language institute, which allows for more flexibility.

PeachTravelingSchool
Spain +34 952 201 742
www.peachtravelingschool.com
Learn Spanish in Spain and experience its most authentic customs, talk to its most genuine people, and discover its most incredible and hidden beauties, whilst having an expert teacher travelling with you 24/7.

363

Pichilemu Institute of Language Studies

Chile +56 (72) 842488/449
info@studyspanishchile.com
www.studyspanishchile.com

The Pichilemu Language School offers accredited Spanish language courses next to the beach in central Chile. We have Spanish crash courses, intensive Spanish classes, Spanish and Surf programs, and Study Abroad for credit courses. We help arrange accommodation and activities for all our students.

Simón Bolivar Spanish School

Ecuador +593 (2) 2234 708
info@simon-bolivar.com
www.simon-bolivar.com

One of the biggest Spanish schools in Ecuador. Spanish lessons are offered at the main building in Quito, the Pacific coast and the Amazon jungle.

Universidad de Navarra - ILCE

Spain +34 948 425 600
ilce@unav.es
www.unav.es/ilce/english/

A wide range of programmes are offered for people who wish to travel to Spain to learn about the culture and the language.

TEFL

Cactus TEFL

UK +44 (0)1273 830960
www.cactustefl.com

Cactus TEFL is an independent advice and admissions service working with over 125 TEFL course providers in 35 different countries.

LoveTEFL

UK +44 (0)113 829 3300
info@lovetefl.com
www.lovetefl.com

TEFL (Teaching English as a Foreign Language) is all about exploring the world while learning new skills and getting useful experience for 'real life'. LoveTEFL offer internationally recognised TEFL training, and unique teaching/travel adventures and internship.

For further information see page 228

Sport

Air

Mokai Gravity Canyon
New Zealand +64 6 388 9109
www.gravitycanyon.co.nz
Mokai Gravity Canyon boasts three world-class adventure activities: our extreme flying fox; our mighty 80-metre bungy; or feel the thrill of a 50-metre freefall on our bridge swing.

New Zealand Skydiving School
New Zealand +64 (03)3029 143
bookings@skydivingnz.com
www.skydivingnz.com
New Zealand's longest established skydiving school with more programmes, facilities and experience than any other in the country.

Nimbus Paragliding
New Zealand 64 03 326 7373
contact@nimbusparagliding.co.nz
www.nimbusparagliding.co.nz
Nimbus Paragliding provides Paragliding courses and paragliding equipment in Christchurch, New Zealand.

Nzone
New Zealand +64 3 442 5867
skydive@nzone.biz
www.nzone.biz
Experience the ultimate adrenaline rush of tandem parachuting while on vacation in New Zealand. Or train to be a Sport Skydiver yourself with an Accelerated Freefall Course, no prior training needed.

Skydive Arizona
USA +1-520 466-3753
jump@skydiveaz.com
skydiveaz.com
Located halfway between Phoenix and Tucson is the largest skydiving resort in the world! The clear desert weather allows over 340 flying days a year.

Skydive Australia
Australia +61 (02) 6684 1323
info@australiaskydive.com
www.australiaskydive.com.au
Skydive Australia is the largest and most professional skydiving company in Australia.

Choose to jump between our 5 unique spectacular locations at East Coast and it will become the experience of your lifetime.

Skydive Las Vegas
USA +1 702 759-3483
www.skydivelasvegas.com
Skydive over the quiet and peaceful views of Hoover Dam, Lake Mead, the Colorado River, the Las Vegas Strip and the entire Las Vegas Valley. Tandem skydiving is the easiest, fastest, cheapest and safest way to make your first skydive.

Skydive Switzerland GmbH
Switzerland +41 (0) 33 821 0011
www.skydiveswitzerland.com
Learn how to skydive in Switzerland. Tandem jumps, fun and glacier jumps also available.

Taupo Bungy

New Zealand +64 27 480 1231

info@tka.co.nz

www.taupobungy.co.nz

Located in the Waikato River Valley, Taupo Bungy is considered one of the world's most spectacular bungy sites. Featuring the world's first cantilever platform and New Zealand's first 'splash cam'.

Earth

Awol Adventures

New Zealand +(+64 9) 834 0501

info@awoladventures.co.nz

www.awoladventures.co.nz

Join us in the Waitakere Rainforest for an amazing Auckland Adventure in the rainforest and beach adventure zone of Piha. We offer canyoning and abseiling experiences, as well as boogie boarding and cater for any level of ability.

Bucks and Spurs

USA +1 417-683-2381

csonny@getgoin.net

www.bucksandspurs.com

Horseback riding vacations in Missouri. Round up cattle, see a horse whisperer use his natural horsemanship, and enjoy the ride at this Missouri Dude Ranch.

Gravity Assisted Mountain Biking

Bolivia +591 767 03000; +591 2 2310218

gravityoffice@gravitybolivia.com; info@gravitybolivia.com

www.gravitybolivia.com

Gravity Assisted Mountain Biking offer various downhill and cross-country mountain bike rides in Bolivia and Peru. We offer one-day to two-week long rides, as well as multi-activity trips that include biking, hiking, mountaineering and much more.

Jagged Globe

UK +44 (0) 845 345 8848

www.jagged-globe.co.uk

Jagged Globe provides mountaineering expeditions and treks. They also offer courses which are based in Wales, Scotland and the Alps for both the beginner and those wishing to improve their skills.

Megalong Australian Heritage Centre

Australia +61 (02) 4787 9116

admin@megalongcc.com.au

www.megalongcc.com.au

Discover the best of the Blue Mountains at this unique venue in stunning wilderness bushland. Experience horse riding, cattle, native wildlife and the rural lifestyle in our guesthouse or camping. Enjoy trail riding in the pristine wilderness of the Megalong Valley.

Mountaineering Council of Ireland

Ireland +353 1 625 1115

info@mountaineering.ie

www.mountaineering.ie

The Mountaineering Council of Ireland has lists of mountaineering clubs in Ireland, useful information and can give advice on insurance.

Quest Japan

Japan +81 (0)3 6902 2551

info@questjapan.co.jp

www.hikejapan.com

Guided walking holidays and tailor-made tours for individuals and small groups, from the island of Yakushima south of Kyushu, to the Kii mountain range in Central Japan, and the island of Hokkaido.

Qufu Shaolin Kung Fu School China
China +86 151 537 30991
shaolinskungfu@gmail.com
www.shaolinskungfu.com
Qufu Shaolin Kung Fu School China is an institute for the teaching and promotion of traditional Shaolin Kung Fu and Chinese Martial Arts in China. Students of all ages and abilities can learn from Shaolin Masters in the beautiful and peaceful UNESCO World Heritage City of Qufu.

Rock'n Ropes
New Zealand +64 800 244 508
info@rocknropes.co.nz
www.rocknropes.co.nz
A Rock'n Ropes course is 'as exciting as skydiving or bungee jumping'. Check out their website for full details.

Sporting Opportunities
UK +44 (0)208 123 8702
info@sportingopportunities.com
www.sportingopportunities.com
Sporting Opportunities offers sports coaching projects and sports tours for gap years, career breaks and volunteer travel.

White Peak Expeditions
UK
mail@whitepeakexpeditions.co.uk
www.whitepeakexpeditions.co.uk
Specialists in trekking and climbing for small groups in Nepal, Tibet, Kazakhstan/Kyrgyzstan, Ecuador and Peru. Climbs are suitable for the less experienced climber and are generally combined with trekking expeditions.

Snow

Alltracks Limited
UK +44 (0)1794 301777
info@alltracksacademy.com
www.alltracksacademy.com
Whether you're looking to spend a fun but challenging career break or gap year on an extended course, perfect your powder turns in a couple of weeks, learn more about backcountry riding and avalanche safety or become a qualified ski or snowboard instructor, Alltracks have a course for you.

Altitude Futures - Gap Course Verbier
Switzerland +44 7539 071166
info@altitude-futures.com
www.altitude-futures.com
Altitude Futures run official BASI and CSIA ski and snowboard instructor courses in Verbier, Whistler and Tignes. See www.altitude-futures.com for more details.

Basecamp Ski and Snowboard
UK +44 (0) 20 8789 9055
www.basecampgroup.com
Basecamp is the no. 1 choice for anyone looking to take their skiing and snowboarding to the next level as part of a gap year or career break.

BASI (British Association of Snowsport Instructors)
UK +44 (0)1479 861717
basi.org.uk
www.basi.org.uk
Fast track your snowsport career and become a qualified ski or snowboard instructor in 10 weeks with approved BASIGap.

Cardrona Alpine Resort

New Zealand +64 3 443 7341

info@cardrona.com

www.cardrona.com

Skiers and Snowboarders of all ages and abilities will enjoy a trip to Cardrona Alpine Resort. With wide open beginner trails, pristine groomers, fun freeride terrain and world class parks and pipes, Cardrona is a great way to enjoy the Southern Alps.

Harris Mountains Heli-Ski

New Zealand +64 3 442 6722

hmh@heliski.co.nz

www.heliski.co.nz

If you are a strong intermediate skier or ski-boarder, then try this for that extra thrill!

ICE Snowsports Ltd

UK +44 (0) 870 760 7360

info@icesi.org

www.icesi.org

With ICE you can attend official BASI courses in Val d'Isere, including a range of ski instructor courses and snowboard instructor courses.

Interski

UK 01623 456 333

enquiries@interskisnowsportschool.co.uk

www.interskisnowsportschool.co.uk

Interski Gap Year Instructor Training Courses run in the resorts of Aosta/Pila and Courmayeur. The only fully-inclusive gap course on the market with guaranteed employment for all successful students.

Non-Stop Ski & Snowboard

UK +44 (0)1225 632 165

info@nonstopsnow.com

www.nonstopsnow.com

Offering a variety of ski and snowboard instructor courses in western Canada, New Zealand and France. An ideal gap-year, career break or chance to fast track into the ski industry.

OnTheMountain Pro Snowsports Instructor Training in Switzerland

Switzerland +41 27 288 3131

gap@onthemountainpro.co.uk

www.onthemountainpro.co.uk

Provides exceptional training and loads of fun, after training stay and enjoy the slopes until the end of the season at no extra cost.

Outdoor Interlaken AG

Switzerland +41 (0) 33 826 77 19

mail@outdoor-interlaken.ch

www.outdoor-interlaken.ch

Ski/Snowboard school for complete beginners and for those who wish to brush up their skills. Have local guides who know the best trails, snow and shortest lift lines.

Oyster Worldwide Limited

UK +44 (0) 1892 770 771

anne@oysterworldwide.com

www.oysterworldwide.com

Paid work opportunities in top Canadian ski resorts: Whistler, The Rockies and Tremblant or join an 11 week ski and snowboarder courses in Jasper, France or Romania. Intermediate skiers can become ski instructors in world-renowned Whistler with CSIA Level 1 course and qualification included.

For further information see page 140

SITCo Ski and Snowboard Training New Zealand

New Zealand +64 21 341 214

ski@sitco.co.nz

www.sitco.co.nz

SITCo has been training keen skiers and snowboarders since 2002. Come to Queenstown NZ to start living the dream. Accommodation, lift pass, training, qualifications, and a Heli-ski, plus much more are all included.

Ski Instructor Academy
Austria +44 7528 131 567
info@siaaustria.com
www.siaaustria.com

Ski Instructor Academy offers high quality, good value ski instructor courses and private improver clinics. We have the unique ability to offer you a guaranteed job as a snow sports instructor in Austria after completing your training, giving you peace of mind that you can put your new skills straight to the test, gain valuable experience and gives you the confidence to book with Ski Instructor Academy leading to a long and successful career in the snow sports industry.

Ski le Gap
UK +44 (0)3309 001032 / 0800 160 1981
info@skilegap.com
www.skilegap.com

Offers ski and snowboard instructor training courses based in the popular Canadian resort of Tremblant.

Ski-Exp-Air
Canada +1 418 520 6669
info@ski-exp-air.com
www.ski-exp-air.com

Ski-exp-air is a Canadian ski and snowboard school offering quality, professional instruction in a fun atmosphere.

SnowSkool
UK +44 (0)1962 713342
team@snowskool.co.uk
www.snowskool.co.uk

Ski and Snowboard instructor courses in Canada, New Zealand, France and the USA. SnowSkool offers four, five, nine and eleven week programmes earning internationally recognised qualifications.

The Winter Sports Company
UK +44 (0)1736 763402
info@wintersportscompany.com
www.wintersportscompany.com

The Winter Sports Company all-inclusive ski patrol courses, ski instructor courses, snowboard instructor courses and internships, with internationally recognised qualifications, in Canada, Europe and New Zealand.

Whistler Summer Snowboard Camps
Canada +1 604 902 9227
info@whistlersnowboardcamps.com
www.whistlersnowboardcamps.com

Treeline is a residential summer ski and snowboard camp, located in beautiful Whistler, British Columbia, Canada. Improve your snowboarding skills with 1-2 week sessions for Kids (7-18), as well as an Adult's Only session for 19+.

Yamnuska Mountain Adventures
Canada +1 403 678 4164
info@yamnuska.com
yamnuska.com

Located in Canmore, Alberta at the Banff National Park gates, Yamnuska are a premier provider of mountaineering, ice climbing, rock climbing, backcountry skiing, avalanche training and trekking experiences in the Canadian Rockies.

Various

Bear Creek Outdoor Centre
Canada +1 888 453 5099
info@bearcreekoutdoor.com
www.bearcreekoutdoor.com

Located on 500 acres, Bear Creek Outdoor Centre contains two private lakes and miles of wooded trails perfect for nature exploration, orienteering, and hiking.

the gap-year guidebook 2016

Camp Challenge Pte Ltd
Singapore +65 6257 4427

enquiries@camp-challenge.com

www.camp-challenge.com

At Camp-Challenge, we believe that every youth is a cell of this global community. We provide the platform for this growth through our programmes.

Canyon Voyages Adventure Co
USA +1 435 259 6007

www.canyonvoyages.com

River rafting, kayaking, canoeing, hiking, horseback, mountain bike and 4x4 trips available in the canyons of Utah.

Class VI River Runners
USA +1 888 383 9985

info@class-vi.com

www.class-vi.com

River Runners offers a variety of organised sporting trips for students, families and corporate groups.

Donegal Adventure Centre (DAC)
Ireland +353 71 984 2418

info@donegaladventurecentre.net

www.donegaladventurecentre.net

DAC offers various camps and activities for all ages and abilities. Try your hand at surfing, high-rope climbing, archery, zip wire, abseiling, cliff jumping, body boarding and many more.

EBO Adventure
UK 0800 781 6861

info@eboadventure.com

www.eboadventure.co.uk

Get adventurous with a wide range of training activities, survival courses and outdoor instructor courses in the UK and abroad.

G2 Outdoor
UK

www.g2outdoor.co.uk

The centre, based in the Highlands of Scotland offers a full range of outdoor activities for both winter and summer.

Mendip Snow Sport
UK 01934 852335

info@mendip.me

www.mendipsnowsport.co.uk

Centre is on the edge of the Mendip hills, where you can ski, snowboard, mountain board, as well as pursue archery, rifle shooting, power kiting, 4x4 driving, quad biking, rock climbing, abseiling and more.

Peak Leaders
UK 01337 860 079

info@peakleaders.com

www.peakleaders.com

Make the most of your once in a lifetime experience in some of the world's leading resorts whilst gaining internationally recognised instructor qualifications, plus plenty of CV enhancing extras.

Raging Thunder
Australia +61 (0)7 4030 7990

info@ragingthunder.com.au

www.ragingthunder.com.au

Selection of day tours, once in a lifetime experiences available, such as Great Barrier Reef excursions, sea kayaking, ballooning and white water rafting.

Rapid Sensations Rafting
New Zealand +64 7 374 8117;
0800 35 34 35

info@rapids.co.nz

www.rapids.co.nz

White water rafting, kayaking and mountain biking on offer. They also have a kayaking school.

River Deep Mountain High

UK +44 (0) 15395 28666

info@riverdeepmountainhigh.co.uk

www.riverdeepmountainhigh.co.uk

Outdoor activities and activity Holidays in the Lake District. Where you can try canoeing, kayaking, gorge walks, abseiling, climbing, sailing, walking, trail-cycling or mountain biking.

River Rats Rafting

New Zealand +64 7 345 6543

www.riverrats.co.nz

River Rats are located in Rototua, New Zealand and are specialists in rafting. They also offer a gondola ride up Mount Ngongotaha other activities.

Rogue Wilderness Adventures

USA +1 (541) 479 9554

webmaster@wildrogue.com

www.wildrogue.com

Hiking, fishing and rafting trips are designed to give you a thrilling, relaxing and fun experience. Based in Rogue River Canyon.

Sport Lived Ltd

UK 0844 858 9103

www.sportlived.co.uk

Sporting gap-year company which arranges for young people to play sport overseas.

Wilderness Aware Rafting

USA +1 719 395 2112

rapids@inaraft.com

www.inaraft.com

At Wilderness Aware Rafting we offer a variety of white water rafting trips suitable for all skill levels, including mild water float trips, fast-paced and splashy beginner/intermediate trips and action-packed advanced white water.

Water

Adventure Bound

USA +1 970 245 5428

info@adventureboundusa.com

www.adventureboundusa.com

Discover the relaxation of drifting down the river without a care in the world, experience the excitement of paddling an inflatable kayak through an exhilarating rapid, or feel the power of laughter and intrigue while sharing campfire stories with Adventure Bound.

All Outdoors California Whitewater Rafting

USA +1 925 932 8993

rivers@aorafting.com

www.aorafting.com

Explore the rivers of California with All Outdoors. Choose from a choice of 10 Rivers, with mild to wild rapids and scenic canyons for beginners or advanced rafters. These professionally guided whitewater rafting trips are available in 1-day & multi-day options.

Allaboard Sailing Academy

Spain +350 200 50202

info@sailing.gi

www.sailing.gi

Whether you are an enthusiastic novice, looking to learn the ropes and sail safely, or a seasoned mariner seeking to hone your skills and achieve the next qualification, Allabroad have the perfect course for you.

Alpin Raft

Switzerland +41 (0) 33 823 41 00

info@alpinraft.com

www.alpinraft.com

Located in Interlaken in the Swiss Alps, Alpin Raft offers fantastic fun and adventures - join us for some thrilling and scenic rafting, canyoning or bungy-jumping!

Aquatic Explorers
Australia +61 2 9523 1518

www.aquaticexplorers.com.au

Aquatic Explorers is an SSI (Scuba Schools International) Facility offering new divers, as well as local and international scuba divers the best scuba diving training at Cronulla Beach in Sydney, Australia.

Barque Picton Castle
Canada +1 (902) 634 9984

info@picton-castle.com

www.picton-castle.com

Explore Europe, Africa and the Caribbean as crew on a three-masted tall ship. No experience needed. Join Barque Picton Castle. Come aboard, come alive!

Bermuda Sub-Aqua Club
Bermuda + 1 441 291 5640

chairman@bsac.bm

www.bsac.bm

The Bermuda Sub-Aqua Club is a branch of the British Sub-Aqua Club and offers members a varied programme of club-organised dives; a safe, structured, proven training programme.

Cairns Dive Centre
Australia +61 7 40 510 294

info@cairnsdive.com.au

www.cairnsdive.com.au

CDC offers daily day or live aboard snorkel and dive trips to the Outer Great Barrier Reef. We also offer SSI learn-to-dive courses from beginners through to instructor level.

Catalina Tours
USA +1 310 510 0211

catalinatours@gmail.com

www.catalinaoceanrafting.com

Catalina Tours provide a variety of ocean and land tours, day packages and overnight packages. Explore the island via electric bike or Jeep, or take to the seas for snorkelling, scuba diving, jet-skiing and paragliding. Discover the local wildlife, including dolphins and sea lions. Situated on Catalina Island itself, all of our staff live on the Island and we know the area well.

Challenge Rafting
New Zealand +64 3 442 7318

challenge@raft.co.nz

www.raft.co.nz

Challenge Rafting offers exciting half-day whitewater rafting trips on the Shotover and Kawarau Rivers.

Dart River Safaris
New Zealand +64 3 442 9992

info@dartriverjetsafaris.co.nz

www.dartriver.co.nz

Jet boat up the Dart River and kayak back or take the bus back. In between explore the ancient forest. The Dart River Valley featured in the Lord of the Rings films.

Deep Sea Divers Den
Australia +61-7-4046 7333

info@diversden.com.au

www.diversden.com.au

Your guide to the finest Great Barrier Reef scuba diving and snorkelling off Cairns Tropical Queensland, Australia.

Dive Kaikoura
New Zealand +64 03 319 6622

divekaikoura@xtra.co.nz

www.divekaikoura.co.nz

Professional instructors and small groups make Dive Kaikoura the ideal place to start your diving journey or advance your diving qualification.

Dvorak Expeditions
USA +1 719 539 6851
www.dvorakexpeditions.com
White water rafting, kayaking and fly fishing trips offered in Colorado, Utah, New Mexico, Idaho, Texas and Mexico.

Elite Sailing
UK 01634 890512
sue@elitesailing.co.uk
www.elitesailing.co.uk
Sailing school and RYA Training Centre based at Chatham, Kent. Suitable for absolute beginner to professional skippers and crew.

Errant Surf
UK +44 (0)208 133 6438
www.errantsurf.com
An award-winning worldwide surf company offering cost effective global surf trips to the most beautiful corners of the globe.

Gap Year Diver Ltd
UK +44 (0)1608 738 419
www.gapyeardiver.com
Diver training and a wide range of activities and excursions included which make the entire experience more exciting and enjoyable.

Island Divers
Thailand +66 (0)898732205
www.islanddiverspp.com
Looking for a new adventure? Then join our friendly and highly qualified staff for dive courses and dive trips for all levels, from beginner to professional.

Island Star Excursions
USA +1 808 661 7238
info@islandstarexcursions.com
www.hawaiioceanrafting.com
Whale watching, rafting, sailing and speed boating all off the coast of Hawaii. Small groups only.

Jubilee Sailing Trust
UK +44 (0) 23 8044 9108
info@jst.org.uk
www.jst.org.uk
Tall Ships Sailing Trust. Join their JST Youth Leadership@Sea Scheme, no sailing experience needed. Registered Charity No. 277810.
For further information see page 246

Learn In Asia (Mermaids Dive Center)
Thailand +66 38 303 333
dive@mermaidsdivecenter.com
www.learn-in-asia.com
Mermaids offers a variety of PADI scuba diving courses, scuba diving internships, coral and wreck diving trips every day, open to complete beginners and experienced divers alike.

National White Water Centre
UK 01678 521083
info@ukrafting.co.uk
www.ukrafting.co.uk
Known as the home of white water rafting and kayaking, the Snowdonia-based centre boasts fantastic water conditions for paddlesports alongside beautiful scenery.

Ocean Rafting
Australia +61 7 4946 6848
crew@oceanrafting.com.au
www.oceanrafting.com
Ocean rafting around the coast of Queensland and the Whitsunday Islands which includes exploring Whitehaven Beach.

Ocean Tribe Ltd
Kenya +254 (0)700 934 854
www.oceantribe.co
Ocean Tribe Ltd organize professional scuba diving training packages, dive training courses and dive career internships where you can go all the way to instructor in just a few short months.

OzSail

Australia +61 7 4946 6877
bookings@ozsail.com.au
ozsail.com.au

OzSail presents an extensive range of sailing and diving holidays from which to choose.

Penrith Whitewater Stadium

Australia +61 2 4730 4333
www.penrithwhitewater.com.au

Introduction packages and courses in whitewater rafting offered and whitewater kayaking.

Plas Menai

UK +44 (0) 1248 670964
info@plasmenai.co.uk
www.plasmenai.co.uk

Plas Menai, the National Watersports Centre in North Wales, offers RYA training courses in dinghy sailing, windsurfing, powerboating and cruising throughout the year and also run kayaking courses and sea kayak expeditions.

Pocono Whitewater

USA +1 570 325 3655
info@poconowhitewater.com
www.poconowhitewater.com

Trail biking, paintball skirmish, kayaking and whitewater rafting available in the LeHigh River Gorge.

River Expeditions

USA +1 800 463 9873
www.raftinginfo.com

Rafting in West Virginia on the New and Gauley Rivers.

Sabah Divers

Malaysia +6088256483
sabahdivers2u@yahoo.com
www.sabahdivers.com

Sabah Divers operate one of the leading scuba diving education & training centres in South East Asia, running a full-service dive shop and offer scuba diving courses as well as recreational dives.

Scuba Duba Dive

UK +44 (0)1224 900640
dive@scubadubadive.com
www.scubadubadive.com

Scuba Duba Dive offers numerous dive holidays and training packages all over the world to suit all levels of diver, from absolute beginners to those with years of experience. Destinations include Egypt, Thailand, Malta and Honduras.

Scuba Junkie

Malaysia +60 89 785372
info@scuba-junkie.com
www.scuba-junkie.com

Scuba Junkie is a fully licensed and insured PADI operation offering courses for beginners to advanced in the Celebes Sea.

Shotover Jet

New Zealand +64 3 442 8570
info@shotoverjet.com
www.shotoverjet.com

World famous as the ultimate jet boat experience, Shotover Jet has thrilled over 3 million people since 1970, and now it's your turn!

South Sea Nomads

Indonesia +6282145804522
info@southseanomads.com
www.southseanomads.com

A floating backpackers' hostel. Our aim is to provide dive and exploration safaris to locations that will appeal to anyone with a love of the sea and a sense of adventure.

Sunsail

UK +44 (0)844 2732 454

www.sunsail.com

Sunsail offers the full range of RYA yacht courses as well as their own teaching programmes. Their instructors are RYA qualified.

Superior Dive Training

USA +1 386 965 5832

richard@superiordivetraining.com

www.superiordivetraining.com

Superior Dive Training is dedicated to providing the highest quality technical diving instruction available, offering a wide range of technical diving courses and instructor programs.

Surf Camp Australia

Australia +61 407 787 346 / 1800 888 732

info@surfcamp.com.au

www.surfcamp.com.au

Surf Camp Australia offers 2-10 day courses for both experienced and beginner surfers, complete with accommodation in beachside cabins just a short distance from the beach and a variety of meals.

Surfaris

Australia 1800 00SURF

surf@surfaris.com

www.surfaris.com

Surfaris - licensed to a greater range of surf breaks than any other operator in Australia. Located on the east coast of NSW, half-way between Sydney and Byron Bay in the coastal surfing village of Crescent Head.

Surfing Queensland

Australia +61 07 552 011 65

info@surfingqueensland.com

www.surfingqueensland.com.au

Surfing Queensland has a surf school system with over 20 licensed surf schools operating on beaches from Coolangatta to Yeppoon.

Tall Ships Youth Trust

UK 02392 832055

info@tallships.org

tallships.org

The Tall Ships Youth Trust is dedicated to the personal development of young people through the crewing of ocean going sail training vessels. It is the UK's oldest and largest sail training charity for young people aged 12-25.

Taupo Kayaking Adventures

New Zealand 027 480 1231

info@tka.co.nz

www.tka.co.nz

Specialising in kayaking trips around the crystal clear water of Lake Taupo, under the shadow of an active volcano, and metres away from Maori rock carvings.

Ticket To Ride

UK +44 (0) 20 8788 8668

info@ttride.co.uk

www.ttride.co.uk

Ticket to Ride develop all of our worldwide surfing adventures around the combination of doing something for yourself, something for others, travelling the world and having something to show for it all at the end.

Torquay Wind & Surf Centre

UK +44 (0)1803 212411

info@kitesurfingtorquay.co.uk

www.kitesurfingtorquay.co.uk

Courses available in kitesurfing, kitebuggying and stand up paddle surfing.

Wavehunters UK

UK +44 (0)1208 880617

mail@wavehunters.co.uk

www.wavehunters.co.uk

Wavehuntyers excel in providing people of all ages personal attention and specifically tailored surf lessons from experienced committed and professional surf coaches.

Sport Instructors

Britannia Sailing East Coast

UK +44 (0) 1473 787019

enquiry@britanniasailingschool.co.uk

www.britanniasailingschool.co.uk

Based at Shotley Marina near Ipswich, Britannia Sailing is a well-established company with first-class facilities offering all aspects of sailing instruction and yacht charter.

Coaches across Continents

USA

brian@coachesacrosscontinents.org

www.coachesacrosscontinents.org

The world's only development organization with a proven track record in using soccer as a vehicle for social change in developing communities, mobilizing volunteers, financial resources, and equipment to work with local teachers and community leaders in disadvantaged communities on three continents

EA Ski & Snowboard

UK +44 (0)20 7193 2647

sstraining@educatingadventures.com

www.easkiandsnowboard.com

EA Ski & Snowboard provides a variety of ski instructor courses at top ski resorts in Canada, New Zealand, Japan, Switzerland and the USA, which arm you with a range of internationally recognised ski instructor qualifications.

Those interested in a full season and wanting to step right into an instructor uniform with a paid Ski Instructor Job should check out the Season Internship Courses. Or, for those looking for a part season training and certification program, check out the 3 to 12 Week Ski Courses.

Flying Fish UK Ltd

UK +44 (0)1983 280641

mail@flyingfishonline.com

www.flyingfishonline.com

Flying Fish trains and recruits over 1000 people each year to work worldwide as yacht skippers and as sailing, diving, surfing, windsurfing, ski and snowboard instructors.

For further information see page 242

International Academy

UK +44 (0)2380 206 977

info@international-academy.com

www.international-academy.com

Become a ski or snowboard Instructor on a gap-year or career break course. Experience world class resorts and gain recognised CSIA, CASI, NZSIA or SBINZ instructor qualifications.

Oyster Worldwide Limited

UK +44 (0) 1892 770 771

anne@oysterworldwide.com

www.oysterworldwide.com

Choose between an 11 week instructor programme in Jasper, Canada and our 5 month course + instructor job in Whistler. Excellent Oyster support throughout.

For further information see page 140

PJ Scuba

Thailand +66 (0) 382 322 19

pjscuba@gmail.com

www.pjscuba.com

Offers the chance to study scuba diving to instructor level (PADI) and then teach in Thailand.

Ski Academy Switzerland

UK +44(0)113 3141510

info@skiacademyswitzerland.com

www.skiacademyswitzerland.com

Provider of quality ski instructor programmes for gap-year students and for those on a career break or just fancy a challenge!

skivo2 Instructor Training

UK +44 (0)1635 278847

dave.beattie@skivo2.co.uk

www.skivo2.co.uk

For those wanting to become Ski Instructors, an opportunity to train with the highest qualified coaches in the world's largest ski area! Courchevel Trois Vallées.

The Instructor Training Co

New Zealand +64 (0)21 341 214

info@sitco.co.nz

www.sitco.co.nz

The Instructor Training Co offers you the opportunity to train for your ski instructor qualification in New Zealand. Five, eight and ten week courses available.

Welcome to the NEW gap-year website!

www.gap-year.com

Festivals

Brighton Festival
UK +44 (0) 1273 700747
info@brightonfestival.org
www.brightonfestival.org
A handful of volunteer posts are open during the festival in May, working in the education and press office departments.

Cheltenham Festivals
UK 0844 880 8094
www.cheltenhamfestivals.com
This company runs festivals throughout the year, including jazz, science, music, folk, fringe and literary events.

Edinburgh Festival Fringe
UK +44 (0) 131 226 0026
admin@edfringe.com
www.edfringe.com
Big and long-established late summer festival that has managed to stay cutting-edge.

Harrogate International Festival
UK +44 (0) 1423 562 303
info@harrogate-festival.org.uk
www.harrogate-festival.org.uk
Harrogate International Festival hosts a number of arts festivals, and offers internships and short-term work experience placements during festivals.

Hay Festival
UK +44 (0) 1497 822 620
admin@hayfestival.com
www.hayfestival.com/wales/jobs.aspx
One of the most famous literary festivals in the UK. Most departments take on extra workers for festival fortnight, including stewards, extra staff for the box-office and the bookshop and three interns.

Holloway Arts Festival
UK 020 7700 2062
info@therowanartsproject.com
www.therowanartsproject.com
Volunteering opportunities include being a steward for a day. Check out their website for further details.

Ilkley Literature Festival
UK +44 (0) 1943 601 210
info@ilkleyliteraturefestival.org.uk
www.ilkleyliteraturefestival.org.uk
If you want to become a volunteer at the Ilkley Literature Festival fill in their online form. Jobs include stewarding and helping with mailouts.

Lichfield Festival
UK +44 (0) 1543 306 270
info@lichfieldfestival.org
www.lichfieldfestival.org
Volunteers required backstage, to assist with stage management and to help with the education programmes. Contact Richard Bateman, volunteer coordinator, for more details.

Mananan International Festival of Music and the Arts
UK +44 (0) 1624 835 858
information@erinartscentre.com
www.erinartscentre.com/get_involved/volunteer.html
Volunteers needed for stewarding duties, programme selling, transportation of artists, administration, catering, bar duties, technical support and manning galleries and shops.

Norfolk and Norwich Festival Ltd
UK +44 (0) 1603 877 750
info@nnfestival.org.uk
www.nnfestival.org.uk
Volunteers needed from January to May to help out with administration, marketing and even event production.

Portsmouth Festivities
UK +44 (0)23 9268 1390
info@portsmouthfestivities.co.uk
www.portsmouthfestivities.co.uk
Volunteers required to help out with the many varied festivities in Portsmouth.

Salisbury International Arts Festival
UK +44 (0) 1722 332 241
info@salisburyfestival.co.uk
www.salisburyfestival.co.uk
Volunteering opportunities include stage manager, helping out with crowd management and leaflet distribution. Registered charity No. 276940.

Winchester Hat Fair
UK +44 (0)1962 844600
info@hatfair.co.uk
www.hatfair.co.uk
This vibrant and entertaining festival takes over the centre of Winchester each year during the first weekend in July. Volunteers are needed to help out before and during the festival.

Youth Music Theatre
UK +44 (0) 844 415 4858
www.youthmusictheatreuk.org
Internships are available in their London office for recent arts graduates or for professionals looking to change career direction. Also need UK-wide volunteers for one to two days per week.

Graduate opportunities & work experience

3M United Kingdom Plc
UK +44 (0)8705 360036
www.3m.com
3M offer internships and Graduate programmes in industry and development. Gain valuable experience in an environment where you'll develop marketable skills and work on exciting projects. Whether you're heading into manufacturing, distribution, or marketing, our programs will put you in position for continued success and advancement in your career.

Absolute Radio
UK 020 7434 1215
www.absoluteradio.co.uk/about
Absolute Radio are looking for individuals with a love of music and a passion for radio broadcasting to experience working behind the scenes at some of the UK's biggest radio stations. Spend two weeks learning how radio stations work, from on-air presentation and production, through to the website, marketing and operation.

Accenture
UK +44 (0) 500 100 189
ukgraduates@accenture.com
www.accenture.com/ukschemes
Apply for graduate placements with Accenture, a global management consulting, technology services and outsourcing company.

Arcadia Group plc
UK 0844 243 0000
www.arcadiagroup.co.uk
They have placement postions in their finance and HR departments, suitable for those undertaking a year's placement as part of their degree. See their website for more details.

BBC Recruitment
UK

www.bbc.co.uk/careers

Work experience placements available across the UK in all areas. These are unpaid placements that can last up to four weeks. Competition is fierce so you need to apply at least a year in advance.

Cancer Research UK
UK

volunteering@cancer.org.uk

www.cancerresearchuk.org

Internships of 12 week duration for people who wish to gain valuable work experience in fundraising, as well as marketing, campaigning and communications. Registered Charity No. 1089464.

Civil Service Recruitment
UK

www.civilservice.gov.uk/recruitment

There are a number of specific schemes open to new and experienced graduates looking for a career change. If you're successful, you could be posted to a number of government departments.

Engineering Development Trust (EDT)
UK 01707 871520

info@etrust.org.uk

www.etrust.org.uk

The EDT is the largest provider of STEM (science, technology, engineering and mathematics) enrichment activities for UK youth.

Foreign & Commonwealth Office
UK +44 (0) 20 7008 1500

www.fco.gov.uk

See their website for more about careers and opportunities in the Diplomatic Service.

GlaxoSmithKline UK
UK +44 (0) 20 8047 5000

www.gsk.com/careers/uk-students-graduates.htm

Industrial placements available.

HSBC Holdings plc
UK +44 (0) 20 7991 8888

www.hsbc.com/1/2/student-careers

HSBC has a worldwide graduate and internship programme. See their website for further details.

IBM UK Ltd
UK 023 9256 1000

ibmstudent@uk.ibm.com

www-05.ibm.com/employment/uk/

IBM run a number of Student Schemes for 'very talented individuals' in all aspects of their business.

IMI plc
UK +44 (0)121 717 3700

info@imiplc.com

www.imiplc.com

IMI operates a global graduate development programme and offers vacation work from June to September to penultimate year engineering (mechanical, electrical or manufacturing) students leading to possible sponsorship through the final year at university.

Kraft Foods
UK

www.kraftfoodscompany.com

Each year Kraft Foods offer plenty of graduate and internship opportunities across Europe.

L'Oréal (UK) Ltd

UK

www.loreal.co.uk

L'Oréal offers internships to students in universities, business and engineering schools from diverse backgrounds and provide the opportunity to acquire substantial initial work experience in one of our areas of expertise: Operations, Finance, Marketing, Sales, Communications, Digital, and Human Resources. For three to twelve months you become a member of our teams, working on projects and achieving concrete objectives on which you are assessed.

Marks & Spencer Plc

UK +44 (0) 20 7935 4422

http://corporate.marksandspencer.com/mscareers/opportunities/graduates

The M&S Graduate scheme offers many different opportunities in Retail Management, Head Office and HR.

Penguin Group UK

UK

jobs@penguin.co.uk

www.penguin.co.uk

Penguin offers business internships which last for eight weeks, journalism internships at the Financial Times which last for twelve weeks, the Pearson Diversity Summer Internship Programme as well as two-week work experience placements throughout the year.

RAF

UK +44 (0) 845 605 5555

www.raf.mod.uk/careers/

Work experience places are available in RAF bases all over the UK. As each base runs its own work experience programme you need to check the RAF website to find one near you.

Rock UK

UK +44 (0)844 8000 222

job.enquiry@rockuk.org

www.rockuk.org

As an experienced Christian provider of Outdoor Adventure residentials and day visits for young people, Rock UK offer an exciting Gap Year Instructor Training Course. Contact us to find out more! www.rockuk.org/work-for-us/gap-year-programme

For further information see page 254

S & N Genealogy

UK +44 (0) 1722 717007

manager@genealogysupplies.com

www.sandn.net/vacancies.htm

Gap-year students required to do office work such as document scanning.

Santander UK

UK

www.santanderukgraduates.com

If you are a graduate interested in working with Santander UK, submit an application for consideration when a position arises.

The Random House Group Ltd

UK +44 (0)20 7840 8400

www.careersatrandom.co.uk/rhc_workexperience.asp

Work experience opportunities are available in editorial, publicity and marketing. Complete their online form to apply.

UNHCR

UK +44 (0) 20 7759 8090

gbrloea@unhcr.org

www.unhcr.org.uk/interns/index.html

The UNHCR have six month internships which give the participant the opportunity to gain valuable experience working with refugees.

Wesser Fundraising UK
UK 01462 704 865
recruitment@wesser.co.uk
www.wesser.co.uk
Wesser offers "live in" fundraising positions nationwide working in behalf of UK charities. All fundraisers are provided with a great pay package plus free accommodation including bills. No experience necessary.

Wii Select
UK 0207 801 2490
enquires@wiiselect.co.uk
events.wiiselect.co.uk
Looking to earn some money to pay for your gap-year? Wii Select is a hospitality recruitment company that supply temporary staff to events and hospitality industry.

Seasonal

Brightsparks Recruitment
UK +44 (0)20 3627 9710
recruitment@brightsparksUK.com
www.brightsparkslife.com
Brightsparks offers job opportunities to students, graduates and young professionals, providing guidance and support to help them get into their dream careers.

Facilities Management Catering
UK +44 (0) 20 8971 2465
resourcing.fmc@aeltc.com
www.fmccatering.co.uk
If you would like to work at the most prestigious sporting event of the year then log onto our website now and click on the work opportunities page to apply online.

Fish4jobs
UK 0345 3000 406
customerservices@fish4.co.uk
www.fish4.co.uk
Search for temporary work, paid or unpaid, charity and fundraising jobs and seasonal holiday jobs abroad.

PGL
UK 0844 3710 123
recruitment@pgl.co.uk
www.pgl.co.uk/jobs
As the UK's market-leading provider of residential activity holidays and educational courses for children, PGL have an immense variety of Gap Year Jobs to offer for your Gap Year: and we pay you!

For further information see page 154

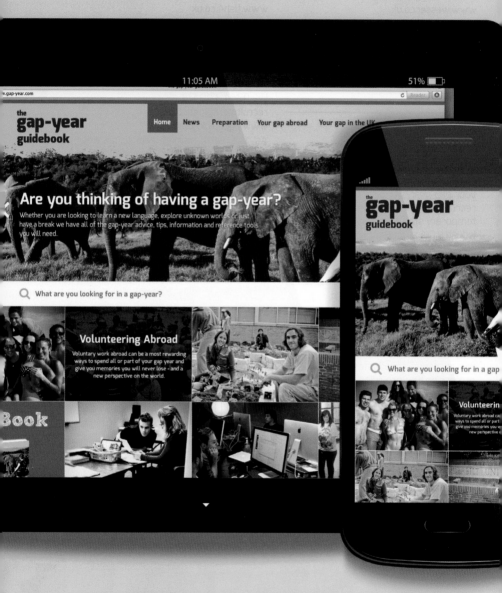

Welcome to the NEW gap-year website!

www.gap-year.com

Fundraising

Marie Curie Cancer Care (Head Office)
UK 0800 716 146
supporter.relations@mariecurie.org.uk
www.mariecurie.org.uk
Volunteer. Help in their shops, hospices and/or offices, or get involved in fundraising for Marie Curie (Registered Charity No. 207994).

Scope
UK +44 (0)20 7619 7100
supportercare@scope.org.uk
www.scope.org.uk
Scope is a registered charity (No. 208231) for the disabled which needs your help in raising funds. Whether it's running, swimming, cycling or trekking, there is plenty you can do to help.

SOS Rhino
Malaysia +60 88 388 405
info@sosrhino.org
www.sosrhino.org
SOS Rhino needs donations to help them in their work to save the Borneo rhinoceros. Why not choose them as your charity fundraising beneficiary?

War on Want
UK +44 (0)20 7324 5040
support@waronwant.org
www.waronwant.org
Run, walk, cycle, swap, bake, party - there are lots of ways to raise money for War on Want (Charity No. 208724). Whatever your fundraising challenge, your work will help in the fight against global injustice.

Volunteering

Action Centres UK
UK +44 (0)1604 499 699
isabelharlow@actioncentres.co.uk
www.go-gap.com
Go-Gap provides international volunteers with the opportunity to gain valuable service-work experience in a safe and comfortable Christian environment.

Amnesty International
UK +44 (0) 20 7033 1777
sct@amnesty.org.uk
www.amnesty.org.uk/volunteer
Amnesty International (registered charity No: 1051681) have a selection of volunteering vacancies throughout their UK offices. Volunteer roles are advertised on their website. Speculative applications are not accepted.

Beamish, The Living Museum of the North
UK +44 (0)1913 704003
volunteering@beamish.org.uk
www.beamish.org.uk/volunteering
Beamish has hundreds of volunteers who make a huge contribution to all areas of the Museum in a wide range of diverse roles, and are always looking for more enthusiastic volunteers to join the team. Contribute to the running of Beamish across all areas in a wide range of roles, including engaging the visitors in the period areas, delivering family learning activities, assisting the Curatorial and Costume Teams behind the scenes and much more.

Beanstalk

UK +44 (0)20 7729 4087

www.beanstalkcharity.org.uk

Volunteer Reading Help is a national charity, helping children who struggle with their reading to develop a love of reading and learning.

Blue Cross

UK +44 (0) 300 777 1897

info@bluecross.org.uk

www.bluecross.org.uk

The Blue Cross is Britain's pet charity (No. 224392), providing practical support, information and advice for pet and horse owners. For information on volunteering visit their website.

Born Free Foundation

UK +44 (0)1403 240 170

info@bornfree.org.uk

www.bornfree.org.uk

The Born Free Foundation has grown into a global force for wildlife. Volunteer with their major international projects devoted to animal welfare, conservation and education. They also list other possible overseas volunteering vacancies.

Camphill Communities in England & Wales

UK

www.camphill.org.uk

Camphill Communities in England and Wales offer opportunities for people with learning disabilities, mental health problems and other special needs to live, learn and work with others of all abilities in an atmosphere of mutual care and respect.

They welcome people from all over the world to join their work as resident Volunteers for a period of six months, a year or more.

Camphill Scotland

UK +44 (0)1316 291520

info@camphillscotland.org.uk

www.camphillscotland.org.uk

Camphill communities in Scotland have a mixture of salaried staff, long term vocational co-workers and short term volunteers, who usually join the community for a year or two, though shorter placements may also be considered.

Cats Protection League

UK +44 (0) 8707 708 649

helpline@cats.org.uk

www.cats.org.uk

Volunteering opportunities available in a wide variety of roles, please see our website for more details. Registered charity No. 203644.

Central Scotland Green Network Trust

UK +44 (0)1501 822015

contact@csgnt.org.uk

www.csgnt.org.uk

CSGN organises volunteers to help with ecological improvements in Central Scotland. Work includes fence repairing and path building. Reg Charity SC015341

Centre for Alternative Technology

UK +44 (0) 1654 705 950

vacancy@cat.org.uk

www.cat.org.uk

CAT has volunteer placements. Reg Charity 265239

Challenge Team UK

UK (+44) 01323 721047

info@challengeteamuk.org

www.challengeteamuk.org

The Challenge Team UK is a group of young volunteers who educate teenagers about healthy sexuality.

Change Agents UK
UK 01572 723419
contact@changeagents.org.uk
www.changeagents.org.uk
CHANGE AGENTS UK are creating a force for a sustainable future; working with young people, graduates, businesses and communities motivated by sustainability to create change.

Children with Cancer
UK +44 (0)20 7404 0808
info@childrenwithcancer.org.uk
www.childrenwithcancer.org.uk
Volunteer with us and help to save young lives. If you've got some spare time, and would like to help our charity, why not join our volunteer team.

Children's Country Holidays Fund
UK +44 (0) 1273 847 770
volunteering@cchf-allaboutkids.org.uk
www.cchf-allaboutkids.org.uk
CCHF (registered charity number 206958) Volunteers required to help out on week long or weekend activity breaks for severely disadvantaged children.

Christian Aid Gap Year
UK +44 (0)20 7620 4444
info@christian-aid.org
www.christianaid.org.uk
Have placements between mid-August and June each year for volunteers in their offices around the UK.

Dogs Trust
UK +44 (0)20 7837 0006
www.dogstrust.org.uk
Volunteers needed to help out in the following areas: fundraising, dog walking, dog socialising and pre-adoption home visiting. Registered Charity No. 227523.

Elizabeth Finn Care
UK +44 (0) 20 8834 9200
info@elizabethfinn.org.uk
www.elizabethfinncare.org.uk
Charity (No. 207812) that aims to help those with limited resources who live in their own homes, or by providing accommodation for older people in their own care homes. Volunteers always needed.

Emmaus UK
UK +44 (0) 1223 576 103
contact@emmaus.org.uk
www.emmaus.org.uk
Emmaus Communities (Registered Charity No. 1064470) offer homeless people a home and full time work refurbishing and selling furniture and other donated goods. They list various volunteer opportunities on their website.

English Heritage
UK +44 (0)870 333 1181
volunteer.enquiries@
english-heritage.org.uk
www.english-heritage.org.uk
English Heritage are looking for people who are aged 18 and over to assist with workshops, tours and other activities associated with learning and school visits.

Friends of The Earth
UK 0207 490 1555
info@foe.co.uk
www.foe.co.uk
Friends of The Earth welcomes volunteers at their head office in London, or at any of their regional offices. Registered Charity No. 281681

Global Adventure Challenges Ltd
UK +44 (0) 1244 676 454
enquiries@
globaladventurechallenges.com
www.globaladventurechallenges.com
Raise money for your chosen charity
whilst having the adventure of a lifetime.
Many adventures to choose from are
listed on their website.

Greenpeace
UK +44 (0) 20 7865 8100
recruitment.uk@greenpeace.org
www.greenpeace.org.uk
Greenpeace need volunteers either as an
active supporter or in their London office
to help out with their administration.

Groundwork Oldham & Rochdale
UK +44 (0) 161 624 1444
www.northwest.groundwork.org.uk
Whether you're looking to gain work
experience, fulfil your passion in
environmental issues or simply want to
give a few hours a week to a cause that
benefits your community Groundwork
can help you to do something special.

Hearing Dogs for Deaf People
UK +44 (0)1844 348 100
volunteer@hearingdogs.org.uk
www.hearingdogs.org.uk
Become a volunteer with Hearing Dogs
for Deaf People (Registered charity
No.293358). Contribute to the life
changing work of this Charity by visiting
their website and clicking on 'Get involved'.

Hebridean Whale & Dolphin Trust
UK +44 (0)1688 302620
info@hwdt.org
www.whaledolphintrust.co.uk
Spend your break living and working
aboard the Silurian, aiding in research and
data collection of the Hebrides marine
life. Learn about the UK's marine life with
full cetacean and sea bird identification
training, and gain sailing experience as you
travel the British Isles.

ILA (Independent Living Alternatives)
UK 0208 906 9265
paservices@ilanet.co.uk
www.ilanet.co.uk
Aims to enable people who need personal
assistance, to be able to live independently
in the community and take full control of
their lives.

Latin Link
UK +44 (0)118 957 7100
www.stepteams.org
Latin Link sends teams and individuals
to work in mission with Latin American
and Spanish Christians for between three
weeks and four months. Registered
Charity No. 1020826.

Macmillan Cancer Support (UK Office - Volunteering)
UK +44 (0) 20 7840 7840
recruitment@macmillan.org.uk
www.macmillan.org.uk
Share your skills to improve the lives
of people affected by cancer. Assist our
fundraising activities or support us in our
offices and gain new experience whilst
having fun. Registered Charity No. 261017.

Mind

UK +44 (0) 20 8519 2122
contact@mind.org.uk
www.mind.org.uk

Mind (Registered Charity No. 424348) would like to hear from you if you would like to take part in a fundraising event, or have an idea for fundraising for the charity.

Museum of London

UK +44 (0) 20 7814 5792
recruitment@museumoflondon.org.uk
www.museumoflondon.org.uk

The Museum of London offers opportunities in a wide variety of departments across the Museum's three sites, enabling volunteers to get an insight into museum life and get involved in a number of different tasks and activities.

NSPCC

UK +44 (0)20 7825 2500
recruitmentenquiry@nspcc.org.uk
www.nspcc.org.uk

Volunteers needed to help with fundraising, office work, manning the switchboard at Childline or even helping on a specific project. (Reg. Charity No. 216401)

PDSA

UK 0800 854 194
www.pdsa.org.uk

A wide range of volunteering opportunities offered. Use the contact form on their website to find out about opportunities in the UK and Ireland. Registered Charity No. 208217.

Rainforest Concern

UK +44 (0)1225 481 151
info@rainforestconcern.org
www.rainforestconcern.org

Sends volunteers to Ecuador, Costa Rica and Panama to work with important conservation programmes.

RNLI

UK +44 (0) 845 045 6999
www.rnli.org.uk

From crewing the lifeboats and volunteer lifeguarding, to raising vital funds or awareness, or using your professional skills in our offices, there are a wide range of volunteer roles available at RNLI. You will receive first class training and equipment, guidance and support and be given the opportunity to make a difference in your local community, to save lives and be part of the larger RNLI family.

Rock UK

UK +44 (0)844 8000 222
job.enquiry@rockuk.org
www.rockuk.org

At Frontier Centre (Northants), Rock UK operates a volunteer programme taking on overseas volunteers. Placements are for 9 months. Volunteers must be at least 18 years old and are typically up to 28 years old.

For further information see page 254

Royal Botanic Gardens

UK +44 (0) 20 8332 5655
info@kew.org
www.kew.org/about-kew/volunteers

Volunteers can help out at the Royal Botanic Gardens in four different areas: school & family, discovery, information and horticultural volunteers.

RSPB (Royal Society for the Protection of Birds)

UK 01767 680 551
volunteers@rspb.org.uk
www.rspb.org.uk/volunteering/residential

Want a career in conservation? Check out the volunteering pages on the RSPBs website for advice, volunteering opportunities and case studies (Registered Charity No. 207076)

RSPCA
UK
www.rspca.org.uk/volunteer
The RSPCA (registered charity no. 219099) are always looking for volunteers. Check out their website for vacancies in a home near you.

Samaritans
UK +44 (0)8705 62 72 82
volunteering@samaritans.org
www.samaritans.org
The Samaritans (Registered Charity No. 219432) depend entirely on volunteers. They are there 24/7 for anyone who needs help. Can you spare the time to help them?

Sense
UK
info@sense.org.uk
www.sense.org.uk
Volunteers always required by Sense (Registered Charity No. 289868) in a variety of areas. See their website for further details of how you can help.

Shelter
UK +44 (0) 844 515 2000
info@shelter.org.uk
www.shelter.org.uk
Volunteers are integral to Shelter's fight against bad housing and homelessness. There are a range of different volunteering opportunities available and we support volunteers with a range of skills, experiences and backgrounds. (Charity No. 263710.)

TCV The Conservation Volunteers
UK +44 (0) 1302 388 883
information@tcv.org.uk
www.tcv.org.uk
The Conservation Volunteers have been reclaiming green places since 1959.

The National Trust
UK 0844 800 1895
enquiries@nationaltrust.org.uk
www.nationaltrust.org.uk/get-involved/volunteer
Learn new skills whilst helping to conserve the UK's heritage. Volunteering opportunities can be found on their website. Registered Charity No. 205846.

The National Trust for Scotland
UK +44 (0) 844 493 2100
www.nts.org.uk/Volunteering
The National Trust for Scotland is a conservation charity that protects and promotes Scotland's natural and cultural heritage. Contact them to find out about volunteering opportunities.

The Prince's Trust
UK +44 (0)20 7543 1234
webinfops@princes-trust.org.uk
www.princes-trust.org.uk
Volunteer with the Prince's Trust (Registered Charity No. 1079675) and help young people achieve something with their lives. Opportunities in fundraising, personal mentoring, volunteer co-ordinator and training.

The Simon Community
UK 0207 485 6639
info@simoncommunity.org.uk
www.simoncommunity.org.uk
The Simon Community is a partnership of homeless people and volunteers living and working with London's homeless. They need full-time residential volunteers all year round. Registered Charity No. 283938.

The Waterway Recovery Group
UK 01494 783453
iwa@waterways.org.uk
www.waterways.org.uk
WRG has helped restore many derelict waterways throughout Britain. Thanks to the hard work of the volunteers many canals have been reopened.

The Wildlife Trusts
UK +44 (0) 1636 6777 11
enquiry@wildlifetrusts.org
www.wildlifetrusts.org
The Wildlife Trusts (Registered Charity No. 207238) always need volunteers. Check out their website or contact your local office for information about vacancies in your area.

UNICEF UK
UK +44 (0) 844 801 2414
www.unicef.org.uk
UNICEF UK regularly recruit voluntary interns to support teams within the UK. These internships usually last between two and six months and are based at offices in London or Billericay.

vInspired
UK +44 (0) 800 089 9000
info@vinspired.com
www.vinspired.com
At vInspired we believe that your creativity, energy and optimism can change the world. We're dedicated to helping you improve your skills, confidence and employability whilst you raise vital funds to make a real difference.

Vitalise
UK +44 (0) 845 330 0148
volunteer@vitalise.org.uk
www.vitalise.org.uk
Vitalise is a national charity providing short breaks and other services for people with physical disabilities, visually impaired people, and carers. They offer inspirational opportunities for volunteers through one of the largest, most diverse volunteer programmes in the UK.

Whizz-Kidz
UK +44 (0)20 7233 6600
volunteers@whizz-kidz.org.uk
www.whizz-kidz.org.uk
Whizz-Kidz is looking for volunteers to join their national Volunteer Network, you just need to be 16 or older. If you have an open mind, tons of enthusiasm and a positive attitude there are opportunities to suit you!

Wild Futures' Monkey Sanctuary
UK 0844 272 1271
volunteer@wildfutures.org
www.wildfutures.org
Residential volunteering opportunities available, offering an ideal opportunity to learn more about primates and their conservation and welfare whilst also helping with the day-to-day running of a busy sanctuary.

Youth Hostel Association
UK 0800 0191 700
volunteers@yha.org.uk
www.yha.org.uk/volunteering
If you've got some free time and would like to support YHA, there are many volunteering activities you can get involved with.

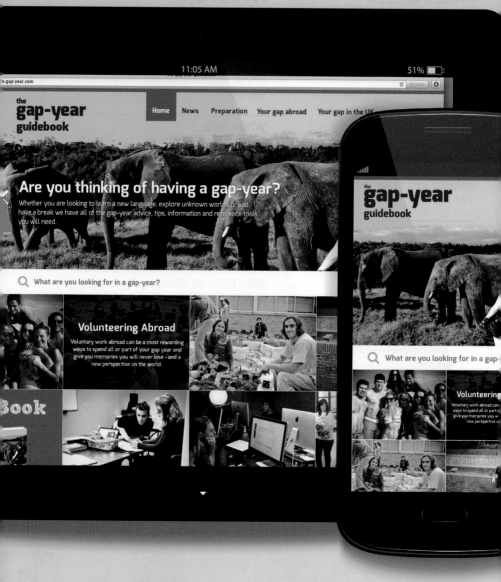

Archaeology

Council for British Archaeology
UK +44 (0) 1904 671 417
info@britarch.ac.uk
www.britarch.ac.uk
CBA's magazine, British Archaeology, contains information about events and courses as well as digs. Reg Charity 287815.

School of Archaeology & Ancient History
UK +44 (0) 116 252 2611
arch-anchist@le.ac.uk
www.le.ac.uk/archaeology/dl/dl_intro.html
Offers a series of modules in archaeology which can be studied purely for interest, or as part of a programme towards a Certificate in Archaeology.

University College London - Institute of Archaeology
UK +44 (0) 207 679 7495
ioa-ugadmissions@ucl.ac.uk
www.ucl.ac.uk/archaeology/
UCL offers a range of short courses in archaeology many of which are open to members of the public.

University of Bristol - Department of Archaeology & Anthropology
UK +44 (0)117 954 6050
sart-ugadmin@bristol.ac.uk
www.bristol.ac.uk/archanth
A variety of short courses offered, including: anthropology, archaeology, egyptology, history, Latin, Minoan, Roman and techniques. They also have a one week intensive 'get started in archaeology' course.

Art

Cardiff School of Art and Design
UK +44 (0) 29 2041 6154
csad@cardiffmet.ac.uk
www.cardiff-school-of-art-and-design.org
They run a ten week summer school programme designed to introduce you to the variety of art and design.

Heatherley School of Art
UK +44 (0) 20 7351 4190
info@heatherleys.org
www.heatherleys.org
Offers various summer courses in art as well as part-time and full-time courses.

The Prince's Drawing School
UK +44 (0) 20 7613 8568
admin@princesdrawingschool.org
www.princesdrawingschool.org
The Prince's Drawing School is an educational charity (No. 1101538) dedicated to teaching drawing from observation. Daytime, evening and summer school courses are run for artists and the general public.

University College London - Slade School of Fine Art
UK +44 (0) 20 7679 2313
slade.enquiries@ucl.ac.uk
www.ucl.ac.uk/slade
The Slade offers various qualifications in Fine Art, in addition to evening, Saturday and Easter courses and summer school.

University of the Arts London - Camberwell College of Arts

UK +44 (0) 20 7514 6302

info@camberwell.arts.ac.uk

www.camberwell.arts.ac.uk

The college offers undergraduate and postgraduate courses in Design and Fine Art, including Book Arts, Conservation, Designer-Maker, Fine Art Digital, Illustration and Printmaking.

University of the Arts London - Central Saint Martins

UK +44 (0)20 7514 7000

info@csm.arts.ac.uk

www.csm.arts.ac.uk

The college offers foundation, undergraduate, postgraduate and short courses in Acting, Directing, Graphic Design, Animation, Textile Design, Fashion, Ceramic Design, Architecture, Fine Art and more.

University of the Arts London - Chelsea College of Arts

UK +44 (0) 20 7514 7751

info@chelsea.arts.ac.uk

www.chelsea.arts.ac.uk

The college offers undergraduate and postgraduate courses in Fine Art, Graphic Design Communication, Textile Design, Interior and Spatial Design and Curating and Collections.

University of the Arts London - Wimbledon College of Arts

UK +44 (0) 20 7514 9641

info@wimbledon.arts.ac.uk

www.wimbledon.arts.ac.uk

The college offers undergraduate and postgraduate courses in Fine Art, Theatre and Screen, Drawing, Digital Theatre, Painting and Theatre Design.

Cookery

Ashburton Cookery School

UK +44 (0) 1364 652784

info@ashburtoncookeryschool.co.uk

www.ashburtoncookeryschool.co.uk

Cookery courses available from one to five days.

For further information see page 276

Belle Isle School of Cookery

UK +44 (028) 95810546

info@belle-isle.com

www.irishcookeryschool.com

Essential Cooking is an intensive four week course designed for people who are interested in learning the key skills for a gap-year job in cooking

CookAbility

UK +44 (0) 1823 461394

venetia@cookability.com

www.residentialcookery.com

CookAbilty caters for all types of gap-year students. Whether you have set your sights on a chalet cooking season, self-catering at university or a new life skill, then this is the place to become inspired in the culinary arts.

Cookery at The Grange

UK 01373 836 579

info@cookeryatthegrange.co.uk

www.cookeryatthegrange.co.uk

Cookery at the Grange has been running the outstanding four week, residential Essential Cookery Courses since 1981. Fantastic local ingredients from the Somerset countryside near Bath, are used to learn to cook really good food, for fun, for a gap year or for a career.

Cookery School at Little Portland Street

UK 0207 631 4590

info@cookeryschool.co.uk

www.cookeryschool.co.uk

Cookery School at Little Portland Street has something to offer all food lovers: check out the huge array of classes on offer on our website.

Edinburgh New Town Cookery School

UK +44 (0)131 226 4314

info@entcs.co.uk

www.entcs.co.uk

1, 3 and 6 month courses designed for gap year students who want to work in ski chalets, luxury live aboard yachts or shooting lodges.

Edinburgh School of Food and Wine

UK 0131 333 5001

info@esfw.com

www.esfw.com

Courses of interest to gappers are the four week Intensive Certificate Course which is geared towards chalet work, and the one week Survival Course which is ideally suited to those leaving home for the first time.

Food of Course

UK +44 (0) 1749 860116

info@foodofcourse.co.uk

www.foodofcourse.co.uk

A four-week residential course providing all essential skills to cook in a ski chalet, on a yacht or in holiday homes worldwide.

Gordon Ramsay's Tante Marie Culinary Academy

UK +44 (0) 1483 726957

info@tantemarie.co.uk

www.tantemarie.co.uk

Tante Marie Culinary Academy is the UK's oldest independent cookery school and is now the only school in the world able to award both the internationally acclaimed Cordon Bleu Diploma and the CTH Level 4 Diploma in Professional Culinary Arts.

Le Cordon Bleu

UK +44 (0) 20 7400 3900

london@cordonbleu.edu

www.lcblondon.com

Le Cordon Bleu has courses ranging from their famous diplomas in 'Cuisine and Pâtisserie' to shorter courses in techniques, seasonal cooking, essentials and healthy eating.

Leiths School of Food and Wine

UK +44 (0) 122 5722983

info@leiths.com

www.leiths.com

Learn how to cook and earn money from it on your gap year. Leiths certificate cookery courses will give you the confidence and skill to achieve this.

Orchards Cookery

UK +44 (0) 1789 490 259

www.orchardscookery.co.uk

Specialises in training and recruiting chalet cooks. Courses are one or two weeks long, residential and great fun with 24 students trained in three separate kitchens.

Swinton Park Cookery School

UK +44 (0) 1765 680900

cookeryschool@swintonpark.com

www.swintonpark.com

Overlooking the exquisite parkland of Swinton Park, the school offers two-day, one-day and half-day classes in a range of themes from Game to Foraging courses.

The Avenue Cookery School
UK +44 (0) 208 788 3025
info@theavenuecookeryschool.com
www.theavenuecookeryschool.com
Offer one and two week courses aimed specifically at gap-year students, chalet assistants and undergraduates.

The Bertinet Kitchen
UK +44 (0) 1225 445531
info@thebertinetkitchen.com
www.thebertinetkitchen.com
The Bertinet Kitchen offers a range of relaxed and fun courses for food lovers of all abilities and specialist baking and bread-making courses for amateurs and professionals alike.

The Cook Academy (Hampshire)
UK 01252 793648
kate@cookacademy.co.uk
www.cookacademy.co.uk
The Cook Academy offers cookery tuition and experiences for all ages, abilities and occasions.

The Cordon Vert School
UK +44 (0)161 925 2015
enquiries@cordonvert.co.uk
www.cordonvert.co.uk
The Cordon Vert School is the world's premier vegetarian cookery school. We teach both the general public and professionals the many aspects of vegetarian cuisine through workshops held at our venues in Altrincham & London. Our courses are open to everyone, whether vegetarian or not.

The Gables School of Cookery
UK +44 (0) 1454 260 444
info@thegablesschoolofcookery.co.uk
www.thegablesschoolofcookery.co.uk
Achieve your dreams through a professional four week cookery course where you can learn the skills required to work your gap-year in a ski resort or on a yacht.

The School of Artisan Food
UK 01909 532171
info@schoolofartisanfood.org
www.schoolofartisanfood.org
Based in the heart of Sherwood Forest, The School of Artisan Food teaches all aspects of artisan food production including baking and patisserie, butchery and charcuterie, cheese making, brewing, preserves, ice cream and chocolate making for people of all skill levels to. Offers a wide range of short courses, and a one year Advanced Diploma.

Webbe's Cookery School
UK +44 (0)1797 222226
www.webbesrestaurants.co.uk
Respected five-day, complete, hands-on, intensive, cutting edge foundation cooking certificate course for healthy eating and cooking for friends on a budget at university and beyond.

White Pepper Cookery School
UK +44 (0) 1202 280050
www.white-pepper.co.uk
With informative and engaging cooking classes, White Pepper offers classes in a variety of cuisines including Japanese, Italian, Thai as well as courses in Foraging, French Patisserie and more.

Yorkshire Wolds Cookery School
UK 01377 227723
info@yorkshirewoldscookeryschool.co.uk
yorkshirewoldscookeryschool.co.uk
Situated in the picturesque Yorkshire countryside, the school offers Gold Residential Duke of Edinburgh courses as well as "Student Gap Year Survival Skills".

Drama

Peer Productions
UK 01483 476825
admin@peerproductions.co.uk
www.peerproductions.co.uk/
participation/actor-training/
This free intensive one year, full time course for 17-23-year-olds, offers practical experience, the opportunity for artistic development and support moving forward.

RADA (Royal Academy of Dramatic Art)
UK +44 (0) 20 7636 7076
enquiries@rada.ac.uk
www.rada.org
This legendary drama college runs a variety of summer school courses.

Royal Central School of Speech and Drama
UK +44 (0) 20 7722 8183
enquiries@cssd.ac.uk
www.cssd.ac.uk/gapyear
Central offers short courses in acting, singing, stand-up comedy, puppetry, cabaret and burlesque, and directing.

For further information see page 278

Springs Dance Company
UK +44 (0)1634 817523
info@springsdancecompany.org.uk
www.springsdancecompany.org.uk
Springs Dance Company offers a 3 or 9 month intensive dance course that focuses on the creation, performance and teaching of dance work inspired by and expressive of the Christian faith.

The Oxford School of Drama
UK +44 (0) 1993 812883
info@oxforddrama.ac.uk
www.oxforddrama.ac.uk
The Oxford School of Drama runs a six-month Foundation Course, including acting, voice, movement, music and stage fighting. Registered Charity No. 1072770.

Year Out Drama
UK 01789 266 245
yearoutdrama@stratford.ac.uk
www.yearoutdrama.co.uk
Full-time practical drama course with a unique Company feel; work with theatre professionals to develop a wide range of skills; perform in a variety of productions; write and direct your own work; benefit from close contact with the RSC.

Driving

AA (Automobile Association)
UK +44 (0) 161 495 8945
www.theaa.co.uk
The AA website has lots of useful information on driving in the UK and abroad, including stuff about breakdown, insurance and travel planning. You can find hotels, good places to stop whilst driving and you're even able to find out about up-to-date traffic news.

DVLA (Driver & Vehicle Licencing Agency)
UK
www.dvla.gov.uk
UK government agency responsible for driving licences and vehicle registration.

DVSA (Driver & Vehicle Standards Agency)
UK 0300 200 1122
customer.services@dsa.gsi.gov.uk
www.gov.uk/dvsa
Information on theory and practical driving tests, fees and other relevant information.

RAC Motoring Services
UK +44 (0)1922 437000

www.rac.co.uk

The RAC website has lots of useful information on driving in the UK and abroad, with breakdown, insurance and other services.

Fashion & Design

Leicester College - St Margaret's
UK +44 (0) 116 224 2240

info@leicestercollege.ac.uk

www.leicestercollege.ac.uk

Has part-time courses in footwear, fabrics and pattern cutting.

Newcastle College
UK +44 (0) 191 200 4000

enquiries@ncl-coll.ac.uk

www.ncl-coll.ac.uk

Short courses available in fashion illustration, bridalwear design, textile dyeing and printing, pattern cutting and embroidery.

The Fashion Retail Academy
UK +44 (0) 20 7307 2345

info@fra.ac.uk

www.fashionretailacademy.ac.uk

Short courses available in visual merchandising, styling, PR, buying and range planning there are also tailor-made courses for those wishing to run their own retail business.

The Session School
UK +44 (0)20 7998 7353

info@thesessionschool.com

www.thesessionschool.com

Independent make-up school for professional make-up courses, workshops and masterclasses for all levels and abilities, with tuition by make-up experts.

University of the Arts London - London College of Fashion
UK +44 (0) 20 7514 7566

shortcourses@fashion.arts.ac.uk

www.fashion.arts.ac.uk

Short courses available in pattern cutting, principles of styling techniques, film and TV make up, childrenswear and maternitywear, retro fashion design and how to recycle your second hand clothes.

University of Westminster - School of Media, Arts & Design
UK +44 (0)20 7911 5000

www.westminster.ac.uk/about-us/schools/media

Westminster offers a range of short courses in fashion, including fashion design, textile printing, and pattern cutting.

Land studies

Bishop Burton College
UK +44 (0)1964 553 000

www.bishopburton.ac.uk

Short courses available in tractor driving, pest control, tree felling, sheep shearing, animal husbandry and more...

Capel Manor College
UK +44 (0) 8456 122 122

enquiries@capel.ac.uk

www.capel.ac.uk

They have short courses in lorinery, flower arranging, CAD in garden design, practical gardening, aboriculture, botanical illustration, leathercraft and more ...

Chichester College
UK +44 (0) 1243 786321

www.chichester.ac.uk

Short courses available in animal care, farming, bushcraft, coppicing, hedgerow planting and managment, watercourse management, moorland management and more ...

Plumpton College

UK +44 (0) 1273 890 454

www.plumpton.ac.uk

Courses available in animal care, welding, tractor driving, machinery, wine trade, aboriculture, chainsaw, bushcraft, pond management, wildlife, woodcraft and more...

Rodbaston College

UK +44 (0)1785 712209

rodenquiries@rodbaston.ac.uk

www.southstaffs.ac.uk

Short courses available in keeping chickens, tractor driving, animal care, hurdle fencing, machinery, pest control and chainsaws.

Royal Agricultural College

UK +44 (0) 1285 652531

www.rac.ac.uk

Have a two day residential taster course in April which gives an insight into the career options in land-based industries.

Sparsholt College

UK +44 (0) 1962 776441

enquiry@sparsholt.ac.uk

www.sparsholt.ac.uk

Have part-time courses in forklift operation, tractor driving, health & safety, horticulture, floristy, landscaping and more.

The Open College of Equine Studies

UK +44 (0)1284 811 401

info@equinestudies.co.uk

www.equinestudies.co.uk

The college offers a series of short courses available in horse and pony care, behaviour, training, physiology and breeding as well as stable and business management courses.

Warwickshire College - Moreton Morrell

UK 0300 45 600 47

info@warkscol.ac.uk

www.warkscol.ac.uk

The college spans 750 acres of countryside, offering agriculture and equine studies. Courses range from brickwork, carpentry and joinery to forestry, tree management and arboriculture, with floristry and flower arranging also available. Courses also include animal welfare and vet nursing in addition to equine and farriery.

Languages

Berlitz - London

UK +44 (0) 20 7611 9640

www.berlitz.co.uk

International language school. Intense courses in Chinese French, German, Italian, Japanese, Portuguese, Russian and Spanish available. Other schools in the UK can be found in Birmingham, Brighton, Bristol, Edinburgh, Manchester and Oxford.

Canning House

UK +44 (0)20 7811 5600

enquiries@canninghouse.org

www.canninghouse.org

Canning House runs evening courses in Brazilian Portuguese, as well as a wide range of events on Latin America, Spain and Portugal.

International House London

UK +44 (0)207 394 6580

info@ihworld.com

www.ihworld.com

Worldwide network of language schools offering courses in Arabic, Chinese, French, German, Italian, Japanese and Spanish.

Italian Cultural Institute in London

UK +44 (0) 20 7235 1461

icilondon@esteri.it

www.icilondon.esteri.it/IIC_Londra

The Italian Cultural Institute has a wide programme of Italian language courses as well as a mass of information about Italy and its culture.

Languages @ Lunchtime

UK +44 (0) 141 330 6521

student.recruitment@glasgow.ac.uk

www.gla.ac.uk/schools/mlc/languagecentre

Small informal classes run at Glasgow University for two hours per week over 18 weeks.

Rosetta Stone (UK) Ltd

UK 0800 005 1220

cs@rosettastone.co.uk

www.rosettastone.co.uk

Learn languages with Rosetta Stone's interactive CD-ROM software plus online features.

The Japan Foundation - London Language Centre

UK +44 (0) 20 7436 6698

info.language@jpf.org.uk

www.jpf.org.uk/language

The Japan Foundation London Language Centre provides courses in Japanese. Also has regular newsletter and resource library.

Music

BIMM - Brighton Institute of Modern Music

UK +44 (0) 844 2 646 666

info@bimm.co.uk

www.bimm.co.uk

Various part-time courses available, also summer schools, for bass, drums, guitar, vocals, songwriting and live sound/tour management.

Dartington International Summer School

UK +44 (0) 1803 847 080

summerschool@dartington.org

www.dartington.org/summer-school

Dartington International Summer School (Registered Charity No. 279756) is both a festival and a music school. Teaching and performing takes place all day, every day.

English Camerata

UK 01923 853309

www.englishcamerata.org.uk

English Camerata offer a Chamber Music Summer Course which provides extensive coaching in an exciting classical chamber music environment for ensembles and instrumentalists playing a variety of instruments.

Lake District Summer Music

UK +44 (0) 845 6 44 25 05

info@ldsm.org.uk

www.ldsm.org.uk

The Lake District Summer Music School is an ensemble-based course for string players and pianists intending to pursue careers as professional musicians. Registered Charity no 516350.

London Music School

UK +44(0)208 986 7885

info@londonmusicschool.com

www.tlms.co.uk

The London Music School offers a Diploma in Music Technology, open to anyone with musical ability aged 17 or over. The course explores professional recording and you get to use a 24-track studio.

London School of Sound

UK +44 (0) 20 7720 6183
info@londonschoolofsound.co.uk
www.londonschoolofsound.co.uk
Based in the recording studio previously owned by Pink Floyd, we offer part and full-time courses of between five weeks and two years in music production, sound engineering and DJ skills.

Music Worldwide Drum Camp

UK +44 (0) 1603 462907
gary@musicworldwide.org
www.musicworldwide.org
Drum Camp is an annual worldwide percussion event in Norfolk specialising in world rhythms and drum and dance programs. Offers an amazing variety of classes over four days, in music, singing and dance.

NLMS Music Summer School

UK
c.gomme@btinternet.com
www.nlmsmusic-summerschool.co.uk
Each year over 100 enthusiastic adult amateur musicians get together for a week of enjoyment.

North London Piano School

UK +44 (0) 20 8958 5206
www.learn-music.com/nlps2
The North London Piano School runs an annual International Summer Course. Courses are intensive and tailored to each participants' skills, needs and aspirations and offer a record number of tuition hours within a week long course.

The British Kodály Academy

UK +44 (0) 208 651 3728
enquiries@britishkodalyacademy.org
www.britishkodalyacademy.org
The Academy runs various music courses for teachers and young children, but also have courses for those wishing to improve their skills.

The DJ Academy Organisation

UK 07980 915424
andyking221@btinternet.com
www.djacademy.org.uk
Offer an eight-week part time DJ course (in various cities in the UK), private tuition, one day superskills course, the ultimate mobile DJ course and the superclub experience.

The Recording Workshop

UK +44 (0) 20 896 88 222
recordingworks@btconnect.com
www.recordwk.dircon.co.uk
The Recording Workshop offer part time and full time courses on all aspects of music production, sound engineering and music technology.

UK Songwriting Festival

UK +44 (0) 1225 876 133
www.uksongwritingfestival.com
Five-day event held at Bath Spa University every August. The Songwriting Workshop includes daily lectures on the craft of songwriting, small group sessions, live band sessions, studio sessions with a producer and an acoustic live recording on CD.

Photography

DigitalMasterclass Ltd

UK +44 (0)1303 230958
brian@digitalmasterclass.co.uk
www.digitalmasterclass.co.uk

London School of Photography

UK +44 (0) 20 7659 2085
lsp@lsptraining.co.uk
www.lsptraining.com
Short courses available in digital photography, photojournalism, as well as travel, adventure and street photography. Small classes of up to eight people. One to one training also available.

Photo Opportunity Ltd
UK +44 (0) 20 8940 0256
chris@photoopportunity.co.uk
www.photoopportunity.co.uk
Courses offered lasting from one to five days in length. Tailored to suit your own particular needs and classes are small.

Photofusion
UK +44 (0) 20 7738 5774
info@photofusion.org
www.photofusion.org
This independent photography resource centre, situated in Brixton, offers digital photography courses.

Picture Weddings - Digital wedding photography workshops
UK (+44) 01793 780501
info@pictureweddings.co.uk
www.pictureweddings.co.uk
Fast-track workshops in digital wedding photography.

The EOS Training Academy
UK 07810 551662
info@eostrainingacademy.co.uk
www.eostrainingacademy.co.uk
Experience Seminars hosts a range of workshops throughout the UK, which are designed to provide a fast track way of learning photography and digital imaging techniques.

The Photography Institute
UK
info@thephotographyinstitute.co.uk
www.thephotographyinstitute.co.uk
The Institute provides an online diploma course in photography, with contributions from leading photographers.

The Photography School
UK +44 (0)1189 483502
info@thephotographyschool.co.uk
www.thephotographyschool.co.uk
Try your hand at photography with intensive photography courses for beginners and professionals alike at The Photography School.

The Royal Photographic Society
UK +44 (0) 1225 325 733
reception@rps.org
www.rps.org/workshops
The RPS holds various photography workshops for human, landscape and floral photography, printing and development and digital manipulation software.

The Trained Eye
UK +44 (0)1494 353637
info@thetrainedeye.co.uk
www.thetrainedeye.co.uk
Offer creative courses in wedding and portrait photography, for amateurs or advanced photographers to improve their skills.

Sport

Ace Adventure
UK +44 (0)330 555 0313
info@aceadventures.co.uk
www.aceadventures.co.uk
Ace Adventure offers numerous activities, situated in the beautiful Scottish highlands. Activities include exciting water and land sports such as white water rafting, canoeing, kayaking, canyoning, paintball and even bungee jumping.

Active Outdoor Pursuits
UK +44 (0)1540 210000
info@activeoutdoorpursuits.com
www.activeoutdoorpursuits.com
Active Outdoor Pursuits provides a range of sports for all weathers. Summer activities include water sports such as white water rafting, canoeing or kayaking, whilst land sports include rock climbing & abseiling and mountain biking. Winter sports include skiing, snowboarding and mountaineering are available.

BASP UK Ltd
UK +44 (0) 1855 811 443
skipatrol@basp.org.uk
www.basp.org.uk
BASP offers First Aid and Safety Training courses designed specifically for the outdoor user, suitable for all NGB Awards.

Big Squid Scuba Diving Training and Travel
UK 0207 627 0700
info@bigsquid.co.uk
www.bigsquid.co.uk
Big Squid offers a variety of dive courses using the PADI and TDI systems of diver education.

British Hang Gliding & Paragliding Association Ltd
UK +44 (0)116 289 4316
office@bhpa.co.uk
www.bhpa.co.uk
The BHPA oversees the standards of instructor training and runs coaching course for pilots. They also list all approved schools in the field of paragliding, hang gliding and parascending.

British Mountaineering Council
UK +44 (0) 161 445 6111
office@thebmc.co.uk
www.thebmc.co.uk
BMC travel insurance covers a range of activities and is designed by experts to be free from unreasonable exclusions or restrictions, for peace of mind wherever you travel.

British Offshore Sailing School - BOSS
UK +44 (0) 23 8045 7733
www.boss-sail.co.uk
BOSS offers complete RYA shore-based and practical training courses, also women only courses, from Hamble Point Marina.

British Sub Aqua Club
UK +44 (0) 151 350 6200
info@bsac.com
www.bsac.com
With 1,000+ friendly dive clubs all around the UK (and some overseas) BSAC offers accessible, affordable scuba diving lessons. With the right training and support, you could be very soon enjoying your own scuba diving adventure.

CricketCoachMaster Academy
UK +44 (0) 7815 081744
info@ccmacademy.co.uk
www.ccmacademy.co.uk
The CCM Academy has a coaching programme to further develop players with the recognised potential to play at county and international level.

Curling in Kent
UK +44 (0)1892 826 004
info@curlinginkent.co.uk
www.fentonsrink.co.uk
Come to Fenton's Rink and try your hand at this exciting Olympic sport. New season begins 1st October.

Dream Fencing Club
UK 07581 782848
dreamfencing@gmail.com
www.dreamfencing.co.uk
Dream Fencing Club aims to introduce this Olympic sport to adults and children in the London area, offering first-class and well-coached fencing opportunities for all ages. The club is for beginners and experienced fencers alike and provides high quality training which not only improves your physical condition but also your mental concentration, coordination, self-discipline and emotional control.

Fly Sussex Paragliding
UK +44 (0) 1273 858 170
info@sussexhgpg.co.uk
www.flysussex.com
Learn to paraglide or hang glide over the beautiful Sussex countryside.

Glasgow Ski & Snowboard Centre
UK +44 (0) 141 427 4991
info@ski-glasgow.org
www.ski-glasgow.org
Learn to ski, improve your existing skills or learn to snowboard. Fully qualified instructors waiting to teach you.

Green Dragons
UK 01883 652 666
fly@greendragons.co.uk
www.greendragons.co.uk
Paragliding and hang gliding centre. You do not need any experience or knowledge, just the desire to fly and follow your instructor's guidance on positions for take off, time spent in the air and landing.

Jubilee Sailing Trust
UK +44 (0) 23 8044 9108
info@jst.org.uk
www.jst.org.uk
Tall Ships Sailing Trust. Join their JST Youth Leadership@Sea Scheme, no sailing experience needed. Registered Charity No. 277810.

London Fencing Club
UK +44 (0)7951 414409
www.londonfencingclub.co.uk
Fencing tuition available in various centres in London - beginners to advanced training available.

London Scuba Diving School
UK 0845 544 1312
info@londonscuba.com
www.londonscuba.com
The London Scuba Diving School teaches beginners in swimming pools in Battersea and Bayswater. They also offer advanced courses for the experienced diver.

Mendip Outdoor Pursuits
UK +44 (0)1934 834 877
info@mendip.me
www.mendipoutdoorpursuits.co.uk
Lessons in abseiling, archery, bridge building, caving, climbing, bush craft, kayaking, navigation, orienteering and more available.

Nae Limits
UK 01796 482600
info@naelimits.co.uk
www.naelimits.co.uk
Nae Limits has over 14 adrenaline-fuelled water and land adventure activities for you to experience, whether you are planning a stag do activity, family activity break, team building event or just fancy a day out to remember! Tackle some of the best White Water Rafting Scotland has to offer or kick up your canyoning a gear in one of our private exclusive venues or get dirty on our Quad Biking Trek.

New Forest Activities
UK +44 (0) 1590 612 377
info@earth-events.co.uk
www.newforestactivities.co.uk
Organises group activities such as canoeing, rope work, cycling and climbing. Also offer environmental courses in the New Forest.

Newquay Activity Centre

UK +44 (0)1637 879571
info@newquayactivitycentre.co.uk
www.newquayactivitycentre.co.uk

Newquay Activity Centre offers great opportunities for lovers of water-sports. Activities include surfing, coasteering and bodyboarding. Available to beginners or experts, with provision for Hen & Stag parties, school outings, family groups and military exercises.

North London Skydiving Centre Ltd

UK +44 (0) 871 664 0113
office@ukskydiving.com
www.ukskydiving.com

Experience the thrill of tandem skydiving from 15,000 feet with North London Skydiving Centre. Alternatively, try out the wind tunnel or ride the hovercraft. Capture the moment with NLSC's photography and video services for an unforgettable experience.

Plas y Brenin - The National Mountain Centre

UK +44 (0) 1690 720 214
info@pyb.co.uk
www.pyb.co.uk

For those hoping to reach dizzy heights, Plas y Brenin offers a vast range of activities and courses.

Pod Zorbing

UK 0845 430 3322
info@zorbing.co.uk
www.zorbing.co.uk

Ever fancied hurtling down a hill in a huge inflatable ball? With a choice of Harness or Hydro Zorbing, Pod Zorbing offers great, professional Zorbing experiences with a true fun factor.

Poole Harbour Watersports

UK +44 (0) 1202 700503
info@pooleharbour.co.uk
www.pooleharbour.co.uk

Learn to windsurf and kitesurf at Poole in Dorset. Courses available for both beginners and improvers.

ProAdventure Limited

UK 01978 861 912
sales@proadventure.co.uk
www.proadventure.co.uk

Based in Wales, ProAdventure offers different activity courses around the UK, including canoeing, kayaking, rock climbing and mountain biking.

Skydive GB

UK +44 (0)1262 228033
info@skydivegb.com
www.skydivebrid.co.uk

Skydive GB specialises in introducing people to the exciting sport of skydiving, whether it's jumping for charity, a one-off experience or something you want to take up as a hobby or sport.

South Cambridgeshire Equestrian Centre

UK +44 (0) 1763 263 213
www.scec.co.uk

This riding school is set in 260 acres of Cambridgeshire countryside. They offer riding tuition to the beginner and also more advanced teaching for experienced riders.

Sportscotland National Centre Cumbrae

UK +44(0) 1475 530757
cumbraecentre@sportscotland.org.uk
www.nationalcentrecumbrae.org.uk

Sportscotland national watersport centre offer a range of courses from a fully residential three weeks Powerboat Instructor or 18 weeks Professional Yachtmaster Training, to a one day introduction to Windsurfing.

Suffolk Ski Centre
UK +44 (0) 1473 602347
info@suffolkskicentre.co.uk
www.suffolkskicentre.co.uk
Learn to ski or snowboard in Suffolk. Courses also available for those wishing to improve their existing skills.

Sussex Polo Club
UK +44 (0) 1342 714 920
info@sussexpolo.co.uk
www.sussexpolo.co.uk
Sussex Polo is a professional and welcoming club, popular with players, sponsors and spectators. Ideal for players wanting high standards of low goal polo or to learn to play in a relaxed and friendly atmosphere all year round.

The Talland School of Equitation
UK 01285 740 155
secretary@talland.net
www.talland.net
World renowned BHS and ABRS approved equestrian centre offering top class training for professional qualifications. Variety of courses including competition training on quality horses.

Tollymore Mountain Centre
UK +44 (0)28 4372 2158
livetheadventure@tollymore.com
www.tollymore.com
Tollymore have a range of courses designed to suit your own skills and experience. Their courses include rambling, mountaineering, climbing, canoeing and first aid.

UK Parachuting
UK 07769 721036
jump@ukparachuting.co.uk
www.ukparachuting.co.uk
AFF courses available. Also tandem skydiving and Accelerated Free Fall tuition slots available every day.

UKSA (United Kingdom Sailing Academy)
UK +44 (0)1983 294941
info@uksa.org
www.uksa.org
Entry level training for work crewing on superyachts, employment in the yachting industry, or train to become a watersports instructor. Spend a few weeks at UKSA and be ready for the working season. Funding options. Travel the world!

Vertical Descents Ltd
UK 07891 264342
cornwall@verticaldescents.com
www.verticaldescents.com
Vertical Descents offer a variety of water and land sports - from surfing, body boarding and white water rafting to climbing & abseiling, go-karting and paintball - plus many more, including extreme sports. Perfect for school trips and corporate and school outings.

Wellington Riding
UK +44 (0) 118 932 6308
info@wellington-riding.co.uk
www.wellington-riding.co.uk
A riding school and livery yard set in 300 acres of the Hampshire countryside. Wellington Riding offers junior courses for children and adult tailor-made courses to enhance riding and horse care at any level.

TEFL

CELTA - INTO University of Gloucestershire
UK +44 (0)844 846 4846
into@glos.ac.uk
insight.glos.ac.uk/departments/into/tefl/pages/celta.aspx
Gloucestershire University offer intensive courses in TEFL leading to the Cambridge ESOL CELTA award.

ETC - The English Training Centre
UK +44 (0) 121 449 2221
info@englishtc.co.uk
www.englishtc.co.uk
Professionally-designed TESOL courses offered accredited by ACTDEC. Experienced tutors provide comprehensive feedback and helpful support. Free grammar guide and teaching resource book.

Golders Green Teacher Training Centre
UK +44 (0) 208 905 5467
www.englishlanguagecollege.co.uk
Full-time and part-time TEFL/TESOL courses available.

ITC - Intensive TEFL Courses
UK +44 (0) 8456 445464
info@tefl.co.uk
www.tefl.co.uk
Intensive TEFL Courses (ITC) have been running weekend TEFL (Teach English as a Foreign Language) courses throughout the UK since 1993.

LTTC - London Teacher Training College
UK +44 (0)208 133 2027
lttc@teachenglish.co.uk
www.teachenglish.co.uk
Over the years the college has trained a vast number of teachers from around the world, and prides itself on the quality of its courses and the individual attention it provides every student who enrols.

OxfordTEFL
UK +34 93 458 0111
tesol@oxfordtefl.com
www.oxfordtefl.com
OxfordTEFL offer a four week training course, accredited by Trinity College London, at the end of which you should get a Certificate in TEFL.

Windsor TEFL
UK +44 (0) 1753 858 995
info@windsorschools.co.uk
www.windsorschools.co.uk
Offer their TEFL course in their centres in London and Windsor as well as in Europe. Also offer the CELTA TEFL course in various places worldwide.

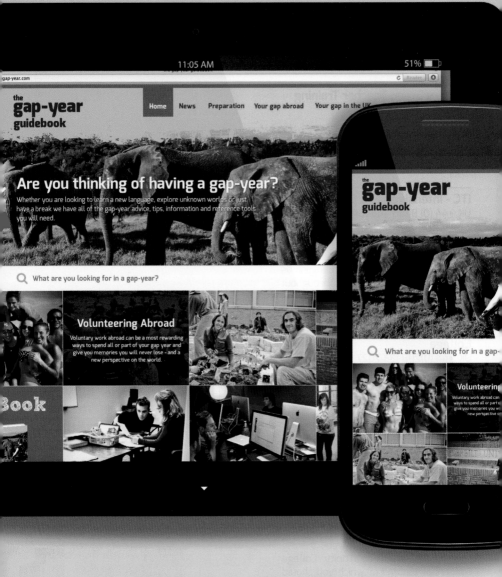

Welcome to the NEW gap-year website!

www.gap-year.com

Appendix

Country info

Once you have chosen where you want to go, whether one country or a dozen, do some research. It would be a shame to travel to the other side of the world and then miss what it has to offer. There are loads of websites giving interesting and useful factual advice (weather, geographical, political, economic) as well as those that are more touristy.

Foreign Office warnings

It's worth bearing in mind that economic and political situations can change rapidly in countries, so check with the Foreign and Commonwealth Office that the country is still safe to travel to before you go. There's a link to their website on: **www.gap-year.com**

It's important to look at the lists of specific areas which travellers should avoid. It's also worth noting the phone numbers of all British embassies and consulates in areas where you may be travelling, in case you need to contact them for help.

Telephone, text or email home regularly to save your family a lot of worry and British embassies a lot of wasted time. The following pages contain data for countries: make sure you check with the FCO for up-to-date information.

Afghanistan, The Islamic Republic of
Capital: Kabul
Currency: Afghani (AFN)
Religion: mainly Sunni Muslim
Languages: Farsi (Dari), Pashtu (Pashto or Pukhto)
British Embassy, Kabul: +93 (0) 700 102 000

Albania, The Republic of
Capital: Tirana
Currency: Lek (ALL)
Religion: Sunni Muslim, Albanian Orthodox, Roman Catholic
Languages: Albanian (Tosk is the official dialect), Greek, Vlach, Romani, Slavic dialects
British Embassy, Tirana: +355 4 223 4973/4/5

Algeria, The People's Democratic Republic of
Capital: Algiers
Currency: Algerian Dinar (DZD)
Religion: Sunni Muslim, Christian, Jewish
Language: Arabic (official language), French and Amazigh
British Embassy, Algiers: +213 77 00 85 000

Andorra, The Principality of
Capital: Andorra la Vella
Currency: Euro (EUR)
Religion: Roman Catholic
Language: Catalan (official), French, Spanish
British Consulate-General, Barcelona: +34 933 666 200

Angola, The Republic of
Capital: Luanda
Currency: Kwanza (AOA)
Religion: Indigenous beliefs, Roman Catholic, Christian, Muslim
Language: Portuguese (official), local African languages
British Embassy, Luanda: +244 (222) 334582

Anguilla (British Overseas Territory)
Capital: The Valley
Currency: Eastern Caribbean Dollar (XCD); US dollars accepted (USD)
Religion: Christian
Language: English
Government House, Anguilla: +1 (264) 497 2621/2

Antigua and Barbuda
Capital: Saint John's City
Currency: East Caribbean dollar (XCD)
Religion: Anglican, Moravian, Methodist and Roman Catholic
Language: English
St John's, Honorary British Consul: +1 268 561 5046

Argentina (The Argentine Republic)
Capital: Buenos Aires
Currency: Peso (ARS)
Religion: Roman Catholic, Protestant, Jewish and Muslim
Language: Spanish
British Embassy, Buenos Aires: +54 (11) 4808 2200

Armenia, The Republic of
Capital: Yerevan
Currency: Dram (AMD)
Religion: Armenian Orthodox, Christian, Yezidi
Language: Armenian, Russian, Yezidi
British Embassy, Yerevan: +374 (0) 10 264 301

Ascension Island (British Overseas Territory)
Capital: Georgetown
Currency: St Helena/Ascension Pound (SHP)
Religion: Christian
Language: English
Government House, Georgetown: +00 247 7000

Australia, The Commonwealth of
Capital: Canberra
Currency: Australian dollar (AUD)
Religion: Christian, Buddhist, Jewish, Muslim
Language: English, Aboriginal
British High Commission, Canberra: +61 (0) 2 6270 6666

Austria, The Republic of
Capital: Vienna
Currency: Euro (EUR)
Religion: Roman Catholic, Muslim and Protestant
Language: German
British Embassy, Vienna Tel: +43 (1) 716 130

Azerbaijan, The Republic of
Capital: Baku
Currency: Manat (AZN)
Religion: Muslim, Russian Orthodox, Armenian Orthodox
Language: Azeri, Russian, Armenian
British Embassy, Baku: +994 (12) 437 7878

Bahamas, The Commonwealth of The
Capital: Nassau
Currency: Bahamian Dollar (BSD)
Religion: Baptist, Anglican, Roman Catholic, Methodist, Church of God, Evangelical Protestants
Language: English, Creole (among Haitian immigrants)
refer to British High Commission, Kingston, Jamaica: +1 (876) 936 0700

Bahrain, The Kingdom of
Capital: Manama (Al Manamah)
Currency: Bahraini Dinar (BHD)
Religion: Muslim
Language: Arabic, English
British Embassy, Manama: +973 1757 4100; +973 1757 4167 (Information)

Bangladesh, The People's Republic of
Capital: Dhaka
Currency: Taka (BDT)
Religion: Muslim, Hindu, Buddhist, Christian
Language: Bangla, English, some tribal languages
British High Commission, Dhaka: +880 (2) 882 2705/6/7/8/9

Barbados
Capital: Bridgetown
Currency: Barbadian Dollar (BBD)
Religion: Protestant, Roman Catholic, Jewish, Muslim
Language: English
British High Commission, Bridgetown: +1 (246) 430 7800

Belarus, The Republic of
Capital: Minsk
Currency: Belarusian Ruble (BYR)

Religion: **Eastern Orthodox Christian, Roman Catholic, Protestant, Jewish, Muslim**
Language: Belarusian, Russian
British Embassy, Minsk: +375 (17) 229 8200

Belgium
Capital: Brussels
Currency: Euro (EUR)
Religion: Roman Catholic, Protestant
Language: Dutch, French, German
British Embassy, Brussels: +32 (2) 287 6211

Belize
Capital: Belmopan
Currency: Belizean Dollar (BZD)
Religion: Roman Catholic, Protestant, Muslim, Buddhist, Hindu, Bahá'í
Language: English, Creole, Spanish, indigenous languages
British High Commission, Belmopan: +501 822 2981/2717

Benin, The Republic of
Capital: Porto-Novo
Currency: CFA Franc BCEAO (XOF)
Religion: Indigenous beliefs, Christian, Muslim
Language: French, Fon, Yoruba, other African languages
Community Liaison Officer, Contonou: +229 21 30 32 65

Bermuda (British Overseas Territory)
Capital: Hamilton
Currency: Bermuda Dollar (BMD)
Religion: Christian, African Methodist Episcopalian
Language: English, Portuguese
Government House, Hamilton: +1 (441) 292 3600

Bhutan, The Kingdom of
Capital: Thimphu
Currency: Ngultrum (BTN), Indian Rupee (INR)
Religion: Buddhist, Hindu
Language: Dzongkha, various Tibetan and Nepalese dialects, English widely spoken

UK has no diplomatic representative in Bhutan. Contact British Deputy High Commission, Kolkata (Calcutta), India: +91 33 2288 5173-76

Bolivia, The Republic of
Capital: La Paz
Currency: Boliviano (BOB)
Religion: Roman Catholic, Evangelical Methodist
Language: Spanish, Quechua, Aymara and Indigenous dialects
British Embassy, La Paz: +591 (2) 243 3424

Bosnia and Herzegovina
Capital: Sarajevo
Currency: Convertible Mark (BAM)
Religion: Roman Catholic, Orthodox, Muslim
Language: Bosnian, Serbian, Croatian
British Embassy, Sarajevo: +387 33 282 200 (main); +387 33 20 4780 (Consular/Visa)

Botswana, The Republic of
Capital: Gaborone
Currency: Pula (BWP)
Religion: Christian, indigenous beliefs
Language: English, Setswana
British High Commission, Gaborone: +267 395 2841

Brazil, The Federative Republic of
Capital: Brasilia
Currency: Real (BRL)
Religion: Roman Catholic, Pentecostal, Animist
Language: Portuguese
British Embassy, Brasilia: +55 61 3329 2300

British Antarctic Territory
Currency: Sterling
Language: English
refer to Foreign & Commonwealth Office, London: +44 (0) 20 7008 1500

British Virgin Islands
Capital: Road Town, Tortola
Currency: US Dollar (USD)
Religion: Christian
Language: English
Government House, Tortola: +1 284 494 2345/2370

Appendix

411

Brunei (Darussalam)
Capital: Bandar Seri Begawan
Currency: Brunei Dollar (BND)
Religion: Muslim
Language: Malay, English, Cantonese,
Mandarin, Hokkein, Hakka
British High Commission, Bandar Seri
Begawan: +673 (2) 222 231;
+673 (2) 226 001 (Consular/Visa)

Bulgaria, The Republic of
Capital: Sofia
Currency: Lev (BGN)
Religion: Bulgarian Orthodox, Muslim, Roman
Catholic, Jewish
Language: Bulgarian
British Embassy, Sofia: +359 (2) 933 9222

Burkina Faso
Capital: Ouagadougou
Currency: CFA Franc BCEAO (XOF)
Religion: Animist, Muslim, Christian
Language: French, indigenous languages
British Honorary Consul, Ouagadougou: +226
(50) 30 88 60

Burma (The Union of Myanmar)
Capital: Rangoon
Currency: Kyat (MMK)
Religion: Buddhist, Christian, Muslim, Animist
Language: Burmese, ethnic minority
languages
British Embassy, Rangoon: +95 (1) 380 322

Burundi, The Republic of
Capital: Bujumbura
Currency: Burundi Franc (BIF)
Religion: Muslim, Roman Catholic, Animist
Language: Kirundi, French, Swahili
British Embassy, Liaison Office, Bujumbura:
+257 22 246 478

Cambodia, The Kingdom of
Capital: Phnom Penh
Currency: Riel (KHR), and US Dollar (USD)
Religion: Buddhist, Muslim, Christian
Language: Khmer, Cambodian
British Embassy, Phnom Penh: +855 23
427124/48153

Cameroon, The Republic of
Capital: Yaounde
Currency: CFA Franc BEAC (XAF)
Religion: Christian, Muslim, indigenous beliefs
Language: French, English, Pidgin, numerous
African dialects
British High Commission, Yaounde: +237 2222
05 45

Canada
Capital: Ottawa
Currency: Canadian Dollar (CAD)
Religion: Roman Catholic, Protestant, Muslim
Language: English, French
British High Commission, Ottawa: +1 (613) 237
1530

Cape Verde, The Republic of
Capital: Praia
Currency: Escudo (CVE)
Religion: Roman Catholic
Language: Portuguese, Crioulo
British Honorary Consulate, Sao Vincente:
+238 232 3512

Cayman Islands (British Overseas Territory)
Capital: George Town (Grand Cayman)
Currency: Caymanian Dollar (KYD)
Religion: Christian
Language: English
Government House, George Town, Grand
Cayman: +1 345 949 7900

Central African Republic, The
Capital: Bangui
Currency: CFA Franc BEAC (XAF)
Religion: Christian, Muslim, indigenous beliefs
Language: French, Sangho
refer to British High Commission, Yaoundé,
Cameroon: +236 2161 8513

Chad, The Republic of
Capital: N'Djamena
Currency: CFA Franc BEAC (XAF)
Religion: Muslim, Christian, indigenous beliefs
Language: French, Arabic, local languages
refer to British High Commission, Yaoundé,
Cameroon: +237 2222 05 45

Chile, The Republic of
Capital: Santiago de Chile
Currency: Peso (CLP)
Religion: Roman Catholic, Evangelical, Jewish, Muslim
Language: Spanish, Mapuche, Aymara, Quechua
British Embassy, Santiago: +56 (2) 370 4100

China, The People's Republic of
Capital: Beijing
Currency: Yuan Renminbi (CNY)
Religion: Officially atheist. Daoist, Buddhist, Muslim, Roman Catholic, Protestant (the 5 state-registered religions)
Language: Putonghua (Mandarin), many local Chinese dialects
British Embassy, Beijing: +86 (10) 5192 4000

Colombia, The Republic of
Capital: Bogotá
Currency: Peso (COP)
Religion: Roman Catholic, Evangelical
Language: Spanish, indigenous languages
British Embassy, Bogotá: +57 (1) 326 8300

Comoros, The Union of The
Capital: Moroni (Ngazidja)
Currency: Comoros Franc (KMF)
Religion: Muslim, Roman Catholic
Language: Comoran, French, Arabic
refer to British High Commission, Port Louis, Mauritius: +230 202 9400

Congo, The Republic of The
Capital: Brazzaville
Currency: CFA Franc BEAC (XAF)
Religion: Roman Catholic, Christian, Muslim, traditional beliefs
Language: French (official), Lingala, Kikongo, Munukutuba
refer to British Embassy, Kinshasa, Democratic Republic of Congo: +243 81 715 0761

Congo, The Democratic Republic of the
Capital: Kinshasa
Currency: Congolese Franc (CDF)
Religion: Roman Catholic, Protestant, Kimbanguist, Muslim, indigenous beliefs
Language: French (official), Lingala (trade language), Swahili, Kikongo, Tshiluba
British Embassy, Kinshasa: +243 81 715 0761

Costa Rica, The Republic of
Capital: San José
Currency: Colon (CRC)
Religion: Roman Catholic, Evangelical Protestant
Language: Spanish
British Embassy, San José: +506 2258 2025

Côte d'Ivoire, The Republic of (Ivory Coast)
Capital Yamoussoukro
Currency: CFA Franc BCEAO (XOF)
Religion: Muslim, Christian, indigenous beliefs
Language: French (official), Dioula, Baoule and other local native dialects
British Embassy, Côte d'Ivoire: +225 (22) 442 669

Croatia, The Republic of
Capital: Zagreb
Currency: Kuna (HRK)
Religion: Roman Catholic, Orthodox, Muslim
Language: Croatian
British Embassy, Zagreb: +385 (1) 6009 100

Cuba, The Republic of
Capital: Havana
Currency: Convertible Peso (CUC) or Peso (CUP)
Religion: Roman Catholic, Santeria, Protestant
Language: Spanish
British Embassy, Havana: +53 (7) 214 2200

Cyprus, The Republic of
Capital: Nicosia
Currency: Euro (EUR), Turkish Lira (in the north) (TRY)
Religion: Greek Orthodox, Muslim, Maronite, Armenian Apostolic
Language: Greek, Turkish, English
British High Commission, Nicosia: +357 22 861100

413

Czech Republic, The
Capital: Prague
Currency: Czech Koruna (Crown) (CZK)
Religion: Roman Catholic, Protestant, Orthodox, Atheist
Language: Czech
British Embassy, Prague: +420 257 402 111

Denmark, The Kingdom of
Capital: Copenhagen
Currency: Danish Krone (DKK)
Religion: Evangelical Lutheran, Christian, Muslim
Language: Danish, Faroese, Greenlandic (an Inuit dialect), English is the predominant second language
British Embassy, Copenhagen: +45 35 44 52 00

Djibouti, The Republic of
Capital: Djibouti
Currency: Djiboutian Franc (DJF)
Religion: Muslim, Christian
Language: French (official), Arabic (official), Somali, Afar
British Honorary Consul, Djibouti: +253 (3) 250915

Dominica, The Commonwealth of
Capital: Roseau
Currency: East Caribbean Dollar (XCD)
Religion: Roman Catholic, Protestant
Language: English (official), French patois (Creole)
British High Commission, Roseau: +767 275 7800

Dominican Republic, the
Capital: Santo Domingo
Currency: Dominican Peso (DOP)
Religion: Roman Catholic
Language: Spanish
British Embassy, Santo Domingo: +1 809 472 7111

East Timor - see Timor-Leste

Ecuador, The Republic of
Capital: Quito
Currency: US Dollar (USD)
Religion: Roman Catholic
Language: Spanish (official), Amerindian languages (especially Quechua)
British Embassy, Quito: +593 (2) 2970 800/1

Egypt, The Arab Republic of
Capital: Cairo
Currency: Egyptian Pound (EGP)
Religion: Muslim (mostly Sunni), Coptic Christian
Language: Arabic (official), English and French
British Embassy, Cairo: +20 (2) 2791 6000

El Salvador, The Republic of
Capital: San Salvador
Currency: US Dollar (USD), Colon (SVC)
Religion: Roman Catholic
Language: Spanish
British Honorary Consulate, El Salvador: +503 2236 5555

Equatorial Guinea, The Republic of
Capital: Malabo
Currency: CFA Franc BEAC (XAF)
Religion: Christian (predominantly Roman Catholic), indigenous religions
Language: Spanish (official), French (official), Fang, Bubi, Ibo
Refer to British High Commission, Abuja, Nigeria: +234 (9) 413 2010

Eritrea
Capital: Asmara
Currency: Nafka (ERN)
Religion: Christian, Muslim
Language: Tigrinya, Tigre, Arabic, English
British Embassy, Asmara: +291 1 12 01 45

Estonia, The Republic of
Capital: Tallinn
Currency: Kroon (EEK)
Religion: Lutheran, Orthodox Christian
Language: Estonian (official), Russian
British Embassy, Tallinn: +372 667 4700

Ethiopia, The Federal Democratic Republic of
Capital: Addis Ababa
Currency: Ethiopian Birr (ETB)
Religion: Orthodox Christian, Muslim, Animist, Protestant
Language: Amharic, Tigrinya, Oromigna, Guaragigna, Sidaminga, Somali, Arabic, other local dialects, English (major foreign language taught in schools)
British Embassy, Addis Ababa: +251 (11) 661 2354

visit: www.gap-year.com

Falkland Islands (British Overseas Territory)
Capital: Stanley
Currency: Falkland Island Pound (FKP)
Religion: Christian, Roman Catholic, United Reformed Church, Anglican
Language: English
Government House, Stanley: +500 282 00

Fiji (The Republic of the Fiji Islands)
Capital: Suva
Currency: Fijian Dollar (FJD)
Religion: Christian, Hindu, Muslim
Language: English (official), Hindustani, Gujarati, numerous Fijian dialects
British High Commission, Suva: +679 3229 100

Finland, The Republic of
Capital: Helsinki
Currency: Euro (EUR)
Religion: Lutheran, Orthodox
Language: Finnish (official), Swedish (official), growing Russian speaking minority and small Sami speaking community
British Embassy, Helsinki: +358 (0) 9 2286 5100/5210/5216

France (The French Republic)
Capital: Paris
Currency: Euro (EUR)
Religion: Roman Catholic, Protestant, Jewish, Muslim
Language: French
British Embassy, Paris: +33 1 44 51 31 00

Gabon (The Gabonese Republic)
Capital: Libreville
Currency: CFA Franc BEAC (XAF)
Religion: Christian, Muslim, indigenous beliefs
Language: French (official), Fang, Myene, Bateke, Bapounou/Eschira, Badjabi
British Honorary Consulate, Libreville: +241 762 200

Gambia, The Republic of
Capital: Banjul
Currency: Dalasi (GMD)
Religion: Muslim, Christian, indigenous beliefs
Language: English (official), Mandinka, Wolof, Fula, indigenous languages
British High Commission, Banjul: +220 449 5133

Georgia
Capital: Tbilisi
Currency: Lari (GEL)
Religion: Georgian Orthodox, Muslim, Russian Orthodox, Armenian Apostolic
Language: Georgian (official), Russian, Armenian, Azeri, Abkhaz
British Embassy, Tbilisi: +995 32 274 747

Germany, The Federal Republic of
Capital: Berlin
Currency: Euro (EUR)
Religion: Protestant, Roman Catholic, Muslim
Language: German
British Embassy, Berlin: +49 (30) 20457-0

Ghana, The Republic of
Capital: Accra
Currency: Cedi (GHS)
Religion: Muslim, Christian, indigenous beliefs
Language: English (official), African languages (including Akan, Mossi, Ewe, and Hausa), Fante, Ga-Adangme, 75 spoken languages
British High Commission, Accra: +233 (302) 213250

Gibraltar (British Overseas Territory)
Capital: Gibraltar
Currency: Gibraltar Pound (GIP)
Religion: Roman Catholic, Protestantism, Muslim, Hindu, Jewish
Language: English
Governor's Office, Main Street: +350 200 45 440

Greece (The Hellenic Republic)
Capital: Athens
Currency: Euro (EUR)
Religion: Greek Orthodox, Muslim
Language: Greek
British Embassy, Athens: +30 210 727 2600

Grenada
Capital: St George's
Currency: East Caribbean Dollar (XCD)
Religion: Roman Catholic, Anglican, Protestant
Language: English (official), French patois
Honorary British Consul, St George's: +473 405 8072

Guatemala
Capital: Guatemala City
Currency: Quetzal (GTQ)
Religion: Roman Catholic, Protestant, Judasim, Muslim, indigenous Mayan beliefs
Language: Spanish, there are 23 officially recognized Amerindian languages
British Embassy, Guatemala City: +502 2380 7300

Guinea, The Republic of
Capital: Conakry
Currency: Guinean Franc (GNF)
Religion: Muslim, Christian, traditional beliefs
Language: French (official), eight local languages taught in schools (Basari, Pular, Kissi, Koniagi, Kpelle, Loma, Malinke and Susu)
British Embassy, Conakry: +224 63 35 53 29

Guinea-Bissau, The Republic of
Capital: Bissau
Currency: CFA Franc BCEAO (XOF)
Religion: Muslim, Christian, indigenous beliefs
Language: Portuguese (official), Crioulo, indigenous African languages
Honorary British Consulate: +245 320 1224/1216

Guyana, The Co-operative Republic of
Capital: Georgetown
Currency: Guyanese Dollar (GYD)
Religion: Christian, Hindu, Muslim
Language: English, Amerindian dialects, Creole
British High Commission, Georgetown: +592 226 58 81

Haiti, The Republic of
Capital: Port-au-Prince
Currency: The Gourde (HTG)
Religion: Roman Catholic, Protestant, Baptist, Pentecostal, Adventist, also Voodoo
Language: French (official), Creole (official)
British Consulate, Port-au-Prince: +509 3744 6371

Holy See, Rome (Vatican City State)
Capital: Vatican City
Currency: Euro (EUR)
Religion: Roman Catholic
Language: Latin, Italian, English and French
British Embassy, Rome: +39 06 4220 4000

Honduras, The Republic of
Capital: Tegucigalpa
Currency: Lempira (HNL)
Religion: Roman Catholic, Protestant
Language: Spanish, English (business), Amerindian dialects
British Embassy, Tegucigalpa: +504 237 6577/6459

Hong Kong (The Hong Kong Special Administration of China)
Currency: Hong Kong Dollar (HKD)
Religion: Buddhist, Taoist, Christian, Muslim, Hindu, Sikhist, Jewish
Language: Chinese (Cantonese), English
British Consulate General, Hong Kong: +852 2901 3281

Hungary, The Republic of
Capital: Budapest
Currency: Forint (HUF)
Religion: Roman Catholic, Calvinist, Lutheran, Jewish, Atheist
Language: Hungarian
British Embassy, Budapest: +36 (1) 266 2888

Iceland, The Republic of
Capital: Reykjavik
Currency: Icelandic Krona (ISK)
Religion: Evangelical Lutheran, Protestant, Roman Catholic
Language: Icelandic
British Embassy, Reykjavik: +354 550 5100

India
Capital: New Delhi
Currency: Rupee (INR)
Religion: Hindu, Muslim, Christian, Sikhist
Language: Hindi (official), 18 main and regional official state languages, plus 24 further languages, 720 dialects and 23 tribal languages, English (officially an associate language, is used particularly for political, and commercial communication)
British High Commission, New Delhi: +91 (11) 2419 2100

visit: www.gap-year.com

Myanmar (see Burma)

Namibia, The Republic of
Capital: Windhoek
Currency: Namibian Dollar (NAD)
Religion: Christian
Language: English (official), Afrikaans,
German, and several indigenous languages
British High Commission, Windhoek: +264 (61)
274800

Nauru, The Republic of
Capital: Yaren District (unofficial)
Currency: Australian Dollar (AUD)
Religion: Protestant, Roman Catholic
Language: Nauruan (official), English
(commerce and government, widely
understood)
refer to British High Commission, Suva, Fiji:
+679 322 9100

Nepal
Capital: Kathmandu
Currency: Nepalese Rupee (NPR)
Religion: Hindu, Buddhist, Muslim
Language: Nepali (official), Newari (mainly in
Kathmandu), Tibetan languages (mainly hill
areas), Indian languages (mainly Terai areas).
Nepal has over 30 languages and many
dialects.
British Embassy, Kathmandu: +977 (1) 441
0583/1281/4588/1590

Netherlands, The Kingdom of The
Capital: Amsterdam
Currency: Euro (EUR)
Religion: Roman Catholic, Protestant, Muslim
Language: Dutch
British Embassy, The Hague: +31 (0) 70 4270
427

New Zealand
Capital: Wellington
Currency: New Zealand Dollar (NZD)
Religion: Anglican, Presbyterian, Roman
Catholic, Methodist, Baptist
Language: English, Maori
British High Commission, Wellington: +64 (4)
924 2888

Nicaragua, The Republic of
Capital: Managua
Currency: Cordoba (NIO)
Religion: Roman Catholic, Evangelical
Protestant
Language: Spanish (official), English, Miskito,
Creole, Mayanga, Garifuna, Rama
British Honorary Consul, Managua: +505 254
5454/3839

Niger, The Republic of
Capital: Niamey
Currency: CFA Franc BCEAO (XOF)
Religion: Muslim
Language: French (official), Arabic, local
languages widely spoken
British Honorary Consul, Niamey: +227 9687
8130

Nigeria, The Federal Republic of
Capital: Abuja
Currency: Naira (NGN)
Religion: Muslim, Christian, traditional beliefs
Language: English (official), Hausa, Yoruba,
Igbo
British High Commission, Abuja: +234 (9) 413
2010/2011/3885-7

Norway, The Kingdom of
Capital: Oslo
Currency: Norwegian Kroner (NOK)
Religion: Church of Norway (Evangelical
Lutheran)
Language: Norwegian (bokmål and nynorsk),
Sami
British Embassy, Oslo: +47 23 13 27 00

Oman, The Sultanate of
Capital: Muscat
Currency: Oman Rial (OMR)
Religion: Ibadhi Muslim, Sunni Muslim, Shi'a
Muslim, Hindu, Christian
Language: Arabic (official), English, Farsi,
Baluchi, Urdu
British Embassy, Muscat: +968 24 609 000;
(out of hours emergencies) +968 9920 0865

Pakistan, The Islamic Republic of
Capital: Islamabad
Currency: Rupee (PKR)
Religion: Muslim, Hindu, Christian
Language: Punjabi, Sindhi, Pashtun, Urdu,
Balochi, English and other local languages
British High Commission, Islamabad: +92 51
201 2000

Palau, The Republic of
Capital: Suva
Currency: United States Dollar (USD)
Religion: Christian, Hindu, Muslim
Language: English, numerous Fijian dialects,
Gujarati, Fijian Hindi
refer to British Ambassador, Manila, The
Philippines: +63 (2) 858 2200

Palestine (The Occupied Palestinian Territories)
Currency: New Israeli Shekel (ILS), Jordanian
Dinar (JOD) (West Bank Only)
Religion: Muslim, Christian
Language: Arabic, English widely spoken
British Consulate-General, Gaza: +972 (08)
283 7724

Panama, The Republic of
Capital: Panama City
Currency: US Dollar (USD) (known locally as
the Balboa (PAB))
Religion: Roman Catholic, Protestant, Jewish,
Muslim
Language: Spanish (official), English
British Embassy, Panama City: +507 269
0866

Papua New Guinea, The Independent State of
Capital: Port Moresby
Currency: Kina (PGK)
Religion: Christian according to its
constitution, Roman Catholic, Evangelical
Lutheran, Evangelical Alliance, Pentecostal,
Baptist, Anglican, Seventh Day Adventist,
United Church, Buddhist, Muslim, Hindu
Language: English, Pidgin, Hiri Motu, over 820
different languages
British High Commission, Port Moresby: +675
325 1677

Paraguay, The Republic of
Capital: Asunción
Currency: Guarani (PYG)
Religion: Roman Catholic, Mennonite,
Protestant, Latter-day Saints, Jewish, Russian
Orthodox
Language: Spanish (official), Guaraní (official)
British Honorary Consulate, Asunción: +595
(21) 210 405

Peru, The Republic of
Capital: Lima
Currency: Nuevo Sol (PEN)
Religion: Roman Catholic
Language: Spanish (official), Quechua (official),
Aymara and several minor Amazonian languages
British Embassy, Lima: +51 (1) 617 3000
(main); 3053/3054 (consular)

Philippines, The Republic of the
Capital: Metro Manila
Currency: Peso (PHP)
Religion: Roman Catholic, Protestant, Muslim
Language: Filipino (official), English (official)
British Embassy, Manila: +63 (2) 858 2200

Pitcairn, Henderson, Ducie & Oeno Islands (British Overseas Territory)
Capital: Adamstown
Currency: New Zealand Dollar (NZD)
Religion: Seventh Day Adventist
Language: English, Pitkern (a mix of English
and Tahitian)
British High Commission, Auckland, New
Zealand: +64 (9) 366 0186

Poland, The Republic of
Capital: Warsaw
Currency: Zloty (PLN)
Religion: Roman Catholic, Eastern Orthodox,
Protestant
Language: Polish
British Embassy, Warsaw: +48 (22) 311 00 00

Portugal (The Portuguese Republic)
Capital: Lisbon
Currency: Euro (EUR)
Religion: Roman Catholic, Protestant
Language: Portuguese
British Embassy, Lisbon: +351 (21) 392 4000

Qatar, The State of
Capital: Doha
Currency: Qatari Riyal (QAR)
Religion: Muslim
Language: Arabic (official), English, Urdu
British Embassy, Doha: +974 4496 2000

Romania
Capital: Bucharest
Currency: New Leu (RON)
Religion: Orthodox, Roman Catholic,
Protestant, Reformed, Greek Catholic, Unitarian
Language: Romanian (official), English, French,
German
British Embassy, Bucharest: +40 (21) 201 7200

Russia Federation, The
Capital: Moscow
Currency: Ruble (RUB)
Religion: Orthodox Christian, Muslim, Jewish,
Buddhist
Language: Russian, Tatar
British Embassy, Moscow: +7 (495) 956 7200

Rwanda, The Republic of
Capital: Kigali
Currency: Rwandan Franc (RWF)
Religion: Roman Catholic, Protestant, Muslim,
indigenous beliefs
Language: Kinyarwanda (official), French
(official), English (official), Kiswahili (used in
commercial centres and by army)
British Embassy, Kigali: +250 252 556000

Saint Helena (British Overseas Territory)
Capital: Jamestown
Currency: St Helena Pound (SHP)
Religion: Christiantiy, Bahá'í
Language: English
Governor's Office, Jamestown: +290 2555

Saint Kitts & Nevis (The Federation of St Christopher & Nevis)
Capital: Basseterre
Currency: East Caribbean Dollar (XCD)
Religion: Anglican, Roman Catholic,
Evangelical Protestant
Language: English
Honorary British Consul, Basseterre: +1 (869)
764 4677

Saint Lucia
Capital: Castries
Currency: East Caribbean Dollar (XCD)
Religion: Roman Catholic, Anglican, Methodist,
Baptist, Jewish, Hindu, Muslim
Language: English (official), French patois
(Kweyol)
British High Commission, Castries: +1 (758)
452 2484/5 (resides in Barbados)

Saint Vincent and the Grenadines
Capital: Kingstown
Currency: East Caribbean Dollar (XCD)
Religion: Anglican, Methodist, Roman Catholic,
Seventh-Day Adventist, Hindu, other Protestant
Language: English
British High Consul, Kingstown: +784 457 6860

Samoa, The Independent State of
Capital: Apia
Currency: Samoan Tala (WST)
Religion: Roman Catholic, Methodist, Latter-
day Saints
Language: Samoan, English
British Honorary Consulate, Apia: +685 27123

São Tomé & Príncipe, The Democratic State of
Capital: São Tomé
Currency: Dobra (STD)
Religion: Christian
Language: Portuguese, Lungwa Santomé, and
other creole dialects
Refer to the British Embassy in Luanda,
Angola: +244 222 334582

Saudi Arabia, The Kingdom of
Capital: Riyadh
Currency: Saudi Riyal (SAR)
Religion: Muslim (Sunni, Shia). The public
practice of any other religion is forbidden
Language: Arabic, English
British Embassy, Riyadh: +966 (0) 1 488 0077

Senegal, The Republic of
Capital: Dakar
Currency: CFA Franc BCEAO (XOF)
Religion: Muslim, Christian, indigenous beliefs
Language: French (official), Wolof, Malinke,
Serere, Soninke, Pular (all national)
British Embassy, Dakar: +221 33 823 7392/9971

423

the gap-year guidebook 2016

Serbia, The Republic of
Capital: Belgrade
Currency: Serbian Dinar (RSD)
Religion: Serbian Orthodox, Muslim, Roman Catholic, Christian
Language: Serbian (majority), Romanian, Hungarian, Slovak, Croatian, Albanian (Kosovan), Ukranian, Bosniak, Montenegrin, Bulgarian, Ruthenian, Roma. Vlach, Macedonian
British Embassy, Belgrade: +381 (11) 2645 055

Seychelles, The Republic of
Capital: Victoria
Currency: Seychelles Rupee (SCR)
Religion: Roman Catholic, Anglican, Muslim, Hindu
Language: English, French, Creole (Seselwa)
British High Commission, Victoria: +248 4283 666

Sierra Leone, The Republic of
Capital: Freetown
Currency: Leone (SLL)
Religion: Muslim, Christian, indigenous beliefs
Language: English (official), Krio (English-based Creole), indigenous languages widely spoken
British High Commission, Freetown: +232 (0) 7689 25634

Singapore, The Republic of
Capital: Singapore
Currency: Singapore Dollar (SGD)
Religion: Taoist, Buddhist, Muslim, Christian, Hindu
Language: Mandarin, English, Malay, Tamil
British High Commission, Singapore: +65 6424 4200

Slovakia (The Slovak Republic)
Capital: Bratislava
Currency: Euro (EUR)
Religion: Roman Catholic, Atheist, Protestant, Orthodox
Language: Slovak (official), Hungarian
British Embassy, Bratislava: +421 (2) 5998 2000

Slovenia, The Republic of
Capital: Ljubljana
Currency: Euro (EUR)
Religion: Roman Catholic
Language: Slovene, Italian, Hungarian, English
British Embassy, Ljubljana: +386 (1) 200 3910

Solomon Islands
Capital: Honiara
Currency: Solomon Islands Dollar (SBD)
Religion: Christian, traditional beliefs
Language: English, Pidgin, 92 indigenous languages
British High Commission, Honiara: +677 21705/6

Somalia (The Somali Democratic Republic)
Capital: Mogadishu
Currency: Somali Shilling (SOS)
Religion: Sunni Muslim
Language: Somali (official), Arabic, Italian, English
British Office for Somalia, Nairobi, Kenya: +254 (20) 2844 000

South Africa, Republic of
Capital: Pretoria/Tshwane
Currency: Rand (ZAR)
Religion: Predominately Christian but all principal religions are represented
Language: 11 official languages: Afrikaans, English, Ndebele, Sepedi, Sesotho, Swati, Tsonga, Tswana, Venda, Xhosa, Zulu
British High Commission, Pretoria: +27 (12) 421 7500

South Georgia & South Sandwich Islands (British Overseas Territories)
Capital: King Edward Point
Currency: United Kingdom Pound Sterling (GBP)
Language: English
Governor's Office, Stanley, Falkland Islands: +500 282 00

Spain, The Kingdom of
Capital: Madrid
Currency: Euro (EUR)
Religion: Roman Catholic, Protestant
Language: Castilian Spanish (official), Catalan, Galician, Basque
British Embassy, Madrid: +34 (91) 714 6300

Sri Lanka, The Democratic Socialist Republic of
Capital: Colombo
Currency: Rupee (LKR)
Religion: Buddhist, Hindu, Muslim, Christian
Language: Sinhalese, Tamil, English
British High Commission, Colombo: +94 (11)
5390639

Sudan, The Republic of
Capital: Khartoum City
Currency: Sudanese pound (SDG)
Religion: Muslim, Christian, indigenous religions
Language: Arabic (official), Nubian, Ta
Bedawie, dialects of Nilotic, Nilo- Hamitic,
Sudanic languages, English
British Embassy, Khartoum: +249 (183) 777 105

Suriname, The Republic of
Capital: Paramaribo
Currency: Suriname Dollar (SRD)
Religion: Hindu, Muslim, Roman Catholic,
Dutch Reformed, Moravian, Jewish, Bahá'í
Language: Dutch (official), English, Sranan
Tongo (Creole), Hindustani, Javanese
British Honorary Consulate, Paramaribo: +597
402 558

Swaziland, The Kingdom of
Capital: Mbabane
Currency: Lilangeni (SZL)
Religion: Christian, indigenous beliefs
Language: English, Siswati
British Honorary Consulate, Mbabane: +268
551 6247

Sweden
Capital: Stockholm
Currency: Swedish Krona (SEK)
Religion: Lutheran, Roman Catholic, Orthodox,
Baptist, Muslim, Jewish, Buddhist
Language: Swedish, English widely spoken
British Embassy, Stockholm: +46 (8) 671 3000

Switzerland
Capital: Berne
Currency: Swiss Franc (CHF)
Religion: Roman Catholic, Protestant, Muslim
Language: Swiss German (official), French,
Italian, Rhaeto-Rumantsch
British Embassy, Berne: +41 (31) 359 7700

Syria (The Syrian Arab Republic)
Capital: Damascus
Currency: Syrian Pound (also called Lira) (SYP)
Religion: Sunni Muslim, Shi'a Muslim, Alawite,
Druze, other Muslim sects, Christian, Jewish
Language: Arabic (official), Kurdish, Armenian,
Aramaic, Circassian, some French, English
British Embassy, Damascus: +963 (11) 339
1513/1541 (consular)

Taiwan (Province of the People's Republic of China)
Capital: Taipei
Currency: New Taiwan Dollar (TWD)
Religion: Buddhist, Taoist, Christian
Language: Mandarin Chinese (official),
Taiwanese, Hakka
British Trade & Cultural Office, Taipei: +886 (2)
8758 2088

Tajikistan, Republic of
Capital: Dushanbe
Currency: Somoni (TJS)
Religion: Sunni Muslim, Ismaili Shiite, Russian
Orthodox Christian, Jewish
Language: Tajik, Russian
British Embassy, Dushanbe: +992 372 24 22 21

Tanzania, United Republic of
Capital: Dodoma (official)
Currency: Tanzania Shilling (TZS)
Religion: Christian, Muslim, indigenous beliefs
Language: Kiswahili, English
British High Commission, Dar es Salaam: +255
(022) 229 0000

Thailand, Kingdom of
Capital: Bangkok
Currency: Baht (THB)
Religion: Buddhist, Muslim, Christian, Hindu
Language: Thai, Yawi
British Embassy, Bangkok: +66 (0) 2 305 8333

Tibet – see China

425

the gap-year guidebook 2016

Timor-Leste, Democratic Republic of
Capital: Dili
Currency: US Dollar (USD)
Religion: Roman Catholic (majority),
Protestant, Muslim, Hindu, Buddhist
Language: Tetum (official), Portuguese
(official), Bahasa Indonesian, English
refer to British Embassy, Jakarta: +62 (21)
2356 5200

Togo (Togolese Republic)
Capital: Lomé
Currency: CFA Franc BCEAO (XOF)
Religion: Christian, Muslim, indigenous beliefs
Language: French, Kabiye, Ewe
The British Ambassador to Togo resides in
Accra, Ghana: +223 21 221665; in a genuine
emergency contact the Honorary Consul in
Togo: +228 2222714

Tonga, Kingdom of
Capital: Nuku'alofa
Currency: Pa'anga (TOP)
Religion: Christian
Language: Tongan, English
refer to British High Commission, Suva, Fiji:
+679 322 9100

Trinidad and Tobago, Republic of
Capital: Port of Spain
Currency: Trinidad and Tobago Dollar (TTD)
Religion: Roman Catholic, Hindu, Anglican,
Muslim, Presbyterian
Language: English (official), Spanish
British High Commission, Port of Spain: +1
(868) 622 2748

Tristan da Cunha (British Overseas Territory)
Capital: Edinburgh of the Seven Seas
Currency: Sterling (GBP)
Religion: Christian
Language: English
Administrator's Office: +870 764 341 816

Tunisia (Tunisian Republic)
Capital: Tunis
Currency: Tunisian Dinar (TND)
Religion: Muslim, Christian
Language: Arabic, French
British Embassy, Tunis: +216 71 108 700

Turkey
Capital: Ankara
Currency: New Turkish Lira (TRY)
Religion: Muslim
Language: Turkish, Kurdish
British Consulae, Izmir: +90 (232) 463 5151

Turkmenistan
Capital: Ashgabat
Currency: Manat (TMM)
Religion: Sunni Muslim
Language: Russian, Turkmen
British Embassy, Ashgabat: +993 (12) 363
462/63/64

Turks and Caicos Islands
Capital: Grand Turk
Currency: US Dollar (USD)
Religion: Christian
Language: English, some Creole
Governor's Office: +1 (649) 946 2309

Tuvalu
Capital: Funafuti
Currency: Australian Dollar (AUD), Tuvaluan
Dollar (TVD) (coinage only)
Religion: Church of Tuvalu, Bahá'í
Language: Tuvaluan, English, Samoan, Kiribati
refer to British High Commission, Suva, Fiji:
+679 322 9100

Uganda Republic
Capital: Kampala
Currency: Uganda Shilling (UGX)
Religion: Christian, Muslim
Language: English (official national language),
Luganda, Swahili
British High Commission, Kampala: +256 (31)
231 2000

Ukraine
Capital: Kyiv (Kiev)
Currency: Hryvna (UAH)
Religion: Ukrainian Orthodox, Ukrainian Greek
Catholic, Jewish, Muslim
Language: Ukrainian (official), Russian,
Romanian, Polish, Hungarian
British Embassy, Kyiv: +380 44 490 3660

426

United Arab Emirates
Capital: Abu Dhabi
Currency: Dirham (AED)
Religion: Muslim, Hindu
Language: Arabic (official)
British Embassy, Abu Dhabi: +971 (2) 610 1100

United Kingdom
Capital: London
Currency: United Kingdom Pound Sterling (GBP)
Religion: Church of England, although all other faiths are practised
Language: English, Welsh (in Wales), Gaelic (in Scotland)
Foreign & Commonwealth Office: +44 (0) 20 7008 1500

United States of America
Capital: Washington, DC
Currency: US Dollar (USD)
Religion: Protestant, Roman Catholic, Latter-day Saints, Jewish, Muslim
Language: English, Spanish
British Embassy, Washington DC: +1 (202) 588 6500

Uruguay
Capital: Montevideo
Currency: Peso Uruguayan (UYU)
Religion: Roman Catholic, Protestant, Jewish, Atheist
Language: Spanish
British Embassy, Montevideo: +598 (2) 622 36 30/50

Uzbekistan, Republic of
Capital: Tashkent
Currency: Som (UZS)
Religion: Sunni Muslim
Language: Uzbek, Russian, Tajik
British Embassy, Tashkent: +998 71 120 1500/1516 (consular/visa)

Vanuatu, Republic of
Capital: Port Vila
Currency: Vatu (VUV)
Religion: Presbyterian, Anglican, Roman Catholic, Seventh Day Adventist
Language: Bislama (offical), English (official), French (official), plus over 130 vernacular languages
refer to British High Commission, Suva, Fiji: +679 322 9100

Venezuela, The Bolivarian Republic of
Capital: Caracas
Currency: Bolivar Fuerte (VEF)
Religion: Roman Catholic
Language: Spanish
British Embassy, Caracas: +58 (212) 263 8411

Vietnam, The Socialist Republic of
Capital: Hanoi
Currency: Vietnamese Dong (VND) (US dollar widely accepted)
Religion: Buddhist, Roman Catholic, Protestant, Cao Dai, Hoa Hao
Language: Vietnamese, minority languages also spoken
British Embassy, Hanoi: +84 (4) 3936 0500

Yemen, Republic of
Capital: Sana'a
Currency: Yemeni Rial (YER)
Religion: Muslim
Language: Arabic
British Embassy, Sana'a: +967 (1) 302480-5

Zambia, Republic of
Capital: Lusaka
Currency: Kwacha (ZMK)
Religion: Christian, Muslim, Hindu, indigenous beliefs
Language: English (official language of government), plus six further official languages
British High Commission, Lusaka: +260 (211) 423200

Zimbabwe, Republic of
Capital: Harare
Currency: Zimbabwean Dollar (ZWD)
Religion: Christian, indigenous beliefs, small communities of Hindu, Muslim and Jewish
Language: English (official), Shona, Ndebele
British Embassy, Harare: 0772 125 160-167

Appendix

428

Index

the gap-year guidebook 2016

visit: www.gap-year.com

433

visit: www.gap-year.com

435

visit: www.gap-year.com

Y

440